THE COMPLETE
AVENGERS

THE COMPLETE
AVENGERS

Dave Rogers

**Everything you ever wanted to know about
The Avengers and The New Avengers**

St. Martin's Press   New York

First published in Great Britain in 1989
by Boxtree Limited

Text Copyright © Dave Rogers

Edited by John Gilbert
Designed by Julia Lilauwala
Typeset by Bookworm Typesetting, Manchester

Library of Congress Cataloging-in-Publication Data

Rogers, Dave.
    The complete Avengers.

    Includes index.
    1. Avengers (Television program) 2. New avengers
(Television program) I. Title.
PN1992.77.A923R64   1989   791.45'72   89-5985
ISBN 0-312-03187-4

First U.S. Edition

Note that where the abbreviation ABC is used throughout the
text, this refers to Associated British Corporation and not
American Broadcasting Corporation unless otherwise stated.

CONTENTS

ACKNOWLEDGEMENTS

THIS BOOK would not have been possible without the contribution of a great many people who agreed that the time was right for the whole story to be told. So thanks are due to the following individuals and organisations for their cordial help during the preparation of this, and the original volumes.

Martin Bigham, John Herron, Ray Jenkins, Vicky Hillard, Jim Tong of the Weintraub Entertainment Group. Brian Clemens, Albert Fennell and Laurie Johnson of The Avengers (Film & TV) Enterprises. Jack Breckon and his staff of Thames Television. Dick Blaney of Eurotel Distribution.

The Brookes Family (Josie, Lewis and Carl) for their continued support. Stephen and Joy Curry, Colin Bayley, Bill Bradshaw, Graham P. Williams, Chris Clazie (UK). David Caruba, Dan Recchia, Dave Schleicher (USA). Geoff and Pauline Barlow (Queensland, Australia).

I would also like to thank John Doyle, Jennie Davis and Jane Struthers, for their work on the previous volumes – and of course, my publisher, Boxtree, for having faith in the new product.

The following companies for allowing me to use extracts from their publications: The London Express News and Features Service. The Mirror Group Newspapers. World International Publishers Ltd., and Harmsworth Publishers Ltd.

A special thank you is given to *Avengers* stars Honor Blackman, Linda Thorson, Joanna Lumley, Gareth Hunt and Patrick Newell, for taking the time to reply to my requests for interviews. Thanks are due also to Brian Clemens for penning the Foreword and allowing me to print extracts from his script; and, last but not least, to Patrick Macnee for his continued support.

Though mentioned last, thanks first and foremost to my wife Celia, who never doubted the cause.

This book is respectfully dedicated to the memory of Albert Fennell, Patrick Newell and in particular, Bud Payton, without whom *Avengers* fans everywhere would be that much the poorer.

FOREWORD

by Brian Clemens

DESPITE BEING SO closely associated with *The Avengers* since its first, faltering inception way back in 1961, it is a tribute to Dave Rogers's immaculate scholarship that I often turn to *his* books on the series for verification of facts I was probably responsible for in the first place!

These days, and especially since the tragic death of my long-time partner and unequalled friend, Albert Fennell, I find the pages unbearably nostalgic.

The spoofy Avengers with their glitter, outrageous plots and (hopefully) wit, have now become part of television legend, but a legend stronger than most; almost every year a revival is threatened, and about once a week I am asked: 'When's it coming back?' I think much of its strength lay in its originality, predating, as it did, the Bond movies by a year or three. A child spawned out of the Sixties, yet with the class and legs on it to keep it cheerfully striding on almost into the Eighties – and still being shown and enjoyed, after almost three decades, all around the world.

What is the secret of its longevity? A carefully contrived, *dateless* fantasy world depicting a Britain of bowlers and brollies, of charm and muffins for tea, a Britain long since gone – if it ever really existed! But above all, John Steed, a character who, if I did not actually create, I certainly helped to hone: Steed, played with consummate, urbane charm by Patrick Macnee, always willing to stand back unselfishly and allow the limelight to fall on his female partners, confident that he was the bedrock of the show, the pivot around which a series of delectable actresses whirled. It is hard to imagine anyone other than Patrick ever playing the role; and yet, should there come such a time, he will surely have the satisfaction of knowing that it was *he* who elevated Steed, in such definitive terms, to a proud position alongside other imperishables such as Bulldog Drummond, Sherlock Holmes and Richard Hannay.

This book is far more than just the work of a devoted fan; it commemorates and documents a remarkable television series. For me it provides the key to many memories. It is an ironic truth that The Golden Age of anything is always 'then', and never 'now'; and it is only with time and hindsight, *and* Dave Rogers, that the realisation eventually dawned that I had actually lived and participated in such an age.

And very grateful I am too. Thanks Dave, for jogging my elbow.

Brian Clemens 1988

Opposite, clockwise from top:
Scenes from *Honey for the Prince*, *Trap*, *The Undertakers* and *Killerwhale*.

INTRODUCTION

PRIOR TO MY first book on the subject (was it really over five years ago?) no one had seen fit to research and publish a volume on *The Avengers* – odd really, when one considers the niche it has notched for itself in television history.

The purpose of that book, and a subsequent volume published eighteen months later, was primarily to give aficionados an account of the series' chronological production history, from the very first episode *Hot Snow*, to the wrap-up story *Bizarre*. That book, containing a reference to all the 161 episodes that made up *The Avengers'* story, together with the second volume, which took the story full circle and covered the production history behind the making of *The New Avengers*, nevertheless failed to document the full story – not because I was frugal in my research, but because at the time I was unable to unearth further information.

Since then, however, by digging deeper into the archives, I have been able to gather together a selection of scripts, film and video material, plus other production documentation which, together with conversations with past and present employees of the companies who produced the programmes, sheds further light on the subject and has enabled me to revise my earlier text and fill in the gaps left unanswered in the previous volumes.

There was also the added bonus of being given the opportunity to conduct interviews with the stars of the show and allow the artists themselves to talk about their own tenure with the series.

So what is 'new' this time around? For a start, the irritating omissions of full-length synopses to four of the first season (Hendry/Macnee) stories have been rectified – giving, for the first time anywhere, a *complete* episode by episode account of the series. In chapters one to three you'll find production briefs issued by the producers of the day to familiarise their technical personnel with the new characters being introduced. A synopsis for the projected (but unmade) 'Cathy Gale'/'John Steed' cinema screen adventure film; additional material on *The Avengers on Stage* and the South African radio series; a 3-page reprint of dialogue from *Avengers*-sage Brian Clemens' script for the projected 1985 *Avengers International* American television pilot – the list is endless. Suffice to say that this time around, I'm confident that no stone has been left unturned to give you what I believe will be accepted as *the* definitive work on the subject.

Yes, of course some of the text remains unchanged. By its very nature the chronology (i.e. dates and situations) *must* remain constant, as must the episode synopses (although these have been updated to include the two-line subtitles, the pre-title teasers and tag scenes to every filmed story). However, with well-over 24,000 new words and the inclusion of over 200 new photographs, this book is *not* a reprint, but an ongoing celebration of my 'love-affair' with one of the most popular television series of all time. As I've stated previously, for sheer unabashed style there has never been another programme quite like it!

This volume also allows me the opportunity to reply to a list of questions that continue to appear in my correspondence with *Avengers* fandom: How do the Honor Blackman/Patrick Macnee stories compare with say, the Diana Rigg monochrome series? How many Honor Blackman stories exist in the archives and, most frequent of all, what is the correct chronological order of the episodes, that is, the order in which the stories were filmed or, in the case of the pre-Rigg series, videotaped?

Having viewed around 25 or so Blackman/Macnee stories, in the majority of cases the contrast between the '63/64 videotaped series and the first (Rigg) filmed series isn't as pronounced as one would expect – given the fact that the Blackman shows were 'studio-bound' and lacked the technical expertise of film. Containing very few exterior location scenes (the cameras in those days were bulky and difficult to manoeuvre – resulting, sometimes, in shuddery visuals), they certainly make for enjoyable viewing and, given their age and the conditions under which they were made, compare very favourably with the series that followed.

How many of the episodes still exist? At the last count, 48 of the 52 stories exist in the 16mm film format – some of which we may well have the opportunity of seeing. As I write this, plans to issue *The Avengers* to the pre-recorded video market have reached an advanced state of negotiations – and don't be too surprised if a *Hendry/Macnee* story is part and parcel of the package! Courtesy of some prudent sifting through film canisters by yours truly, I recently unearthed a 'lost' Hendry/Macnee episode – *complete* and in near-perfect condition! (Score one for perseverance!)

As for *The Avengers*' chronology, I attempted to answer this one in the listing printed in my second book – but found it totally impossible to substantiate the correct order of filming for the Rigg monochrome series, for which *no production records exist*. Ergo, I have little new to add in relation to that series, and the filmed order of the first nine Rigg colour stories. However, I have amended the order slightly, with information gleaned from the shooting scripts and have added further

'working titles' throughout the listing (that is to say the writer's *original* story title as it appeared on the script *before* production began, at which time the transmitted story title was substituted). The listing has been amended further to include the production order of the Hendry/Macnee series and *The New Avengers* episodes now appear in the *order in which they were filmed!*

Author's note: Some of the storylines to the Rigg monochrome and colour series may differ slightly from the episodes that eventually reached the screen. This is because in each case I have used official shooting scripts and synopses as a working guide. A typical example of this can be found in the synopsis for the story *Never, Never Say Die*. The version that finally reached the screen has one or two minor changes to the breakdown given here. However, as I (still) believe that most fans of the show will welcome the extra information, I offer no apology for not having changed these this time around. They are, after all, based on the stories as written, and as such provide an insight into what changes were actually made from the storyboard stage to the actual filming of the episodes.

Happy reading.

Dave Rogers   August 1988

THE DOCTOR AND THE SPY

HOW DID it all start, the series that swept the world, made the sophisticated adventures of that imperturbable cloak-and-dagger man, John Steed, and his succession of glamorous but highly lethal, leather-clad partners into weekly 'not to be missed' television fare for millions of fans and established star Patrick Macnee as a household name and face?

The history of *The Avengers* spans a quarter of a decade to a day in 1960 when Howard Thomas, then Managing Director of ABC, suggested to Canadian-born Sydney Newman, Head of Drama and originator of *Armchair Theatre* for the company, that he should balance ABC's drama schedules with a more light-hearted drama series, along the lines of the thrillers that were being popularised by film directors like Alfred Hitchcock and novelists like Ian Fleming in his James Bond books, thrillers that were as tough and exciting as ever, but were also sophisticated and tongue-in-cheek. Audiences were being invited to laugh as well as gasp, and they showed every sign of enjoying the experience.

It was Newman's daring idea to adapt this format into an off-beat formula for television – but to expand it to include the buccaneering spirit of the day by having the main characters outwit murderers, kidnappers and assassins in an outrageous, tongue-in-cheek, but imaginative fashion.

Above: *A rare publicity shot of Patrick Macnee.*

Opposite: *The Avengers Steed and Dr Keel take to the London streets in pursuit of villainy.*

Newman decided to accomplish this by redeveloping another ABC series, *Police Surgeon*, a standard cops-and-robbers show, then nearing the end of its run. Although the series had failed to make too much impression on viewers, Newman noticed that their letters indicated they liked the brash appeal of its young star, Ian Hendry. If Ian Hendry could be combined with this new formula, Sydney Newman was sure they'd have a success. With this in mind, Newman, together with *Police Surgeon*'s co-producer, Leonard White, came up with the idea of teaming Hendry with another actor: Hendry again playing a doctor, who would set out to avenge the death of his fiancée, shot in a London street by thugs during a drugs investigation. The doctor's crusading zeal against these plug-uglies would lead to his being co-opted to assist the British Secret Service by shadowy undercover agent John Steed.

But they first had to find an actor to play Steed. It was then that Newman remembered Patrick Macnee, an actor he'd worked with in Canada, and invited him to lunch. There was a role he wanted to discuss. 'Patrick, you could play this fellow I've been thinking about,' said Newman, 'a sort of George Sanders type. You'd be perfect for the part. You ought to wear a moustache, though.' Macnee flatly refused to wear a moustache. 'Okay. But will you take the part?' asked Newman. 'We're calling it *The Avengers*.'

Any actor would have been interested, but Macnee was not sure that he wanted to remain an actor. He'd just completed producing a television documentary series based on Sir Winston Churchill's memoirs, *The Valiant Years*, and saw this as the beginning of a new career in television production. On the other hand, the role did sound appealing. Unsure what to do, Macnee demanded a ridiculously high fee for each instalment and decided to let fate take its course. To his astonishment, the following week Newman rang to accept the terms, and Macnee signed to play John Steed.

The rest is history. Twenty years later Patrick Macnee was still playing the key figure in a series that had become cult viewing all over the world.

In November 1960, Leonard White issued an inter-departmental memo to his *Police Surgeon* production staff, confirming that Ian Hendry would now be playing a totally different character to the one he had played in that show – although the new character would continue to be a doctor – and their new show *The Avengers* would have absolutely nothing to do with the previous series. He added that Patrick Macnee had been engaged for the new series to share the lead and would play a new

character to be known as John Steed. The scripts for the first three stories were in active preparation, and White himself was investigating the possibility of engaging top composer Johnny Dankworth to arrange the theme music and incidental scores for the new series.

Ian Hendry was enthusiastic about the format. On the face of it Dr David Keel was rather similar to Dr Brent in *Police Surgeon*, but this time the doctor would have a private practice and would no longer be directly aiding the police. 'Keel is a most attractive character,' Hendry said at the time. 'He combines toughness with compassion, and serves as the conscience of the team. The role will be a kind of extended version of the police surgeon, because Keel will be more directly involved with fighting crime. And as he tangles with villains himself, he'll have more of the action. The accent is on authenticity, with vigorous, fast-moving action and well-researched stories.'

Like Hendry, Macnee was captivated by the role he was asked to play. In the first few stories Steed claimed to be a Secret Service agent, but for whom or what he was working nobody knew. 'He is a wolf with the women and revels in trouble,' said Macnee. 'He doesn't think so much about saving hoodlums as just getting them out of the way. By the same token, he doesn't follow the Queensberry rules, and though he works indirectly with the police, he is not too popular with them.' When I spoke to him recently, he added, 'The character of John Steed was created purely as a name, as an opposite type to the rather steady doctor. At first you never quite knew if he was evil or good. He was a shadowy sort of character who emerged through windows with a pistol and impeccable brolly. After we had completed a couple of shows, Sydney Newman came to me and told me that the character didn't seem very interesting, and asked me to make the character a bit more lively. They gave me a bit more freedom and the character evolved from there. I decided to base him on various people: my father; the foppish, witty Scarlet Pimpernel, daringly snatching prisoners from the guillotine; Ralph Richardson in *Q Planes*; and my commanding officer in the Royal Navy, who was an incredibly brave man. I thought of Regency days – the most flamboyant, sartorially, for men – and imagined Steed in waisted jackets and embroidered waistcoats. Steed I was stuck with as a name and it stayed. Underneath he was steel. Outwardly he was charming and vain and representative, I suppose, of the kind of Englishman who is more valued abroad. The point about Steed was that he led a fantasy life – a hero dressed and accoutred like a junior cabinet minister. An Old Etonian whose most lethal weapon was the hallmark of the English gentleman – a furled umbrella.' He added, 'Ian Hendry was such a volatile character, and he put a great deal more into the series than was really there. That's how it started. We had this great feeling of alertness and it came mainly from Ian's mind. The show was based entirely on the inherent skills of Sydney Newman, Leonard White, Peter Hammond, Don Leaver and Ian Hendry, but most of all, Ian Hendry, because he wasn't just an actor, he was a writer, an innovator, a wonderful artistic influence – a great and talented man.'

Ian Hendry and Ingrid Hafner who played his receptionist, Carol Wilson.

In keeping with other videotaped programmes of the period ('filmed' inserts to pep up the studio action were well established by this time), the first ever filmed material for *The Avengers* – the sequence in which Peggy, Dr Keel's fiancée, was gunned down in a London street – was completed on 20 December 1960 at a location in Chelsea. Meanwhile the actors due to appear in the first two stories began rehearsals at Teddington Studios.

Keel and Steed were formally introduced to the British public on 7 January 1961 and the partnership would last for a total of 26 episodes before Steed was introduced to Mrs Catherine Gale, the first (some say the best?) of his world-famous female partners. That, however, was still some time away and the programmes' format would undergo several changes of direction before *The Avengers*' format as we know it was firmly established.

Barely six weeks into production, Leonard White, dissatisfied with the way the series was heading, drew up the following production directive.

THE AVENGERS

At this time it is well that we remind ourselves of certain fundamentals concerning the series.
1. Keel and Steed are essentially UNDERCOVER. They are *not* private or public detectives and any story which follows the usual 'Private Eye' pattern is *not* right for us.

They do *not* work *with* the police and usually cannot call upon more police aid than would normally be available to ordinary citizens.
2. KEEL, being a doctor, is the 'amateur'. This does not mean that he is less good at the 'job' but simply that his motives for concerning himself with a mission are quite different from Steed's. Without being at all 'goody-goody' he will, usually, be fired by a sense of public service, kindled by his humanitarian instincts.

He is an excellent doctor and this proficiency is a specific help in the joint missions.

He is a mature man. Any tendency to make him like a 'little boy' tagging along behind Steed, asking all the questions, and making silly mistakes' MUST be eradicated.

Women find him attractive. Usually, however, he will keep them at a distance. His sincerity does not allow him to flirt and he still has deep feelings for the fiancée he lost.

He is tough, but *not* hard. Can be very gentle: loves children. Likes sport (would be a keen rugby player if he had the time). Product of a 'red-brick' University.

A wry sense of humour. Quite serious normally, but when he smiles – it's wonderful!

Being a good doctor he is well trained to *think* out a problem and resolve it by *positive action*.

His 'practice' (Chelsea-Victoria district) includes an interesting area comprising city, river, village communities of all 'social' classes.

He has a partner in 'Dr Tredding' – a much older man – whom we rarely see, but who 'allows' Keel to be absent from time to time on his 'missions' (Tredding *never* knows the nature of Keel's escapades, however).

Another, more active link with the 'surgery' and Keel's professional background is:
3. CAROL. As his Nurse/Receptionist, she must be used to keep alive the *duality* of Keel's life. She does not know of his *undercover* work – but she may have her suspicions.

Her integrity and great admiration (it might be more) for the doctor prevent her from stepping outside the bounds of her professional status. She is not beyond 'looking after him' in the most innocent (but telling) ways, however. She will 'mother' him but never allow it to become unpleasant or possessive.

She is attractive – very efficient, with great common-sense.

She is NOT part of the undercover team, but *can* be used obliquely to assist either Keel or Steed or both where justifiable. Essentially this means that whatever she does will be quite attractive or natural, irrespective of any undercover uses which may be made of her participation.
4. STEED is the professional undercover man. He is suave, debonair, a 'man-about-town'. A sophisticate but not lacking in virility. His 'sports' are probably horse-racing, dograning, beauty competitions, etc.

He has an eye for the beautiful and unusual – be it objects d'art or women. He will never be serious with any one woman, however. He is very experienced.

He is an expert at his job (but not perfect). He handles the 'tools of his trade' with great proficiency. Probably, gun-handling, ju-jitsu and turkish baths are part of the ritual for him.

His flat is an indication of his 'special' tastes. Some might think these slightly decadent – but they would be wrong. He has owned a Great Dane (now dead) – but will have another unusual hound. He has a man-servant. He has a Rolls Royce. He dresses superbly – but not altogether conventionally. His motives are not necessarily as 'moral' as Keel's. To him the *success* of the mission is the only important thing and therefore his *means* may sometimes be questionable. The success of the mission, however, is a *wrong put right*, and therefore sometimes necessitates these means being used to this end.

He is very highly paid for his work. It is VERY, VERY dangerous. He has NO ORGANISATIONAL ties whatsoever. He has no one 'working for him' except such as may be paid or persuaded (by him) to do a specific job. He certainly has *no* 'plain clothes' types waiting to assist him at the right moment.

His only 'organisational' contact is to *One-Ten* who feeds him assignments and information. Once on assignment, however, Steed (or Keel) are essentially relied upon to work out their own salvation.

Steed has a quick wit. A very persuasive tongue. Lots of old-world charm. He is *not* a lounge-lizard: he is ACTIVE.

5. ONE-TEN is our only link with apparent official-dom. His 'establishment' is necessarily very obscure. He contracts the 'undercover' work, but he will always keep the arrangements on a PERSONAL basis. He knows of Keel's activity but doesn't recognise him as anything more than an 'extension' of Steed's work. Very useful of course, but not a 'professional'.

One-Ten is very intelligent. He might be an 'Oxford Don' who has been assigned to highly specialised work in big crime detection where normal police activity has to be augmented.

He is usually on a 'phone' – but the 'phone' always seems to be in interesting places.

'AVENGERS' INGREDIENTS should always be:

(A) GLAMOUR. Beautiful, attractive, unusual women.
(B) UNUSUAL & EXCITING LOCALES. Good visual value and enjoyment to the audience.
(C) AN IMPORTANT MISSION. Much more than a usual 'police' story and one that provides the correct motives for *Keel's inclusion* in the mission. The problem should be a BIG one (Steed's work) and have relation to individual humans (Keel's interest).
(D) STORY BALANCE. 1. A predominance of attractive recognisably human characters. 2. Something to intrigue the intelligence, however lightly. 3. Some WIT, HUMOUR and GRACE in the dialogue. 4. A constant awareness of the viewers' capacity for friendly affection for our characters. 5. In such context – violence sinks into place.
(E) ACTION. As much as is compatible with 'live' studio production – plus a little more?

NOTES:

'The Avengers' is a SERIES, not a SERIAL. Therefore nothing should be included in scripting, performance or direction, in the nature of 'running gags'. (Character-building or visual treatment) which are not perfectly acceptable to an audience which has *not* seen other episodes.

A few days later, White added the following comments:

(1) Because we are 'new' and will face fierce competition from other productions, our episodes must get BETTER – and *not* slip away as we become established.
(2) The series' title MUST be remembered and each episode MUST be firmly motivated by this.
(3) It appears that the Keel stories seem to be the most difficult to write. Without unbalancing our format, we should therefore try to find opportunities for KEEL to get *closer* to the character than is perhaps necessary in Steed's case.
(4) Generally a KEEL story should *not* be one that could be transferred to a STEED story and vice versa.
(5) The 'locale' of each episode should be EXOTIC, EXCITING and UNUSUAL. Perhaps a good story could be found in the 'Horse Racing World' to take advantage of Macnee's background – and also one in which we could use Hendry's ability as a 'Stunt Motorcyclist'.

Ian Hendry as David Keel was a mainstay of the first Avengers season.

Neither idea was used, but it is interesting to reflect if the latter suggestion – combined with Honor Blackman's prowess at handling a two-wheeled machine – formed the thinking behind making Cathy Gale a dab hand with a high-powered motorcycle.

With a few other minor changes (Ingrid Hafner's role was beefed-up to give 'Carol' a bigger slice of the action), the series progressed comfortably to nationwide acclaim – and the beginnings of the *Avengers'* format destined to make its stars world famous – a wacky but sophisticated, comedy thriller, with a sideline in topsy-turvy, but thoroughly entertaining, mad-cap antics.

Incidentally, it is interesting to note that though Patrick Macnee's portrayal of the unconventional Steed gathered momentum and swiftly became *the* firm viewers' favourite – with Hendry's character placed a comfortable second – the latter continued to receive star billing *above* the title credits, while Macnee's name was credited immediately *after* the *Avengers'* title logo.

HOT SNOW

Teleplay by Ray Rigby
Based on a story by Patrick Brawn

Dr Tredding	**Philip Stone**
Peggy	**Catherine Woodville**
Dr David Keel	**Ian Hendry**
Spicer	**Godfrey Quigley**
Charlie	**Murray Melvin**
Johnson	**Charles Wade**
Det-Supt Wilson	**Alister Williamson**
Stella	**Moira Redmond**
Sgt Rogers	**Astor Sklair**
Steed	**Patrick Macnee**
Mrs Simpson	**June Monkhouse**
Ronnie Vance	**Robert James**

Designed by Alpho O'Reilly

Directed by Don Leaver

THE EPISODE opens with Dr David Keel feeling on top of the world. He has just announced his engagement to his secretary, Peggy. Later that day, however, a gang of drug peddlers mistakenly deliver a packet of heroin to Keel's surgery. Realising their mistake, the gang sends two of its members to retrieve the package, but Peggy disturbs them. They escape but, because Peggy can identify them, lie in wait and gun her down in the street. Keel calls in the police, only to find they have insufficient evidence on which to act. Heartbroken at Peggy's death, Keel vows to find the killers himself. He follows the trail to the consulting rooms of a shady medical practitioner (who should have received the heroin in the first place) but he, too, has been murdered by the gang. As he leaves, Keel is stopped and questioned by a mysterious stranger who introduces himself as John Steed. Steed tells Keel that he is after the gang and enlists his help to track them down. Using a fake package of heroin as bait, Keel contacts the gang but tells them that he will only deal direct with their boss, Vance. The gang, however, are suspicious and decide that Keel must be killed. They lay a trap for Keel, but as they are about to dispose of him, Steed arrives and rescues him. A furious fight breaks out, in which the police arrive and arrest the gang, but the gang leader, Vance, is able to escape.

How it all began. In Hot Snow, Peggy, Dr Keel's fiancée, is shot down in a London street.

BROUGHT TO BOOK

Teleplay by Brian Clemens

Prentice	Lionel Burns
Lale	Redmond Bailey
Pretty Boy	Clifford Elkin
Bart	Neil McCarthy
Nick Mason	Charles Morgan
Spicer	Godfrey Quigley
Dr David Keel	Ian Hendry
Dr Tredding	Philip Stone
Carol Wilson	Ingrid Hafner
Chinese Girl (Lila)	Joyce Wong Chong
John Steed	Patrick Macnee
Ronnie Vance	Robert James
Det-Supt Wilson	Alister Williamson
Det-Sgt	Michael Collins
Jackie	Carol White

Designed by Robert Fuest

Directed by Peter Hammond

ONCE AGAIN, Dr David Keel meets the mysterious John Steed. Steed invites him to ingratiate himself with Vance, leader of a notorious gang of protection racketeers. Steed explains that he has managed to become a member of a similar gang led by Mason, who wants to poach Vance's territory. When Steed explains that Peggy's killer is implicated with Mason, Keel accepts the challenge, and a police raid is staged in Vance's presence, which makes Keel appear crooked. To test Keel's loyalty, Vance asks him to attend to his brother, Pretty Boy, who has been razor-slashed by Mason's gang. Keel does this, and is readily accepted by Vance. Keel is then told that one of Mason's gang, Spicer, has been hired to kill the Vance brothers. Keel tells Steed, who arranges for the police to be present at the killing. Mason, however, suspects Steed and, instead of Spicer, arrives himself and warns Vance that there are traitors in both camps – adding that he has sent Spicer to kill Steed. Keel overhears and rushes to rescue Steed. In threatening Spicer with instant death by an injection from his hypodermic needle in revenge for his fiancée's murder, he extracts a confession which the police arrive in time to hear. Spicer successfully dealt with (by a trick – there was nothing harmful in the hypodermic), Steed enlists Keel's permanent help in the undercover police's constant fight against organised crime.

Medical practitioner turned undercover man. Ian Hendry in a scene from Brought to Book.

SQUARE ROOT OF EVIL

Teleplay by Richard Harris

John Steed	Patrick Macnee
5	Heron Carvic
Secretary	Cynthia Bizeray
Bloom	Michael Robbins
Hooper	George Murcell
Warren	Vic Wise
The Cardinal	Alex Scott
Lisa	Delphi Lawrence
Carol Wilson	Ingrid Hafner
Dr David Keel	Ian Hendry

Designed by Patrick Downing

Directed by Don Leaver

AWARE THAT Riordan, a convicted forger, is due to be released from prison within a few hours, '5', One-Ten's colleague, has the forger taken to a safe-house, then arranges for Steed to impersonate the convict and infiltrate Riordan's gang, part of a large criminal ring, planning to flood the country with forged banknotes. Hooper, the gang's leader, accepts Steed at face value but his second-in-command, The Cardinal, is suspicious of the newcomer and sets out to expose him as a fraud. One evening, as Steed is rifling through the contents of Hooper's safe, he is caught in the act by Lisa, The Cardinal's wife. He persuades her not to give him away by telling her that he knows that her husband is a murderer, and unless she helps him to expose the gang she could be arrested as an accomplice, Steed is forced to intervene when The Cardinal finds them together and attacks the woman, knocking her to the ground. Steed thrashes the man within an inch of his life. That night Hooper receives a telephone call telling him to be ready to receive Bloom, the head of the organisation, who will then arrange the next step in the operation – distribution. Overhearing this, Steed realises that he must get a message to Dr Keel, but how? The Cardinal is still watching his every move. An opportunity arrives as Steed is helping other gang members to load the forged currency into a van. Stumbling and feigning injury to his arm, Steed begs to be allowed to visit his doctor. Ignoring objections from The Cardinal, Hooper allows him to do so and Steed informs his colleague of the gang's plans. That evening, on the pretext of tending his patient, Keel arrives at the gang's headquarters. Furious with Steed for allowing the doctor to learn of their base, The Cardinal attacks Steed with a knife. Keel intervenes and a fight breaks out in the printing room where good – Steed and Keel, assisted by Lisa – overpower the bad – The Cardinal, Hooper and Bloom. Allowing Lisa to get away, Steed telephones the police, while Keel attends The Cardinal's injuries; unlike Steed, the man's arm really is broken!

NIGHTMARE

Teleplay by Terence Feely

Williams	Gordon Boyd
Dr David Keel	Ian Hendry
Carol Wilson	Ingrid Hafner
Faith Braintree	Helen Lindsay
Commander Reece	Michael Logan
John Steed	Patrick Macnee
Dr Brown	Robert Bruce
Dr Jones	Redmond Bailey
Dr Miller	Robert Sansom

Designed by Robert Fuest

Directed by Peter Hammond

AN EERIE telephone call from one of his patients, Faith Braintree, leads Dr Keel to investigate the disappearance of her husband, an eminent scientist engaged on top secret work. While he is attending Faith, a fake MI5 man arrives and, assuming Keel to be the professor, tries to kidnap him. Keel is saved, but recovers from the attack in hospital where Steed persuades him to impersonate Braintree and draw the enemy's attention from the real professor (who is still missing). The ruse works, and a second attempt is made to kidnap Keel. He escapes, but during the ensuing fight is shot in the chest. A minor operation is needed but Carol, Keel's receptionist, learns that the anaesthetist is one of the enemy. But before she can tell Steed, she is caught and tied up by the assassins. During the operation, Keel's oxygen is tampered with and he is dying when Steed arrives and unmasks the anaesthetist. Carol is freed and Keel recovers. The real Braintree, suffering from amnesia due to overwork, is found and Steed, Keel and Carol have a celebratory drink with the professor and his wife.

David Keel receives a telephone call from Faith Braintree, in Nightmare.

CRESCENT MOON

Teleplay by
Geoffrey Bellman and John Whitney

Senora Mendoza	**Patience Collier**
John Steed	**Patrick Macnee**
Bartello	**Harold Kasket**
Carmelite Mendoza	**Bandana Das Gupta**
Luis Alvarez	**Nicholas Amer**
Paul	**Eric Thompson**
Fernandez	**Jack Rodney**
Vasco	**Roger Delgado**
Carlos (policeman)	**George Roderick**
Dr David Keel	**Ian Hendry**

Designed by Alpho O'Reilly

Directed by John Knight

STEED is sent to a Caribbean island, to investigate the kidnapping of a young girl, Carmelite Mendoza. Although the family jewels are missing, Steed suspects a political motive, for the girl's father, pro-Western General Mendoza, was officially reported killed in a mysterious accident only a week earlier. Steed's questioning of Senora Mendoza and her family retainer, Vasco, reveals nothing. Later, however, Vasco is seen killing Carmelite's kidnapper and abducting the girl himself. Having intercepted a police report about the murder, Steed beats the police to the scene of the crime and follows up a clue naming the man behind the abduction as Senor Paul. Meanwhile, in London, Dr Keel is told to expect a new patient – General Mendoza! By clever questioning of Vasco, Steed discovers where Carmelite is being held prisoner, but when he attempts to rescue her, Paul attacks him. Steed soon overpowers Senor Paul and takes him and the girl to the police. Paul admits being behind the original kidnapping, but states that he only wanted to take her to her father, who had to flee and fake his own death to escape the plotting of his wife. Senora Mendoza and Vasco wanted his vast fortune to bring their political party to power. Back in London, Keel tells Steed that when the General was in England he was ill and he had attended him.

GIRL ON THE TRAPEZE

Teleplay by Dennis Spooner

Vera	**Delena Kidd**
Anna Danilov	**Nadja Regin**
Dr David Keel	**Ian Hendry**
Carol Wilson	**Ingrid Hafner**
Policeman	**Ian Gardiner**
Zibbo	**Kenneth J Warren**
Supt Lewis	**Howard Goorney**
Stefan	**Edwin Richfield**

Designed by Paul Bernard

Directed by Don Leaver

A GIRL jumps into the Thames but the body which is rescued and which Dr Keel tries to revive is that of another girl, whose face seems familiar to Keel. The girl dies, having murmured the word 'Danilov', and Keel is convinced that she is the victim of foul play. With the help of his receptionist, Carol, Keel finds the dead girl's photograph in a newspaper and they discover that she was the trapeze artist with the Radeck State Circus, now on the last night of its visit to Britain. They visit the circus and discover that one of the performers, Vera (the girl who jumped from the bridge), is guarding a girl whose face is masked by bandages. The owner tells them that the trapeze girl had a slight accident during her performance but is now recovering in her dressing room. Suspicious, Keel calls in the police, who tell him that Professor Danilov, a Radeck scientist, has fled to the West with his young daughter, Anna. Keel investigates the trapeze girl's dressing room and finds the heavily bandaged figure. But before Keel can question her, Zibbo the clown traps him, and he and Carol are held prisoner. Zibbo informs them that Anna Danilov, bandaged to avoid recognition, will take the place of the dead girl and be smuggled back to Radeck to compel her father to return. Keel is told that unless he tells the police that he has made a mistake, Carol will be shot. Keel does so, but the police sergeant remains suspicious, and has the circus secretly surrounded. That night, Keel arranges for Carol to escape by having her swathed in bandages and pretending to be Anna. Then he himself escapes and takes the real Anna to safety. Carol, however, is trapped by Zibbo, who threatens her at gunpoint. As he is about to shoot her, the police close in and the gang is arrested.

DIAMOND CUT DIAMOND

Teleplay by Max Marquis

John Steed	**Patrick Macnee**
One-Ten	**Douglas Muir**
Fiona Charles	**Sandra Dorne**
Dr Collard	**Hamlyn Benson**
Carol Wilson	**Ingrid Hafner**
Dr David Keel	**Ian Hendry**
Stella Creighton	**Joy Webster**

Designed by Robert Fuest

Directed by Peter Hammond

HOT ON the trail of an organisation who specialise in smuggling illicit diamonds to New York by air, Steed, masquerading as John Ryan, an airline steward arrested in Australia on suspicion of smuggling – but released for lack of evidence – is living in a bungalow near to Heathrow Airport; a place once owned by Harcourt, a suicide whom One-Ten's department suspected of being a member of the organisation. Before long Steed meets Fiona Charles, a nurse employed by Dr Collard, medical adviser to Globe Airlines, and subsequently, Sharp, the pilot with whom Steed will be flying to New York the following morning. After an uneventful trip and a party to celebrate the flight, Steed returns home somewhat the worse for drink. The following morning a voice on the telephone advises him to read the morning papers. Each carries the story that a 25-year-old woman was run down and killed by a hit-and-run driver, a man driving like a maniac who was obviously intoxicated. The police are confident of an early arrest as the car must have sustained considerable damage. Told by the caller to check his garage, Steed does so and finds his car fender covered in dried blood, its front wing and radiator bent askew. Baffled and unable to recall the previous night's events clearly, Steed visits Dr Keel. After taking blood and urine tests, his colleague confirms Steed's suspicions, he was given a massive dose of barbiturates, and couldn't have possibly driven a car in such a condition: Steed isn't responsible for the woman's death. Nevertheless, when Steed is contacted by Fiona and asked to deliver a 'package' to someone in New York, he does so. Returning home, he finds Fiona and Dr Collard waiting for him, gun at the ready. His usefulness over – the gang are clever enough to use a courier once only, like Harcourt before him – Steed is to take his own life. So too will Fiona, whom Collard says knows too much for her good: she will meet her death at Steed's hand; then, full of remorse, Steed will commit suicide. At the eleventh hour Collard's plans are foiled by the arrival of Dr Keel. The medico is arrested and Fiona turns Queen's evidence.

THE RADIOACTIVE MAN

Teleplay by Fred Edge

Marko Ogrin	**George Pravda**
Mary Somers	**Christine Pollon**
Carol Wilson	**Ingrid Hafner**
Dr David Keel	**Ian Hendry**
John Steed	**Patrick Macnee**
Dr Graham	**Gerald Sim**

Designed by Alpho O'Reilly

Directed by Robert Tronson

MARKO, AN immigrant working as a cleaner at a top secret government Medical Research Laboratory, picks up and takes away a radioactive isotope capsule, unaware that possession of it could kill him within a few hours and seriously harm anyone coming into close contact with him. Informed of the theft, Dr Graham, head of the establishment, seeks help from One-Ten's department. With Steed about to depart on a mission abroad, it is left to Dr Keel to help the police in their search for the missing man. Marko, meanwhile, hearing that he is wanted by the authorities and believing that the police wish to prosecute him for having a forged passport, goes into hiding and telephones his girlfriend, Mary Somers. That afternoon Mary receives a visit from Police Inspector Tudor, who tells her that Marko is in trouble and asks her to call him immediately her boyfriend makes contact. Keel, meanwhile, visits the research laboratory and learns the full extent of the danger; unless Marko is found soon he will become a harbinger of death: anyone touching him will die in agony within 36 hours of contact. That evening, Marko slips through the police cordon surrounding Mary's home and enters the house unobserved. Unaware of Inspector Tudor's real reason for hunting her boyfriend, and believing Marko's forged passport theory, Mary gives her lover some cash and the immigrant joins some fellow compatriots who are hiding in the cellar of a shop owned by Milan, a ruthless crook who has promised to get them safely out of the country: in reality he means to kill them and pocket their savings. Following a lead given to them by Steed, who telephones Keel, the doctor, Police Inspector and Dr Graham step up their search. Mary Somers and her son are tested for radioactivity and the results prove positive. Told the truth about her boyfriend's condition, the woman is able to remember the name of one of Marko's contacts, Frane. With his help and a geiger-counter trace, the immigrant is traced to Milan's shop. But Marko defies the police with a gun until, with the arrival of Dr Keel and Mary, who convinces him of his plight, he hands the deadly capsule to Dr Graham. Milan and his cohorts are taken to hospital and Keel returns to his surgery – in time to welcome home a sun-tanned Steed.

ASHES OF ROSES

Teleplay by Peter Ling and Sheilagh Ward

John Steed	Patrick Macnee
Olive Beronne	Olga Lowe
Jacques Beronne	Mark Eden
Johnny Mendelssohn	Peter Zander
Dr David Keel	Ian Hendry
Carol Wilson	Ingrid Hafner
Denise	Hedi Erich

Designed by Patrick Downing

Directed by Don Leaver

WHEN A watchman dies in a warehouse fire, Steed is convinced that it was murder and that the fire was started deliberately – one of several recent cases of suspected arson. Steed has only one lead – a telephone number – and it belongs to a hairdressing salon run by Olive and Jacques Beronne. Steed asks Dr Keel to let Carol have some time off to go to the hair salon. Carol, eager for adventure, and what she imagines is some smart detective work at the salon, does so, but finds nothing of interest. Sitting under her hairdrier, she presses the heating switch. Suddenly, there is a loud explosion and the hairdrier bursts into flames. Steed, waiting outside in his car, hears the explosion and rushes to Carol's rescue. He takes her back to his apartment and when she revives he tells her that fortunately, the extra current had blown the hairdrier's fuses and saved her life. He has also discovered that Jean, one of the salon assistants, and not Carol, was meant to be the next under the hairdrier. Visiting the salon, Steed questions another of the assistants, Denise, and learns that the salon is near bankruptcy. Leaving, he spots Jacques Beronne talking to a man called Mendelssohn, a convicted criminal. Carol questions Jean, who tells her to come to her flat later that evening. But their conversation is overheard by Olive Beronne and when Steed and Carol arrive at Jean's flat they find she has been strangled. When he discovers that the Beronnes are about to leave for Paris, Steed intercepts them at the station and Jacques confesses that the salon will be set on fire that evening so that the Beronnes can collect the insurance. Meanwhile, Denise has told Carol that she suspects Mendelssohn of intended arson and together they drive to the salon to stop him. They are both saved from being burned alive when Steed arrives and knocks out Mendelssohn as he is about to light the fuse to an incendiary bomb.

HUNT THE MAN DOWN

Teleplay by Richard Harris

John Steed	Patrick Macnee
Paul Stacey	Maurice Good
Dr David Keel	Ian Hendry
Carol Wilson	Ingrid Hafner
Stella Preston	Melissa Stribling
Nurse Wyatt	Susan Castle

Designed by Robert Fuest

Directed by Peter Hammond

WHEN FRANK PRESTON is released after a long prison sentence for robbery, the proceeds of which (more than £100,000) have never been traced, he drives to a sewer in which he had hidden the money, but is disturbed and attacked by two thugs, Stacey and Rocky, who then try to force him to reveal where the money is hidden. Preston is rescued by John Steed, who has been assigned to follow Preston and find the stolen loot. Steed takes the injured man to Dr Keel's surgery, and under anaesthetic and in delirium, Preston murmurs 'That's where we hid it'. Unknown to Keel and Steed, Stella, Preston's wife, who has been brought to the surgery by Steed, has joined forces with Stacey and Rocky and tells them she thinks Keel knows where the

Dr Keel enters a sewer to track down a gang of thieves in a scene from **Hunt the Man Down.**

money is buried. The two thugs kidnap Keel's receptionist, Carol, and tell Keel that she will be killed unless he divulges the whereabouts of the money. Keel tells Steed of the threat, and he promises to use his department's resources to find the thugs' hideout. Before he can do so, however, Preston, worried about his wife, breaks out of hospital and arrives home to see her kissing Stacey. He goes to Keel's surgery and, at gunpoint, forces Keel to give him further medical attention and then enlists his help in finding the money. He and Keel then drive to an entrance to the sewer and go down, followed by Stacey and Rocky, who have brought Carol along as hostage. When Preston finds the money, there is a chase through the sewers and finally Preston and Dr Keel are cornered by the thugs. Steed arrives with the police in tow, the thugs are arrested and Carol is freed.

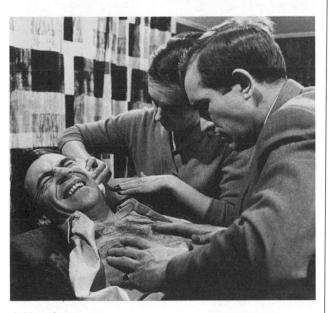

In **Hunt the Man Down**, *Dr Keel and Carol attend the injured Frank Preston.*

PLEASE DON'T FEED THE ANIMALS

Teleplay by Dennis Spooner

John Steed	**Patrick Macnee**
Felgate	**Tenniel Evans**
Carol Wilson	**Ingrid Hafner**
Dr Keel	**Ian Hendry**
Christine	**Carole Boyer**
Kollakis	**Harry Ross**
Renton-Stephens	**Alastair Hunter**
Yvonne	**Catherine Ellison**
Sarah	**Genevieve Lyons**
Barman	**Mark Baker**

Designed by Patrick Downing

Directed by Dennis Vance

FELGATE, a minor Whitehall civil servant dealing with secret cyphers, is being blackmailed by the owner of a Soho club. He is being watched by Steed, who has been planted in the same office. Steed and Dr Keel follow Felgate to a private zoo in the country where he throws a packet of the blackmail money into the reptile pit. Though Steed keeps close watch on the package, it mysteriously disappears. The next day, the blackmailer, finding Felgate has no money left, orders him to steal a top-secret file from his office. Felgate refuses and the club owner has him beaten up, but Dr Keel saves the civil servant from serious injury. Later at the club, Steed, knowing the conversation is being recorded, allows himself to be put into an embarrassing position with one of the club hostesses. He is soon contacted by the blackmailer who threatens Steed about the recording and orders him to steal the secret file. Acting on written instructions, Steed throws the package (containing false secret information) into the reptile pit of the zoo. Keel, keeping watch, sees a small monkey enter the pit and make off with the package. Questioning the zoo manager and his daughter, Steed decides that though they have no knowledge of the affair the girl's pet monkey was the one used to collect the packages. He discovers that a girl who runs the drinks kiosk next to the reptile pit is friendly with the daughter, and the monkey plays party tricks for her and her customers at the kiosk. Steed discovers that the girl is the ringleader behind the blackmail gang and she is arrested.

DANCE WITH DEATH

Teleplay by Peter Ling and Sheilagh Ward

Dr David Keel	Ian Hendry
Carol Wilson	Ingrid Hafner
Elaine Bateman	Caroline Blakiston
Trevor Price	David Sutton
Beth Wilkinson	Angela Douglas
Major Caswell	Ewan Roberts
Valerie Marne	Pauline Shepherd
Mrs Marne	Diana King
Philip Anthony	Geoffrey Palmer
John Steed	Patrick Macnee
Porter	Norman Chappell

Designed by James Goddard

Directed by Don Leaver

ELAINE Bateman, the owner of a ballroom dancing school, is gassed. When Dr Keel revives her, she insists that someone is trying to murder her. The police say that though she has already reported one attempt on her life, they have been unable to prove her story. Keel, however, is sympathetic and puts her under his care. Visiting the dancing school, he meets Elaine's partner, Major Caswell, and the school pianist, Anthony, and is forced to intervene when one of the pupils, Price (who is in love with Elaine), gets jealous. During the rumpus, Keel drops his scarf but next day, when he returns to collect it, he finds it has been used to strangle Elaine. Steed, when told, promises to help clear Keel's name. Steed enrols as a student at the school and meets the rich Mrs Marne and her spoiled young daughter, Valerie. Anthony's face seems familiar to Steed, who checks the files and tells Keel that the man was acquitted years ago of murdering his wife. Steed, however, is convinced that the man was guilty. He is also wanted by the police for a more recent crime. However, when Steed and the police go to arrest Anthony, they find he has eloped with Valerie – and her mother's diamonds. Steed tells Keel that the man is suspected of electrocuting his victims in the bath, and they set out to find him. Meanwhile, in a hotel room, Anthony, having first confirmed with the infatuated Valerie that the diamonds are in her possession, suggests that she has a nice hot bath. Keel visits the dancing school and catches Price searching Anthony's belongings for evidence that Anthony has been blackmailing him. Fortunately, Price has discovered where Anthony has taken Valerie, and Keel drives frantically to the hotel. He meets Steed there, who, having had Anthony's taxi traced, has arrived before him. They break into the room just in time to save Valerie from electrocution and arrest Anthony.

In a scene from Dance with Death, *The Avengers take to the rooftops to track down a murderer who electrocutes his victims in the bath.*

ONE FOR THE MORTUARY

Teleplay by Brian Clemens

Benson	Peter Madden
John Steed	Patrick Macnee
Dr David Keel	Ian Hendry
Carol Wilson	Ingrid Hafner
Scott	Ronald Wilson
Pallaine	Dennis Edwards
Yvette Declair	Malou Pantera
Dubois	Frank Gatliff
Maid	Irene Bradshaw
Bernard Bourg	Toke Townley

Designed by Robert Fuest

Directed by Peter Hammond

STEED HAS to get an important new medical formula to a health conference abroad. Unknown to Dr Keel, Steed conceals the formula, in microdot form, on a document belonging to one of Keel's partners. Keel will take it with him when he attends the conference in Geneva. On the flight, Keel meets a girl who is taken ill and after attending to her, he invites her to go to the conference with him, unknowingly giving her the invitation card on which the medical formula is hidden. When Steed arrives in Geneva, he finds Keel is under arrest. He has been accused by the police of murdering a man who was actually killed by one of the thugs seeking the formula. Keel is released into Steed's custody and Keel takes him to meet the girl at his hotel, but when they arrive she has gone. Keel remembers that the girl said she was going to visit her uncle, and he goes to the address, but finds only a weird taxidermist who says he has never heard of the girl. He suggests, however, that Keel has confused his name with that of a nearby town. Keel traces the girl and makes an appointment to see her. Steed and Keel visit the girl's room and Keel is astonished when Steed informs them of the importance of the invitation card. Steed then phones a doctor to whom the formula was meant to be delivered. But the doctor arrives accompanied by two heavies. He confesses that he is behind the attempts to steal the formula and intends to sell it to the highest bidder. His plans are foiled by the arrival of the police, and Steed takes possession of the formula until a new, safe, contact can be made.

THE SPRINGERS

Teleplay by John Whitney
and Geoffrey Bellman

John Steed	Patrick Macnee
Dr David Keel	Ian Hendry
One-Ten	Douglas Muir
Pheeney	David Webb
Straker	Charles Farrell
Haslam	Brian Murphy
Mr Groves	Arthur Howard
Caroline Evans	Margo Andrew
Neame	Donald Morley

Designed by Alpho O'Reilly

Directed by Don Leaver

STEED asks Dr Keel to impersonate a convict who he believes will shortly be helped to escape from a particular prison. Steed is anxious to trap the organisers of the escape route who will help any prisoner, even the dangerous ones, providing they have the funds to pay their price. Keel enters the prison and he soon receives a message giving a date for the escape. Believing that the escape route is by water, Steed visits a town served by a canal. A clue leads him to a girl's finishing school, and masquerading, with a young female agent, as father and daughter, they visit the school. However, Steed cannot be sure that this is to be Keel's destination. Later, Keel, helped by a warder, makes his escape, while at the finishing school Neame, the gang's organiser, catches Steed trying to break into the school to find information. When Steed fails to return to his hotel room, his female partner informs Steed's superior, One-Ten, but he tells her that to rescue Steed at this point would jeopardise the whole project. Meanwhile, Steed tries to convince Neame that he is simply a thief, but he is locked in a room at the school. When Keel is brought there, they devise an escape. When one of the gang recognises Keel as an impostor, however, it is left to Steed's quick-thinking to get them out of their predicament. The super-cool Steed soon outwits the gang and Neame is placed under arrest.

In The Springers, *Dr Keel watches Steed turn on the heat to discover who is behind the prisoners' escape route.*

THE FRIGHTENERS

Teleplay by Berkely Mather

Moxon	**Philip Locke**
Deacon	**Willoughby Goddard**
John Steed	**Patrick Macnee**
Carol Wilson	**Ingrid Hafner**
Jeremy de Willoughby	**Philip Gilbert**
Nigel	**David Andrews**
Sir Thomas Waller	**Stratford Johns**
Marilyn Waller	**Dawn Beret**
Mrs Briggs	**Doris Hare**

Designed by Robert Fuest

Directed by Peter Hammond

STEED and Keel are on the trail of an organisation which arranges the beating-up of subjects for money, and intercept two thugs who have been hired to beat-up a young society man, Jeremy de Willoughby. When de Willoughby refuses to press charges, Steed and Keel try to learn something from one of the thugs, but he refuses to divulge anything. Keel, however, tricks him into leading him to the hideout of the organiser, who is known as the Deacon. Keel learns that the Deacon has been paid by a business tycoon, Sir Thomas Waller, to prevent de Willoughby from marrying his daughter. Steed, meanwhile, makes enquiries about de Willoughby and discovers that he is a 'professional marrier'. Meanwhile, Waller refuses to pay the Deacon his fee because de Willoughby has not been frightened off. The Deacon now decides to settle with Waller. Dr Keel invites de Willoughby and his fiancée Marilyn Waller to his home to arrange their elopement. While they are there, a scruffy woman appears, claiming to be de Willoughby's mother. Now, faced with Marilyn's disenchantment and the threat of arrest by her father, de Willoughby flees. Keel pays off de Willoughby's 'mother' – an actress hired for the occasion – and the police arrest the Deacon before he and his men can carry out their threat on Waller.

THE YELLOW NEEDLE

Teleplay by Patrick Campbell

Sir Wilberforce Lungi	**Andre Dakar**
Dr David Keel	**Ian Hendry**
Carol Wilson	**Ingrid Hafner**
Inspector Anthony	**Eric Dodson**
Jacquetta Brown	**Margaret Whiting**
John Steed	**Patrick Macnee**
Chief Bai Shebro	**Bari Johnson**
Ali	**Wolfe Morris**

Designed by Alpho O'Reilly

Directed by Don Leaver

AN ATTEMPT is made on the life of Sir Wilberforce Lungi, an African leader visiting London for friendly negotiations leading to independence for his country, Tenebra. Steed asks Dr Keel, an old friend of Lungi's, to help his investigations of Lungi's secretary/companion, Jacquetta Brown. Steed flies to Tenebra, in the guise of a journalist, to meet Lungi's rival and enemy, Chief Bai Shebro, a passionate tribal nationalist. Keel finds Steed was right to suspect Jacquetta Brown. In Africa, Steed is befriended by a servant, and one of Shebro's wives, Judith, both of whom know and like Keel. Steed gathers more information which points to Jacquetta's unreliability. Shebro discovers Steed's impersonation is false and has him arrested and held prisoner. Judith helps Steed escape, and tells him that a final attempt is to be made on Lungi's life some time during the next 48 hours. In London, Jacquetta (who is a member of a sinister African secret society) substitutes a dose of yellow fever for the insulin with which Lungi has to inject himself. Steed rings Keel to say that he is not to leave Lungi for the next 48 hours. The call, however, is overheard by Jacquetta, and she drugs Keel. Steed returns the following morning, and overpowers Jacquetta as she tries to give Keel a second dose of the drug.

DEATH ON THE SLIPWAY

Teleplay by James Mitchell

Kolchek	Peter Arne
Dr David Keel	Ian Hendry
John Steed	Patrick Macnee
Sir William Bonner	Frank Thornton
Liz Wells	Nyree Dawn Porter
Sam Pearson	Paul Dawkins
Fleming	Sean Sullivan
Geordie Wilson	Redmond Bailey
Jack	Robert G Bahey
Insp Georgeson	Barry Keegan
PC Butterworth	Tom Adams
One-Ten	Douglas Muir
Pardoe	Gary Watson
PC Geary	Patrick Conner
Sgt Brodie	Hamilton Dyce
Chandler	Billy Milton

Designed by Robert Fuest

Directed by Peter Hammond

STEED IS sent, masquerading as a metallurgist, to a dockyard where a nuclear submarine is being built. A secret sevice man has been murdered there by a foreign spy, Kolchek, an old enemy of Steed's, who wants the plans of the submarine's reactor and is being helped by Fleming, the yard's personnel manager. Kolchek recognises Steed and arranges an accident for him but to no avail. Worried that time is running out, Kolchek orders Fleming to place a time-bomb in his briefcase and leave it on board the submarine during his next inspection. Steed returns to his hotel room to find Liz, Fleming's secretary, searching his suitcase – she believes he is a snooping detective. She explains that Fleming was once her lover and that a year ago his drunken driving killed a child. Steed now suspects that Fleming is being blackmailed into treachery by Kolchek and when an astute policeman observes that Fleming has left his briefcase behind, Steed realises that a bomb may be on board, and goes to search for the briefcase. Meanwhile, Kolchek, believing that Liz suspects him, locks her in a cupboard. Steed manages to find the deadly briefcase and hurries to confront Fleming with the evidence, only to see Kolchek pull a gun on Fleming. Kolchek turns the gun on Steed as he enters, but Fleming knocks the gun from his hand. Steed then throws the briefcase into the water, where the bomb explodes, harming no one.

DOUBLE DANGER

Teleplay by Gerald Verner

Mark Crawford	Charles Hodgson
Harry Dew	Robert Mill
Al Brady	Peter Reynolds
Bert Mills	Ronald Pember
Dr David Keel	Ian Hendry
Carol Wilson	Ingrid Hafner
Lola Carrington	Vanda Hudson
John Steed	Patrick Macnee
Bruton	Kevin Brennan
Bartholomew	Gordon Phillott

Designed by James Goddard

Directed by Roger Jenkins

DISCOVERING THAT Mace, a man he's been called upon to attend, is dying from gunshot wounds and not, as he was told, from the results of an accident, Dr Keel demands that the patient be taken to hospital. Ignoring the doctor's advice at gunpoint, Brady, the wounded man's partner, orders Keel to give Mace immediate treatment. Connecting the man's injuries to a recent diamond robbery being investigated by Steed, during which one of the thieves was shot by security guards, on the pretext of needing medical instruments and anaesthetic, the doctor persuades Brady to allow him to write a prescription which Mills, Brady's cohort, takes to Keel's surgery. The surly man's arrival disturbs Carol, Keel's receptionist, as does the cryptic prescription entry 'Fonus Equus'. Concerned that her employer is being held against his will and the entry is a clue, Carol rings Steed: 'Equus' means horse – or Steed. 'Fonus' is obvious – 'phone' . . . telephone Steed: the doctor is in trouble! Keel, meanwhile, becomes worried as Mace lapses into unconsciousness. Before doing so he whispers the words 'Hot Ice . . . Bartholomew's Plot' to the doctor. Minutes later the man dies. Furious that Keel has allowed his friend to die, Brady demands to know the man's dying words. When Keel laughs in his face, Brady orders Mills to dispose of the doctor. A fight breaks out and Keel makes good his escape. When Bruton, the gang's leader, arrives and Brady tells him that Mace died before revealing where he had secreted the proceeds of the diamond heist – but did whisper some words to the doctor – Bruton determines to make Keel talk: Carol is abducted from the surgery and Keel receives a telephone call intimating that the woman will be killed unless Keel discloses what Mace told him. Keel does so and Brady recalls that Bartholomew is the owner of the cottage used as a meeting place by Mace. Leaving Carol locked in a cellar, the crooks race to the cottage. But Steed has beaten them to the punch; having rescued Carol during their absence, both he and Dr Keel are waiting when the heavies arrive – the missing diamonds safely in Steed's possession. The police are called and Steed invites Carol and the doctor to join him for dinner – paid for from the proceeds of the insurance company reward!

TOY TRAP

Teleplay by Bill Strutton

John Steed	Patrick Macnee
Dr David Keel	Ian Hendry
May Murton	Hazel Graeme
Henry Burge	Tony van Bridge
Alice	Nina Marriott
Bunty Seton	Sally Smith
Mrs McCabe	Ann Tirard
Freddie	Brandon Brady
Johnnie	Brian Jackson
Photographer	Lionel Burns
Lennie Taylor	Tex Fuller
Ann	Mitzi Rogers

Designed by Douglas James

Directed by Don Leaver

BUNTY, daughter of a country doctor, who is a friend of Dr Keel, is working in a large department store. Worried by the disappearance of her friend May, she asks Keel for his help. Keel believes May is involved in a call-girl racket and enlists Steed's help in finding her. The trail leads to an ex-shop girl, Chrissie, and when she is murdered, Keel tells Steed he is worried about Bunty's safety. Steed visits the department store and learns from the supervisor, Hearn, that Chrissie had recently stopped working there. Meanwhile, Keel visits the hostel where the shop girls live, and is warned off by the housekeeper, Mrs McCabe. Steed learns that one of the store's assistants, Lennie, has a criminal record, and he and Keel trail him to his apartment. When Lennie leaves, they enter and find Bunty's friend May. May says that Lennie has been hiding her from the boss of the call-girl organisation. Steed asks Bunty to act as a decoy and pretend that she is interested in the gang's offer to work as a call-girl. Bunty is soon approached by the boss of the gang – Mrs McCabe. Steed arrives with the police and Mrs McCabe is arrested.

THE TUNNEL OF FEAR

Teleplay by John Kruse

Maxie Lardner	Stanley Platts
Jack Wickram	John Salew
Dr David Keel	Ian Hendry
Carol Wilson	Ingrid Hafner
Harry Black	Murray Hayne
John Steed	Patrick Macnee
One-Ten	Douglas Muir
Mrs Black	Doris Rogers
Madame Zenobia	Nancy Roberts
Claire	Miranda Connell
Billy	Douglas Rye
Sergeant	Morris Perry

Designed by James Goddard

Directed by Guy Verney

WHEN AN escaped convict, Harry Black, appears at Dr Keel's surgery bearing injuries caused by broken glass, Steed investigates and discovers that Black, who insists he was framed, has recently been working in a funfair at Southend. Steed tells Keel that top-secret information has been leaked to foreign countries, and it seems that Southend is the source of the leaks. He tells Keel to go to the funfair and make enquiries about Black, while Steed gets a job at the fairground. When Black returns to the funfair, his former colleague, Maxie, tips off the police. Keel, having visited Black's mother who also says that her son was framed, helps Black, who takes refuge on board the boat of his girlfriend, Claire. Maxie soon becomes suspicious of Steed and informs his boss, Wickram, who sets a trap. Maxie knocks Steed out in his hotel room. Steed is then hypnotised by a fairground hypnotist, working for Wickram, but he will not divulge any information. Keel, meanwhile, has realised that Black must have been hypnotised and framed, in order to get him out of the way. He drives to Claire's boat, where Black tells him that Claire has been kidnapped by Wickram and his henchmen. They rush to the funfair and find Claire and Steed trussed and gagged in the tunnel of the Ghost Train, with a machine which is tapping information from a telephone line to Europe. Disturbed and threatened by Wickram, they are saved when Steed conducts a gigantic bluff with an apparently explosive cigarette. Keel and Steed soon overpower the rest of the gang and end the leaks.

THE FAR DISTANT DEAD

Teleplay by John Lucarotti

Zun Garcia	Reed de Rouen
Dr David Keel	Ian Hendry
Dr Ampara Alverez Sandoval	Katharine Blake
Hercule Zeebrugge	Francis de Wolff
Rayner	Tom Adams
Godoy	Andreas Malandrinos
Mateos	Michael Mellinger
Inspector Gauvreau	Guy Deghby

Designed by Robert Fuest

Directed by Peter Hammond

RETURNING TO England from Chile, Dr Keel's flight stops over in Mexico City and, learning that a cyclone has struck a small Mexican sea-port, he volunteers to help the victims. En route, he meets a young Mexican woman doctor who is also going to help the disaster victims. Keel and the woman soon decide to continue their journey together. At the emergency hospital in town, a patient is brought in suffering from severe food poisoning, and Keel discovers that the cooking oil flown in as rations is, in fact, hydraulic fluid. He learns that the oil was donated by an old warehouse-man who had been storing the tins for an unknown customer. Returning to his hotel room, Keel finds an anonymous letter, informing him that the first victim of the cooking oil died in Vera Cruz two years before. In Vera Cruz, Keel and the woman doctor visit the victim's widow, who tells them that her husband stole the oil from a tramp steamer. A check with the shipping company shows that the oil came from Marseilles. In Marseilles, they meet a man named Caron who tells them that the oil came from Zeebrugge. Keel's companion discovers that this is not the port of Zeebrugge, but the name of a financier and, making an excuse to Keel, she leaves. Keel soon discovers his mistake and finds the financier's address. He drives to Zeebrugge's home in time to stop the woman doctor taking revenge for the deaths of the villagers by killing the financier. Sympathetic to her cause, however, he allows her to escape before calling the police to arrest Zeebrugge.

KILL THE KING

Teleplay by James Mitchell

King Tenuphon	Burt Kwouk
Prince Serrakit	James Goei
General Tuke	Patrick Allen
Mei Li	Lisa Peake
John Steed	Patrick Macnee
Crichton-Bull	Peter Barkworth
Dr Keel	Ian Hendry
Carol	Ingrid Hafner
Zoe Carter	Moira Redmond
Major Harrington	Ian Colin
Ingrid Storm	Carole Shelley
U Meng	Andy Ho
Suchong	Eric Young

Designed by Paul Bernard

Directed by Roger Jenkins

KING Tenuphon, who is in London to sign an oil treaty, is threatened with assassination by dissidents in his country, and Steed is instructed to guard him until the treaty is signed. An attempt has already been made on the King's life when, on the plane carrying him to England, a steward tried to shoot him, wounding instead Prince Serrakit, the King's adviser. The steward was killed by Tuke, the royal bodyguard. Meanwhile, a Major Harrington arrives at a flat opposite the King's hotel suite and tells the owner, Mrs Carter, that her husband – a missing secret service agent – will be shot unless she lets him use her window to shoot the King. Steed discovers that U Meng, leader of the dissidents, has paid someone to carry out the killing. Worried that the King may be shot by a sniper close to the hotel, Steed checks for possible sniper points. But when he arrives at Mrs Carter's boarding-house, she tells him nothing of Major Harrington. Later that day, a low-flying helicopter attracts the King and his entourage to their hotel balcony. Suspicious, Steed throws himself at the King just as Major Harrington shoots from across the street. Prince Serrakit is killed, and the King's bodyguard, Tuke, shoots the major.

DEAD OF WINTER

Teleplay by Eric Paice

Harry	John Woodvine
Syd	Blaise Wyndham
Schneider	Carl Duering
John Steed	Patrick Macnee
Dr David Keel	Ian Hendry
Dr Brennan	David Hart
Inez	Sheila Robins
Carol Wilson	Ingrid Hafner
Willi	Michael Sarne
Margarita	Zorenah Osborne
Weber	Neil Hallett
Ted	Norman Chappell
Kreuzer	Arnold Marle

Designed by Robert Fuest

Directed by Don Leaver

STEED INVESTIGATES when the body of Gerhardt Schneider, a wanted Nazi war criminal who had tried to raise a new Fascist party to be called Phoenix, is discovered among the deep-frozen consignment of meat unloaded at the London docks. Having questioned the dockers and Weber, the head of the meat importing firm, about the body, Steed and Dr Keel go to the mortuary where Dr Brennan, a friend of Keel's, is to do the autopsy on Schneider's body. On arrival, however, they find the body gone and Brennan murdered. Steed persuades Keel to impersonate a doctor member of Phoenix who is about to arrive in London. Willi, a young member of Phoenix, takes Keel to the distinguished Dr Kreuzer, who shows him Schneider's body. To Keel's amazement the body blinks and sits up. Kreuzer explains that he can suspend life by deep-freezing and later resuscitate his patients. But he knows Keel to be a fraud, and has him bound and gagged and made ready for his next experiment. Steed meanwhile receives a visitor – Margarita, Willi's girlfriend, and she takes him to Keel. They arrive at the docks, where Steed is attacked by Kreuzer's henchmen. The dockers, however, have been primed by Steed and make a surprise rescue. Steed is in time to prevent his friend from being used in Kreuzer's experiment and releases him from his cold-room prison. Phoenix is totally destroyed and Keel's only after-effect is a cold.

THE DEADLY AIR

Teleplay by Lester Powell

Barbara Anthony	Ann Bell
Dr Philip Karswood	Michael Hawkins
Heneger	Keith Anderson
John Steed	Patrick Macnee
Herbert Truscott	Richard Butler
Dr David Keel	Ian Hendry
Dr Hugh Chalk	Allan Cuthbertson
Dr Owen Craxton	John Stratton
One-Ten	Douglas Muir
Carol Wilson	Ingrid Hafner
Dr Harvey	Cyril Renison
Keo Armstrong	Anthony Cundell
Professor Kilbride	Geoffrey Bayldon

Designed by Robert Macgowan

Directed by John Knight

STEED and Dr Keel are called in when Heneger, a scientist working on top-secret experiments to prove a vaccine for a serious disease, is attacked and a whole batch of the precious vaccine wasted. Two other scientists, Chalk and Craxton, decide on a final test of the vaccine, but one of the doctors enclosed in a hygienic test room collapses with a fatal dose of the disease. It is suspected that the vaccine is faulty, but when a monkey is injected, it remains healthy, leading Dr Keel to suspect sabotage. Investigating the machinery used in the test, Steed finds traces of glass inside the air duct that feeds sterilised air into the test chamber. He tells Keel he believes the man was murdered by a phial of the vaccine being broken and introduced into the air-feed to the room. Steed and Keel volunteer to carry out the next test when, unaccountably, the air intake fan begins to work, and the door is locked from the outside. An engineer in charge returns to find that Heneger is responsible for the murder attempt. Heneger, however, shoots the engineer and makes his escape. Fortunately, the engineer manages to shut off the air to the test room and release the door, before dying. Steed finds an unbroken phial of the vaccine taped to the fan blade and has it analysed. The vaccine is proved to be over 100 times more potent than the rest of the batch, and Steed seeks the help of Professor Kilbride. Then the remaining six phials of the vaccine are stolen. Heneger next tries to kill the Professor, but Keel prevents him by throwing the contents of a test-tube in his face. Heneger now admits his part in the crime but says that Dr Craxton is the mastermind behind the murders. He wants to discredit the vaccine so he can sell it, suitably disguised, elsewhere. Craxton, meanwhile, has trapped Steed in the test room, taped a new phial to the intake fan, and set it working. Keel manages to rescue his partner, who now believes that this time he has received a fatal dose, and hasn't long to live. Truscott, head of the project, says the phial used by Craxton was harmless – he had taken the six lethal ones home and replaced them with phials of pure water. Craxton is arrested by the security guards.

A CHANGE OF BAIT

Teleplay by Lewis Davidson

Archie Duncan	**Victor Platt**
Lemuel Potts	**John Bailey**
Peter Sampson	**Henry Soskin**
Carol Wilson	**Ingrid Hafner**
John Steed	**Patrick Macnee**
Herb Thompson	**Robert Desmond**
Nat Fletcher	**Graham Rigby**
Dr David Keel	**Ian Hendry**
Barker	**Gary Hope**
André	**Arthur Barrett**
Bryan Stubbs	**Norman Pitt**
Ivy	**Gillian McCutcheon**
Charlie	**Harry Shacklock**
Steed's helper	**Michael Hunt**

Designed by James Goddard

Directed by Don Leaver

ARCHIE, AN elderly man seriously ill with a heart disease, has bought a cargo of bananas which he hopes to sell at a profit. But Potts, a crooked businessman, knowing Archie's difficulty in finding a buyer, organises a sale. But he then tells Sampson, a shop steward at the docks, to organise a strike so that Barstow, another businessman to whom Potts offers the bananas, will be able to claim insurance when the fruit goes rotten. Keel, called in when Archie has a heart attack, discovers that Steed already knows about Potts' scheme. Steed blackmails Sampson into calling off the strike, and arranges that when Potts telephones Barstow to warn him that the fruit will be delivered after all, Steed himself takes the message. Barstow is now forced to accept delivery of the rotten bananas, and it seems that Potts will now have to pay Archie for the consignment. Potts, however, decides to delay payment until Archie's heart gives out from the suspense. Steed, realising this, decides to take part in another of Potts' shady deals – a plan to set alight an antique shop for the owner, who needs the insurance money. Steed and Keel conceal themselves in the shop and extinguish the flames. The shop keeper, furious, telephones Potts, who hurries to the shop, and is photographed by Steed as he is about to re-start the fire. Once arrested, he is invited by Steed to telephone Barstow, incriminating him. Steed explains that if he does this he will be allowed to telephone the bank and stop Archie's cheque. Potts telephones Barstow, but when he tries to phone his bank, discovers that Steed has put the clock forward, and the bank is not yet open. As the police take Potts away, Steed gives Archie his cheque while Keel breaks into laughter.

DRAGONSFIELD

Teleplay by Terence Feely

John Steed	**Patrick Macnee**
Lisa Strauss	**Sylvia Langova**
Saunders	**Alfred Burke**
Reddington	**Ronald Leigh-Hunt**
Susan Summers	**Barbara Shelley**
Jack Alford	**Thomas Kyffin**
Technician	**Keith Barron**
Secretary	**Amanda Reeves**
One-Fifteen	**Eric Dodson**
Boris	**Steven Scott**
Landlord	**Michael Robbins**
Peters	**Herbert Nelson**
Second Technician	**Morris Perry**

Designed by Voytek

Directed by Peter Hammond

STEED IS sent to a research centre at which a team of scientists is working against time to produce a material which will shield space travellers from radiation. One of the scientists has recently been badly exposed to radiation, and cannot work. Steed discovers that Saunders, the unpopular security officer, has warned Dr Alford, one of the team, about fraternising with Susan Summers, his pretty assistant. Alford takes this badly, but Susan believes that Saunders is simply jealous. Later, Steed overhears a quarrel between Susan and another female member of the team, Lisa Strauss, whom Susan accuses of being in love with Dr Reddington, the head of the project. When Alford is attacked by an unknown assailant, Steed rescues him, though Alford receives injuries and is put out of action. Meanwhile, unknown to Steed, Saunders has managed to break the code used by the saboteurs, and sends a message making a rendezvous at the local pub. Arriving for the show-down, Saunders is captured and held at gunpoint by two thugs. In the meantime, Steed, having volunteered to act as a guinea-pig in an experiment, is almost killed when someone tampers with the laboratory equipment. From Saunders' report, Steed learns of the trap he has set and arrives at the pub to find Saunders has been taken away by two gunmen. He tracks them to a disused flour mill and arrives in time to disarm the gunmen and rescue Saunders. Steed forces one of them to reveal that the saboteur is Susan Summers and Steed quickly drives back to the research centre, while Saunders rings the authorities to arrest the gunmen. However, Lisa and Dr Reddington have just discovered a fatal error in their calculations. They agree to run one final test, assisted by Susan Summers. Steed arrives, to be told by Dr Reddington that Susan and Lisa have gone to the laboratory ahead of him to set up the experiment, and he gets there in time to stop Susan strangling Lisa.

GALE FORCE/HIGH FASHION AND DERRING-DO

Patrick Macnee/Honor Blackman 1962

IN DECEMBER 1961, a decision was taken to extend the Hendry series to 39 episodes and plans were made to introduce a new female partner to the team. However, as one might expect, this was not to be Catherine Gale. The new girl was to be a young nightclub singer named Venus Smith, who would be introduced in episode 27 and then alternate with Keel as Steed's partner on a fortnightly basis.

As history shows, this never happened. Ten months after its first successful series was closed down by an actors' dispute (Equity, the actors' union, forbade any of its members to appear in film work) the show returned – this time without Ian Hendry, who had left the production to pursue a career in the cinema. This time around Steed had *three* new helpers – all unofficial, all much more concerned than he was with man's behaviour towards his fellow man.

First of these was Mrs Catherine Gale, a character created by producer Leonard White who, finding that he had a half-dozen or so unused scripts commissioned for the previous series, decided to change the Keel role to that of a woman, 'a 1960's version of Shaw's emancipated young woman, providing the Conscience in combat with Patrick Macnee's contemporary Chocolate Soldier', based (or so the story goes) on two famous women: Margaret Mead, the anthropologist, and Margaret Bourne-Smith, the photographer for *Life Magazine*.

Cathy was to be a cool blonde with a PhD in anthropology, who had married a farmer in Kenya and become adept with a gun during the Mau Mau troubles in which her husband was killed. When Cuba's Fidel Castro was leading a democratic rebellion against dictatorship, she fought in the hills with him. But as soon as Dr Castro achieved power, he deported her because of her opposition to certain aspects of his regime and she returned to Britain to take up a position at the British Museum. Unlike Steed, she was not a professional undercover agent, but her existence was known and accepted by Steed's superiors. A judo expert and three times runner-up at Bisley, her resourcefulness and scientific knowledge were often in demand by Steed, but her attitude to any mission was totally different. A woman of unshakable moral principle, the end, to her, could never justify the means, and she disliked Steed's cavalier treatment of people. Nevertheless, she assisted him as a crusading amateur with a genuine desire to help the victims of crime.

Plans to introduce nightclub singer Venus Smith were placed on hold while White and his team began their search for an actress with the right qualities to become John Steed's first ever female colleague. After ABC had spent six months considering the right girl for the part, Honor Blackman was chosen to join Patrick Macnee in his fight against crime – but not before Leonard White had whittled down his shortlist of would-be hopefuls to six names.

Among these were Honor Blackman and, favourite to get the part, Nyree Dawn Porter. Convinced that the latter stood head and shoulders over the former, producer Sydney Newman, who was about to go on holiday for a fortnight, told White 'Get Nyree Dawn Porter, but *not* Honor Blackman', whom he believed was too saccharine and genteel for the role. Imagine his surprise when, upon his return to the studio, he was greeted with the news that the new Avengers girl had been signed – Honor Blackman was to play Mrs Catherine Gale! (It transpired that Miss Porter was unable to accept the role due to prior commitments.) Honor Blackman signed in June 1962, her original contract being for six episodes only, but the studio retained the option which allowed them to pick up her services for further episodes between that date and January 1963.

Prior to the series being screened in September 1962, Honor said, 'I'm a first for television. The first feminist to come into a television serial; the first woman to fight back. Cathy is all anthropologist, an academic, all brain and what she doesn't have in the way of brawn, she makes up for in motorbikes, black boots, leather combat suits and judo.' She told me recently, 'We had enormous problems with rewrites at the beginning. My part had been written for a man and when they started writing it for me, my problem was that they continued to write it as they'd *always* written women's parts until then; she waited for the man to make the decision; she had no mind of her own and was incapable of any logical thought process. I was going mad at the time. In fact I was going mad just *learning* it. Then my husband at the time, Maurice Kauffman, said, "Why don't you *pretend*

that you're a man and *play* it that way?" So I did, then gradually we changed the scripts as we went along and the writers soon got used to writing for me, once they'd seen on screen just what *sort* of character I was producing.'

Macnee's role was also revamped. Although he had been wearing his Edwardian-style clothes for the final episodes of the Hendry series, the producers asked him to dandify the role more than ever. A return visit to his tailor brought him embroidered waistcoats, and a visit to a well-known London hatter brought him a variety of bowlers and trilby hats.

Steed immaculate in formal garb complete with bowler.

'I design all my own Avenger suits,' Patrick said. 'I like the idea of velvet for the collars, it helps mould and complement the suits. There are no breast pockets and only one button to give the best moulding to the chest. Plus a deliberatcly low waist, to give the effect of simplicity, but with an individual style.' Expensive shirts, many of them striped, elegant embroidered waistcoats, expensive cuff-links and tie-pins, plus hand-made Chelsea boots, completed the wardrobe. 'I visual-ised Steed as a modern-day Beau Brummell – with an iron exterior. In developing Steed's character, I consi-dered one of the most important facets was to give him good manners. You did not complain about the food, you always opened doors for ladies. You could bash someone over the head but you always observed the social proprieties.'

Upon his partnership with Honor Blackman he told me, 'Honor Blackman was by far and away *the* most suitable lady for the part. It was a choice between her and another very fine actress. Honor won the part and then, with her incredible beauty, energy, attack and originality, she created Cathy Gale, who was *the* first English television lady. The part she played was virtually that of a man and in her own inimitable way she turned it into a female character-like person who had strong tendencies which were met by my own, seemingly disarming, outward casualness. We trod a very, very

gentle, narrow line. We had a nice submerged sense of humour and a deep respect for each other.'

One of the main contributing factors to the program-me's success was the judo-influenced fighting style of Cathy Gale. Apparently, this wasn't a calculated plan on the part of the producers.

Originally, Cathy was to have carried an assortment of miniature pistols in her handbag. But after two or three weeks of Cathy reaching for her .25 calibre gun, or her powder compact which concealed a miniature gold pistol, they got bored with the gun's limitations and decided to change the format. They first tried fitting Cathy with a garter holster, but feminine though the garter proved, it made Honor bow-legged. (There was also the added drawback of Cathy having to raise her skirts every time she met a possible assailant.) Next they tried concealing firearms about her person. Under-arm holsters are fine for men, but men don't have breasts or tight-fitting sweaters. Miniature swords, daggers and a Kongo-stick were the next idea, but they also proved no good – too many cut or broken bra straps. So they were left with purely physical attacks. Honor and Patrick were sent to see René Burdet, ex-head of the Resistance in Marseilles during the war, who taught them how to throw people. Realising that she was expected to fight an average of once each episode, and aware that each fight *had* to look right first time (in those early days it wasn't possible to edit videotapes prior to transmission, and what happened in the studio found its way into viewers' homes), Honor discussed her fighting technique with Leonard White, who urged her to take up judo seriously.

Cathy Gale typically combining glamour with menace.

Recalling that Douglas Robinson, a Black Belt of the 9th Dan, had played a small part in an earlier Avengers story, White arranged for Honor to meet him. Within days she was learning the ropes the hard way, thrashing about on the straw mats and concrete floor of Robinson's gym. Given barely five weeks to teach the actress the basic judo moves, the instructor achieved the impossible. Within the time allocated, Honor had mastered enough of the technique to make her on-screen fights convincing. Within months her technique blossomed and, slowly, her judo expertise was worked into the part. 'It's fascinating,' she said at the time. 'It makes you feel quite splendid. Anyway, I couldn't go on stopping villains by producing a gun. I'm not a killer and at the same time I couldn't *pretend* to heave men over my shoulder. It had to be the real thing.' (Rumour has it that during the recording of each story, male studio technicians placed side bets on whether she *could* actually throw a man across the room. They always lost! As a worker on the set said: 'To see her in action before the camera, you'd think she'd eat a man for breakfast. She puts everything she's got into her judo moves.')

Meanwhile, the search continued to find an actress to play Venus Smith. In August 1962, ten days after 51 actresses had descended upon Teddington Studios to audition for the role, five were requested to return to strut their stuff for the producers. Of these, Angela Douglas, Julie Stevens and Vera Day were shortlisted. Three weeks later Julie Stevens was signed for the role.

As with the earlier series, in order that the writers could familiarise themselves with the new character concept, Leonard White presented them with a new, updated directive.

THE AVENGERS

Name: CATHERINE GALE (Cathy)   Age 28/30

A widow. She is very attractive, intelligent and has a vital personality.

Her BACKGROUND includes a good education. She has been to a University and gained an honours degree – BA/Anthropology.

Her intention was to continue research for her PhD but she met, and fell in love with, a young farmer on holiday in London from his home in Africa. The idea of sharing his life abroad appealed to her *lively spirit of adventure*.

She married him.

Her experiences, during several years on their isolated homestead in Africa, toughened her and she came to accept and thrive in their new environment. Carrying *firearms* was second nature to her and she became *expert in their use*. She learned to cope with the practicalities of isolated living as well as any man. She could equally well deal with the mechanics of a car engine as with the delivery of a baby.

After several years her husband was killed on their farm.

Cathy returned to this country and resumed her studies to pick up the threads of her original career. She gained a PhD in Anthropology.

She has become a first class photographer. She has presented a paper to the Royal Geographical Society on her recent photographic expedition to the Amazon. During this expedition she was separated from the party and attacked by natives: she escaped only after shooting three of them.

She is essentially a *strong, lively personality*. She is an individualist. She doesn't make friends too easily but such as she may have are friends for life. Her experiences may have made her a little withdrawn: she may even appear to be a somewhat lonely person. She may repress the sensual side of her nature but nevertheless all these characteristics only *enhance our desire to get to know her better*.

She is sophisticated but *not* upper-class.

She has a *strong sense of humour*.

Her flat reflects her personality and interests. There are some *special firearms*: some *prizes of her expeditions*: some of her *African treasure* and examples of *her photography* and equipment. There is nothing flamboyant and the effect is *not* of luxury. It is obviously a *woman's* flat and strong touches of femininity are seen. In all *good taste* is evident.

Only fools would dare to tangle with the delectable Cathy Gale.

In her 'undercover' activities she is fired by the desire to fight against evil and essentially help those who are victims of crime.

During *her joint missions with Steed* she will, more often than not, provide the *moral attitude*. She may not always approve of Steed's methods. His is the attitude of the ruthless professional and hers may be that of the crusading 'amateur', who *cares deeply for the people involved*.

We will *care deeply about her*.

Name: VENUS SMITH   Age: 20-ish

She is a vivacious nightclub singer.

Her father was a barge owner and her early years were spent with her family on a barge travelling the canals of England. She is the youngest of three children. Her two brothers, much older than she, both emigrated when she was 12 years old. Her formal education was rather sporadic but her lack of academic prowess is compensated for by her *alert commonsense*.

At 17 she decided to leave 'home'. In London she found ways of developing her *natural talent* to entertain. At first with amateur and semi-pro jazz groups and then, recently, club work.

The nature of her formative years has created a *resilient* character quite able *and eager to cope with the rough and tumble of her career in show-business*.

Steed joins Venus Smith to discover who is leaking government secrets in Box of Tricks.

Her character is NOT that of a corny 'sex bombshell' type of entertainer. She is well able to put over a sexy number if necessary, but essentially she is a *warm-hearted, lovable, gay* girl. She may be earthy, but NEVER coarse or jaded.

Others feel they would like to take care of her.

She makes friends easily. She accepts people as she finds them. This does not mean that she is lacking in perception, but that *she prefers to think well of people.* She hates gossip.

She is by no means a 'goody goody', but she *is* a good person.

She has a special *radiant quality* which is her great attraction both on-stage and off.

She does not know anything of the true nature of Steed's work.

She is NOT an undercover agent. She is involved in Steed's 'escapades' for several reasons. She does it for the *excitement*; for the opportunity to go places and do things otherwise not possible to her.

She likes Steed, and the aura of mystery surrounding him is an intriguing attraction for her.

There is NO suggestion of any 'affair' between them. If anything she probably regards Steed as a 'special' elder brother. This attitude he finds rather flattering and he may feel that she 'needs looking after'. Very often, in fact, on her adventures she may indeed *need* Steed's timely aid to get her out of trouble.

Steed usually calls her 'Smith', but to her friends and associates at the club she is known as 'Vee'. 'Vee' for vitality!

Always on target. Honor Blackman and Patrick Macnee were voted Independent Television's Personalities of 1963.

Name: ONE-TEN.   Age: 55/60

He is our only link with apparent officialdom. His 'establishment' is necessarily very obscure.

He contracts the 'undercover' work but he will always keep the arrangements on a PERSONAL basis.

He may know that Steed and Cathy use other people, but they are not 'recognised' by him (and neither are they his responsibility).

One-Ten is very intelligent. He might be an Oxford Don who has been assigned to his highly specialised work in big crime detection where it is necessary to use undercover agents.

He is often on the telephone – but the 'phone always seems to be in an *interesting* place.

If and when he has to make physical contact with Steed or Cathy, it will probably be in the most *unlikely* places – say a launderette, a barber's shop, an auction, etc., etc.

His use in the stories should be kept to the absolute minimum, and it is not necessary that he should be involved in every episode.

GENERAL:

We will woo our audience in the *first minute* of each story. Whatever happens later, *the first minute* MUST establish *excitement* and *provocation.*

Our HEROES are people we (the audience) will *like and admire.* We should like them because of the virtues they display: we will admire them for the *dexterity and intelligence* with which they win their battles.

The CAUSES our heroes defend are *good causes,* and the people they help and protect are people like ourselves.

The stories will be set in environments which are *exciting and different* (scenes set in 'offices', 'drawing rooms', 'flats', etc. are very dull visually). We need some *special quality* to make them acceptable. One main exciting and unusual locale (atomic energy plants, zoos, breweries, mass-production factories, etc.) gives more value than an endless number of small box sets of dull rooms.

Our leading characters are essentially UNDERCOVER. They are NOT private or public detectives. Any story which follows this pattern is NOT right for us.

On their missions they do NOT work with the police. If the police are involved at all (and this should be *very rare*) then it is most likely that they believe our undercover characters are *on the wrong side!*

STEED and CATHY will generally work *jointly* on their missions, but occasional episodes using them individually will be used. When working together, the means they use individually and the differing attitudes they adopt will often give rise to some sort of *conflict.* Development of CHARACTER is of great importance. On occasion CATHY may do even better than STEED. Nevertheless they retain a *deep respect* and regard for each other. They are NOT in conflict over either the importance of their mission or the need to bring it to a successful conclusion.

VENUS must only be used as an 'extension' of STEED. She will of course have her own separate private life and career, but as she CANNOT be 'in the know' her use is oblique to the main issue. Normally she will only appear in stories with STEED.

You will note that the directive made no mention of Dr Martin King, the character who shared three adventures with Steed in the series. I have it on good authority that actor Jon Rollason was contracted solely to 'bridge the gap' between the introduction of Mrs Gale and Venus Smith, and make use of three scripts originally written for Ian Hendry's character.

The new direction planned for the series wasn't without its critics. Prior to the production of the first Blackman episode, the Controller of Programmes for ABC voiced his concern that several high-ranking company executives had expressed the comment that 'the replacement of Ian Hendry by a woman would a) alienate female viewers, b) lose viewers who had obviously enjoyed the bantering camaraderie between Hendry and Macnee, and c) would tend to introduce elements of sex and sexual violence into the series.' Alarmed that such might be the case, the producers were directed to ensure that item c) in particular was given 'careful attention' and that the scripts avoided this 'unsavoury element'.

Commenting recently on the relationship Cathy Gale shared with John Steed, Honor Blackman told me, 'Leonard White particularly wanted Cathy to be pure. As a contrast really, because first of all, Steed's character *was* wicked, devilish and saucy, so Cathy *had* to be a contrast. This made her so much more entertaining – and certainly more *acceptable*. She did all the fighting and therefore it was important that she remained a woman who defended herself for only *good* reasons and went after the baddies because she *cared* very much about right and justice. What was so lovely was the sense of humour that was retained throughout – the sort of sexual sparring that went on between them, particularly from Steed, which she warded off, but with humour.

This made it much more entertaining. Let's face it, you could hardly have a series with a man and a woman who were both perfectly normal, *without* having *that* sort of relationship. Some *sexual* relationship *had* to be brought into it because it would have been rather bizarre without it over such a long period.' (In fact there was just enough innuendo and fade-outs over popping champagne corks at the end of each story to leave the viewer wondering 'do they or don't they?' – go to bed, that is.) 'Cathy was a creature of fantasy. A girl who could toss minions all over the room and manhandle even the toughest villains with nonchalant disdain. No one could be so brainy and remote and physical and sexy and untouchable and wear leather and high boots and be perfectly normal as well.'

As perfection in clothes was to play an important part of Cathy's character, Leonard White, still with his finger on the pulse (and setting a precedent that would permeate throughout all future Avengers series), circulated a memo to his staff stressing the importance of taking full advantage of the publicity surrounding the introduction of Honor Blackman to make her character a leader of fashion. 'It is,' he said, 'the programme makers' declared intention to *set* fashion – not to *follow* it!'

When recording began, fashion expert Michael Whittaker designed some sensational outfits for Cathy, and predicted that tailored styles and high boots were coming into vogue. As this was absolutely in line with Cathy's character and the job she had to do as the undercover agent with a passion for high fashion, derring-do and derringers, her entire wardrobe was planned with an eye to these trends. But her leather fighting gear came about by accident.

Honor Blackman told the press at the time, 'The leather thing was extraordinary. The fact that I happened to choose leather for my fighting kit was a pure accident. Cathy led a very active life and I soon realised that I needed something that wouldn't rip. Skirts were out of the question. When your legs are flying over your head, the last thing you want to worry about is whether your stocking-tops are showing. It happened that right at the beginning of the series, I split my trousers in close-up, with my rear in full view of the camera. So it became obvious that I had to find some tougher gear. Somebody suggested suede, but we found suede didn't "light" on television. Then someone, Patrick, I think, suggested leather and after trying it, the producers said "Great", so I wore it throughout the rest of the show. The only thing you can wear with leather trousers are boots, so they kitted me out with calf-length black boots, and the leather thing was born.' (Incidentally, she told me recently that her first leather outfit was *green*. However, because the show was shot in black and white it didn't really matter. Once the viewers had accepted that it was *black* leather, it became black leather.)

Patrick Macnee told me, 'We had Honor Blackman in black leather, partly because it was better than wearing skirts when she was doing lots of violent action, and it evolved, of course, in comic strip form, to a woman sending thugs flying in all directions and doing karate chops. I recommended it when Honor needed costumes for her fights. At first, no one realised the importance of the idea. Studio technicians disliked it because black wouldn't televise. The leather had to be green, or tan. But the lighting techniques soon improved and Honor ended up wearing black leather. We used a lot of sexual fetishes, leather, bondage, whatever, but in a very very light way. But then Cecil B. DeMille had been doing that in the 20s and the 30s, under much heavier censorship. In other words, we titillated. It was an attractive fashion that soon caught on.'

Honor Blackman wears her famous leather action suit designed by Michael Whittaker for her role as Cathy Gale.

Michael Whittaker, who took on the job as a special favour to Honor Blackman, for whom he had designed many film wardrobes, used leather for many of Cathy's clothes: slacks suits, worn with a long line, vee-necked pullover jacket and tapered slacks in soft kid leather, teamed with long leather boots; a cocktail dress with a full skirt which could be removed in a moment, to show a slim pair of Spanish brocade trousers; a fine woollen dinner dress with a plain, tight-fitting bodice and culottes hidden by a panel in the skirt. He made everything to fit skin-tight and every outfit accentuated Honor's slim waist. Many of Cathy's outfits were interchangeable. A skirt and jacket worn with a non-creasing blouse could be switched about to become a dress suit or simply a skirt and blouse. Other outfits included divided skirts, trench coats and draped pyjamas – leading one critic to comment, 'Steed's Girl Friday has more curves than a runaway bus!'

Whereas the formula remained the same – a series of wildly over-animated adventures treated as an enjoyable dramatisation of, say, a Boys Own paperback yarn, laced with plenty of action and worldly dialogue, this time Steed had a new canine sidekick, Freckles, a two-year-old Dalmatian puppy, who was brought in to replace Juno, the Great Dane who was Steed's regular companion in the Hendry series, until he lost his life in an accident on London's underground when en route to film an Avengers story.

Patrick Macnee as Father Christmas, Honor Blackman as Robin Hood, and Juno, the Great Dane.

The theme music was slightly different, too. Johnny Dankworth had revamped his original score by adding extra percussion and a xylophone middle phrase.

The series got off to a cracking start with a thrill-packed story called *Mr Teddy Bear*. However, this was not intended to be the first Cathy Gale episode. That distinction was held by the script called *Warlock*. Penned by scriptwriter Doreen Montgomery, this contained passages in which Steed and Cathy met for the first time (when Steed was ordered by his superiors to seek expert advice on a Black Magic grimoire he'd found at the scene of a crime, from anthropologist Cathy, then working at the British Museum), and several other 'character establishing' scenes. However, because several other Cathy Gale stories had already been transmitted prior to this story, the 'introductory' scenes were trimmed prior to transmission.

MR TEDDY BEAR

Teleplay by Martin Woodhouse

Interviewer	**Tim Brinton**
Col Wayne-Gilley	**Kenneth Keeling**
John Steed	**Patrick Macnee**
Dr Gilmore	**John Horsley**
One-Ten	**Douglas Muir**
Catherine Gale	**Honor Blackman**
Henry	**Michael Robbins**
Mr Teddy Bear	**Bernard Goldman**
Café girl	**Sarah Maxwell**
Dr James Howell	**John Ruddock**

Designed by Terry Green

Directed by Richmond Harding

COLONEL Wayne-Gilley is publicly murdered during a television interview. The method used is so diabolically clever that One-Ten is certain that the killer can only be Mr Teddy Bear – a professional assassin, of no political allegiance, who works for the side that pays him best. Steed's department has long been after the killer, and to finally trap him, One-Ten tells Cathy Gale to commission him to murder John Steed. Contact made, Cathy is summoned to a remote country house where she meets a toy teddy bear. The assassin's voice is relayed through the toy, and he agrees to kill Steed for £200,000. Cathy is asked to leave something as surety and places a diamond pendant on the desk, at the same time smuggling a cigarette case into her handbag. But it provides no clue to Teddy Bear's identity – it bears only the fingerprints of a chimpanzee. Via a false newspaper advertisement, Steed is lured to the apartment of an informer who has been helping in the hunt for the assassin, but he finds the informer dead. Disturbed, he returns to his flat. The telephone rings. It is Mr Teddy Bear, who informs Steed that he is dead – the phone has been smeared with a deadly poison which enters the skin's nerve endings. Steed struggles to inject the antidote and falls to the floor. Cathy now receives a bill for £200,000. She begins to wrap up the money but is interrupted by an old professor friend who tells her that he has been asked to collect a package and deliver it to a man named Bruin. As she hands over the package, the phone rings. It is Steed, who tells her to disregard the professor and meet him at a warehouse. Unknown to her, the caller is not Steed, but Steed's voice recorded earlier by Teddy Bear. At the warehouse, Cathy is held at gunpoint by the assassin. He tells her that although he knows she has tried to trick him, he couldn't kill a woman and offers Cathy a knockout pill to give him time to get away. Steed, now fully recovered, enters the warehouse and throws the bolt on the steel doors. Cathy snatches the assassin's gun and forces him to swallow one of his own knockout pills. Teddy Bear has, however, tricked them both. The knockout pills contain a fast-acting poison and he falls to the floor, dead.

In Mr Teddy Bear, *Cathy forces the unseen assassin to swallow one of his own deadly knockout pills.*

PROPELLANT 23

Teleplay by Jon Manchip White

Jules Meyer	Frederick Schiller
Jeanette	Justine Lord
Capt Legros	Nicholas Courtney
Co-pilot	Michael Beint
Paul Manning	Geoffrey Palmer
Catherine Gale	Honor Blackman
John Steed	Patrick Macnee
Laura	Catherine Woodville
Jacques Tissot	Trader Faulkner
Lieut 'Curly' Leclerc	John Crocker
Siebel	John Dearth
Roland	Ralph Nossek
Pierre	Barry Wilsher
Gendarme	Graham Ashley
Shop assistant	Deanna Shendery
Baker	John Gill

Designed by Paul Bernard

Directed by Jonathan Alwyn

STEED AND CATHY are told to meet a passenger en route from Tripoli to Marseilles. He will be carrying a sample of new liquid rocket fuel, Propellant 23. At Marseilles airport, they await the courier's arrival but as the man enters the airport customs centre, he collapses and dies. A silver liquor flask in his hand falls unnoticed among some flowers. The man's briefcase is confiscated by the customs officials, and a bottle of hair-restorer in it is given to a police officer, Curly, who suffers from baldness. Later, Steed breaks into the room where the briefcase is hidden. He finds the case but is attacked by Siebel, a foreign agent, already there. Steed soon overpowers the man and escapes with the briefcase. Meanwhile, Manning, an English passenger on the plane, has been questioning the stewardess about the dead man, and is told that he died from poisoning. Cathy has learned that Jacques, a hotel tout, was seen picking up a silver liquor flask. Then, the customs official tells her of the hair-restorer given to Curly. She goes to his flat, where she is disturbed by Siebel. She knocks him out and finds the bottle of hair-restorer – empty. Cathy reports to Steed and together they visit Jacques' apartment. On the floor they find the dead body of the air stewardess. Frantically, they search for the missing Jacques and he is finally found drinking in a bakery. Their recovery of the flask is interrupted by the arrival of Siebel and Manning. Cathy holds Siebel at gunpoint while Steed neatly disposes of Manning with a sharp tap from his umbrella.

THE DECAPOD

Teleplay by Eric Paice

Girl in shower	Pamela Conway
Yakob Borb	Paul Stassino
Stepan	Philip Madoc
John Steed	Patrick Macnee
Bodyguards	{ Douglas Robinson
	Valentine Musetti
Venus Smith	Julie Stevens
Cigarette girl	Valerie Stanton
Edna Ramsden	Lynne Furlong
Ito	Wolfe Morris
Harry Ramsden	Raymond Adamson
Guards officer	Harvey Ashby
and	The Dave Lee Trio

Designed by Terry Green

Directed by Don Leaver

STEED IS assigned to ensure the safety of Yakob Borb, President of the Balkan Republic, who is in London to negotiate a huge loan. When Borb's English secretary is murdered, Steed arranges for Venus Smith to take her place, allowing Venus to believe that Borb might grant her a singing tour of his country. Borb is a wrestling enthusiast, and he and Venus go to a fight where one of his bodyguards is wrestling The Decapod, a ten-limbed squid whose emblem is used by an old professional, Harry Ramsden. The bout is over in minutes, for The Decapod deliberately kills his opponent and escapes. Steed is told by Stepan, the Balkan Ambassador, that the bodyguard's death was meant to isolate Borb and warn him off completing the loan. Steed visits Ramsden's wife, who works at Venus' club. She says her husband is innocent. He then appears and says he was paid to keep away from the fight. The Decapod in the ring was an impostor. Borb and his second bodyguard, closely followed by Steed, are at the club watching Venus' cabaret act, when suddenly the lights go out. Borb and the bodyguard leave, and when Steed follows them, he finds Borb safe, but a Decapod mask is hanging in the cloakroom and the bodyguard is dead. Although he believes the bodyguard's death was his final warning, Borb insists on completing the loan. He then tells Venus that he has become infatuated with her, proposes to buy a luxury yacht and cruise the world, and will she join him? Venus says she will consider his offer. Steed, meanwhile, has accused Stepan of the murders and forces him to confess – he had engaged the bodyguards, not to protect Borb but to prevent him abandoning the Presidency. (Borb now wants only to live the life of a playboy.) Steed goes to the club, and finds himself face to face with the Decapod. As they begin to fight, Ramsden arrives and challenges The Decapod to one final bout. Ramsden wins and Steed lifts his mask to reveal Yakob Borb. Stepan, having followed Steed, learns of Borb's treachery and exacts his own justice on him by shooting the President.

BULLSEYE

Teleplay by Eric Paice

Jean	Mitzi Rogers
Miss Ellis	Judy Parfitt
Brigadier	Charles Carson
Foreman	Robin Wentworth
Catherine Gale	Honor Blackman
Calder	Ronald Radd
Young	Felix Deebank
Reynolds	John Frawley
Shareholder	Graham Bruce
Karl	Bernard Kay
John Steed	Patrick Macnee
Dorothy Young	Laurie Leigh
Inspector	Fred Ferris

Designed by Robert Macgowan

Directed by Peter Hammond

BRITISH weapons are being smuggled to trouble-spots abroad, creating a dangerous political situation. Steed arranges for Cathy, armed with 20 per cent of the shares, to join the board of Anderson's Small Arms Ltd – a firm whose chairman has just been killed, and which is fighting a take-over bid from Calder, a tycoon. Cathy meets other board-members, including a Brigadier, and the super-efficient Miss Ellis. Cathy is invited to visit the butts and fire one of the new Anderson rifles. When she goes to collect her target, she finds the shot body of one of the directors. Though the death occurred before Cathy entered the butts, the murder bullet came from her rifle and hers are the only fingerprints on it, so the police are suspicious. Young, another board-member, invites Cathy aboard his powerful motor launch and tries to persuade her to sell him her shares. She refuses. Meanwhile, Calder visits the Brigadier and makes him a substantial offer for his shares. Later that day, the Brigadier is found in his office, dead. Suspecting Calder, Cathy visits his sumptuous office, and when he offers her a large sum for her shares, she accepts. He then informs her that the three dead directors sold out to him but they had been killed before they could implement the sale. Someone is desperate to stop his takeover. That evening, when Miss Ellis calls a shareholder's meeting, Calder (Cathy's shares giving him the necessary advantage) interrupts the meeting and calls for an immediate inventory and sales check. This move panics the criminals, Young, his wife, and their accomplice, Karl, into escaping in Young's boat. But before they can depart, Cathy denounces Miss Ellis as the ringleader and murderer. The rest of the gang are arrested and Steed is delighted at the outcome – Cathy's shares are now showing a handsome profit.

MISSION TO MONTREAL

Teleplay by Lester Powell

Carla Berotti	Patricia English
Film director	Harold Berens
Peggy	Pamela Ann Davy
Brand	Alan Curtis
Receptionist	Angela Thorne
Pearson	Eric McCaine
Nicholson	Mark Eden
Stewards	{ Peter Mackriel William Swan
Budge	Gerald Sim
Marson	John Bennett
Reporters	{ Malcolm Taylor Terence Woodfield Leslie Pitt
Photographer	William Buck
Sheila Dowson	Iris Russell
Dr Martin King	Jon Rollason
Judy	Gillian Muir
John Steed	Patrick Macnee
Passenger	John Frawley
Barman	Allan Casley

Designed by Terry Green

Directed by Don Leaver

STEED TAKES advantage of the fact that his friend Dr King needs a holiday, to put him aboard a luxury liner cruising to Canada, as private doctor to Carla Berotti. She is a beautiful but neurotic film actress whose stand-in was murdered in London, in mistake for her. Steed also joins the crew as a steward. Dr King witnesses a secret meeting between Carla and the ship's Second Officer, Nicholson, which reduces Carla to tears. When telling Steed of this, he is informed that a microfilm of the Dew Line – the early-warning system in North America – has been stolen and Carla is suspected of carrying it for a group of agents. This disturbs King, for he likes Carla, and she has come to rely on him. Carla is frightened when Nicholson tells her that Brand, who murdered her stand-in, is on board. She hides the microfilm in a bottle of tablets and puts them in King's medicine bag. That night one of the guests passes out from too much drink and he is put into King's cabin to sleep it off. Next morning, he is found dead. While investigating, Steed discovers the microfilm in the medicine bottle, but Carla refuses to answer Dr King's questions, except to swear she meant him no harm. Later, Steed receives a message giving him the identification code used by the agents to contact each other. The code is used by Brand, and Sheila, Carla's secretary. Steed now tells Sheila, in confidence, that he has the microfilm and Carla is willing to divulge the necessary information to implicate the rest of the gang. Sheila and Brand decide Carla must die, and Nicholson is persuaded to do the deed. That night on deck, he takes Carla in his arms and attempts to throw her overboard, but Steed and King are waiting and save her. The gang are taken into custody. So is Carla, and a sad Dr King watches as she is taken down the gangplank at Montreal.

THE REMOVAL MEN

Teleplay by Roger Marshall
and Jeremy Scott

Jack Dragna	Reed de Rouen
Bud Siegal	Edwin Richfield
Godard	Donald Tandy
John Steed	Patrick Macnee
Cecile Dragna	Patricia Denys
Binaggio	George Goderick
Venus Smith	Julie Stevens
One-Ten	Douglas Muir
Waiter	George Little
Jailer	Hugo de Vernier
Nicole Cauvin	Edina Ronay
Charlie	Hira Talfrey
Harbour officer	Ivor Dean
and	The Dave Lee Trio

Designed by Patrick Downing

Directed by Don Leaver

The Removal Man *found Steed and Venus Smith face to face with a gang of ruthless assassins, led by Jack Dragna.*

Her cover story blown, Cathy is captured and interrogated by members of the New Rule, determined to retain the secret of The Mauritius Penny.

WHEN AN eminent British politician is murdered, Steed flies to the Riviera on the trail of a gang which kills for money. To be accepted into the gang, Steed gives himself a criminal record and robs the home of the gang boss, Dragna. But there is no vacancy, so Steed arranges for one of the gang members to be arrested. Dragna now admits Steed into the gang and tells him that in order to ensure the prisoner's silence one of the gang has entered the prison and killed him. At a local nightclub where Venus is appearing, Steed receives his first assignment – the murder of a young French film actress. Steed visits the girl, tells her of the murder plot, and says he knows of a safe hiding place. As they climb into the actress's car, Steed sees Venus. Not wishing to answer questions, Steed snubs her. Once the girl is safely hidden, Steed drives her sports car off a cliff and reports her successful killing to Dragna. He believes Steed, but next day Venus mentions her chance meeting with Steed and the actress to Siegal, the club owner. Siegal reports to Dragna that Steed was seen with the actress moments before her death and Dragna orders Venus to be silenced. Rebuked by Dragna for his carelessness in allowing Venus to see him with the actress, Steed is ordered to kill Venus. Meanwhile, Siegal, suspicious of Steed, makes his own investigation to find out if the actress really is dead. Later that day, he shows Dragna photographs he has taken that afternoon of the actress, alive and well, at the hideout, and Dragna orders the killing of both Steed and Venus. At the nightclub, Steed tries to warn Venus, but is unable to do so as Siegal keeps a close watch on both of them. Dragna enters and orders the club to be emptied. Once alone, Siegal pulls a gun on Steed. Dragna, however, not wishing to rush, orders Venus to make her final curtain call, and Venus is forced to sing for the gang boss. During one of her numbers she distracts his attention sufficiently for Steed to break free and in the ensuing fight both Siegal and Dragna are killed.

THE MAURITIUS PENNY

**Teleplay by Malcolm Hulke and
Terence Dicks**

Goodchild	Philip Guard
Percy Peckham	Harry Shacklock
John Steed	Patrick Macnee
Catherine Gale	Honor Blackman
Boy	Anthony Rogers
Gerald Shelley	David Langton
Maitland	Edward Jewesbury
Brown	Alfred Burke
Lord Matterley	Richard Vernon
Porter	Raymond Hodge
Burke	Alan Rolfe
Andrews	Edward Higgins
Charlady	Grace Arnold
Lorry driver	Edwin Brown
Lorry driver's mate	Anthony Blackshaw
Miss Power	Delia Corrie
Sheila Gray	Sylvia Langova
Foreign delegate	Theodore Wilhelm

Designed by Philip Harrison

Directed by Richmond Harding

WHEN THE Mauritius Penny, a very rare stamp, is offered for sale in an ordinary sale catalogue, a stamp collector informs Steed, and is killed for his trouble. Steed visits the stamp dealer's shop and gets a lead to the stamp auction room where he meets Lord Matterley, a rich collector, and Shelley, owner of the auction room – and actually second-in-command of a secret organisation. Shelley decides that Goodchild, the stamp dealer's assistant, who has panicked after the murder, is a risk, and has him killed during the auction. Steed and Cathy find more dealers' lists in the dead man's pockets and realise that all the stamps offered form a coded message. Cathy gets a job at the stamp shop but Brown, Goodchild's murderer, discovers she is working for Steed and tries to kill her. Cathy overpowers him and in his pocket finds an invitation to a philatelic convention at the auction room. Meanwhile, Steed keeps an appointment written in Goodchild's diary, and finds himself at a lady dentist's. She doesn't know Goodchild, but when she checks his dental chart against Steed's teeth, she realises he is a fake and anaesthetises him. Steed recovers, and is questioned and threatened by Shelley. But a lorry driver who has come to collect a packing case rescues him. He tells Steed that he has been carrying packing cases to and from the shop all week. One case fell open and it was full of guns. Cathy has discovered that the convention is really a planning meeting for an extremist political group, heavily armed, which plans to take over the country and begin New Rule. Brown, recovered, arrives and Cathy is caught and questioned. But Steed has been delivered to the convention by the driver and he breaks out of the packing case in time to rescue Cathy. The head of the organisation arrives – it is Lord Matterley. Steed and Cathy overpower him, and when he rises to address his followers, they both have guns trained on him – and Matterley announces the unavoidable postponement of New Rule.

DEATH OF A GREAT DANE

Teleplay by Roger Marshall and
Jeremy Scott

Minister	**Billy Milton**
Gravedigger	**Herbert Nelson**
Gregory	**Leslie French**
Catherine Gale	**Honor Blackman**
John Steed	**Patrick Macnee**
Mrs Miller	**Clare Kelly**
First assistant	**Dennis Edwards**
Second assistant	**Anthony Baird**
Getz	**Frederick Jaeger**
Miller	**Frank Peters**
Policeman	**Michael Moyer**
Sir James Mann	**John Laurie**
First winetaster	**Eric Elliott**
Second winetaster	**Roger Maxwell**
Man from kennels	**Kevin Barry**

Designed by Patrick Downing

Directed by Peter Hammond

STEED IS on the trail of a gang that smuggles fantastic sums of money out of the country. When he is told that Miller, a man badly injured in a road accident, is carrying a great number of diamonds in his stomach, he is sure that there is a connection with the gang. Steed sees Miller's wife, who says her husband was working for Alex Litoff, a multi-millionaire financier and renowned philanthropist. Steed visits Litoff, and is received by Gregory, Litoff's butler, who is about to walk a Great Dane – the companion, he says, of a similar dog which died some weeks before. Litoff is apparently ill, so Steed meets Getz, his assistant. Producing the diamonds, Steed tries to blackmail Getz, who immediately agrees his price, saying that Litoff would dislike the publicity of taking Steed to the police. When Cathy discovers that Litoff has withdrawn all his financial support from numerous charitable organisations, most of which he had founded, Steed in convinced that Getz is unloading all Litoff's assets, and realising millions of pounds in the process. Steed visits Sir James Mann, Litoff's personal doctor, who admits his patient is seriously ill with a bad heart. When Steed tells him about Getz selling off Litoff's assets, Sir James, certain of Litoff's ignorance, is horrified. Steed breaks into Litoff's home. The millionaire's bed is empty, and Steed finds Sir James Mann waiting with a loaded gun. Cathy meanwhile discovers that Miller has been murdered, and decides to call on his wife – whom she finds dead at her practical joke shop. Cathy finds a Great Dane locked in a back room and takes it home with her. The captive Steed is told by Gregory about Getz's plan, conceived when Litoff died of thrombosis, to seize the financier's fortune and divide it between himself, Gregory and Sir James. They pretended that Litoff was still alive, but he was secretly

Steed shares afternoon tea with villains Sir James Mann and Getz in Death of a Great Dane.

buried in a pets' cemetery, in the supposed grave of the Great Dane. Miller was ordered to destroy the dog, but gave it to his wife. When Cathy arrives – on the pretext of collecting the remaining dog for the kennels – she is recognised and taken prisoner. Getz decides to kill them, but they turn the tables and as Steed and Cathy escort the three out at gunpoint Gregory, butler to the end, holds the door open for them.

THE SELL-OUT

Teleplay by Anthony Terpiloff and
Brandon Brady

Dr Martin King	Jon Rollason
John Steed	Patrick Macnee
M Roland	Carleton Hobbs
Policeman	Anthony Blackshaw
Gunman	Storm Durr
One-Twelve	Arthur Hewlett
Frazer	Michael Mellinger
Harvey	Frank Gatliff
Lilian Harvey	Anne Godley
Judy	Gillian Muir
Workman	Richard Klee
Reporter	Henry Rayner

Designed by Terry Green

Directed by Don Leaver

STEED IS assigned to guard a United Nations official, M Roland, secretly in London for high-level talks. An assassination attempt on Roland's life is made and although it fails, an innocent man is killed. Dr King, having seen the killing, is enraged at Steed's apparent casualness about the murder. Steed tells his superior, One-Twelve, that he believes the assassination attempt, and the failure of several others, has been the work of an informer. Steed suspects Harvey, an associate who is also responsible for the security of the talks. Before the next meeting, at which Steed pretends to be M Roland, he asks King to help him, but he says he is tired of the bloodshed which is involved in Steed's job. As Steed arrives at the hotel for the talks, a workman tries to shoot him. Dr King is passing and helps. Meanwhile Harvey tells another associate, Frazer, that he believes that Steed is the informer, and learns that Frazer has been ordered by One-Twelve to follow Steed. At the next session of talks – which masquerade as a cocktail party – Steed, suspecting that Harvey's health is bad, dopes his drink, having first ensured that Mrs Harvey will call on Dr King, who will then report to Steed on Harvey's illness. One-Twelve is called away from the party and Steed follows him. He finds Frazer dead, and One-Twelve knocks Steed unconscious. Meanwhile, Harvey discovers it was Steed who suggested that his wife call in Dr King, and he holds the doctor at gunpoint. Harvey tells King that because he was dying he'd turned informer to secure what future he had left. One-Twelve meanwhile tells Steed that although he'd always suspected Harvey of being the informer, he had knocked Steed out hoping to convince Harvey that Steed was the one under suspicion. One-Twelve leaves to ensure the safety of M Roland. Steed goes to King's surgery, rescues the doctor and takes Harvey into custody.

DEATH ON THE ROCKS

Teleplay by Eric Paice

Mrs Ross	Annette Kerr
Liza Denham	Ellen McIntosh
Diamond dealers	{ Jack Grossman
	Vincent Charles
John Steed	Patrick Macnee
Max Daniels	Hamilton Dyce
Van Berg	Richard Clarke
Catherine Gale	Honor Blackman
Painter	Haydn Ward
Fenton	Gerald Cross
Nicky	David Sumner
Samuel Ross	Meier Tzelniker
Jackie Ross	Toni Gilpin
Sid	Douglas Robinson
Mrs Daniels	Naomi Chance

Designed by James Goddard

Directed by Jonathan Alwyn

WHEN MRS ROSS, the wife of a diamond merchant, is murdered by a beautician who smothers her with a quick-hardening face pack, Steed – having heard that an enormous influx of illegal stones is swamping Hatton Garden – enters the diamond business. He buys Ross' house and persuades Mrs Gale to move in and pose as his wife. Fenton, part of the illegal smuggling ring, tells Nicky, one of his henchmen, to investigate Steed's activities. This is easy, as Steed has entered into partnership with Ross, whose daughter, Jackie, Nicky is courting. At a party held in Steed's new house, Nicky suggests he buys some illicit diamonds, but Steed is non-committal. Meanwhile Cathy breaks into Nicky's cellar, and discovers some crystals on the floor, but is interrupted and attacked by one of Fenton's men, whom

In Death on the Rocks, *Cathy poses as Steed's wife as they join an illegal smuggling ring.*

she fights off. Nicky arrives and she persuades him that she had come about a business matter. She invites him to leave the gang he was blackmailed into joining but Nicky declines. After she has left, Nicky notices that the wires to the alarm system have been cut. He does not tell Fenton of Cathy's visit. Cathy is later visited by Mrs Daniels, the wife of another diamond merchant, who tells her that her husband is being threatened by the gang. Steed has made Ross admit that his wife was killed so as to blackmail him into buying from the gang. He is now afraid for Jackie's safety, as Fenton plans to drive the Diamond Federation out of business. Cathy arrives and shows Steed what she found in the cellar – rock salt crystals, in which the diamonds are smuggled into the country. Meanwhile, Mrs Daniel's body is found in Cathy's flat. Steed accepts the diamonds from Nicky, and is given a few hours to produce the cash. Ross has refused to join the gang, so Fenton has Jackie kidnapped. When Fenton's man tries to kill both Ross and Jackie, Steed – who has found them in Fenton's salt warehouse – intervenes. Fenton arrives, but with Ross and Nicky's help (the latter wants to protect Jackie) Steed captures him. Meanwhile Liza, the beautician who killed Mrs Ross and Daniels and is the real leader of the gang, tries to murder Cathy. But Mrs Gale throws Liza in the way of Daniels' gun and knocks him cold with a stuffed animal's head.

Out to expose the Traitor in Zebra, *Steed finds time to display his snooker expertise to Sub Lt Graham.*

TRAITOR IN ZEBRA

Teleplay by John Gilbert

Escorting Officer	**Richard Pescud**
Nash	**Noel Coleman**
Crane	**Danvers Walker**
Maggie	**June Murphy**
Catherine Gale	**Honor Blackman**
John Steed	**Patrick Macnee**
Mellors	**Ian Shand**
Wardroom steward	**Michael Browning**
Graham	**William Gaunt**
Franks	**Richard Leech**
Rankin	**John Sharp**
Linda	**Katy Wild**
Thorne	**Jack Stewart**

Designed by Terry Green

Directed by Richmond Harding

INVESTIGATING reports that an officer on HMS Zebra – a shore establishment – is giving secret information to the enemy, Steed joins the unit as a naval psychiatrist and Cathy goes undercover in the control room. Crane, the suspected officer, is accused of leaking information so the enemy can jam the navy's new device for tracking enemy missiles and satellites. At the base, Steed meets Captain Nash, his secretary, Lieutenant Mellors, and Sub-Lieutenant Graham – a friend of the accused, who says he has submitted a report which proves that people other than Crane had access to the formula. This alarms Mellors, who is using a code (via a dartboard at the local inn) to pass on information to Rankin, a local artist. He collects the information and uses his dog to convey the message to a local sweet shop, where it is received by Linda, a counter assistant. Mellors anxiously consults Rankin, who in turn phones someone else, and that night Mellors is strangled in his car. Cathy forms a friendship with Franks, a local newspaper proprietor, and he invites her to his offices. While there, she notices a piece of paper bearing a darts score. When Franks next visits the sweet shop to collect the information from Rankin, Steed follows him. At the shop Steed questions Linda, but she reveals nothing. When the next tracking test is jammed, it becomes obvious that Crane is not guilty. Graham, believing his friend's innocence is proven, receives a message from Linda asking him to meet her but Franks, suspecting that Linda might give him away, slips a pill into Graham's drink, and within minutes, the officer is dead. Steed questions Linda again and she confesses her guilt, but refuses to disclose Frank's name. Cathy searches Rankin's room when he arrives and attacks her. Steed arrives but Rankin escapes through the window and goes to warn Franks. Franks, believing that the game is up, murders Rankin and booby-traps his office, then sets out to plant a bomb at the base. Steed narrowly escapes death from the booby-trap and follows Franks to the naval base. He reaches the control room just as Franks has planted his bomb. By locking Franks in with his own device, he forces him to defuse it, and saves the day.

THE BIG THINKER

Teleplay by Martin Woodhouse

Dr Clemens	Walter Hudd
Catherine Gale	Honor Blackman
Dr Farrow	David Garth
Dr Hurst	Tenniel Evans
Janet Lingfield	Marina Martin
Dr Kearns	Anthony Booth
John Steed	Patrick Macnee
Broster	Allan McClelland
Clarice	Penelope Lee
Blakelock	Ray Brown

Designed by James Goddard

Directed by Kim Mills

THE FINAL tests on Plato, the largest and most advanced computer ever built, are being sabotaged. When the computer breaks down a second time, and a dead professor is found frozen stiff inside it, Cathy, posing as a language specialist, is sent to investigate. She meets Dr Clemens, head of the project, an old friend, Professor Farrow, and Kearns, a brilliant mathematician. Steed – posing as a government official – appears and tells Cathy that Plato could be a major advance in missile interception, and encourages her to become friendly with Dr Kearns. Kearns takes Cathy to Broster's gambling club, and joins a poker game, but soon runs into debt through his opponent's skilful play. Steed believes that getting Kearns into debt is an attempt to soften him up and enlist him into treachery. Later, Broster and his girlfriend, Clarice, are surprised when Cathy offers to pay Kearns' debts. When Broster tries to intimidate Cathy, he is defeated by her expert judo. Next day, Clemens dismisses Kearns, but Kearns insists he is valuable and stays for the next test on Plato. But someone has tampered with the fuses and Cathy is almost killed when they blow up. When Cathy and Kearns enter Plato to check, they find the dead body of Dr Clemens. Kearns is immediately suspected, but disappears. Later that night, Cathy returns to the Plato project and finds Kearns hiding inside the building. He says Clemens was killed because he had evidence that the murderer was one of his own staff. Kearns believes that Clemens may have fed the information into the computer before he died, so they enter Plato and Kearns begins the test. But someone has locked them in, the refrigeration system has been sabotaged and the temperature is falling rapidly. Kearns sends out an SOS through the computer which Steed picks up, as he has been keeping an eye on Cathy. Steed rescues them and Kearns checks the tape for Clemens' message. Professor Farrow arrives and tries to stop the computer. In his attempt to destroy the evidence of his crime, he accidentally switches on the main fuses and is electrocuted.

In The Big Thinker, *Dr Kearns puts the byte on Cathy's computer investigations.*

DEATH DISPATCH

Teleplay by Leonard Fincham

Baxter	Hedger Wallace
Pasco	Alan Mason
John Steed	Patrick Macnee
One-Ten	Douglas Muir
Catherine Gale	Honor Blackman
Thugs	Geoff L'Cise
	Arthur Griffiths
Miguel Rosas	Richard Warner
Anna Rosas	Valerie Sarruf
Muller	David Cargill
Chambermaid	Bernice Rassin
Rico	Michael Forrest
Singer	Maria Andipa
Customer	Jerry Jardin
Travers	Gerald Harper

Designed by Anne Spavin

Directed by Jonathan Alwyn

A BRITISH COURIER is murdered in Jamaica but he manages to prevent his diplomatic bag, containing dispatches, from being stolen. Steed and Cathy are flown to the scene of the crime, but Steed cannot understand why it happened, as the bag contains only routine information. Steed masquerades as the replacement courier and, with Cathy keeping watch, sets out to complete the dead courier's itinerary. When they arrive in South America, Steed is attacked and an attempt made to steal the bag, but Cathy is at hand and the attempt fails. Rosas, an ambitious South American politician, is angry when his assistant, Pasco, fails to get the bag, and orders another man, Muller, to get rid of Pasco and intercept Steed. Steed and Cathy meanwhile have flown to Santiago and Steed leaves the bag in his hotel room as bait, should another theft be attempted. That night he observes Pasco enter his room but when Steed goes in after him, he finds Pasco dead and the bag's contents disturbed. Steed realises that the murderer must have entered his room through the window, having climbed down from the balcony of the room above, so Cathy impersonates a chambermaid and checks the room, to find it occupied by Muller, but she gets away safely. When Steed arrives at Buenos Aires – the last stop on the courier's route – the police question him about the body in his hotel room. Meanwhile, Cathy has followed Muller from Santiago, but she is spotted and taken to Rosas' home. When Steed discovers Cathy's fate, he goes after her but Muller is waiting for him and at gunpoint takes Steed to Rosas. Muller then explains that Rosas wants the itinerary of the visit of an American envoy, whose assassination will trigger a revolt planned to put Rosas in power. Just then, Rosas' young daughter arrives and Steed disarms Muller and arrests Rosas. Their mission accomplished, Steed and Cathy are invited to the reception for the visiting envoy.

DEAD ON COURSE

Teleplay by Eric Paice

Pilot	Trevor Reid
Bob Slade	Bruce Boa
Margot	Margo Jenkins
Freedman	John McLaren
John Steed	Patrick Macnee
Deidre O'Connor	Elisabeth Murray
Dr Martin King	Jon Rollason
Sister Isobel	Janet Hargreaves
Mother Superior	Peggy Marshall
Hughes	Nigel Arkwright
Michael Joyce	Liam Gaffney
Vincent O'Brien	Donal Donnelly
Gerry	Edward Kelsey

Designed by Robert Fuest

Directed by Richmond Harding

STEED AND Dr King investigate a suspicious plane crash on the Irish coast. The bodies have been taken to a nearby convent and while King is there, the sole survivor of the crash, the stewardess, is brought in, still unconscious. Steed has discovered that the plane's load of bank notes has disappeared. He visits the convent and King tells him that the pilot of the plane was strangled. At the local inn, King meets a villager, Vincent, who hints at knowing something about the crash. He tells King he saw a man in pilot's uniform after the crash. Suspicion now falls on the missing co-pilot. Steed discovers that the co-pilot is secretly married to an air-hostess, Deidre. She tells him nothing, but Steed is not convinced and believes that the crash was no accident, even though there is no sign of any sabotage. At the convent, the injured stewardess recovers consciousness but is strangled before she can be questioned. The Mother Superior, however, refuses to allow a search for the murderer – or let her nuns break their vows of silence – so Steed taps the telephone lines in the convent and overhears Deidre telling someone in the convent the call sign of the aircraft which is to carry the remainder of the bank shipment. At the inn, King finds a nun's habit and a concealed passage leading to the convent. He asks Vincent to tell Steed, which he does, but begs an air passage to America on a plane carrying Deidre, and piloted by Steed. Meanwhile, King goes to the convent and is held at gunpoint by the Mother Superior – one of the gang who has been using the convent as cover. King is locked in a cell with the missing co-pilot, who says Deidre was told he would be killed if she did not reveal the plane's call sign. The gang then talk-down the plane on a crash course, but it is Steed's plane which reponds to the call sign. Realising they are heading for a crash, Vincent breaks down and confesses to being the ring-leader. Steed lands the plane safely and he and Dr King, helped by the co-pilot, round up the rest of the gang.

Dr King and Steed discover how a pilot was Dead on Course *and a prisoner of an inhospitable convent.*

Posing as an arms dealer, Steed infiltrates the Intercrime *organisation and meets gun-runner Palmer.*

INTERCRIME

Teleplay by Terrance Dicks and Malcolm Hulke

Palmer	**Donald Webster**
Sewell	**Rory MacDermot**
Moss	**Alan Browning**
John Steed	**Patrick Macnee**
Catherine Gale	**Honor Blackman**
Hilda Stern	**Julia Arnall**
Trusty	**Charlotte Selwyn**
Prison officer Sharpe	**Bettine Milne**
Felder	**Kenneth J Warren**
Lobb	**Jerome Willis**
Manning	**Patrick Holt**
Pamela Johnson	**Angela Browne**
Kressler	**Paul Hansard**

Designed by Richard Harrison

Directed by Jonathan Alwyn

TWO PETTY thieves are caught rifling a safe by Moss, who represents Intercrime, the international crime organisation for which they work, and he shoots them. One of them, Palmer, survives and tells Steed that a woman, Hilda Stern, is arriving in England to work for the gang. Steed has her arrested at London Airport, and Cathy follows her to Holloway, where she learns that Hilda's escape is already planned. Steed persuades Cathy to take the woman's place in the escape and Felder, the British organiser of Intercrime, accepts Cathy as Hilda, and tells her she has been engaged as a professional assassin. Palmer meanwhile has had a change of heart and telephones Felder to warn him about Steed. Deciding that Palmer is a risk, Felder orders Cathy and Moss to kill Palmer and Steed. Cathy soon returns and tells Felder that Moss was ambushed by Palmer, but she has dealt with him and Steed. Meanwhile Pam Johnson, a girlfriend of Manning, one of Felder's business associates, learns about the gang and Steed warns her that Felder will try to kill her. Cathy attends a trial held by Intercrime in which one of its members, Lupescu, is accused and found guilty of stealing £500 out of the proceeds of a robbery. Then the real Hilda Stern, having escaped from Holloway, arrives. Cathy says that the new Hilda is the impersonator, but when Felder orders her to shoot Lupescu, she can't, and is discovered. Manning – now revealed as the supreme organiser behind Intercrime – is told that Felder intends to take over from him. During the ensuing dispute, Steed arrives and manages to free Cathy. A fight takes place, in which Cathy grabs Hilda's gun, and Steed subdues Manning and the rest of the gang. Unfortunately, Steed is mistaken for one of the gang and is taken away by the police. Visiting him in his cell, Cathy promises to put matters right – soon!

IMMORTAL CLAY

Teleplay by James Mitchell

Catherine Gale	Honor Blackman
Allan Marling	Gary Watson
Mara Little	Didi Sullivan
Richard Marling	Paul Eddington
John Steed	Patrick Macnee
One-Ten	Douglas Muir
Miller	James Bree
Anne	Rowena Gregory
Josh Machen	Bert Palmer
De Groot	Steve Plytas
Blomberg	Frank Olegario

Designed by James Goddard

Directed by Richmond Harding

WHEN ALLAN MARLING claims to have created an unbreakable ceramic, One-Ten tells Steed to see if such a thing really exists. Knowing Cathy is writing a book on china, Steed sends her to the Marling factory. She is being shown round the factory by Allan's brother, Richard, when the body of a man, Lander, is found dead in a slip tank of clay. Cathy discovers that Lander had been seeing Richard's wife, and that Marling was jealous. She meets a man named De Groot, who says he is buying Marling ware to show at the Leipzig Trade Fair. Steed arrives and, entering the laboratory, finds De Groot's right-hand man, Blomberg, searching the premises. He overpowers Steed and escapes. Meanwhile, in another part of the factory, Miller, the Marlings' chief designer, is offered £20,000 by De Groot to steal the ceramic. Miller, wanting to impress his beautiful assistant, Mara, accepts. De Groot tells him to remould the tile into a cup, so it can be smuggled out in the consignment of pottery meant for the Leipzig Fair. Next day, Allan Marling arranges to demonstrate the unbreakable ceramic to Steed. He is about to hand it to Steed, when his brother arrives. Richard scoffs at Allan's claim and knocks the tile from his hand. It falls to the floor and shatters. Miller gives De Groot a glove marked with Allan's name, which he found near the slip tank in which Lander was killed. De Groot phones Allan and tells him he has the glove and Allan agrees to meet him in the laboratory. De Groot arrives with Cathy, who has said she is interested in the tile. They are joined by Blomberg and Miller, and as Miller hands over the cup, and demands his £20,000, De Groot shoots him. The cup falls from Miller's hands – and shatters! De Groot turns the gun on Cathy and Allan. Steed meanwhile has been told by Mara that she loves Allan and wants to steal back the glove. She introduces him to Richard's wife, who confesses that Lander offered her a vast sum for the tile. But when Lander tried to make love to her, Allan fought to protect her, and Lander struck his head and fell into the slip tank. Steed dashes to help Cathy, and arrests De Groot and Blomberg. As they depart, Josh, the night-watchman, arrives – carrying the real unbreakable cup. He explains that he saw Miller making it, then stole it and locked it in the firm's safe.

BOX OF TRICKS

Teleplay by Peter Ling and
Edward Rhodes

Gerry	Ian Curry
Venus Smith	Julie Stevens
John Steed	Patrick Macnee
Henrietta	Jacqueline Jones
Manager	Dallas Cavell
Denise	April Olrich
General Sutherland	Maurice Hedley
Kathleen Sutherland	Jane Barrett
Dr Gilham	Edgar Wreford

Designed by Anne Spavin

Directed by Kim Mills

NATO SECRETS are being leaked and Steed is convinced that this is tied up with the death of a magician's girl assistant during a vanishing cabinet trick at the club where Venus is working. He gains entrance by pretending to be a masseur and meets General Sutherland, a NATO Commander, who agrees that there has been a serious leakage of secrets within his command. Meanwhile, in the cabaret room, Denise, the new assistant, has a row with the magician. Later, when Denise is demonstrating the vanishing cabinet's workings to Venus, she too, is killed. Venus tells Steed that she overheard a conversation between the General and his daughter Kathleen, in which the General told off his daughter for consulting a faith-healer, Dr Gilham. Kathleen believed that Gilham could cure her ill father with one of his sealed healing boxes, which contain a balanced assortment of minerals. Steed, posing as a rich hypochondriac, calls on Dr Gilham, who agrees to send one of the healing boxes to Venus for Steed to collect. The box arrives but is stolen from Venus' dressing-room. When Steed discovers it, hidden in the well of a lift that forms part of the cabinet apparatus, Venus and Steed are nearly killed by a concealed trip-wire hidden in the lift. Meanwhile Kathleen has been told by Gilham to take the latest healing box to the club and replace the one she had previously concealed in her father's wheelchair. As she is about to change the box, Steed intervenes and, breaking open the seal, reveals a portable tape-recorder, which has recorded all her father's conversations. Wander, the magician, is in league with Gilham, and kidnaps Kathleen, but Steed sees it and follows them to the magician's dressing-room. He arrives to witness Wander forcing Kathleen into the vanishing cabinet and overpowers the magician, then he and Venus leave to arrest Dr Gilham.

In Immortal Clay, *Steed's mission leads him to the Potteries in search of an unbreakable ceramic.*

WARLOCK

Teleplay by Doreen Montgomery

Cosmo Gallion	Peter Arne
Neville	Allan Blakelock
Mrs Dunning	Olive Milbourne
John Steed	Patrick Macnee
Markel	John Hollis
Julia	Pat Spencer
Mogam	Philip Mosca
Catherine Gale	Honor Blackman
Doctor	Brian Vaughan
Pathologist	Gordon Gardner
Miss Timson	Christina Ferdinando
One-Ten	Douglas Muir
Barmaid	Susan Franklin
Pasco	Herbert Nelson

Designed by Terry Green

Directed by Peter Hammond

Right: *To save Cathy from the overtures of Warlock Cosmo Gallion, Steed finds a novel way of breaking into the magician's lair.*

Below: *What is the secret of The White Dwarf? Cathy enters the observatory telescope chamber to find out.*

WHEN NEVILLE, a scientist who has perfected a new fuel formula, is found in a state of coma, Steed is assigned to the case, and One-Ten takes the formula for safe-keeping. Steed and Cathy discover that Neville was associated with a black magic circle, but before they can question him further, Neville is kidnapped and taken to Gallion, the head of the circle. Gallion is being paid by Markel, a foreign agent, to interest scientists in black magic and then extract their secrets. Markel tries to question Neville and when he realises that the scientist no longer has the formula, he angrily rouses him to ask further questions. The shock is too great for Neville and he dies. One-Ten tells Steed and Cathy that two other security leaks were connected with the circle. They search Neville's library for clues, and find a dated reference to the circle's next meeting. Steed and Cathy attend the meeting and Cathy is introduced to the circle's leader. Gallion asks if he may cast Cathy's horoscope and she agrees. Gallion finds that Cathy would be ideal for one of his experiments. Returning to his room, Gallion is accused by Markel of being a fraud because he failed to produce Neville's formula. Gallion appears to put a 'hex' on Markel – and he falls to the floor, dead. The following morning Steed finds that Cathy has been kidnapped. Suspecting that the circle is involved, he goes to Gallion's home, and arrives to find the experiment in progress. He is cornered by Gallion's henchmen, and Gallion uses all his powers to make Cathy appear. She arrives, and holds Gallion at gunpoint. Steed overpowers his guards and he and Cathy round up Gallion's supporters. When Gallion realises that his evil powers are finished, he mysteriously collapses – and dies?

THE GOLDEN EGGS

Teleplay by Martin Woodhouse

Dr Ashe	Donald Eccles
Elizabeth Bayle	Pauline Delaney
De Leon	Gordon Whiting
John Steed	Patrick Macnee
Catherine Gale	Honor Blackman
Diana	Irene Bradshaw
Hillier	Robert Bernal
Redfern	Peter Arne
Campbell	Louis Haslar
Hall	Charles Bird

Designed by Douglas James

Directed by Peter Hammond

D R ASHE, an experimental scientist, is attacked by a burglar, De Leon, and a refrigerated case containing two gold-plated eggs is stolen. Cathy investigates but on questioning Ashe, he denies the theft and the attack. De Leon is taken ill with a mysterious disease. Hillier, the man who engaged him, and who works for the immensely wealthy Redfern, told De Leon that the job contained no risk and there was nothing extraordinary about the eggs. Because of this, De Leon refuses to reveal where the case is hidden. Ashe's assistant, Elizabeth (also in Redfern's pay), warns him that De Leon must be treated immediately for he caught the fatal virus which Ashe has developed and keeps in the eggs. Redfern arranges for a fake ambulance to collect De Leon from hospital, but on its way to Redfern's it is involved in a road accident. Though the ambulance has been cremated in the crash, Steed identifies De Leon's safe-cracking tools and Cathy takes Ashe to De Leon's home in the hope of finding the missing case. After a fruitless search, Ashe goes home, but Cathy continues and finds the case buried in the ground. She takes it home but Redfern and Hillier arrive. They kidnap both her and the case. Imprisoned, Cathy is visited by Elizabeth, who now realises that when she is no longer of any use to Redfern, she can expect little mercy. She frees Cathy but they are discovered by Redfern and held at gunpoint. Cathy threatens to drop the eggs unless he surrenders. He refuses and Cathy throws the eggs into his face. Instinctively, he tries to catch them, and Cathy is able to disarm him. After Redfern and Hillier are rounded up, Cathy and Steed discover that the eggs are dummies. They visit Dr Ashe who explains he was so convinced of the potential evil of the virus that he destroyed all his experiments and the real, deadly, golden eggs.

SCHOOL FOR TRAITORS

Teleplay by James Mitchell

East	John Standing
Venus Smith	Julie Stevens
Claire Summers	Melissa Stribling
Roberts	Richard Thorp
Higby	Reginald Marsh
John Steed	Patrick Macnee
One-Seven	Frederick Farley
Dr Shanklin	Anthony Nicholls
Professor Aubyn	Frank Shelley
Green	Terence Woodfield
Proctor	Ronald Mayer
Barmaid	Janet Butlin

Designed by Maurice Pelling

Directed by Jonathan Alwyn

W HEN A university tutor who had been working on important research is found dead, suicide is suspected and Steed is sent to investigate. He is sure the man was murdered and hints that the dead man has left a letter addressed to Venus, who is appearing at the University during Rag Week. Meanwhile, Claire, a girlfriend of Roberts, who now has the dead tutor's job, tells him she is in financial trouble and persuades him to forge a cheque – thus placing him in the hands of Higby, a local pub owner. Venus is contacted and ordered to leave the letter in the college quadrangle. But on Steed's instructions, her envelope contains blank paper. While Steed waits to see who collects the letter, a man named East diverts his attention and Green, an undergraduate, makes off with it. Steed follows Green, only to find him dead and the letter gone. When Claire discovers that Venus has tricked her, she sends a pot of beauty cream containing acid to Venus. But Venus does not use the cream and, as she prepares to meet Steed, Roberts breaks into her room and demands the real letter. Steed arrives and questions Roberts, who admits that Higby has blackmailed him into getting the letter, and he agrees to help. Higby, however, suspects Roberts as a risk, and when Roberts discovers that Claire is working for Higby, he is shot. Claire now decides to blackmail East, a promising graduate, with the same technique she used on Roberts. East apparently falls for the trick and Higby orders him to kill Steed. East now confides in his tutor, Professor Shanklin – the master-mind behind the scheme – and he gives him the gun with which to murder Steed. But East has been co-operating with Steed and, together with Venus, they round up Shanklin, Higby and Claire.

THE WHITE DWARF

Teleplay by Malcolm Hulke

Professor Richter	**Keith Pyott**
John Steed	**Patrick Macnee**
Catherine Gale	**Honor Blackman**
Minister	**Daniel Thorndike**
Henry Barker	**Peter Copley**
Cartwright	**Philip Latham**
Fuller	**Vivienne Drummond**
Rahim	**Paul Anil**
Luke	**George Roubicek**
Maxwell Barker	**George A Cooper**
Johnson	**Bill Nagy**
Miss Tregarth	**Constance Chapman**
Butler	**John Falconer**

Designed by Terry Green

Directed by Richmond Harding

PROFESSOR RICHTER, an astronomer, is murdered while observing a star called The White Dwarf. The Ministry of Science, however, refuse to allow his assistant, Cartwright, to reveal the news of Richter's death. Steed tells Cathy that Richter believed The White Dwarf is heading straight for our solar system, and will destroy the Earth. Cathy arrives at the observatory, posing as an astronomer, and is shown around by Richter's son, Luke. They enter the telescope chamber and discover the body of Rahim – an Indian astronomer who was sent to confirm Richter's observations. Meanwhile Steed discovers that Maxwell Barker, a financier, in conjunction with an American financier, called Johnson, is selling the bulk of his stocks and shares. Realising that Barker's brother, Henry, works for the Ministry of Science, Steed accuses Henry of leaking information about The White Dwarf to his brother. Henry threatens to tell the Minister and resign his post. Johnson overhears and decides Henry must be killed. Later that evening, Johnson is discovered dead in Maxwell's apartment. Meanwhile, Luke, enraged by the Ministry's reaction to his father's death, tells Cathy about his father's findings and when Cartwright arrives to make the final observation, Cathy has changed the plates in the telescope. Cartwright focuses on The White Dwarf and is horrified to see that Richter was right – the star is heading towards Earth. When Maxwell appears, Cartwright accuses him of defrauding him over the deal. Steed and Cathy arrive and take Cartwright into custody but Maxwell escapes onto the roof of the observatory where, during a chase, he is shot dead by Steed.

MAN IN THE MIRROR

Teleplay by Geoffrey Orme and Anthony Terpiloff

Betty	**Daphne Anderson**
Strong	**Ray Barrett**
Brown	**Julian Somers**
John Steed	**Patrick Macnee**
Venus Smith	**Julie Stevens**
Jean	**Rhonda Lewis**
Trevelyan	**Hayden Jones**
Iris	**Frida Knorr**

Designed by Anne Spavin

Directed by Kim Mills

STEED INVESTIGATES the suicide of a cypher clerk, Trevelyan. Venus, taking photographs in a funfair, has her camera and films stolen by Betty, a girl who works at the café there. One roll of film, however, is not stolen and when developed it shows Trevelyan's face reflected in the Hall of Mirrors. But the film was taken *after* the clerk's death! Strong, who owns the café, tries to persuade Betty to leave Brown, the owner of the funfair, but Brown warns off Strong, reminding him that he is an accessory to treason. When Steed and Venus visit the funfair, Steed deliberately lets Brown see the photograph of Trevelyan. Steed visits Mrs Trevelyan, who admits that she identified another body as her husband's. He had been kidnapped, and in order to preserve his life she had agreed to co-operate with the criminals. Meanwhile, at the café, Venus recognises a brooch worn by Betty as being one stolen from her at the same time as the camera. She tries to reclaim it, but is caught by Strong. Betty now tries to blackmail Mrs Trevelyan and says she will reveal the whereabouts of her husband for a fee. Mrs Trevelyan agrees to pay £500, but Steed interrupts them and is held at gunpoint by Strong. Strong shoots Brown, who was going to show Steed where Trevelyan was hidden. Mrs Trevelyan takes Strong's gun and trains it on Steed and Venus. She and her husband are, in fact, traitors. Strong ties Venus and Steed up and a time-switch bomb is set to kill them. As Strong leaves, Betty, who loves Brown, turns on him and shoots him. Steed is able to call her, and she turns off the mains supply, which defuses the bomb.

In Man in the Mirror, *Venus unwittingly photographs a 'dead man' and Steed is hard-pressed to save her.*

CONSPIRACY OF SILENCE

Teleplay by Roger Marshall

James	Artro Morris
Sica	Alec Mango
Carlo	Robert Rietty
John Steed	Patrick Macnee
Rickie	Sandra Dorne
Catherine Gale	Honor Blackman
Gutman	Roy Purcell
Leggo	Himself
Terry	John Church
Arturo	Tommy Godfrey
Professor	Willie Shearer
Rant	Ian Wilson

Designed by Stephen Doncaster

Directed by Peter Hammond

WHEN TWO Italians are brought together in the office of a circus artist agency, one, Carlo, knows that the other is a complete stranger to him. The second Italian, Sica, is a member of the Mafia and has been ordered to kill Steed. Sica knows that Carlo joined the Mafia when young, and is still bound by the sacred oath. Sica now orders Carlo to carry out the assassination. When Carlo attempts to kill Steed, his own panic and reluctance make him fail, but he does escape. Steed tells Cathy that the Mafia are smuggling drugs via London to Canada and the States, and that the assassination attempt was meant to silence him. When Cathy discovers that Carlo is a clown, she visits the circus as a photographer/journalist. The proprietor welcomes the publicity and arranges for Cathy to share the caravan of Carlo's wife, Rickie. Later that day Sica arrives and threatens Rickie, demanding to know where Carlo is hiding. Rickie is rescued when one of the stage-hands, Terry, intervenes. Rickie tells Cathy that when Carlo was in the Italian Air Force, one of his bombing raids hit a school and killed 80 children. Unknown to Cathy, Carlo is at the circus dressed as Beppo, another clown. The real Beppo has had an accident. Rickie tells him that he must kill Steed, so the Mafia will leave him alone. Steed receives two tickets, sent anonymously by Carlo, for the next performance. After the show, Carlo confronts Steed – together with Terry, who works for Sica – and says he must die. Meanwhile Cathy has discovered Sica in the clown's quarters and holds him at gunpoint. Sica boasts that Steed cannot escape both his enemies and Cathy swears that if he dies, she will kill Sica. Two shots ring out and Sica is exultant. Footsteps draw near and Cathy is relieved to hear Steed calling her name – Carlo had shot Terry instead of Steed.

A CHORUS OF FROGS

Teleplay by Martin Woodhouse

Staphanopoulus	Makki Marseilles
One-Six	Michael Gover
Mason	Eric Pohlmann
Anna	Yvonne Shima
Venus Smith	Julie Stevens
Ariston	John Carson
Pitt-Norton	Frank Gatliff
Helena	Colette Wilde
Jackson	Alan Haywood
John Steed	Patrick Macnee

Designed by James Goddard

Directed by Raymond Menmuir

STEED, HOLIDAYING in Greece, is asked to investigate the mysterious death of a deep-sea diver, Staphanopoulus. Steed stows away on a luxury yacht, *The Archipelago*, owned by Mason. Experiments are being made on board with a bathyscaphe designed by Pitt-Norton, a scientist in Mason's employ. Venus has been invited on board to entertain Mason's guests, one of whom is a foreign agent, Anna. Three other guests, Jackson, Helena and Ariston – all close friends of the dead diver – decide to dive under the yacht and spy on Mason's laboratory, so as to discover the cause of Staphanopoulus' death. When Jackson and Helena are confronted by Steed, he is held at gunpoint and told to keep out of the way. As Jackson prepares to dive, Anna appears and kills him with a harpoon gun. Mason says that Jackson has drowned while skin-diving and Helena wants to kill Mason in order to avenge the death of her two friends, but Ariston persuades her to talk to Steed first. Venus tells Steed that Mason has a secret laboratory, where delicate fish are kept. They leave to investigate but Mason appears and Steed is questioned. Meanwhile, Ariston and Helena discover the experimental bathyscaphe in which Staphanopoulus died. Ariston goes down in it and when it resurfaces he is unconscious. Steed tells Ariston that he suspects Mason of experimenting with different gas mixtures in the bathyscaphe, in order to discover a mixture that will prevent compression sickness. Anna has taken Venus prisoner and she forces Pitt-Norton to face the truth about his experiments – that Mason is only interested in the bathyscaphe because of its use as a midget submarine. Helena threatens to kill Mason but Steed intervenes. Together they enter the laboratory in time to see Anna and Pitt-Norton forcing Venus to make one final test in the bathyscaphe. Helena overpowers Anna and Steed makes short work of Pitt-Norton.

SIX HANDS ACROSS A TABLE

Teleplay by Reed R De Rouen

Julian Seabrook	Philip Madoc
Sir Charles Reniston	John Wentworth
George Stanley	Campbell Singer
Oliver Waldner	Guy Doleman
Butler	Ian Cunningham
Brian Collier	Edward de Souza
Lady Reniston	Freda Bamford
Catherine Gale	Honor Blackman
Rosalind Waldner	Sylvia Bidmead
Miss Francis	Gillian Barclay
Draughtsman	Stephen Hancock
Bert Barnes	Frank Siemen
John Steed	Patrick Macnee
Receptionist	Ilona Rodgers

Designed by Paul Bernard

Directed by Richmond Harding

CATHY IS invited to spend the weekend at a house party given by an old school friend, Rosalind Waldner, whose father, Oliver, is a member of the powerful Reniston Group of shipbuilders. Rosalind tells Cathy that Herbert Collier, a shipbuilder planning to build a nuclear-powered liner with French collaboration, has been killed in a road accident, leaving his son Brian in control of the shipyards. The Reniston Group is against combining with the French and wants to win the order for the new liner to be built in their yards. Steed meanwhile visits Brian Collier, who intends to continue his father's policy. He admits that the situation is very difficult for him because he is in love with Rosalind. Brian calls Waldner and the other board members – Sir Charles Reniston and George Stanley – to his office and tells them of his intentions. Afterwards, as Cathy and Brian leave together, a heavy block and tackle falls from the roof of the works section, narrowly missing them. Sir Charles is worried about Waldner's attitude to Brian's proposal and suspects that he may be planning something but Stanley says there is nothing wrong. The following day, however, Seabrook, financial adviser to the Reniston Group, tells Brian that his company will shortly be taken over. Brian says he will fight the take-over bid, and Cathy – quite fond of Oliver Waldner – offers her support. Seabrook and Sir Charles resign from the Reniston board and join Brian, so he can buy back control of his own company. That night as Cathy is trying to open the safe in Waldner's study, Waldner finds her. He explains that he and Stanley are trying to take over enough companies to control the British shipyards but only to prevent orders being given to foreign companies. At the next board meeting, the take-over bid is defeated and Cathy and Steed arrest Waldner and Stanley.

KILLERWHALE

Teleplay by John Lucarotti

John Steed	Patrick Macnee
'Pancho' Driver	Patrick Magee
Harry	Morris Perry
Catherine Gale	Honor Blackman
Joey Frazer	Kenneth Farrington
Willie	John Tate
Sailor	Frederick Abbott
Fernand	John Bailey
Angela	Julie Paule
Receptionist	Lyndhall Goodman
Laboratory assistant	Christopher Coll
Brown	Robert Mill

Designed by Douglas James

Directed by Kim Mills

WHEN CATHY introduces Steed to a young boxer named Joey Frazer, Steed suggests that he should start training at a gymnasium run by Pancho Driver. Cathy agrees and decides to manage Joey herself. Joey is introduced to Driver and given a trial bout in the ring against the formidable Tiger. After the fight Joey borrows a bar of soap from a visiting sailor's locker. Pancho enters and takes away the soap, warning Joey not to interfere with other people's property. Next day, when Cathy is binding Joey's hands, she notices a peculiar smell and realises that the soap was, in fact, ambergris. That night she visits the gymnasium and finds a dead sailor's body in the dressing room. She tells Steed, who is very interested, and had suspected that ambergris was being smuggled from the Caribbean to Pancho's gym – now he has the proof. Steed follows Pancho's assistant, Harry, to a couturier's owned by Fernand. While he is there, pretending to buy an outfit for his niece, two men enter and demand money from Fernand. He pays half his debt and they promise to return the next day for the rest. Joey, anxious to help Cathy, searches the dressing room for the silver paper the soap was wrapped in. He has found it in the cellar when Pancho appears and holds him at gunpoint. Cathy arrives at the gym. Worried by Joey's absence, she goes to the cellar and finds Pancho sitting on a vaulting box. She forces Pancho to take the box to pieces, and inside find the unconscious Joey. Cathy tries to revive Joey but Pancho attacks her and takes her and Joey to Fernand's laboratory and locks them in a storeroom. In the meantime, Fernand has discovered the body of the sailor, hidden in the couturier's by Steed. Pancho panics and tries to escape. However, Steed has released Cathy and Joey and they are able to stop Pancho's escape attempt. After a fight, Fernand and Pancho are arrested.

AVENGING CRIME WITH A WINK

USUALLY IT takes several months before a TV series makes sufficient impression on the public, for its particular flavour to become part of the popular folklore. And because Saturday night shows received less attention from the Press than those screened when journalists were on duty, it was some time before *The Avengers* team became aware – through growing Press interest, viewers' letters, requests for personal appearances and their own contact with members of the public – that their programme had become 'the rage'. They were told, for instance, that *The Avengers* was 'The darling of the Primrose Hill set' (Sunday Times). 'It keeps the Bright Young Things of Belgravia and Chelsea at home on Saturday nights.' 'It's trivial and I love it without reservation because it's shrewdly calculated and played with great style' (The Spectator). 'Has started a new fashion in pin-ups – the photographers of a leading Fleet Street tabloid have taken down their pictures of unclad ladies and substituted the elegantly dressed Honor Blackman.' When it was screened for the first time in Scotland it immediately scored the highest viewing figures of any television contractor for the time of day. *The Avengers*, it appeared, had made it and now bore the accolade of television's most 'with it' drama show.

Honor Blackman and Patrick Macnee pose for a publicity session in London's Oxford Street, c. 1963.

But not everyone applauded the programme. As plans were being prepared for a new 26-week run, a financial director of Iris Productions, the subsidiary company set up to produce the show for ABC, decided to examine the overall production cost of each episode produced. Finding that on two occasions only did the cost come below – or break even with – the projected production budget (script, design, music and wardrobe costs had been rising steadily), the executive remitted a memo to ABC, his main cause of concern being the proposed increases of salary for Honor Blackman and Patrick Macnee, both of whom were waiting to learn if their contracts were going to be renewed. Intimating that the company should face up to the fact that they simply could not afford Blackman *and* Macnee, he asked for a decision to be taken as to which star *should be dropped* – or, if neither was to go, whether the company would approve a substantially higher budget. Within seven days the series was allocated an extra £5,000 budget and the stars' contracts were renewed.

Meanwhile, an ABC producer put forward the idea that the series could well use the addition of another male lead, to 'prevent the show from becoming *hag-ridden*', and the company's managing director, Howard Thomas, suggested that should they ever decide to give Steed a new Number 2, the producers should keep in mind actor John Standing, who had played the role of East in the story *School for Traitors*, and would prove a perfect foil for Macnee.

These views were in the minority. Most people enjoyed the show's originality, and the Cathy Gale character, as one of the screen's earliest liberated women, was a revelation. At the time, Honor said, 'I'd been used to playing women of the sweet, fairhaired English rose variety. So when the opportunity of playing a character like Cathy Gale came along, it was like a breath of fresh air. The first few weeks were extremely difficult and for a time I wondered if I'd bitten off more than I could chew. But then I began to cope with the task of licking Cathy into the beginnings of what she is now. Everybody had ideas of what she was going to be like. And all of us, including Leonard White, who was then the producer, wondered how the public were going to receive this 'way-out' woman who was starting to evolve. As far as we were concerned, the more she took shape, the more our image of her crystallised, the more we liked her. Imagine our extra delight, then, when we found that people were thrilled by her way-outness – were even prepared to take more.' It appears that the producers had wanted her to be a *contrast* to Steed. As she told me,

'She would *never* play dirty. She would never *kill* anyone. She was extraordinarily *pure*! Patrick and I were very lucky because we had two weeks of rehearsal before doing it "live" on videotape. So Cathy's character was fleshed-out inasmuch as *I* wouldn't do certain things and Patrick felt that *Cathy* wouldn't do certain things, or *would* do certain things, and from all the banter that went on during rehearsals, the character evolved and Cathy emerged.'

Leonard White, who shaped the first two series, had transferred to ABC's *Armchair Theatre*, and the series' former story editor, John Bryce, was now heading the production team. Gone also were Venus Smith – Julie Stevens had left the show to have a baby – and Dr King, One-Ten, Freckles and company were quietly forgotten. Newcomers this time around were Paul Whitsun-Jones as Charles, Steed's superior in the stories *Man With Two Shadows* and *The Wringer*, and Ronald Radd, as Quilpie, Steed's chief in the episode *The Outside-In Man*. A distinctive character whose office lay hidden behind a butcher's shop, where he passed out prime cuts of meat between briefing his agents, who entered via the cool room, Quilpie, head of PANSAC (Permanent Agency for National Security and Counter-Intelligence), was given the opportunity of uttering a typical Avengers line – 'Come into the fridge – there's something that needs to be done'. A third 'new' character was Junia, an 18-month-old Great Dane. Sister of Juno, the canine who shared Steed's adventures during the Hendry series, Junia had actually made her debut as a replacement for her brother in the story *Death of a Great Dane*, but returned to stardom for six second-season Blackman episodes. Referred to as 'Puppy' by Steed, both dogs were owned and trained by top dog-breeder Barbara 'Walkies' Woodhouse.

One reason for the programme's success was the friendly cooperation that existed between the writers and the production team. *The Avengers* was a show where everyone collaborated in altering or embellishing the scripts to improve the show. Bryce and story editor Richard Bates (son of novelist H. E. Bates), had gathered together the finest writing talent available. Writers of the calibre of Brian Clemens, Roger Marshall and Malcolm Hulke were asked to devise new and exciting stories that were scripted for tension, lacked solemnity and embodied a broad streak of leg-pulling, and would allow the viewer to be carried along with the action and not be dismayed when something outrageously illogical happened to Steed and Cathy. They were also urged to attend readings, rehearsals and recordings, and encouraged to regard themselves as key figures in the shaping of the final production. The team were relentless self-critics, constantly conducting their own audience research and welcoming each and every tuppenny-worth of free advice. They saw their show as a pastiche of the thriller formula which had delighted highbrows and lowbrows alike ever since it was first devised. If some of the fun that they had in putting the show together rubbed off on their audience, they were well satisfied. They relished its bizarre, tongue-in-cheek quality, and refused to treat it seriously – except in their own terms,

which was as an hour of slick, sophisticated, and highly entertaining television. As a result, the scripts became slicker. Week after week the crime-busting duo proved themselves to be a remarkable twosome who, when confronted with all kinds of mysterious and intriguing situations, would somehow or other always overcome the opposition – usually with a wink of the eye or a smile. One special gimmick was to give the viewer only about half the facts necessary for a reasonable understanding of the plot, then shuffle these into a pattern that took 50 minutes to unravel – leaving the onlooker with a kind of guessing game, which was invariably good fun.

In Death Dispatch, *Steed summons Cathy to Santiago.*

However, when a national newspaper called Steed 'a marshmallow Scarlet Pimpernel', and further research indicated that he was becoming too much of a humorous 'feed' to Cathy Gale, steps were immediately taken to toughen up his character and restore the cultivated callousness which had first endeared him to his fans. (An example of this appeared in the story *Man With Two Shadows*, in which Steed, during his interrogation of a prisoner suspected of having been brainwashed by the 'opposition' into becoming a 'double agent', angrily snatched away the chair from beneath the prisoner, then *kicked him in the ribs* as he lay prostrate on the cell floor!)

Similarly, Cathy's role was changed to allow her more opportunity to show the feminine and fallible side of her nature. Throughout the earlier series, Cathy's instinct for self-preservation had never faltered – even when her partner was being threatened by villains no hint of female submission had ever cracked her icy cool. She had come to represent women everywhere who wanted to prove their equality with the opposite sex; a woman who fought like a man, used her wits like a man, yet firmly retained her femininity. Towards the end of the first series, she was also allowed to fall for a tycoon who turned out to be a bad lot (Oliver Waldner, played by Guy Doleman in *Six Hands Across a Table*). She was shown kissing the man and since then Bryce had vetoed such embraces. Though Steed had occasionally made a pass at her, it was usually in fun, and she had always politely resisted his advances. In fact they kissed only once in the entire series – and that was strictly in the line of duty when Steed felt it necessary to do so to save Cathy's life. The story was *The Little Wonders*, where Bryce was finally presented with circumstances in which he could no longer maintain his ban on the kissing of Mrs Gale – a New Year's Eve party, where naturally the ever-gallant Steed would be expected to do just that!

Once again, a new production directive was called for and Bryce issued his technicians with his own ideas for the new format.

Farewell Mrs Gale. Steed kisses his leading lady goodbye on the set of Lobster Quadrille.

THE AVENGERS

A Reappraisal

JOHN STEED:

Steed is a thoroughly professional and efficient undercover man. His 'cover' is that of a 'man about town' with a private income. He is suave, witty, debonair; foppish even. These qualities are conscientiously cultivated to disarm his opponents and lull them into a vulnerable position for the 'kill'.

Steed is an expert; *dedicated, ruthless, unscrupulous*. His MISSION is *all-important* to him and its *success* is the justification of whatever *methods* he has used. He has been thoroughly trained in arson, burglary, forgery, explosives, codes, poisons and murder . . . to name but a few.

He is trained to withstand *torture* and *brainwashing*.

Other than CATHERINE GALE there is no one working *for* STEED or *with* him, except such as may be persuaded (by any means from bribery to blackmail) to help him in a *specific* situation.

Steed's tastes are gentlemanly and slightly self-indulgent. He frequents the best tailor, best bootmaker, best wine merchant, visits the best clubs, best restaurants, reads the Royal Edition of 'The Times', plays bridge, bezique, polo, croquet, etc.

In Death of a Batman, Cathy solves a crossword problem as Steed tests a polo stake in his flat.

Steed's flat reflects family tradition and heritage: e.g. The Hyderabad All India Polo Cup; a tiger skin; hunting trophies; a portrait of his Great Grandfather Steed, etc. Most of STEED's possessions have a history – or at least an anecdotal background to them.

Unlike CATHY, he carries no obvious symbol of his vocation, such as a gun-holster (he uses a gun infrequently). But when necessary he can produce a fund of firearms, poison capsules, time bombs, microscopic transmitters, etc.

When tackling criminals he fights like a cad and uses *every dirty trick in the book* to knock them out with the least inconvenience to himself.

At all times (whether being menaced or menacing) Steed displays GRACE and CHARM.

MRS CATHERINE GALE:

A widow. She is trained as an anthropologist. *She is now a PROFESSIONAL undercover agent.* (The two jobs sometimes get in the way of each other.)

CATHY is essentially humanitarian. She is *loyal, honest* and *compassionate*. She is as much a professional as STEED, but her attitude to the MISSION is totally different. The END can never justify the MEANS for her. She CARES about people and *cannot* USE them like STEED. (She clashes frequently with Steed over the callousness of his methods.)

STEED deceives people fluently. CATHY deceives people with the greatest difficulty and *only* when her role makes it inevitable. She will NEVER deceive people simply in order to discover information; her enquiries are more likely to be straightforward.

Cathy prefers plain speaking: e.g. STEED says 'assassination', CATHY calls it 'murder'.

CATHY carries a gun. She is *expert* with all firearms and at photography and judo. She drives a car fast and well.

CATHY'S flat is modern and functional, predominantly *press-button controlled* (e.g. sliding doors; concealed drinks cabinet, etc.).

Cathy is avant garde in all her tastes. Her clothes are designed to suit her own individual style of cool, uncluttered elegance, masculine in the manner that emphasises femininity and always *practical* for the life she leads.

Her possessions (photographic equipment, etc.) will be the most modern. (STEED is slightly ill-at-ease among CATHY'S 'gadgetry'.)

THE TWO CHARACTERS:

STEED and CATHY'S moral attitudes CONFLICT and this difference is emphasised when they are on a MISSION. (Each character's point of view, although opposed, is of course equally valid).

No matter how they CONFLICT, the two characters retain a TRUST in each other. Cathy, for example, will always leave that important anthropology meeting to HELP Steed. . . . But, of course, each will always be able to SURPRISE the other with some character revelation.

STEED and CATHY are *not*, and could never function as police, private eyes, etc. They are UNDERCOVER agents, and consequently conceal this identity at all times: they have no badge to show or card to flash, nor does the announcement of their names bring automatic recognition or respect.

STEED and CATHY thrive on audience curiosity and speculation.

FIGHTS/ACTION:

There will be at least one fight, and some physical conflict, in EVERY EPISODE.

CATHY is the professional, disciplined judo expert . . . STEED fights like a cad – with little apparent exertion (and without having to remove his bowler). CATHY throws her opponents . . . STEED trips his. CATHY's aim is to close with her opponent in order to use judo . . . STEED stays at a distance by use of props (e.g. his bowler hat, his umbrella, etc.)

STUNTMEN should always be used as opponents and the scripts will be written to make such casting practicable.

FILM:

We will make use of FILM, but never in the conventional way. (i.e. establishing shots; as a link between scenes, etc).

We will only use FILM when we have a self-contained sequence (including CATHY and/or STEED) which typifies the SERIES. i.e. CATHY giving chase on a motorbike; a gunfight during a STEED golf match; CATHY tied to a railway track while the 7.10 thunders closer and closer, etc.

THE AVENGERS is a SERIES with an established popularity. I want to take advantage of this privileged situation and make it an opportunity for Direction, Design, Effects, Casting, Scripting, etc., to encourage and implement NEW ideas. Of course, all EXPERIMENT will be contained within the terms of our existing SUCCESSFUL format, but there is plenty of

scope, so let us take our opportunities to enhance further the Style and Prestige of THE AVENGERS.

DRINKING scenes should be kept to a minimum. SMOKING scenes should be kept to the minimum. BLASPHEMY is OUT!

Steed and Cathy's wardrobes were changed for the new series. Patrick Macnee's clothes became more Edwardian than ever, with braided pin-stripe suits, elegantly embroidered waistcoats, cummerbunds, drainpipe trousers and curly bowlers. Cathy's leather, though not entirely forgotten, gave way to garments that had either a military or Chinese influence. Suits, hats and boots took their flavour from the officers' uniforms of the Napoleonic period, with fobs, waistcoats and cravats. Dresses and jackets had the simplicity of the Chinese line. Frederick Starke, one-time chairman of the London Fashion House Group, was given the task of designing Cathy's new fashions and Honor Blackman wore some sensational creations, such as a cloth of gold sheath with knee-high boots in the story *November Five*. The designs were previewed on 29 October 1963 at the Garrison, Les Ambassadeurs Club, in London's Park Lane, and Honor wore Starke creations in 15 out of the 26 episodes. The other stories were completed before Mr Starke's designs became available. For one episode, *Don't Look Behind You*, Honor's outfits were designed by ABC Television.

Surrounded by mannequins, Honor and Patrick attend the 1963 Avengerwear fashion show.

When asked if wearing the leather fashions influenced her choice of everyday dress, Honor Blackman told me, 'I had the most fearful time during *The Avengers*, because some men felt threatened by Cathy Gale – the *image* of Cathy Gale. I would go to parties and they would try to lure me outside for a fight. It was pretty jokey really, because usually they were sufficiently stoned that one slight push in their stomach and they'd have soon been over. To have worn leather would have been to invite trouble, and in any case, everybody else was wearing leather then – I simply set the fashion. So it certainly affected my choice inasmuch as I didn't wear leather outside the show. As a matter of fact, I bought my first leather jacket just a few months ago.' It appears that Cathy Gale's image problem didn't end there. Pressed further, Honor continued, 'I had this extraordinary fanmail. Some of it quite funny, some of it very sick. We used to have this wonderful publicity woman called Marie Donaldson, who admitted quite frankly that a lot of the letters were kept from me. But some I saw and I suppose around 80% were answered. It created some rather strange invitations – some *very* strange invitations. Some people actually imagined that with all the leather and boots I wore, I also carried a whip! I was frequently asked to attend "strange" parties – provided I carried my whip. I never went, of course!' Mind you, if called upon to do so, Honor Blackman could handle herself in any situation, as this anecdote proves. Prior to a live television appearance in the Midlands to promote the show, Honor asked the interviewer what type of questions he would be putting to her during the programme, a request intended to ensure that she could give adequate answers. 'Oh, I never discuss the questions with a guest,' came the reply – leaving an edge to the relationship as they faced the camera. The interview moved along until out of the blue the pompous questioner said: 'Tell me, Miss Blackman, how does it feel to be half man and half woman?' Without batting an eyelid, the Avengers star, dressed in a low-cut dress which fully displayed her natural contours to the best advantage, leaned across the table and replied: 'Which half are you referring to?' Cue for a red-faced interviewer to fluff his remaining lines.

Cathy finds it amusing to read a headline that Steed has been accused of her 'murder' in Brief for Murder.

Brian Clemens's script for the season's opening episode, *Brief For Murder*, contained some interesting 'facts' about Steed's background. Once again these were cut from the final transmission print. Nevertheless, as they give one writer's view of Steed's formative years, I'll include them here. These suggested that Steed was the younger son of a younger son, a scion of a noble family, but he is the black sheep of the family. He was sent to Eton, but spent most of his time in amateur theatricals. He left Eton shortly before war broke out and had a fine war record, which was distinguished when, as a lieutenant in the Royal Navy, he commanded a motor torpedo boat. After 1945 he ran an ex-naval launch in and around the Eastern Mediterranean ports at a time when cigarette trafficking was in full swing. Later, he turned up in London and, to some extent, re-established himself with his family by taking a respectable job with the Civil Service. Shortly afterwards, he appeared in the Middle East as economic adviser to Sheikh Akbar Ben Sidi Ben Becula, ruler of an oil-rich state. While he was there the Sheikh became involved in a quarrel between two neighbouring states. Some people say this row nearly started World War III, but others say it averted it. However, the Sheikh became richer through oil royalties and Steed returned to England with an award from him, the Order of the Golden Ram (Second Class), and life royalties from two of the oil wells. From this income he lived the life to which he had accustomed himself. At about this time he is said to have done some work for the State, but no official record exists of such work. . . .

To give an added dimension to the characters of Steed and Cathy, they now had resident addresses, and many of the stories opened and closed with Steed and Cathy meeting at home – something which would be continued in later episodes. Steed's flat, at 5 Westminster Mews, was furnished with Victoriana collected during his frequent trips up and down the country. Polo cups and hunting trophies adorned the shelves, complemented by Steed's collection of military paintings. The hearth had a tiger-skin rug and over the fireplace hung a magnificent portrait of his great-grandfather, R.K.J.J. de V. Steed (known in his day as 'Stallion'). The flat was furnished with red upholstery. Concealed behind a false row of books was a secret radio receiver. The spacious window overlooking Parliament Square was built of bullet-proof glass.

Cathy's flat, at 14 Primrose Hill, was modern and functional, predominantly press-button controlled. Her kitchen was superbly equipped and all the rooms had sliding doors. There was a concealed cocktail cabinet in the sitting-room, which was furnished with uncomfortable-looking backless chairs and a sofa. To make life that much easier, a television monitor screen showed her who was at the door, and her photographic studio contained the most modern equipment. One unusual feature was a magnetic chessboard which, when reversed, concealed a telephone.

As the series went before the camera, no one was more pleased than Honor Blackman and Patrick Macnee when regular scriptwriter Malcolm Hulke went on record as saying: 'The dedication and enthusiasm of these two artists is one of the most important factors in the development of the series. Despite working a six- and seven-day week for months on end (and often rehearsing two shows at once), both stars have sacrificed much of their all-too-brief leisure time to activities that would help build up the show: judo and gymnastic sessions to equip them for their fights, endless costume fittings to extend their wardrobes, and of course the personal appearances and press interviews that their popularity has earned them.'

The year ended on a high note, with Honor and Patrick being voted *Independent Television's Personalities of 1963*, in the Variety Club of Great Britain Annual Awards ceremony held at London's Dorchester Hotel.

BRIEF FOR MURDER

By Brian Clemens

Wescott	Alec Ross
Dicey	June Thody
Marsh	Fred Ferris
John Steed	Patrick Macnee
Catherine Gale	Honor Blackman
Wilson	Anthony Baird
Barbara Kingston	Helen Lindsay
Miles Lakin	Harold Scott
Jasper Lakin	John Laurie
Judge	Robert Young
Bart	Michael Goldie
Maisie	Pamela Wardel
Miss Prinn	Alice Fraser
Foreman of the jury	Walter Swash

Designed by James Goddard

Directed by Peter Hammond

WESCOTT, CHARGED with treason at the Old Bailey, is pronounced not guilty. Cathy, however, is certain of his guilt and discovers that Wescott's contact – a man called Jonno who was never caught – is in fact Steed. When Cathy asks him about it, Steed refuses to discuss the matter and threatens to silence her 'once and for all'. Cathy responds by publishing her accusation in the newspapers. Steed contacts Wescott and asks him to put him in touch with the solicitors whose brief got Wescott acquitted. The solicitors are Jasper and Miles Lakin, two elderly brothers. They are glad to help Steed and happily agree to defend him on the murder charge when he commits the murder of Mrs Gale. The brothers tell Steed exactly how to commit the murder. Steed shoots Cathy and the body falls into the Thames. As Steed leaves, he is seen by the principal of a yoga school where Cathy practises. Steed is soon arrested and sent for trial. The prosecution case goes exactly as arranged by the Lakins and Steed is pronounced not guilty. As he leaves the court, he looks up into the public gallery – where Cathy sits. Steed and Cathy meet later at Miss Prinn's yoga school and Steed tells Cathy that her murder is not sufficient to arrest the Lakins. They have safeguarded themselves too well and must be caught out at their own game. Cathy visits them posing as a Miss Patchett, wishing to commit a fraud involving two business partners who must be caught while she goes free. The Lakins are surprised at having to work for a conviction, but agree to help. They carefully arrange all the details, but Steed, by pretending to have been re-arrested, operates their plan so that they become the two business partners and they are caught in the very trap which they so expertly arranged.

THE UNDERTAKERS

By Malcolm Hulke

Green	Howard Goorney
Madden	Patrick Holt
Catherine Gale	Honor Blackman
John Steed	Patrick Macnee
Mrs Sayer	Lally Bowers
Lomax	Lee Patterson
Wilkinson	Ronald Russell
Paula	Jan Holden
Daphne	Mandy Miller
Mrs Lomax	Marcella Markham
Mrs Baker	Helena McCarthy
Reeve	Denis Forsyth

Designed by David Marshall

Directed by Bill Bain

STEED TELLS Cathy that he is disturbed because Professor Sayer – with whom Steed was going to promote a new invention – has apparently gone into meditation at a rest home, the Adelphi Park. Steed has visited the home but was refused entry by the Matron, Mrs Lomax. He shows Cathy a copy of the local electoral register which contains the names of the occupants of Adelphi Park. Cathy realises that they are all millionaires. Meanwhile, Marshall, a multi-millionaire, is murdered by a man called Green, and the body is taken away by three undertakers. Apparently all the millionaires at the rest home have recently signed over their fortunes to their next of kin, to evade death duties. Cathy wonders if the owners of Adelphi Park have discovered a way of keeping the millionaires alive, at least on paper, for the required five-year period after the signing. Cathy applies for the position of Assistant Matron at the home while Steed, posing as a representative of a firm of funeral directors, visits the local undertakers which is run by Green. There in the Chapel of Rest he finds the body of Mrs Lomax. Cathy arrives at Adelphi Park and meets the new Matron, Mrs Sayer – wife of Professor Sayer – who confirms that Adelphi Park is being run by an organisation to help millionaires evade death duties. Meanwhile Marshall, who is still alive, and his 'murderer' Green, are talking in the funeral parlour. Marshall tells Green that he is waiting to take revenge on Lomax – husband of the former Matron – who had ordered Marshall's death. Daphne Marshall now arrives from Switzerland and is told by her stepmother, Paula, that her father is staying at Adelphi Park. Daphne calls at the rest home and demands to see her father but is held captive by Mrs Sayer, Paula and Lomax. They take Daphne away, but they are seen by Cathy who immediately informs Steed. Steed returns to the funeral parlour and sees Marshall and Green leaving. He forces an entry and is attacked by one of Green's undertakers, but he makes short work of him and leaves for the rest home. At Adelphi Park, Cathy has found Daphne locked in a closet. She releases her and they are about to depart when Lomax arrives and holds them at gunpoint. He is disturbed by the arrival of Marshall and Green, and Marshall, swearing vengeance, shoots Lomax. Steed arrives and in the confusion Marshall and Green escape into the grounds – to be pursued and caught eventually by Cathy and Steed.

Steed chases his quarry into the Adelphi Park grounds in The Undertakers.

Steed looks on as Cathy prepares to take up her post as Assistant Matron in The Undertakers.

MAN WITH TWO SHADOWS

By James Mitchell

Gordon	**Daniel Moynihan**
Charles	**Paul Whitsun-Jones**
John Steed	**Patrick Macnee**
Borowski	**Terence Lodge**
Catherine Gale	**Honor Blackman**
Rudi	**Douglas Robinson**
Sigi	**George Little**
Julie	**Gwendolyn Watts**
Dr Terence	**Geoffrey Palmer**
Miss Quist	**Anne Godfrey**
Cummings	**Philip Anthony**
Holiday camp official	**Robert Lankesheer**

Designed by Paul Bernard

Directed by Don Leaver

STEED IS summoned by Charles, his superior, to meet a man named Borowski who has been brainwashed by the 'opposition'. During brief moments of sanity, Borowski speaks of the 'doubles' that the opposition are going to smuggle into the country. Steed and Charles realise that all the men hold top positions in the Ministry of Security. Cathy and Steed watch the newspapers closely for any suggestion of a scientist or politician being murdered. Their first clue is a brochure for a holiday camp found amongst Borowski's possessions. A few days later a man is run over by a car, and since his description fits a scientist called Gordon who is visiting the holiday camp, Steed visits Gordon's doctor and dentist. But the body is so badly damaged that they are unable to confirm that it is Gordon. Cathy meanwhile visits the holiday camp and meets a man named Gordon. She returns convinced that he is the real Gordon. Steed visits the man and tells him that he must have a medical check-up. Gordon agrees and both doctor and dentist say that the man is the real Gordon. Steed, however, is unconvinced. Gordon returns to the camp, calls his superiors and relates what has happened. They decide to put the next part of their plan into action – the new double will be John Steed. Steed books into the camp and that night he is attacked by his double. There is a fierce fight and 'Steed' tells Gordon and Cummings (a visiting politician and the third doppleganger) that the real Steed is dead. Cathy is summoned by Charles and told that if the real Steed is dead, she will have to kill his double. At the same time, Steed is told by Cummings that if Cathy suspects anything, Steed will have to kill her. When Cathy learns that Gordon has left the camp and returned to his research station, she approaches Cummings and asks for his help. At Steed's chalet Cathy pulls a gun on Steed and asks Cummings to keep him under surveillance while she goes for help. When she has left, Steed immediately attacks Cummings. The following day, Cathy returns home to find Steed waiting for her. He tells her he disposed of his double and went along with the plan to discover the identity of the gangleader – Cummings. He has since been placed under arrest, along with his associates, and Gordon is now feeding back secret information to the opposition supplied by Steed!

THE NUTSHELL

By Philip Chambers

Elin Strindberg	Edina Ronay
Catherine Gale	Honor Blackman
John Steed	Patrick Macnee
Laura	Patricia Haines
Military policeman	Edwin Brown
Disco	John Cater
Venner	Charles Tingwell
Susan	Christine Shaw
Anderson	Ian Clark
Jason	Jan Conrad
Alex	Ray Browne

Designed by Philip Harrison

Directed by Raymond Menmuir

STEED AND CATHY are called to The Nutshell – a vast underground shelter to be used by the security forces in the event of World War III – where the Director of Operations (Disco) tells them that a file listing double agents, codenamed Big Ben, has been copied. They have photographs taken by hidden cameras during the break-in, and the thief is an attractive young girl. Cathy is sent to Central Security to find out from Venner if the girl is on their files. Steed is ordered to Special Branch but instead visits a rehearsal room where he meets the girl, Elin. She gives him the microfilm she has taken of Big Ben and Steed tells her to leave the country. He then telephones Disco to say he has found the girl. Disco sends Venner to arrest Elin but when he reaches the rehearsal room she is dead. Venner returns to Disco with several photographs of Elin. Steed is seen in the background of one of them. Disco suspects him of being a traitor and Venner is ordered to bring him in for questioning. Venner visits Steed's flat but Cathy refuses to believe that Steed is a traitor or to help, other than telling him that Steed is meeting a man called Jason at an airfield. Venner and his assistant, Anderson, go there and try to arrest Jason but Steed orders them to release him. As Jason hurries to the waiting aircraft Steed gives himself up. He is taken back to The Nutshell and questioned, but refuses to say what has happened to Big Ben and is finally put in a cell. Cathy arrives and, apparently convinced of Steed's guilt, tells Disco that she will try to persuade Steed to tell the truth. As she enters Steed's cell, he attacks her. During the fight, she surreptitiously hands him a gun, then the guards rescue Cathy. Venner arrives and offers Steed his freedom in exchange for the microfilm. That evening, Steed escapes, captures Venner and restores the microfilm to Disco. Steed admits that he bribed Elin to copy Big Ben in order to trap the real traitor – Venner.

DEATH OF A BATMAN

By Roger Marshall

Edith Wrightson	Kitty Attwood
John Wrightson	David Burke
John Steed	Patrick Macnee
Catherine Gale	Honor Blackman
Lord Teale	Andre Morrell
Eric Van Doren	Philip Madoc
Cooper	Ray Browne
Lady Cynthia	Katy Greenwood
Gibbs	Geoffrey Alexander

Designed by Paul Bernard

Directed by Kim Mills

WHEN STEED attends the reading of the will of Wrightson, his one-time batman, he is surprised to find that he is repaid £10 owed since 1942. Lord Basil Teale, an influential merchant banker, is left Wrightson's war medals. To his son John, Wrightson leaves £100 – and £480,000 to his wife Edith. Steed is astonished by the sum and he and Cathy ponder how Wrightson, a draughtsman for a printing firm, could have amassed such a fortune. Steed suspects forgery. Lord Basil and his partner, Van Doren, are also concerned at the amount left by Wrightson and fear that the game is up unless they act quickly. A lovely, though scatterbrained, heiress, Lady Cynthia, arrives and is firmly advised not to sell her profitable investments. When she leaves, however, Van Doren and Teale immediately make arrangements to sell them. Steed and Cathy attend an open day at an electronics firm and Steed tells Cathy that he is concerned about the security implications of Van Doren and Teale having financial control of the firm. It seems they specialise in electronics companies. Steed visits Lady Cynthia, who gives him a list of her investments. Thorpe, a broker, tells Steed that the stock market price on Lady Cynthia's investments indicate selling. John Wrightson now contacts Teale and blackmails him, because he knows that his father's fortune came from Teale and Van Doren for services rendered. His father's firm printed new currencies, share certificates, etc, and Wrightson, as top draughtsman, was first to be told of any new order. Therefore he could inform Teale before the public announcement. Steed, having gained proof from Thorpe of Teale's crooked activities, calls on John and forces him to help him trap Teale. Teale swears his motives were solely patriotic – all his money was used to finance Britain's electronics industry. But Steed has no option but to inform the police and Teale and Van Doren are arrested.

Cornered Secret Service official Venner seems to have the drop on Steed in The Nutshell.

The chances of Steed surviving to collect his £10 inheritance look decidedly slim in this scene from Death of a Batman.

NOVEMBER FIVE

By Eric Paice

Returning Officer	John Murray Scott
Michael Dyter	Gary Hope
Mart St John	Ric Hutton
Gunman	Frank Maher
John Steed	Patrick Macnee
First lady	Aimee Delamain
Major Swinburn	David Langton
Arthur Dove	David Davies
Catherine Gale	Honor Blackman
Fiona	Iris Russell
Joe	Joe Robinson
Mrs Dove	Ruth Dunning

Designed by Douglas James

Directed by Bill Bain

AS THE results of the Parliamentary by-election for South-East Anglia are being announced, the winning candidate, Dyter, is shot by someone in the crowd. Dyter had promised to expose a major security scandal. Steed visits the House of Commons, and sees Major Swinburn, MP, who had employed Dyter. Swinburn tells Steed that there is no substance to the scandal. Later, however, Swinburn hastily arranges a meeting between himself, St John, Dyter's publicity agent, and Arthur Dove, MP, a member of the opposition. They discuss the failure of the government to deal with the theft of a nuclear warhead and decide that Swinburn should put a question before the House to expose the security breach. Steed co-opts Mrs Gale into standing in the by-election caused by Dyter's death and together they visit a ski-school run by Fiona and Ernst. They meet Dove and Swinburn, and Steed tells Swinburn and St John that he is acting as Mrs Gale's election agent. Cathy says she will fight the election on Dyter's platform of exposing the security scandal but that she will do this before the campaign starts. This worries Swinburn. When they go to meet him at the House, they find him murdered. Later, Steed meets Dove and reveals that the government has received a blackmail note asking for £500,000 in return for the warhead. St John meanwhile visits Fiona and Ernst and tells them about Steed's activities. He then returns to his office and is confronted by Dyter, very much alive, who says he has abandoned the ransom threat in favour of a new plan. He will blow up the bomb, which is now hidden on the terrace of the House of Commons. Meanwhile, Steed and Cathy are going through the files in St John's office. They remove some photographs of the murder and realise that Dyter was not killed. That night, when Dyter goes to the House to set off the bomb, he finds Steed there, and then he and Cathy round up the rest of the gang.

Dinner by candlelight with Cathy Gale – a prospect to tempt any man. The lucky recipient in this scene from November Five *is actor David Davies.*

THE GILDED CAGE

By Roger Marshall

John Steed	Patrick Macnee
Catherine Gale	Honor Blackman
Groves	Neil Wilson
JP Spagge	Patrick Magee
Fleming	Norman Chappell
Manley	Frederic Abbott
Westwood	Alan Haywood
Wardress	Margo Cunningham
Benham	Edric Connor
Hammond	Martin Friend
Peterson	Terence Soall
Gruber	Geoff L'Cise
Barker	Douglas Cummings

Designed by Robert Macgowan

Directed by Bill Bain

CATHY HAS been working in a secret gold vault and when she tells Steed that it would only take six men to steal and remove the gold, he sees a way to put her scheme to good use. Steed's department has been on the trail of a man named Spagge, a millionaire from his criminal activities who is suspected to be the mastermind behind several recent big crimes. Steed visits Spagge and tells him that he and Mrs Gale are planning to steal £1,000,000 worth of gold. Spagge refuses to help. The following morning Cathy is arrested and charged with Spagge's murder. As she is led away, Steed arrives and assures her that he will soon have her released. In her cell, she desperately tries to recall what happened after her arrest, but her mind is a blank. Later that day she is visited by Benham, the prison chaplain, who asks why she killed Spagge and what part Steed played in the crime. Cathy continues to protest her innocence. She is called to see the Governor and is led away by a warder and left outside a large door. She finds herself confronted by six men, including Benham. They say that her arrest was a test, and having passed with flying colours, they are now prepared to hear her plans for stealing the gold. Steed is told that Cathy is safe and Spagge is not dead. He takes a case of clothes to Spagge and asks that they be passed on to Cathy. That night, at home, Steed answers his telephone. As he stands silhouetted in the window, somebody shoots him and he falls. The robbery is successfully carried out and the gold taken to Benham's home. Spagge then arrives and orders them to kill Cathy as he has discovered that Steed is working for the police. At this moment Steed arrives and rounds up the gang, leaving Cathy to fight it out with Benham and Spagge.

SECOND SIGHT

By Martin Woodhouse

Dr Vilner	Steven Scott
Neil Anstice	Peter Bowles
Dr Eve Hawn	Judy Bruce
John Steed	Patrick Macnee
Catherine Gale	Honor Blackman
Marten Halvarssen	John Carson
Dr Spender	Ronald Adam
Steiner	Terry Brewer

Designed by Terry Green

Directed by Peter Hammond

STEED hears that blind millionaire Halvarssen wants to bring two eye corneas from Switzerland. They are to travel in a specially sealed container designed by Dr Vilner. Steed tells Cathy that Halvarssen intends to use the cornea grafts on himself, to regain his sight. When Cathy visits Halvarssen's home, she is prevented from seeing him by his assistant, Anstice, but Cathy manages to make him reveal that the grafts are to be taken from a live donor. Steed calls in Dr Spender, a famous eye surgeon who, against Steed's wishes, demands that Halvarssen allows him to attend the operation. Steed decides that Cathy should go too, and Halvarssen agrees. Anstice accuses Halvarssen of jeopardising their plan, but he says that the complications are minor. Anstice can deal with Cathy and Spender later. At the Swiss clinic, Cathy and Dr Spender are told that they cannot see the donor, Hilda Brauer. However, Cathy finds Hilda's room – it is empty but for an unfinished portrait. She tells Spender and they both insist on seeing Hilda Brauer. Anstice finally takes them to her room. The bed is now occupied but the patient's face is totally masked by bandages. Anstice says she is under sedation and therefore no one can talk to her. That afternoon, Cathy receives a phone call from Steed and learns that Halvarssen lost his sight because of a head wound. New corneas are useless because it is physically impossible for him to regain his sight. Meanwhile Spender has been called to Hilda's room, but to his surprise finds only the patient there. He walks to the balcony to see if anyone is there. Hilda Brauer walks up behind him, and pushes him over the balcony rail. Arriving home, Cathy meets Steed at a private airfield where the sealed container is brought through customs by Anstice. Steed is convinced that Halvarssen is smuggling and though Cathy agrees, she is disturbed by Dr Spender's death and does not believe that Halvarssen would condone murder. She tells him of Spender's death and asks Anstice why he has not been told of the killing. Anstice replies that he is a professional and Spender was in the way. Steed now learns that Hilda Brauer died three years before. There was neither patient nor operation. At Halvarssen's home, Anstice hands him the container. The millionaire opens it and removes two large diamonds. He then draws one diamond across a mirror and feels for the scratch, but the mirror is smooth – Anstice has double-crossed him. As Anstice holds Halvarssen at gunpoint, Cathy arrives. Anstice grabs Cathy and, using her as a cover, tries to escape but Steed intervenes and the crooks are arrested.

THE MEDICINE MEN

By Malcolm Hulke

Catherine Gale	Honor Blackman
John Steed	Patrick Macnee
Geoffrey Willis	Peter Barkworth
John Willis	Newton Blick
Frank Leeson	Harold Innocent
Taylor	John Crocker
Fay	Monica Stevenson
Masseuse	Brenda Cowling
Miss Dowell	Joy Wood
Edwards	Peter Hughes

Designed by David Marshall

Directed by Kim Mills

Top: *In* The Gilded Cage, *Cathy organises a bullion robbery to outwit millionaire criminal Spagge.*

Centre: *Inclement weather is no deterrent to Steed and Cathy Gale in* Second Sight.

Bottom: *Cathy is all tied up in* The Medicine Men.

A CHINESE GIRL is murdered in a Turkish bath and Steed asks Cathy to investigate. He visits a pharmaceutical company, Willis Sopwith, which has been badly hit by the sale of imitation products on their overseas markets. Steed learns from Geoffrey Willis that the imitators change the spelling of the brand name as protection against copyright action, and Willis Sopwith have redesigned all their cartons in an effort to get one jump ahead. The company's research scientist, Edwards, tells Steed and Willis that there is a printer's trademark on one of the imitation cartons – if they can trace the printer he may lead them to the imitator. Cathy discovers that the Chinese girl often went to the Turkish bath and sometimes her pores oozed paint, as though she had taken a bath in it. At the baths a girl called Fay is covered in paint and Cathy discovers that she once advertised cosmetics for Willis Sopwith. Cathy gets a job as an efficiency expert at the firm. Miss Dowell, Willis' secretary, shows Cathy around and Edwards' body is discovered in a stationery cupboard. He has hanged himself. Cathy meets Willis' father, John Willis, chairman of the company, and learns that Fay is his girlfriend and she models for Leeson, an artist. Meanwhile, Taylor, a printer, shows replicas of the new Willis Sopwith carton designs to Leeson. That night Steed and Cathy break into Taylor's print shop and discover the copies. Later Steed visits Leeson's studio and overhears him explaining to Fay that this time their cartons will be identical to the originals. They will contain various poisonous ingredients, causing illness and death in the Arabic countries, and so harm the goodwill there of Willis Sopwith and of Britain, thus endangering a forthcoming oil treaty. Fay is horrified and says she will tell John Willis. Steed and Cathy return to the printing shop and replace the printing block with one made by Steed. They discover Fay bound and gagged and release her. But as Cathy searches the rest of the building, she is discovered by Miss Dowell and Steed is held at gunpoint by Geoffrey Willis – the ringleader of the organisation. Taylor arrives with the new cartons but Miss Dowell realises that the Arabic wording on them reads 'Poison. This is an imitation'. Steed manages to break free and Cathy takes care of Miss Dowell while Steed overpowers the rest of the gang, using his bowler.

THE GRANDEUR THAT WAS ROME

By Rex Edwards

Bruno	Hugh Burden
Marcus	John Flint
Estow	Ian Shand
Catherine Gale	Honor Blackman
Octavia	Colette Wilde
John Steed	Patrick Macnee
Appleton	Kenneth Keeling
Lucius	Raymond Adamson
Barnes	Colin Rix

Designed by Stan Woodward

Directed by Kim Mills

WHEN THERE are reports of crop failures, unknown diseases in animals and frequent outbreaks of illness in all parts of the world, Steed and Cathy visit United Foods and Dressings Ltd (UFD), a factory which distributes fertilisers and insecticides. Cathy tells Estow, the public relations officer, of the reports and Estow shows them over UFD. Cathy can see no way the modern equipment could have been tampered with but Steed is not so sure. Meanwhile Sir Bruno Lucer welcomes Marcus Dodds, his right-hand man, who has been touring America on behalf of Sir Bruno's political party. Lucer lives in a villa designed like that of a Roman senator, and clearly has a Caesar fixation. He introduces Marcus to his attractive companion, Octavia. At Steed's flat, Steed and Cathy study specimens of grain and fertiliser from all over the country. Finally, Cathy discovers that some of the UFD grain is infected with ergot, which would account for some of the illnesses. Steed thinks that it is no accident but a deliberate attempt to infect the grain. He shows Cathy an unusual marking which he found on one of the sacks at UFD, but Cathy is unable to identify the marking. Lucer is preparing for the arrival of his deputies from all over the world, and he informs Marcus that the full 'senate' will soon meet to announce his plan to take over the world by spreading bubonic plague. Later, Marcus meets Octavia and tells her that he thinks Bruno is taking the Roman Empire idea too far. Together they plan to kill Bruno and become the new party leaders. Meanwhile Steed has told Cathy that the chairman of UFD is Sir Bruno Lucer, a one-time left-wing politician. Cathy produces some photographs she took at UFD and one of them shows the marking Steed found earlier – a Roman monogram. On the pretext of selling Roman figurines, Steed visits Bruno who confesses that in his opinion the Romans were the greatest civilisation ever, but denies having any strong political feelings. As Steed leaves, he bumps into Marcus and recognises him as Dodds, the organiser of The World Empire Party. That night Cathy breaks into the UFD laboratory but is caught and held prisoner by a security guard. He phones Marcus, who tells Bruno they now have a guinea pig for his experiment with the plague. The following morning,

Steed, concerned at Cathy's disappearance, breaks into Bruno's villa. He is discovered by Estow and locked in the cellar with Cathy. Bruno prepares for the 'senate meeting' and his subsequent coronation. At the height of the celebrations Bruno sends Lucius, an American senator, to fetch Cathy. When he arrives at the cell with a guard, he is surprised to find Steed missing. The guard takes Cathy away, and Steed appears from his hiding place above the door. The senator draws his sword but Steed kills him. In the hall above, Marcus and Octavia prepare a goblet of wine, containing the plague toxin which is meant to be given to Bruno. But Bruno is suspicious, and changes the goblets around, giving the 'doctored' one to Cathy, and orders her to drink it. She hesitates – then throws the wine in his face. At that moment, Steed arrives and the senators flee, leaving Steed and Cathy to fight the guards. They quickly dispose of the opposition and set out in search of Bruno and Marcus, only to find Bruno dead. Marcus has killed him and the debt is paid. Together they arrest Marcus and his accomplice, Octavia.

Cathy is held prisoner by Bruno, determined to recapture The Grandeur That Was Rome.

THE GOLDEN FLEECE

By Roger Marshall and
Phyllis Norman

Captain Jason	**Warren Mitchell**
Major Ruse	**Tenniel Evans**
Sgt Major White	**Barry Lineham**
Mrs Kwan	**Yu Ling**
Mr Lo	**Robert Lee**
John Steed	**Patrick Macnee**
Catherine Gale	**Honor Blackman**
Esther	**Lisa Peake**
Jones	**Michael Hawkins**
Private Holmes	**Ronald Wilson**

Designed by Anne Spavin

Directed by Peter Hammond

AFTER DINNER with Cathy at a Chinese restaurant, Steed deliberately gets the cloakroom attendant to hand him the wrong coat. When they reach Steed's flat he searches the coat pockets and finds a cheque for £2000 made out to Mr Jason and drawn against a Chinese bank. Steed decides to wait and see who collects it. Meanwhile at the restaurant, an elderly Chinese gentleman, Mr Lo, tells the owner, Mrs Kwan, to prepare for the arrival of three guests, one of whom is Mr Jason. During the meeting Mr Lo lets it be known that someone in the organisation has absconded with £10,000. Jason realises that it is one of his men, and promises to investigate. Next morning, Jason visits Steed, having traced him through the address in Steed's coat. When Jason has left, Steed tells Cathy why he is interested in the restaurant – it is being used as a cover by Mr Lo, an international gold smuggler. Jason confers with his associates, Sgt Major White and Major Ruse, who agree that the man responsible for endangering their relationship with Mr Lo and the success of the highly important Golden Fleece Fund must be brought to heel. Jason visits the man, Jones, an ex-corporal who now runs a garage, and asks him to return the money. Jones refuses and that night Mr Lo kills him. Steed has found out that Jason is really Captain Jason and asks Cathy to investigate him. Cathy, however, explains that she cannot as she has been offered a job cataloguing an army museum. At the base she meets an officer named Black. He shows Cathy around the museum and she discovers that Captain Jason is stationed at the base. Cathy phones Steed and tells him. When Jason, White and Ruse discover that Jones has been murdered, they determine that the next assignment from Lo must go through without a hitch. They agree that the Golden Fleece Fund – the proceeds from their smuggling activities with which they are supporting deserving ex-comrades – is the most important thing in their lives. Cathy learns that there is to be a large shipment of ammunition that night and informs Steed. When the ammunition arrives, Steed and Cathy watch as White, Jason and Ruse pack it into specially marked boxes. Steed forces the men to open one of the boxes – the tips of the bullets are made from pure gold. After reassuring the men that the names of the ex-comrades they were helping will never be revealed, Steed and Cathy arrest them.

Steed discovers the secret ammunitions cache hidden by Captain Jason in The Golden Fleece.

DON'T LOOK BEHIND YOU

By Brian Clemens

Catherine Gale	**Honor Blackman**
John Steed	**Patrick Macnee**
Ola	**Janine Gray**
Young man	**Kenneth Colley**
Man	**Maurice Good**

Designed by Terry Green

Directed by Peter Hammond

CATHY IS invited for a weekend at the Devon home of Sir Cavalier Resagne, an authority on medieval costume. Steed drives her there and on the way picks her a bunch of wild flowers. At the house they are welcomed by Ola, a young girl, who says that Sir Cavalier will not be back until later. Steed leaves to spend the weekend on the coast. By dark Sir Cavalier has not returned and Ola insists that Cathy eats without him. After taking a phone call, Ola says she has to visit a friend in the village and Cathy assures her that she does not mind being alone. Later Cathy is disturbed by a noise which she traces to a room at the end of the landing. In the room is an empty rocking horse – still rocking. At this moment the front door bell rings. Cathy answers it to find a young man in dark glasses who says he has run out of petrol – could he use the phone? Reluctantly, Cathy lets him in, but when he picks up the phone the wires have been cut. As he cannot repair the phone, Cathy gives him the keys to the garage so he can find a can of petrol. The young man goes to the garage and a few moments later Cathy hears him drive away. Cathy returns to the room with the rocking horse but the door is locked. She goes to her bedroom and finds Steed's flowers strewn across the floor. She decides to read a book but when she opens it, cut-up pieces of a photograph flutter to the floor. She puts the pieces together – it is a picture of herself. Cathy is startled to hear the phone ringing downstairs and hurries down to answer it – only to find the wires are still cut. As she enters the kitchen she hears a scream from outside. She finds a torch and goes out into the garden to investigate, but finds nothing. In the garage she discovers a Rolls-Royce. She turns on the headlights and tries to start the engine, but without success. Then she sees written on the garage door 'Don't look behind you'. She immediately does so and discovers she is sitting in a hearse. As she jumps out she steps on something – the young man's dark glasses. She has just returned to the house when all the lights go out, and in the dining-room the candles are being snuffed out one by one. She hurries upstairs and hears again the noise of the rocking horse. Rushing to the room – now open – she discovers the young man on the rocking horse, dead. She then hears her name being called, coming first from one part of the house and then another. She runs down to the front door but it is locked. She turns to see the shadow of a man standing in the hall. As she approaches him she realises he is a man she helped Steed arrest years before. Now he has escaped and means to kill her. Cathy backs into the dining-room to find another man there – Steed. He explains he knew the man had escaped and suspected that he might try to avenge himself. Steed, in fact, had never left the house. As the murderer breaks into the dining-room they overpower him.

DEATH A LA CARTE

By John Lucarotti

Catherine Gale	**Honor Blackman**
Emir Abdulla Akaba	**Henry Soskin**
Mellor	**Robert James**
Ali	**Valentino Musetti**
Umberto	**David Nettheim**
Lucien	**Gordon Rollings**
Arbuthnot	**Ken Parry**
John Steed	**Patrick Macnee**
Dr Spender	**Paul Dawkins**
Josie	**Coral Atkins**

Designed by Richard Harrison

Directed by Kim Mills

But will it stop bullets? Steed contemplates some new attire in this scene from Don't Look Behind You.

CATHY IS hired by a London hotel to organise the visit of Emir Abdulla Akaba, who is visiting London for his annual medical check-up. The penthouse and adjacent kitchens are put at his disposal. Steed, suspecting that someone will try to assassinate the Emir, gets a job in the kitchen as a chef. He meets two highly temperamental chefs, Lucien and Umberto, and the head of the kitchen staff, Arbuthnot. Lucien bakes a cake to celebrate the Emir's arrival and as it is presented to him, Pentner, the Emir's adviser, hides a packet under the silver cake cover. After the reception, a young girl, Josie, takes the silver away to be cleaned. That night Lucien breaks into the cleaning room and removes the package, which contains several mushrooms. When he learns that the silver room has been broken into, Steed is worried that his suspicions may be confirmed. Meanwhile the Emir's medical adviser, Dr Spender, confirms that the Emir is ill, but the Emir intends issuing a bulletin saying he is quite well, so as to ease the unrest in his country. Steed tries to make sure that he cooks the Emir's next meal by knocking over Umberto's specially-prepared lasagne. Pentner, however, urges Lucien to ensure that the Emir's next meal is poisoned. That night as the Emir is dining with Dr Spender, he collapses and dies. Steed and Cathy are summoned to the penthouse and when they learn that the Emir is dead, Cathy insists on calling for an ambulance. Pentner refuses, saying that if the news reaches his country there would be a revolt. Dr Spender is asked to wait in one room while Steed and Cathy go into the bedroom. Suspecting that the Emir's death may have been planned, Steed climbs out on to the roof and down to the kitchen. He finds Lucien searching for the mushrooms, now powdered, and overpowers him. Cathy fuses the penthouse lights and when Pentner comes in to investigate she knocks him out and releases Dr Spender. Steed reveals that the mushroom powder was poisoned, although the Emir died of natural causes. Because the poison would not have taken effect for at least ten days, the Emir has died too soon and so Pentner's planned coup is defeated.

DRESSED TO KILL

By Brian Clemens

Newman	Leon Eagles
First officer	Peter Fontaine
John Steed	Patrick Macnee
Catherine Gale	Honor Blackman
Napoleon	Alexander Davion
Pussy Cat	Anneke Wills
Barman	Frank Maher
Highwaywoman	Anthea Wyndham
Policeman	Richard Leech
Sheriff	John Junkin
Robin Hood	Leonard Rossiter

Designed by David Marshall

Directed by Bill Bain

AN EARLY-WARNING station is alerted for World War III, but just in time it is discovered to be a false alarm. Steed explains to Cathy that all the country's early-warning stations were alerted, but as yet, nobody knows how it happened. Steed has found out that land has been bought overlooking the stations, and he himself has bought a plot overlooking the newest early-warning station. Later, Steed arrives at a large railway terminus dressed as a gambler for a New Year's Eve party to be held on a train. He meets two other guests, one dressed as Napoleon and a girl dressed as a cat. More guests arrive, including a monk, who dodges Newman, the conductor, and boards the train unseen. When the train leaves, Steed finds himself in the company of Napoleon, Pussy Cat, a sheriff, Robin Hood, a policeman and a highwaywoman. As they chat, they realise their invitations are false. The coach stops, and they get out, but the train has gone on, leaving their coach stranded at a derelict station. They discover they all have a business meeting in London the next day, taking up their options on plots of land overlooking the new early-warning station. The sheriff, an ex-railwayman, says that this station was closed years ago and he volunteers to go to the nearest village for help. Hearing a scream, they rush outside and find his dead body – an arrow projecting from his back. Robin Hood announces that he has lost his bow and quiver, but denies that he murdered the sheriff. Steed goes to the ticket office and meets the monk – who is Cathy. On the coach the highwaywoman is overcome by the barman and the conductor. Steed searches the coach without success and when he goes back to the station the highwaywoman is there. The policeman says there are six plots of land for sale and seven people who claim ownership. He produces a map of the site and numbers of the plots. They know that the sheriff owned the plot containing the railway station, so if they all write down the number of their plots, someone will give himself away. Steed and the highwaywoman – who is Cathy – have the same plot. The policeman produces a gun and they are handcuffed together and locked in the station-master's office. They soon escape and, in the ticket office, discover Napoleon, Newman

and the barman discussing their plans to take over the early-warning stations. Cathy deals with the barman and Steed calls Napoleon out onto the platform where they have a Western-style shoot-out. Newman appears behind Steed, a shot rings out, and Steed turns to see Cathy, horse pistol smoking.

In Dressed to Kill, *Steed ponders sheriff John Junkin's theory that 'Robin Hood' is guilty of murder.*

THE WHITE ELEPHANT

By John Lucarotti

George	**Martin Friend**
Noah Marshall	**Geoffrey Quigley**
John Steed	**Patrick Macnee**
Catherine Gale	**Honor Blackman**
Brenda Paterson	**Judy Parfitt**
Fitch	**Bruno Barnabe**
Joseph Gourlay	**Toke Townley**
Madge Jordan	**Rowena Gregory**
Lawrence	**Edwin Richfield**
Lew Conniston	**Scott Forbes**

Designed by Philip Harrison

Directed by Laurence Bourne

WHEN SNOWY, a white elephant, is stolen from Noah Marshall's zoo, Cathy joins the staff as a big-game hunter. Noah tells her that Snowy was found by one of his hunters, Conniston, in the Burmese jungle. He brought the elephant home and Noah has kept it as a pet ever since. Cathy discusses Snowy's

Cathy watches apprehensively as zoo keeper Noah Marshall handles one of his pet reptiles in The White Elephant.

disappearance with her keeper, George. He is convinced that the elephant is dead since only one man could have taken her from the zoo alive – Lawrence, who owned the Burmese camp where Snowy was found. But George tells Cathy that Lawrence was killed in the jungle. Brenda, Noah's secretary, seems to be running the organisation almost by herself and even chooses Noah's guns for him. Cathy tells Steed of this and he visits the gun shop and meets Fitch, the owner. While Fitch goes to get a gun to show Steed, Steed notices some fine white powder on the counter and deliberately brushes his sleeve against it. Meanwhile Brenda is inspecting a new supply of cases that have been delivered by Madge, who makes cages for the zoo. The cases contain secret compartments, in which Brenda and Conniston smuggle ivory into the country. The next day, when Cathy is feeding the animals, she goes into the meat cold-room and discovers George hanging from a meat hook. Steed confirms that George was murdered and shows Cathy the sample of dust from the gun shop. When analysed it was found to be ivory dust. Steed tells Cathy ivory smuggling has been on the increase for some time, and is damaging Britain's reputation in Africa. Conniston and Brenda are preparing to ship another consignment of ivory out of the country. As Noah will be on night duty, they decide to drug him. That night Steed breaks into Madge's cage-making factory. He discovers Snowy hidden in a cage and finds Fitch working on the smuggled ivory. A fight breaks out and Steed knocks Fitch unconscious. Cathy meanwhile has returned to the zoo and finds the drugged Noah, but before she can arouse him Lawrence, supposedly dead, arrives. He is, in fact, in league with Conniston and suspects that Conniston and Brenda may be trying to double-cross him. Cathy overcomes Lawrence and ties him up, but Conniston arrives and locks Cathy in a tiger's cage. Steed goes to the zoo and releases Cathy. They set out to find Conniston and Brenda, and find them in the cage-making factory. They try to escape but Cathy and Steed stop them. Once the rest of the gang are under arrest, Steed and Cathy return the elephant to a grateful Noah.

THE LITTLE WONDERS

By Eric Paice

Beardmore	Tony Steedman
Sister Johnson	Lois Maxwell
Bishop of Winnipeg	David Bauer
Catherine Gale	Honor Blackman
John Steed	Patrick Macnee
Gerda	Rosemarie Dunham
Hasek	Frank Maher
Porter	Alex McDonald
Harry	Harry Landis
Big Sid	John Cowley
Fingers	Kenneth Warren

Designed by James Goddard

Directed by Laurence Bourne

MR BEARDMORE, a Harley Street specialist, is visited by the Bishop of Winnipeg and his nurse, Sister Johnson. The Bishop enters the examination cubicle and removes his vestments, beneath which he's wearing two guns. Cathy meets Steed at London Airport, where he shows her a suitcase belonging to the Rev Harbottle who has just been arrested. It contains a gun, ammunition, and a large German doll. The head of the doll is loose and Cathy takes it to a doll's hospital to have it restrung. Steed meanwhile visits Beardmore and learns that the Bishop does not have long to live. Cathy visits the doll's hospital. The next day, Gerda, the owner, rings as promised, to tell Cathy that the doll is ready for collection. But she must pay a restringing fee of £20,000. Cathy refuses to pay, but Gerda insists that she take back the doll. Cathy collects it and goes to Steed's flat. Steed notices that the head is different and they discover it contains microfilm, listing top British secret agents. Steed discovers that the Rev Harbottle was due to attend a convention of the leaders of a criminal organisation called Bibliotek. Next day, the Bishop of Winnipeg receives his guests – the Vicar of Melbourne, the Archdeacon of Singapore, the Dean of Quebec and other gentlemen bearing clerical titles. Steed arrives wearing a dog-collar. He calls himself the Vicar of Salisbury and claims he has taken over from the ailing Harbottle. The Bishop informs the men that they are there to elect a new Bishop, as he is in poor health. That night Sister Johnson appears from behind a secret screen and mows everyone down with a machine gun. Steed is wounded in the leg and visits Beardmore to have the wound dressed. When Steed has left, Sister Johnson appears and asks why Beardmore let him go. He replies that he is not yet sure of Steed's true identity. Sister Johnson visits the doll's hospital and asks Gerda why Cathy did not pay the repair fee. At that moment Steed arrives carrying the doll – whose head has been broken again – and promises to pay the fee once the doll has been repaired. After Steed leaves, Hasek, Gerda's assistant, searches the doll and to his relief finds the microfilm. Steed is at Cathy's flat when he receives a visit from the Dean of Quebec (he mysteriously avoided the machine gunning), who suggests that together they kill the Bishop and take over Bibliotek. Steed promises to think about it. Beardmore meanwhile has discovered that the microfilm is really Steed's laundry list and plans to get rid of Steed, Cathy and the Bishop. That night as Cathy returns to the hospital for the doll, she is captured by the Dean and taken to the school where Beardmore and Sister Johnson are waiting. Just in time, Steed rescues Cathy and arrests the Bishop and his colleagues.

In this scene from The Little Wonders, *Steed, having infiltrated the Bibliotek organisation, masterminded by criminals posing as clerical gentlemen, joins other gang members in a game of chance.*

THE WRINGER

By Martin Woodhouse

Hal Anderson	Peter Sallis
Charles	Paul Whitsun-Jones
Oliver	Barry Letts
John Steed	Patrick Macnee
Catherine Gale	Honor Blackman
Lovell	Gerald Sim
Bethune	Neil Robinson
'The Wringer'	Terence Lodge
Murdo	Douglas Cummings

Designed by Philip Harrison

Directed by Don Leaver

STEED IS told by Head of Operations, Charles, that fellow agent Anderson has not returned from his last mission – investigating a series of mysterious deaths of agents on an escape route between Austria and Hungary. Steed's enquiries lead him to a fire-watching tower in Scotland. There he finds Anderson suffering from shock and unable to remember anything of the last six weeks. Anderson then produces a dossier on Steed and says he remembers now that he can prove that Steed caused the agents' deaths. Anderson takes Steed back to Headquarters, where Charles finds enough evidence to convince him that Steed is a traitor. He turns Steed over to the head of the brainwashing unit, a man nicknamed The Wringer. It soon becomes apparent that The Wringer, with the help of a man called Bethune, captured and brainwashed Anderson and forced him to write up the dossier on Steed. The Wringer wants to sabotage the Service by creating suspicion and mistrust amongst its members. After a long interrogation, The Wringer decides that Steed's mind is ready to be fed false information. Cathy arrives at the unit and when she discovers that Steed is already suffering from the effects of the brainwashing, she overpowers the guard and drags Steed out of the cell through an air vent. She then returns to London and tells Charles that Steed has escaped. Steed returns to the fire-watching tower and tries to make Anderson remember that it was he who compiled the dossier under pressure from The Wringer, but Anderson cannot remember anything. The Wringer and Bethune arrive at the fire-tower and their arrival jolts Anderson's memory. As Charles and Cathy arrive, they are greeted by Steed and Anderson confirms that The Wringer is the traitor.

MANDRAKE

By Roger Marshall

Rev Wyper	George Benson
Roy Hopkins	Philip Locke
Benson	Robert Morris
John Steed	Patrick Macnee
Dr Macrombie	John Le Mesurier
Catherine Gale	Honor Blackman
Sexton	Jackie Pallo
Mrs Turner	Madge Ryan
Judy	Annette Andre

Designed by David Marshall

Directed by Bill Bain

STEED ATTENDS the funeral of an acquaintance, Benson, at a lonely cemetery in Cornwall. He learns from Benson's son that his father died suddenly and was buried in Cornwall at his own request. Visiting Cathy, Steed shows her newspaper cuttings announcing funeral services at the cemetery. The cemetery has not been so busy for years as the villages nearby have become derelict. All the funerals have been for people who lived in London. Meanwhile, young Benson visits the London surgery of Dr Macrombie and together with Roy Hopkins, the doctor's assistant, celebrate the success of their venture. When Benson has left, Macrombie suggests that they should cease their activities and retire. Hopkins, however, says that he has a new client, a Mrs Turner. Cathy photographs some of the more recent headstones in the cemetery. She meets the local vicar, the Rev Wyper, and while they are talking Hopkins arrives with Mrs Turner. Hopkins hopes that Wyper will be able to find a suitable plot for Mrs Turner's husband when he dies. Cathy overhears Hopkins telling the Sexton to keep an eye open for further strangers. Cathy shows Steed her photographs and Steed reveals that out of the eleven names nine were in *Who's Who* and seven of them left estates of over £100,000. He has also discovered that Hopkins owns a cracker factory. It seems, however, that Hopkins has another source of income. Hopkins meanwhile introduces Mrs Turner to Macrombie and together they go over her husband's case history. He is elderly and wealthy and his sudden death would arouse no suspicion. Macrombie agrees to help and gives her a small bottle of arsenic for her husband. Steed discovers that Benson recently visited Dr Macrombie and, at his suggestion, Cathy pays the doctor a visit. She manages to leave a window unlatched so that Steed can break in and study the doctor's files. Cathy returns to the cemetery but is disturbed by the Sexton. They fight and Cathy knocks the Sexton into an open grave. But Rev Wyper appears and holds Cathy at gunpoint. Next morning, Steed visits Benson, who admits his part in the plot. Cathy tells Wyper that she thinks the recent burials have been caused through arsenic poisoning. The soil in the area has a very high arsenic content, so a few weeks after the burials a post-mortem would be unable to prove that arsenic had been the cause of the deaths. Steed arrives in time for the funeral of Mr Turner, and once the service is over, he and Cathy tell Hopkins, Macrombie and Mrs Turner that they have buried a coffin full of sand. Hopkins tries to escape, but the Sexton – having been bribed by Cathy – stops him and the gang are arrested.

Cathy meets Rev Wyper and learns the secret of Mandrake.

THE SECRETS BROKER

By Ludovic Peters

Mrs Wilson	Avice Landon
Julia Wilson	Jennifer Wood
Bruno	Valentine Musetti
Frederick Paignton	John Stone
Catherine Gale	Honor Blackman
John Steed	Patrick Macnee
Marion Howard	Patricia English
Jim Carey	Brian Hankins
Cliff Howard	John Ringham
Allan Paignton	Ronald Allen
Waller	Jack May

Designed by Richard Harrison

Directed by Jonathan Alwyn

WHEN ONE of Steed's associates is murdered, Steed has only two clues – a wine list from Waller and Paignton's wine stores, and a reference to a research establishment called Bridlingtons. Cathy is sent to Bridlingtons while Steed, on the pretext of buying a crate of wine, visits the wine shop. He notices Waller's anxiety when Frederick Paignton knocks over a pile of wine lists, and Steed surreptitiously removes a copy. At Bridlingtons, Cathy meets Marion and Cliff Howard, who are working on a secret underwater tracking device. Cathy learns that Marion has a lover but is unable to discover his name. Meanwhile we learn that the murderer, Frederick Paignton, was blackmailed into committing the crime by Mrs Wilson, a fake medium who holds seances in which she uncovers her client's secrets. That night, Mrs Wilson visits Frederick's brother, Allan – Marion's lover – and tells him that his brother is in trouble and unless he helps her steal the tracking device, she will go to the police. Allan persuades Marion to put the Bridlingtons' alarm system out of action the following Tuesday. If she does not help, Mrs Wilson will tell Marion's husband of their relationship. Reluctantly, Marion agrees to help. That night, Steed and Cathy break into the wine shop and discover an entrance to a photographic studio hidden behind a false wine barrel.

Steed has the wine list examined – the full stops are, in fact, micro-dots containing the stolen plans of new military weapons. He returns to the wine shop the following morning and is invited to a wine-tasting party on Tuesday night. On Tuesday, Marion persuades her husband not to work late, and then goes to the party with Allan. During the party, Steed deliberately leans on the false barrel and to Waller's embarrassment, 'discovers' the photographic studio. Meanwhile Frederick breaks into Bridlingtons but a moment later Cliff returns and sounds the alarm – which still works. In his panic, Frederick shoots Cliff. That night Steed breaks into the wine shop again and discovers Frederick's dead body hidden in a wine barrel. Marion is invited to Mrs Wilson's next seance, where she is forced at gunpoint into the cellar, and meets Waller. Waller tells her that she must bring her husband's plans to him immediately. Allan now tells Steed that Marion is missing and Steed hurries to the seance room. When he arrives, he is held at gunpoint by Julia, Mrs Wilson's daughter, who takes him into the cellar. Waller suggests that Steed be dropped into the Thames in a barrel of cement. At this moment, Allan arrives and Steed overpowers Julia. As Waller turns his gun on Allan and Steed, Cathy appears from out of a wine barrel and knocks Waller out.

THE TROJAN HORSE

By Malcolm Hulke

Johnson	**Derek Newark**
Rt Hon Lucian Ffordsham	**Geoffrey Whitehead**
Kirby	**James Donnelly**
George Meadows	**Arthur Pentelow**
Major Ronald Pantling	**Basil Dignam**
John Steed	**Patrick Macnee**
Ann Meadows	**Lucinda Curtis**
Tony Heuston	**T P McKenna**
Lynton Smith	**John Lowe**
Catherine Gale	**Honor Blackman**
Tote girl	**Marjorie Keys**

Designed by Richard Harrison

Directed by Laurence Bourne

AT A deserted racecourse the Hon Lucian Ffordsham waits with Johnson, a bookie's collector, to interview Kirby, who refuses to pay his debts. Johnson beats up Kirby and Ffordsham drags him away. Kirby fails to get up and Johnson tells Ffordsham he is dead. Frightened, they run away. Kirby gets to his feet, smiles and walks away. Steed visits the stables of George Meadows, a famous racehorse trainer. He tells Meadows that he has been asked by the Foreign Office to keep an eye on a horse, Sebastian the Second, belonging to a wealthy Shah. Steed is introduced to one of Meadows' jockeys, Lynton Smith, who says he will leave the stable after his ride in the Crediton Cup. Steed explains to Cathy his interest in Meadows' stables. Recently there have been a series of apparently unmotivated killings of eminent politicians and businessmen. Watching the Crediton Cup race, Steed and Cathy see Lynton Smith fall. He is carried into the steward's office on a stretcher. Kirby appears, dressed as a doctor, and murders Smith. He then returns to the office of Heuston, owner of a large betting shop syndicate. As Kirby leaves, Cathy arrives and explains to Heuston that she has been swindled by one of his settlers. She gives him the details of an elaborate bet and Heuston agrees that she is right. He is so impressed by Cathy's mathematics that he offers her a job, which she accepts. That night Steed is at the stables and witnesses a secret meeting of the jockeys and stable hands, during which Johnson gives a lecture on the use of poisons and firearms. At the end of the lecture Heuston appears and pays the men off. Steed is seen leaving by one of the hands and when Heuston learns of this, he suggests that Johnson gets rid of Steed. The following morning Ann Meadows discovers that her father is missing – not even Major Pantling, her father's close friend, knows of his whereabouts. Later, Johnson tells Heuston that he was forced to kill Meadows because he threatened to expose Heuston's crimes. Heuston is then confronted by Ann who says she knows her father and Heuston were running a racket together. Heuston confesses to this and tells Ann her father is dead. Ann pulls out a gun, but Cathy appears, disarms Ann, and tells her to call the police. Meanwhile, Steed finds Meadows' body in the back of a horsebox. He is discovered by Johnson who pulls a gun on him and takes him to Heuston. Heuston tells Johnson to carry out his orders and kill Steed. Johnson hesitates, and at that moment Cathy enters the room. Steed is able to disarm Johnson and covers the rest of the gang while Cathy and Major Pantling take Heuston into custody.

Cathy Gale pictured in her Primrose Hill apartment during the story of The Trojan Horse.

BUILD A BETTER MOUSETRAP

By Brian Clemens

Dave	Donald Webster
Catherine Gale	Honor Blackman
Ermintrude	Nora Nicholson
Cynthia	Athene Seyler
John Steed	Patrick Macnee
Harris	Harold Goodwin
Col Wesker	John Tate
Caroline	Alison Seebohm
Stignant	Allan McClelland
Jessy	Marian Diamond
Gordon	David Anderson

Designed by Douglas James

Directed by Peter Hammond

CATHY, HAVING joined a motorcycle gang, calls on two elderly ladies, Ermintrude and Cynthia, who own a watermill and the surrounding meadows, to ask their permission for the gang to use one of the fields for scrambles. Ermintrude refuses and threatens to put a spell on the gang unless she leaves. Meanwhile, Steed, staying at a local inn, learns from the barman, Harris, about the mysterious jammings of all mechanical and electrical devices in the neighbourhood. He meets Stignant, a security officer at the nearby atomic research station, who admits that sometimes all clocks, engines, refrigerators and other apparatus have refused to function. But this has only happened since the arrival of the motorcycle gang. Steed arranges a rally and sends off each of the motorbike riders, including Cathy, across separate parts of the country. All the riders break down, and when she returns, Steed shows Cathy a map of the area and points out where each bike stopped. In the middle of the affected area is the watermill. Steed asks Stignant to find out anything he can about the two sisters. He discovers Ermintrude is the daughter of the late Professor Peck who, at the time of his death, had been working on several interesting experiments. Steed arranges to meet Stignant at the mill that night. Meanwhile at the mill, Ermintrude is working on two experiments. When Steed arrives at the mill, he finds Stignant murdered, in the bushes outside the mill. At the inn, Cathy tells Steed that Dave, leader of the gang, has offered to show her round the mill. Steed says he will follow her later and Cathy leaves. Caroline, the niece of Wesker, a retired army man, insists that Steed has a drink with her. She tries to drug him, but Steed, realising what's happening, pours the drink away. Caroline, believing she has been successful, leaves for the mill. Steed is about to follow her, when Jessy, another member of the motorcycle gang, brings him a letter posted by Stignant before his death. This reveals that Professor Peck had been working on a long-range jamming device, the plans of which he had left with his daughter. Steed hurries out of the inn and bumps into Harris who has just found Dave bound and gagged in the loft of his barn. Steed realises that Cathy has gone off with the wrong man. Meanwhile Cathy has discovered what she believes to be the jamming device but at that moment 'Dave' removes his helmet and goggles to reveal himself as Wesker. Caroline arrives and she and Wesker are about to leave when their exit is blocked by Ermintrude and Cynthia. Wesker escapes and runs out with the jamming device as Dave and Steed appear. In the ensuing fight, the other equipment is destroyed and Cathy is puzzled when Steed explains with a smile that the jamming device Wesker had stolen was really Ermintrude's attempt to build a better mousetrap.

In Build a Better Mousetrap, *Cathy has to stave off the attentions of a gang of motorcycle villains.*

THE OUTSIDE-IN MAN

By Philip Chambers

John Steed	**Patrick Macnee**
Catherine Gale	**Honor Blackman**
Mark Charter	**James Maxwell**
Alice	**Virginia Stride**
Quilpie	**Ronald Radd**
Jenkins	**Ronald Mansell**
Edwards	**Anthony Dawes**
Ambassador	**William Devlin**
Major Zulficar	**Basil Hoskins**
Helen Rayner	**Beryl Baxter**
Michael Lynden	**Arthur Lovegrove**
Sharp	**Philip Anthony**

Designed by David Marshall

Directed by Jonathan Alwyn

In between passing out prime cuts of meat, Quilpie, Steed's superior in The Outside-In Man, *finds time to brief his agents.*

STEED IS put in charge of the security arrangements for the forthcoming visit of Sharp, an Englishman who five years previously started anti-British propaganda and brought about revolution and bloodshed in Abarain. Sharp, termed traitor by the British, was awarded a military title in Abarain, and has now returned to Britain for trade talks, with diplomatic immunity. Steed points out to his superior, Quilpie, the irony of protecting a man they were trying to kill five years earlier. Two agents died in the attempts on Sharp's life – Rayner and Charter. Now, Charter turns up alive. Two days earlier he had been released after five years in prison. Steed is uneasy at the coincidence of the release of a man ordered to kill Sharp, and Charter's visit to England. Steed reads Charter's files and believes that he will still try to kill Sharp. Realising that he will need a car, Steed arranges for Cathy to sell one to Charter. Charter visits Helen Rayner, and obtains a list of their agent friends. He then drives to the garage of one of the agents, Lynden, and makes him respray the car. Cathy calls at the Abarain Embassy but they refuse to cancel Sharp's visit. She next calls on Helen Rayner and discovers that Charter has had the car resprayed. The car is soon traced to a remote cottage in Sussex. Charter meanwhile is caught trying to break into the Abarain Embassy. He is taken to the Ambassador, who tells him that should he be reluctant to kill Sharp, they will help. Sharp arrives in England. At a reception given in his honour, Steed tells Sharp that he has persuaded Charter to pretend to seek revenge on Sharp, in order to confirm his suspicion that Sharp had outlived his usefulness to Abarain and they wanted him dead. Charter had been released in the hope that he would do the job for them – and in so doing, put the British government at a disadvantage. Convinced that Steed's suspicions are correct, Sharp tells Steed that once the trade talks are over, he'll return to Abarain.

Cathy shows off her famous garter-gun to colleague John Steed in The Outside-In Man.

THE CHARMERS

By Brian Clemens

John Steed	Patrick Macnee
Catherine Gale	Honor Blackman
Martin	John Barcroft
Keller	Warren Mitchell
Kim Lawrence	Fenella Fielding
Betty Smythe	Vivian Pickles
Sam	John Greenwood
Harrap	Frank Mills
Horace Cleeves	Malcolm Russell
Mr Edgar	Brian Oulton

Designed by Philip Harrison

Directed by Bill Bain

In The Charmers, *Cathy outfences a gang of saboteurs.*

STEED AND CATHY discuss the mysterious death of Vinkel – a member of the opposition. Steed thinks they are purging the organisation, but then a man, Martin, tries to kill Steed in revenge for Vinkel's death. Steed protests his innocence and Martin is finally persuaded to take Steed to his superior, Keller. Keller and Steed discover that various acts of sabotage, which each attributed to the other's side, have, in fact, been initiated by a third party. Steed suggests they work together to expose the other group but Keller insists that as an act of good faith they should each supply a hostage. Steed agrees to give Keller Cathy, and in return is presented with an attractive woman called Kim Lawrence. Martin and Cathy retrace Vinkel's movements and end up at a dentist's. Cathy goes in to make enquiries and when she returns, Martin has disappeared. Meanwhile Steed and Kim call at an exclusive tie shop, but the owner insists he has never heard of Vinkel. That night, they return to the shop and find Martin dead, in a crateful of bowler hats. Next day, Steed follows the crate, which is carried away by four elegantly-dressed young men. They go to a charm school, where Steed meets Mr Edgar, who tells him that he is training the men to become gentlemen. Steed notices the crate in Edgar's office, but now it only contains bowler hats. Meeting Kim outside, she suggests that maybe they followed the wrong crate, as she saw another one addressed to a dentist's. At the dentist's, he meets Cathy. Cathy tells him that Kim is not a member of Keller's staff but merely an actress hired to play the part. Rushing into the dentist's surgery, where Kim is supposed to be having treatment, Steed finds her gone and the dentist dead. Kim has been bound and gagged and hidden in a crate. As the young men arrive to remove the crate, Steed knocks one of them out and takes his place. Arriving at the charm school, they are greeted by Edgar and Steed discovers that the young men are really being taught how to kill, and all their umbrellas are swordsticks. Steed releases Kim but is interrupted by the arrival of Keller, who unmasks Steed and admits that he runs the third party. Cathy arrives and has a fencing match with one of the young men, and Steed knocks out Edgar. Keller is about to shoot Steed when Kim throws a fencing foil at him, killing him. Her mother, she tells Steed, used to be in a knife-throwing act.

CONCERTO

By Terence Dicks and Malcolm Hulke

Peterson	Bernard Brown
Catherine Gale	Honor Blackman
Polly White	Valerie Bell
Burns	Geoffrey Colville
John Steed	Patrick Macnee
Zalenko	Nigel Stock
Stefan Veliko	Sandor Eles
Darleen	Dorinda Stevens
Receptionist	Carole Ward
Robbins	Leslie Glazer

Designed by Douglas James

Directed by Kim Mills

IMPORTANT TRADE talks are taking place in London between representatives of the Russian senate and their British counterparts. To reinforce goodwill during the talks, a brilliant young pianist, Stefan Veliko from behind the Iron Curtain, is giving his first concert in London. When it is discovered that someone is trying to break up the talks, Steed puts Cathy in charge of security. She acts as a representative of the British Cultural Council and calls on Veliko with Steed. They discover that an attractive young girl, Polly, has accused Veliko of assaulting her and the girl has since been killed. Steed believes that her murder is part of an attempt to blacken Veliko's name and thus create an international incident which would affect the trade talks. Steed and Veliko's manager Zalenko decide to keep the incident from the press. Steed discovers that Polly worked at a strip club, and visits a friend of hers there called Darleen. Darleen says she knows nothing of Polly's last job, but afterwards rings Steed and says she has some information for him. When Steed goes to her flat, he is knocked unconscious by Burns – Polly's murderer – who then forces Darleen to phone Stefan and invite him to the club. Steed discovers from Cathy what has happened and hurries to the club with Zalenko. They arrive in time to save Stefan from being compromised, with Darleen, in some photographs. Steed and Zalenko check the recital room in which Veliko is to give his concert before a distinguished audience – including the Minister responsible for the trade negotiations. Meanwhile at the club, Darleen overhears Burns and Peterson, his assistant, discussing how they plan to murder someone at the recital. She tells Cathy she will provide the name of the person to be murdered for £500. Cathy goes to the club with the money but finds Darleen dead. Before she can escape, she is threatened by Burns. At gunpoint he says he will kill her if she doesn't reveal what she knows. Cathy is rescued by Steed's arrival at the club. He overcomes Burns and they leave for the recital. During the interval, Peterson tells Stefan that he must pretend to shoot the Minister – otherwise he will be involved in another incident, thus ruining his reputation. As Steed and Cathy watch the Minister closely, wondering who will try to kill him, Cathy notices Stefan has a gun and, realising that Peterson is responsible, attacks and overcomes him before anyone is harmed.

ESPRIT DE CORPS

By Eric Paice

Capt Trench	John Thaw
Sgt Marsh	Douglas Robinson
Pte Jessop	Roy Kinnear
Brig Gen Sir Ian Stewart-Bollinger	Duncan Macrae
John Steed	Patrick Macnee
Mrs Craig	Pearl Catlin
Catherine Gale	Honor Blackman
Lady Dorothy Bollinger	Joyce Heron
Pte Asquith	Anthony Blackshaw
Admiral	Hugh Morton
Signaller	James Falkland

Designed by David Marshall

Directed by Don Leaver

AT MARROON Barracks, Captain Trench, of the Highland Guards, commands the execution by firing squad of Corporal Craig. After the execution, Steed meets Private Jessop, a member of the firing squad, who tells him that the regimental post-mortem on Craig will show that he died as a result of an accident while cleaning his rifle. Steed tells Cathy that he knows Craig was killed by bullets from three different rifles, and asks her to check the military establishment. She visits the local civil defence centre to meet Captain Trench and is invited by him to attend a regimental cocktail party that evening. Cathy arrives at the party with Steed, and while she heads for the Mess, Steed breaks into the Barrack Room and discovers huge amounts of ammunition. As he leaves, Jessop arrives and holds him at riflepoint. Steed offers the man a bribe to release him and Jessop accepts. Next day, on the pretext of writing the history of the regiment, Steed meets Lady Bollinger. She says that since her husband's retirement, he has devoted himself to Scottish history and has discovered that his stepson is the rightful heir to the throne of Scotland. The son, however, is a bookmaker in Halifax and is uninterested in making a claim. The final plans for an army exercise are taking place in Trench's office. Also present are an Admiral, a Marine Colonel and an Air Vice-Marshal. They all pledge their support for Operation Claymore, an exercise in capturing London. Listening outside, Steed waits for the men to leave, then climbs into the office and tries to read the secret papers relating to the exercise, but he is caught and arrested by Trench. Cathy is visited by Brig. General Bollinger who tells her that he has traced her family history and discovered that Cathy – after the Colonel's stepson who has disclaimed the title – is in direct line to the throne of Scotland. He tells Cathy to be ready to take up accession. Steed meanwhile has been charged with treason by a court martial and Trench orders his execution. Lady Bollinger visits Cathy and explains that she believes her husband is planning a military coup and for his own sake must be stopped. Steed now faces the firing squad led by Captain Trench. They fire and Steed falls to the ground. The firing squad – with the exception of Jessop, who is left to dispose of the body – is marched away. As they leave, Jessop, having decided to accept a further bribe from Steed, tells

Steed to get up. That night, at the Mess dance, Bollinger appears and denounces the military coup which he says Trench planned. Trench is placed under arrest but Cathy and Steed know that Bollinger means to continue the coup. They capture him as he leaves the Officer's Mess. Bollinger protests his innocence and tries to bribe them, telling Cathy that she could have been the Queen of England. Cathy smiles and replies that she made Steed fake her family tree.

Steed prepares to face a firing squad in Esprit de Corps.

LOBSTER QUADRILLE

By Richard Lucas

Bush	Gary Watson
Quentin Slim	Corin Redgrave
John Steed	Patrick Macnee
Catherine Gale	Honor Blackman
Dr Stannage	Norman Scace
Mason	Burt Kwouk
Capt Slim	Leslie Sands
Katie Miles	Jennie Linden

Designed by Patrick Downing

Directed by Kim Mills

THE AVENGERS visit a hospital mortuary where Steed identifies the body of an agent, Williams, discovered in the ashes of a burnt-out fishing hut. Among the dead man's belongings is an unusual chess piece. They visit the scene of the crime and as Steed pokes about in the ashes, he is discovered by Bush, who says he is trespassing. The hut belongs to his partner, Captain Slim. Steed visits Captain Slim, but is unable to discover how the fire started. He also meets Slim's daughter-in-law, Kate, who tells him that Slim's son, Quentin, has recently drowned when his boat capsized in a sudden storm. Cathy takes the chess piece to Mason, the owner of a chess shop, who says the chess piece is one of a set bought by a man named Williams. When Steed returns to his flat, he finds Cathy trying to solve a list of chess moves that she has found in some letters addressed to Williams – she realises that they don't make sense. Meanwhile Bush phones Mason and tells him of Steed's visit. When Mason tells him about Cathy's visit to the shop, Bush asks Mason to find out her identity. Later that evening, Steed receives a phone call confirming his suspicions about Quentin Slim. Before his death he was under suspicion of smuggling. Steed leaves Cathy working on the chess moves and promises to return soon. Cathy continues her work, convinced that the moves form a code. She breaks the code but is interrupted by a knock at the front door. She answers it and finds herself confronted by Mason with a gun. When Steed returns to the flat Cathy has gone. He notices the original unusual chess piece standing alone on the board and, under a cushion, he finds Cathy's notes. He heads for the chess shop and breaks in. During his search he finds a small quantity of dope hidden in a drawer. As he leaves, Kate arrives and tells him that her husband is not dead but had moved to France. Together they visit Captain Slim and try to convince him that his son is still alive. Slim refuses to believe that Quentin wasn't drowned or that his son was guilty of smuggling dope. Just then Quentin and Bush arrive and, although Steed disarms Bush, Quentin escapes. He goes to the fishing huts and orders Mason to prepare a boat for their escape. He ties Cathy to a rowing boat, and as they leave sets fire to the hut. The following morning, two charred bodies are found among the ashes of the burnt-out fishing hut. Steed is concerned about Cathy's disappearance – until she finally arrives to say that she spent the night at the local police station.

Honor Blackman takes a break during Lobster Quadrille.

THE IMMACULATE EMMA PEEL

Patrick Macnee/Diana Rigg   1965–66

IN DECEMBER 1963, Louis de Rochemont, an American film producer working in association with John Halas, of the Halas and Batchelor Cartoon Films Ltd., approached ABC. He had an idea for putting *The Avengers* onto the cinema screen. Were the company interested? Needless to say they were – provided the proposed film's format retained the spirit of the series and, most important of all, Honor Blackman and Patrick Macnee agreed to take part. Both stated their willingness to do so and within days the company received a summary of the film's format.

Running at between 2/2½ hours, the film would be shot in colour using the newly developed Dimension–150 process; a 70mm, wide-angle, one-lens system which the owners believed to be superior in every way to the new Cinerama process. The screenplay would be based upon a story outline devised by Howard Thomas, and the writer (or writers) would be drawn from the current *Avengers'* production team who in turn would be assisted by John Bryce. Patrick and Honor would star opposite their American counterparts, who would be star names. In the event that the D–150 version was aborted, de Rochemont had expressed his interest in co-producing a 35mm version with Magna Incorporated, a subsidiary company of the United Artistes Theatre Corporation.

Here is an edited version of the film's story outline, as prepared by Howard Thomas.

THE AVENGERS

The location is established: Beirut – the gateway of the East.

> In the School of Asiatic Languages, a classroom of a dozen young Englishmen and Americans are listening intently to their Lebanese teacher. These are the cream of the Foreign Office and the State Department; tomorrow's diplomats and other men who work in less respectable Government departments – the espionage branch.
>
> Enter two masked men in flowing robes, gripping the most modern of automatic weapons. Calmly, methodically, they fire. We see the students slumping defencelessly over their desks.
>
> The chatter of the guns dissolves into the stutter of newspaper tape machines as the story is tapped out:-
>
> 'Young Diplomats Slaughtered
> in Classroom Massacre.'

In Washington, grave-faced men assemble to count their losses and to decide on action. In London, the head of the Secret Service is telephoning Steed, his key man.

Steed is seen in his splendid Belgravia flat. At his side is Mrs Catherine Gale, the tough, judo-trained beauty who has worked with him on so many assignments.

'They've wiped out some of our best men, Steed. Take Mrs Gale with you and you'll be joined by two people from Washington. Your job is to establish our organisation in the Middle East.'

'And there's another job, too,' says Steed grimly, as he replaces the receiver. 'We must avenge our colleagues.'

In Washington, Drew Vernon is packing his gun and answering his telephone at the same time.

'You're teaming me up with a woman!'

The four people set out for Beirut to create new espionage links – and to avenge their friends ... four worldly, elegant Londoners and New Yorkers, two sophisticated men and two women trained to kill, face up to unknown hazards in one of the world's most spectacular and sinister settings.

Meanwhile, an equally intriguing project landed on the desk of Howard Thomas. Having read about *The Avengers* in a *Sunday Times* Colour Magazine, Cheryl Crawford, a well-known American producer of plays, approached ABC about the possibility of producing a *musical* based upon the series! Though unfamiliar with the show's format (the Blackman series was never transmitted in the USA), after viewing several of the stories and reading numerous scripts, she believed that the show could be successfully transferred to the stage. Her idea was to open on Broadway, then bring the cast to London's West End. Recognising that the idea had possibilities, ABC gave their blessing to the project – but stuck firmly to their guns that, musical or not, the production would have to retain the fast-moving, fairytale, *Avengers* format, told against a tough, sometimes bizarre, contemporary setting.

It was then that Honor Blackman dropped her bombshell. She would not be continuing the Cathy Gale role after the end of the current series (due for completion in March 1964). If the producers had become hysterical at this point no one would have blamed them. Not only did they now have to find a new female lead for Steed, they also had to invent a new

character, because Honor Blackman had made the role of Cathy Gale so much her own, it would be almost impossible for another actress to take over. Though several attempts were made to get the actress to change her mind, five weeks later she informed the company that her decision was final – Cathy Gale would disappear from *The Avengers* in the final story of the current season.

Within hours of the announcement that Honor was quitting the show, the British newspapers carried the following headlines. 'CATHY HANGS UP HER BOOTS FOR GOOD!', 'CATHY IS QUITTING THE AVENGERS', 'EXIT CATHY OF THE AVENGERS'.

Ex-champion boxer Freddie Mills takes a tip on self-defence from Avenger girl Diana Rigg.

All editions carried a similar story, 'Cathy Gale, leather-clad heroine of ITV's *The Avengers*, is to leave the programme to step into a five-year film contract. Honor said last night: 'I've got a lot to thank television for, and my biggest debt is Cathy.' Celebrating at her home, she added, 'I'm sorry about having to quit the Cathy Gale role. But I felt it was better to do this than wait until she gets out of fashion. My part in the series was a little different from that of John Steed, the eternal Englishman who can go on forever. Cathy Gale was a child of her times and I feel if I go on too long I will outstay my welcome.' She told me, 'By this time the show had become such a wild success that they didn't imagine that I would actually leave at that point, while the series was such a runaway success. So when we finally achieved what had been our ambition – or certainly Patrick's – to go onto film, I'd already arranged to play Pussy Galore in *Goldfinger*. In any case, as far as I was concerned, I was getting out because two years is enough. You can't sustain *that* kind of show for longer than two years. They were very upset that I didn't stay, because by then the two of us were such national characters that they couldn't imagine replacing me. But that was my decision, so when it came to the final

episode and they knew that I *was* going, Patrick put in a reference to my "pussy-footing around" on some glorious beach in Miami. It was Patrick's "in" joke, because I was going off to play Pussy Galore. It was terribly moving, the last episode, the farewell party and everything.' (In point of fact, none of the cast, not even Patrick Macnee, was made aware of Cathy's final fate. To stave off press disclosures, the script to *Lobster Quadrille* was deliberately left unfinished – with Cathy locked in a burning boathouse, and no escape in sight. A sheet of flame engulfed the screen – and Steed was requested to identify a body in a mortuary. It wasn't Cathy's, and the story ended with a short *unscripted* scene in which the two crimebusters said goodbye – Cathy was off to the Bahamas, for a no-return holiday.) When I interviewed him recently, Patrick Macnee told me, 'The Honor Blackman shows created Cathy Gale and were, as a consequence, new and exciting. Cathy was the springboard that made *The Avengers* what it was.'

Patrick Macnee wonders if he shares anything in common with this gentleman.

With no female lead to offer either de Rochemont or Crawford, ABC were forced to take stock of their position. Some weeks earlier, the American television network had indicated their interest in buying a *filmed* series of *The Avengers* – but not until the autumn of 1965. With obvious reluctance to abandon their successful award-winning product, the company decided to take the show off the air to give them time to mount a 'new improved' 26-episode series, to be made on film. Plans to co-produce the new series in partnership with the Associated Rediffusion TV Company came to nothing, and the role of mounting the new show was handed over to Telemen Limited, a company owned jointly by ABC and well-known British film producer Julian Wintle. He assembled a team of experienced telefilm professionals headed by Albert Fennell and Brian Clemens, who was appointed Associated Producer and Story Editor for the new series, and commissioned 26 scripts from the best British writers in this field.

Auditions were held to find a partner for Patrick Macnee and well over 60 actresses were tested for the as yet unnamed part. (Actually Steed's partner *had* been named. In the first three scripts, the character was known as Samantha, shortened to Mantha in rewrites, but no one, including Brian Clemens, who had originated the name, found the name appealing.) It was then that Marie Donaldson, the production's press officer, had a brainwave. She realised that the new character had to have man appeal, and as she played around with the phrase in her head she couldn't help thinking Man Appeal, M appeal – Emma Peel. She liked the sound of the name and the producers leapt at it.

Emma Peel quickly became the internationally educated daughter of a wealthy shipowner and youthful widow of Peter Peel, a famous test pilot. A woman of independent means, she was the complete one-jump-ahead jet-set female, a cool, luscious British counterspy with wicked brown eyes and auburn hair who would effortlessly karate chop and knee her opponent into submission; an English rose with the ability to toss a man over her shoulder as if he were a sack of feathers – the perfect partner for Steed in the espionage and counter-espionage game. (The fact that these two activities are covered by separate departments, MI6 and MI5 respectively, didn't deter the producers. They cheerfully explained that Steed was an employee of 'MI5 and a half'.) Outwardly Emma was cast in the same image as Cathy Gale. She lived in a streamlined London penthouse, wore avant-garde clothes, drove a high-speed Lotus Elan and fought free and furious by every known technique from judo and karate to her own brand of balletic 'feinting' and a straight left to the jaw. But the relationship between Emma and Steed became much warmer and gayer than the one which Steed had with Cathy – in spite of the fact that, as a ruthless professional agent, Steed continued to use every trick in the book both in dealing with his adversaries and in commandeering help from his amateur assistant. Emma was permanently aware that Steed's charm was a cloak for yet another attempt to involve her in some dangerous mission; but she reluctantly accepted his insistance that her innocence of what was going on was her best protection, so she fell in with his plans good-naturedly enough – but lost no opportunity to get even with him for the indignities inflicted on her person.

It was vital, however, to find the right Emma, and after months of searching it began to look as if she didn't exist. It was then that they found a beautiful actress called Elizabeth Shepherd, daughter of a Welsh Nonconformist minister, who had been dubbed one of the most beautiful of the current British actresses, and she was signed for the role. However, Miss Shepherd failed to impress the producers, or ruffle the characteristic well-bred charm of Patrick Macnee. After viewing rushes of the first episode, *Town of No Return*, they decided that, although an accomplished actress, she didn't give the character the light comedy touch they were looking for. Having spent over £120,000, they stopped the production half-way through *The Murder Market*, and Elizabeth Shepherd was dropped. (A studio memo, written by the series press officer Marie Donaldson, gave an insight into the character the actress *may* have produced. Her £600 wardrobe consisted of clothes created by New York designer Bonnie Cashin. The most startling outfit was a red-leather fighting suit that had a large cowled neck, which could be pulled up into a hood. Worn with poppy red thigh-length boots and a single *black* leather glove with which she could administer her karate blows, Emma Peel, Shepherd-style, was to be a top-flight swordswoman, an expert with firearms and a dab hand with a longbow.) With an impressive range of Shakespearean roles behind her, it is difficult to understand why Miss Shepherd failed to demonstrate her pedigree to the producers. However, a further 20 or so actresses were tested before Dodo Watts, the programme's casting director, asked the producers to look at an actress she'd just used in an *Armchair Theatre* production, 'The Hothouse'.

After viewing a tape of the play, Brian Clemens and Albert Fennell sensed that this could be the girl they'd been searching for and they invited her to take a screen test with Patrick Macnee. Diana Rigg, who believed she wasn't really suitable for the role and remarked later, 'I only did it for a giggle', was required to place a plaster on Patrick Macnee's wrist, and fire a gun at a retreating villain. The results were first class. Macnee and the young actress seemed to find an immediate rapport. She was signed to a long-term contract, and 18 months after the last series had ended, *The Avengers* were on their way back. The rest of course, is history. Patrick Macnee told me, 'The lady before Diana Rigg, Elizabeth Shepherd, was a very beautiful woman and a wonderful actress – but totally miscast. She was far too serene and lovely for anything like *The Avengers*, in which you had to be a bit quick and cocky, the way Diana Rigg was. The woman needs to be a hermaphrodite, a woman, but one who runs like a man. When Diana came into the show she was only 28, but she had this total, complete technical comedic style and sparkle, surety and assurance. In fact she was so good that it sharpened, in a sense, my own comedy style which was there, but dormant. My style changed considerably. We were also doing it on film for the first time, which necessitated a different form of approach. The scenes that we played together, with the full approval of Brian Clemens, were largely rewritten by Diana and myself. She had a very sharp and lively imagination and understanding of what a woman, a woman like her, would say in any given situation – however outrageous or mad. We, and I say *we* advisedly, took perfectly straight situations and made them slightly ludicrous. You had to be slightly mad, but you also had to be basically cool. We tilted everything, made it humorous – and it worked.'

As Steed, Patrick Macnee preferred a vintage mode of transport. In real life he drove around town in his own Jaguar.

If Emma represented the future of Britain, Steed, as before, stood for the best of the past. He still embodied tradition and all that people associated with the British way of life – gracious living; a London home full of family heirlooms and handsome antiques; a cultivated appreciation of food, wine, horseflesh and pretty women; proficiency at gentlemanly sports such as fencing, archery and polo; exquisite tailoring; a high-handed way with underlings and an endearing eccentricity which manifested itself in such preferences as driving a vintage Bentley convertible and fighting with a swordstick, rolled umbrella or any other handy implement, rather than the more obvious weapons.

In the best British stiff-upper-lip tradition, however, this rarified exterior camouflaged a highly efficient operator, who quietly got his man while his opponents were still being distracted by his amusing ways – just as Emma's wit and femininity concealed a cool resourceful woman who was at her best in a crisis.

Consequently there was never a shortage of wisecracks between Steed and Emma; the twosome deliberately echoed the classic partnership of William Powell and Myrna Loy in the famous *Thin Man* films. Their adventures, however, recalled the exploits of early film favourites like Douglas Fairbanks and Pearl White; Steed having spectacular fights on moving trains, and Emma being constantly rescued from appalling hazards, of which being trussed up in a harness, tied to a railway track and clamped into a metal wine press were just a sample. The series embodied the best of the old with many fresh and more spectacular elements (not least of which were the resources of a big motion picture organisation that were not possible in the earlier videotaped series). It was of course, the first programme to exploit this formula on television, and it added an element of its own – labelled by the Press as 'Kinkiness' - which gave a twist to clothes, humour and action that highlighted the flashpoint between comedy, sex-appeal and violence.

Emma's mode of fighting was different, too. Cathy had been the judo expert. Emma's fighting technique was karate-influenced. Villains were attacked with the edge of the hand (palm and fingers held rigidly flat), the elbow, fingers and thumbs, and the foot, which, in action, became part of a graceful, but deadly, balletic movement. A jolting, stiff-legged kick was delivered as high as an adversary's jaw, to great effect. The fight sequences became more ambitious – choreographed mayhem – meticulously planned and arranged by one of Britain's top stuntmen, Ray Austin. The news that Emma would be using her 'bizarre' combat methods to throw a man down a flight of stairs or hurl him through a plate-glass window, led the company's publicity manager to comment, 'I think we must be extremely careful, when arranging fights for this series, to avoid highlighting some of the individual blows. It would be damaging to say the least if, for instance, a teenager were to injure another, having picked up his tuition from one of our episodes. With karate this could happen.' As things turned out, the rough and tumble scenes were mapped out in minute detail long before the series reached the screen. Interviewed at the time, Ray Austin said, 'When Steed meets trouble – and that happens at least once in every story, he does so unarmed. This allows us to show the ruthless streak in his character and stop at nothing in his methods. He uses every trick in the book – and quite a few unwritten ones. His fights are staged extravagantly and always with a sense of humour. His partner, Emma Peel, is a much more conventional fighter. She uses guns, swords, karate, the lot. The vital difference, of course, being that all these arts are employed not by a tough guy but a delectable and intelligent woman.' Unlike her predecessor, Honor Blackman, Diana Rigg wasn't given lessons in self-defence. 'I had a crash course,' she said, 'and a group of wonderful stuntmen did it for me. I'd give them a push with my index finger, and they'd exercise a double-somersault and fall to the floor.'

Emma Peel grapples with a knotty problem involving action man Ray Austin.

Diana Rigg in John Bates's black leather trouser suit.

As the previous Blackman series had made a breakthrough in setting fashion trends, ABC were determined that the new series would once again lead the way, and called in top fashion designer John Bates to produce a new and daring wardrobe for Emma; the first collection of clothes designed specifically for a television programme to be adapted in its entirety for retail distribution.

The project was inspired by the demand which arose from viewers for the type of clothes worn by Honor Blackman in the earlier series. Some of her clothes were made available for sale, but only on a small scale. For the new series, the Jean Varon fashion house sought the cooperation of several well-known firms to make all the clothes designed by John Bates available in stores throughout Britain and overseas.

The Avengers Collection comprised some three dozen items, with all the relevant accessories. The principles on which John Bates designed Diana Rigg's wardrobe were necessarily different from those which guided any ordinary fashion collection. As the new series was being made on film for world distribution, it could expect a screen life of five years or more, so Emma Peel's clothes had to be as modern as her character and yet timeless enough to remain acceptable for a long time afterwards. Also they had to photograph clearly and simply on the small screen; which meant using uncluttered lines and materials that would not 'strobe' in front of the cameras, and that would stand up to the strenuous adventures in which the character became involved. Basically, the collection took as its theme the black and white of the television medium – the 'lines' from which the TV screen is made up. These lines were seen repeatedly in the use of braid on coats and dresses. The other recurring motif was a target, symbolising the op-art designs of the Space Age (as seen in Emma's Avenger beret and the dial of her Avengers watch). Since Emma was to be a younger, more carefree and more feminine character than her predecessor, John Bates's designs included a number of day and evening dresses which were by turns both demure and daring, in womanly materials such as lace, silk, lamé and crepe. Emma's fighting suits largely discarded the old leather image for a different kind of sex appeal based on form-fitting stretch jersey, or (where leather was used) on an 'animal look' conveyed through snakeskin, or a 'soft-centre' look achieved by wearing leather over a crepe blouse. Emma also had some black and white furs by Selincourt, cunningly worked in simple rabbit, which not only looked expensive enough for a lady of means but were so cuddly as to make it hard for any but the most cold-blooded male to keep his hands off her. The new designs were launched in August 1965 at the Courtaulds Fashion Theatre, in London, and ABC commissioned tie-ups with 14 British fashion manufacturers. Soon major stores and boutiques in Britain and overseas were selling what became known as the Jean Varon/Avengers pack.

Femininity and grace, and always on target. Diana Rigg wearing an outfit called 'Flash'.

Steed's address for the series remained the same, but this time we were treated to more interior views. He now had a tape machine that automatically recorded all telephone conversations (in and out). The apartment was on two levels, and the bathroom was reached by climbing three steps which led from the sitting room. Added to his antique collection were a barrel clock, an 18th-century desk, a fox umbrella stand and a cast-iron Victorian juicer. A wrought iron staircase led from the kitchen to his underground garage.

Emma lived in a roof-top penthouse in Hampstead. The flat was basically one large room, which could be converted to a bedroom or whatever she desired by sliding any one of the numerous dividers that skirted all sides of the main living area. Emma's collection of abstract paintings and objets d'art adorned the walls. A nice touch was the introduction of a large automated eye set into her front door which, when the doorbell was pressed, flicked open to allow Emma to see her visitors. (Prior to filming, press officer Marie Donaldson had suggested that the jet-setting Emma should have a push-button wardrobe of super separates stored behind electronically controlled panels in her bedroom which, card-indexed by a computer, would, when she wanted to go, say, to Morocco, shoot out the appropriate garments for that climate at the press of a button. She added that this would give good opportunities for comedic effect if Steed got at the computer and reset it, so that the warm-climate button produced a wardrobe for Alaska!)

Brian Clemens introduced certain ground rules. Interviewed recently, he told me, 'The series had to have unity, and thus enable us to do *anything* – any kind of story at all, *our* way. I laid down the ground rule that no woman should be killed, no extras should populate the streets. We admitted to only one class .. and that was the upper.'

Albert Fennell (who, with Brian Clemens was to become the guiding light throughout the next five years of *The Avengers'* screen life) was responsible for adding that extra touch of gloss to the finished series. An experienced film technician, he put the stamp of technical expertise on the series and (though he stayed somewhat in the background as far as the media was concerned) he deserves as much credit as anyone for shaping the series.

Clemens quickly realised that the only way to break into the American market (and thus ensure a profit) was to create something with which the Americans themselves could not compete. So the formula was to set the stories against a tongue-in-cheek panorama of the picture-postcard Britain illustrated in tourist brochures. Every aspect of British life was incorporated as it was promoted overseas; from atom-stations, bio-chemical plants and modern industry on the one hand to fox-hunting, stately homes and the Olde Englishe Inne on the other. It was all gently sent up as a good-humoured counterpoint to the dangerous adventures of the two secret agents who hid their iron fists beneath the velvet gloves of high-living and sophisticated luxury.

'We became terribly British,' said Clemens. 'A car is a car is a car, and not an automobile. A lift is a lift is a lift, never an elevator. It is this Britishness that fits the fantasy world so appealing to the Americans.'

Aware that the new direction the show was to take required a more distinctive musical theme to complement the way-out situations they planned to introduce, the producers contacted top composer Bob Sharples to undertake the composing and arranging of a new

The late Albert Fennell was responsible for adding that extra touch of gloss to the series.

Brian Clemens took the credit for carrying the filmed series to great heights.

signature tune and background music for the show. Sharples had other commitments and talented composer Laurie Johnson was brought in to provide the music tracks. The new theme was composed after long discussions between Brian Clemens, Albert Fennell, Julian Wintle and Laurie Johnson, during which the style of the show was established.

Mid-way through the production, ABC received correspondence from a representative of the Australian Broadcasting Commission, indicating that the company would be interested in contributing ex-amount of Australian dollars to the production cost of the new series – provided ABC would agree to three of the 26 episodes being shot on location in that country. This never happened. The economic facts of doing so, let alone the cost of flying the stars, the cast and the film unit to Sydney, were prohibitive and the offer was politely refused.

Whereas most of the Honor Blackman stories had been designed as a one-hour thriller series with a tongue-in-cheek slant to offset the off-beat adventures of Steed's chipper secret service agent and Cathy's sylph-like Amazon, the new *Avengers* series became more science-fiction orientated. Plots concerning the efforts of power-mad scientists hell-bent on ruling the world, using such outrageous devices as a giant man-eating plant; torrential rainstorms; agents being brainwashed in a Manchurian concentration camp – situated in the heart of London's West End(!) – and even a pair of steel robots.

The latter, *The Cybernauts*, were selected as the villains to introduce Steed and his colleague, via the American Broadcasting Company (ABC), to American viewers. UK viewers were, of course, well acquainted with the exploits of Steed and his female partners, but the Blackman series, though screened in Canada and Australia, had never been shown in the USA. The problem then, was one of familiarising the American viewers with the characters.

This was solved when Albert Fennell and Brian Clemens decided to film a special 'introductory' teaser sequence which was tagged onto the beginning of the American prints. The sequence began with a man wearing a waiter's jacket, walking into view across a giant chessboard. Suddenly, he falls to the ground and we notice that he has a dagger implanted into a 'target' motif on his back. Enter Emma left and Steed right. They cross to the dead figure and Steed kneels to pick up a bottle of champagne from the dead man's hand. He smiles coyly at his partner as she deftly replaces a small, gold-plated pistol into the top of her black leather boot. Emma returns the smile as, in close-up, Steed fills two glasses.

Proposing a silent toast, they drink the bubbly and, carrying the champagne bottle, walk off into the background – cue *The Avengers* main title.

Throughout this sequence, the music builds to a crescendo of tenor drum rolls, while a voice-over narration tells us that:

Extraordinary crimes against the people and the State have to be avenged by agents extraordinary. Two such people are John Steed, top professional, and his partner, Emma Peel, talented amateur – otherwise known as The Avengers.

The shooting schedule was long and arduous. (Diana Rigg and Patrick Macnee were required to learn over 60 pages of dialogue per week, and work a 14-hour day.) Each episode cost £30,000 to produce and had a 10-day shooting schedule (although most ran over and took an average of 14 days to complete). Because the stories were being filmed for the first time, greater use was made of outdoor locations, with the majority of episodes being filmed in and around the country lanes of Radlett and Shenley, in Hertfordshire, a short drive from EMI's Elstree Studios (known at the time as Associated British) where the principal shooting began in May 1965.

At the beginning of *Town of No Return* (the first episode screened in Britain), Emma and Steed were already known to each other. No mention was made of Cathy's disappearance. However, Cathy Gale is mentioned in *Too Many Christmas Trees*. Steed is opening his Christmas cards and, finding one from Cathy, says to Emma, 'A card from Mrs Gale! Whatever can she be doing at Fort Knox?' A reference, of course, to Honor Blackman's *Goldfinger* Pussy Galore character.

No matter how grim the dangers to which they'd been exposed, Steed and Emma ended every story by driving off into the sunset in/on various forms of transport, except that, being *The Avengers*, there was naturally a twist to their manner of going. I've described the transport used in each case.

Opposite: *Emma and Steed on the giant chessboard used for the USA prologue sequence.*

Above: *LWT's window promotion for the Rigg b/w series.*

THE TOWN OF NO RETURN

In which Steed finds a town full of ghosts –
and Emma gets into harness

By Brian Clemens

John Steed	Patrick Macnee
Emma Peel	Diana Rigg
Brandon	Alan MacNaughtan
Smallwood	Patrick Newell
Piggy Warren	Terence Alexander
Vicar	Jeremy Burnham
Saul	Robert Brown
Jill Manson	Juliet Harmer
School Inspector	Walter Horsbrugh

Directed by Roy Baker

WHEN FOUR special agents in succession vanish without trace in Bazeley-by-the-Sea, a remote village on the Norfolk coast, near a derelict RAF base from World War II, The Avengers are alerted. John Steed, posing as a property dealer, and Emma Peel, as a schoolmistress, arrive at the local inn, where they meet the proprietor, 'Piggy' Warren, a Battle of Britain veteran, Mark Brandon, who is the local headmaster, and Jill Manson, one of his staff. That night Steed and Emma are disturbed by strange sounds – the tramp of an army on the march; the far-off braying of hounds. Their initial attempts to investigate are thwarted, but later they find a mass of bootprints leading up from the sea, and then the body of Jimmy Smallwood, a recent arrival in the village, who has been savaged by the dogs. Smallwood had been visiting his brother, Tom, the blacksmith, but when Steed and Emma go to the forge they realise that the man claiming to be the blacksmith is a phoney. Emma calls in at the village church, but all recent entries in the parish records have been removed. She tells the vicar, but, to her amazement, he holds her at gunpoint. Meanwhile, Steed, touring the derelict airfield, discovers evidence that shows Piggy Warren is also an impostor. When he finds that Emma has disappeared, Steed forces Piggy to talk. The trail takes Steed back to the forge, where Saul, the blacksmith, lashes out at him with red hot steel. Steed eventually wins the fight and finds Emma trussed up. They now realise that the whole village has been over-run by subversive elements who have been training a pocket army to make a take-over bid of all Britain. At the airfield they discover a well-equipped arsenal in the disused underground shelters. They are about to leave when they are cornered by Brandon, Jill Manson and the vicar. The would-be invaders are eventually shut in behind the heavy emergency doors. Steed and Emma leave Bazeley-by-the-Sea on a moped, Emma contemplating the thought of a 3-inch steak just around the corner.

THE GRAVEDIGGERS

In which Steed drives a train –
and Emma is tied to the tracks

By Malcolm Hulke

John Steed	Patrick Macnee
Emma Peel	Diana Rigg
Sir Horace Winslip	Ronald Fraser
Johnson	Paul Massie
Miss Thirwell	Caroline Blakiston
Sexton	Victor Platt
Fred	Charles Lamb
Nurse Spray	Wanda Ventham
Baron	Ray Austin
Sager	Steven Berkoff
Miller	Bryan Mosley
Dr Marlowe	Lloyd Lamble

Directed by Quentin Lawrence

A SUDDEN fault develops in the nation's early-warning radar system. Steed and Emma suspect deliberate jamming by hostile forces, but they are told that no blocking device that powerful yet exists. However, a Dr Marlowe had been working on such a system until his recent death. Steed goes to Pringby, a village lying in the path of the radar block, where Marlowe was buried, and arrives at the cemetery just as Marlowe's exhumed coffin is being loaded onto a hearse. He follows it to the Sir Horace Winslip Hospital for Retired or Ailing Railwaymen, and while making enquiries there, is astonished to recognise a passer-by as the dead Marlowe. It becomes apparent that Marlowe, obsessed with his work, has been frustrated by the lack of government funds and equipment and has sold out to enemy agents. Steed's arrival causes panic, and Johnson, who controls the set-up under the guise of head surgeon, decides that because of Marlowe's premature activation of the device, which has alerted the authorities, he must be eliminated. Enter Mrs Peel, posing as a nurse allocated by the Ministry. She soon befriends Nurse Spray, who says she will have little to do as Johnson performs his operations behind locked doors, with only the senior staff. Steed investigates the hospital's patron, Sir Horace Winslip, an eccentric who lives at Winslip Junction, a house completely full of railway ephemera. Steed notices there is a miniature passenger-carrying railway in Sir Horace's grounds that has a direct line to the hospital, plus a locked signal box inside Winslip Manor. That night, Steed and Emma secretly watch Johnson's latest operation. However, Johnson is soon asking Matron Thirwell to pass the blow-torch. . . . Steed discovers that all the burials have been arranged with a local undertaker up to six weeks ahead. Each one is at a different cemetery in a site at which the coffin-encased devices would completely surround the radar station. Wondering how they would be triggered off, Steed sets off to investigate the signal box at the Manor. Meanwhile Johnson discovers Emma's true identity and wants to kill her. He will incriminate Sir Horace by strapping Emma to his private railway line and driving a steam engine over her neck. Steed is greeted at Winslip Manor by an irate Sir Horace. Steed explains that his wish to prolong the life of the railways was being used for more sinister intentions. Through Sir Horace's telescope, Steed sees Johnson's henchmen start up the engine which will kill Emma, who is tied helpless at the far end of the track. He leaps on the train and fights a furious battle with the men as the train speeds along the track. Finally, Steed switches a vital set of points and the train narrowly misses decapitating Emma. As Steed unties her, Johnson tries to kill them but Emma's karate skill saves the day and the villain is left floundering in deep water. Having disposed of Johnson in style, Emma and Steed exit on Sir Horace Winslip's mini-train.

Top: Town of No Return.

Centre: The Gravediggers.

Bottom: The Cybernauts.

THE CYBERNAUTS

In which Steed receives a deadly gift – and Emma pockets it

By Philip Levene

John Steed	**Patrick Macnee**
Emma Peel	**Diana Rigg**
Dr Armstrong	**Michael Gough**
Benson	**Frederick Jaeger**
Jephcott	**Bernard Horsfall**
Tusamo	**Bert Kwouk**
Sensai	**John Hollis**
Lambert	**Ronald Leigh-Hunt**
Hammond	**Gordon Whiting**

Directed by Sidney Hayers

A KILLER OF fantastic strength wipes out a number of executives in violent succession. Steed and Emma discover that all the men were negotiating for the rights to a new circuit system developed by a Japanese company. Emma suspects that the men were killed by karate and she visits a leading karate school in search of a lead. Steed discovers that, of all the companies interested in the concession, the representatives of all but two of them have been murdered. Emma visits one, a mechanical toy manufacturer, owned by Jephcott. At the other company, United Automation, Steed, posing as a science reporter, meets the head of the company, Dr Armstrong, a cripple confined to an elaborately automated wheelchair, from which he controls a complex web of gadgetry and automata. Armstrong, suspecting Steed of being a spy, gives him a special pen – identical to the ones found on the murder victims. Later, Steed and Emma discover Jephcott dead. His violent assassin apparently reached him by walking through his office wall. Steed returns to Armstrong's hideaway and is trapped there just as he learns that the killings were performed by a radio-controlled robot, so that Armstrong could get the new circuit system – which would enable him to build an empire of robots under his supreme control. These were controlled by a radio transmitter housed in each of the pens given to the representatives. Steed realises that he left his pen with Emma. . . . But she, fearing for Steed's safety, sets off for Armstrong's factory – unaware that the unstoppable killer is on her trail, guided by the pen she has clipped in her pocket. Steed has distracted Armstrong and his assistant, Benson, and escaped. He reaches Emma just as she is cornered by the robot, and shouts to her to throw the pen away. Emma does so – escaping death by seconds – but Armstrong now turns loose an advanced robot which can think for itself. The new robot advances on Steed and Emma, but Steed clips the pen to this robot, leading the first robot to attack its superior counterpart. In an effort to stop the mayhem, Armstrong dies at the hands of his own creations. The remaining Cybernaut breaks the deadly pen, then stands stock still before the mystified duo. An inquisitive Emma prods the robot with her index finger – and the titan crashes to the ground! Leaving United Automation in her Lotus, Emma comes across Steed sitting in the Bentley doing a crossword puzzle. She offers him a pen. He politely declines.

DEATH AT BARGAIN PRICES

In which Steed fights in Ladies Underwear – and Emma tries 'feinting'

By Brian Clemens

John Steed	**Patrick Macnee**
Emma Peel	**Diana Rigg**
Horatio Kane	**Andre Morell**
Wentworth	**T P McKenna**
Farthingale	**Allan Cuthbertson**
Massey	**George Selway**
Marco	**Harvey Ashby**
Jarvis	**John Cater**
Professor Popple	**Peter Howell**
Glynn	**Ronnie Stevens**
Julie	**Diane Clare**

Directed by Charles Crichton

AN AGENT friend of Steed's is shot dead and dumped in an alleyway. A receipt from Pinter's department store, dated on a Sunday, is found on the body. Emma decides to take a job at the shop. At work in the lingerie department, she is approached by Jarvis, the house detective, who remarks on the apparent inexperience of most of Pinter's staff – a fact which dates only from the recent take-over by Horatio Kane, a tycoon known as King Kane, who lives in a penthouse over the store. Kane tells Steed, posing as an efficiency expert, that the store manager, Wentworth, will attend to him. Wentworth does just that, by forcibly evicting Steed. When Emma overhears about plans for the third night meeting of all the senior staff in one week, she asks Jarvis about them. Jarvis says that he, too, is suspicious of the management, and intends to eavesdrop at the meeting that night. He overhears Wentworth finalising a sinister plan, at the crux of which is a Professor Popple, who is being held in enforced detention. Jarvis is discovered by the gang and killed. The next day, Marco, a store executive, makes a play for Emma, and she asks him about the Sunday receipt. He says she must talk to Wentworth and, on the way to do so, Emma discovers a laboratory. In it is a shackled old man whom Emma recognises as Professor Popple, a missing atom scientist. As she leaves, Wentworth and Marco corner her. Steed calls at Pinter's and is told that Emma has been sacked. Suspecting that she is in trouble, Steed hides in the store until it closes. He then disposes of the nightwatchman and releases Emma, who is trussed up in a carpet in the furniture department. They enter the laboratory, where Popple lies in a drugged stupor, and discover that the receipts are, in fact, feed cards for an atomic computer. The whole store has been converted into a giant atomic bomb! Kane enters with Farthingale, his assistant, and at gunpoint, Steed and Emma are told Kane's plans for the biggest take-over bid of all – he is about to hold all Britain to ransom under the threat of the bomb. A fight breaks out and Steed and Emma soon dispose of the villains. Kane, however, makes one last bid to detonate the bomb and sets a disused lift in motion. The descending lift will operate the detonator mechanism exploding the bomb. The Avengers struggle to open the lift gates and jam the progress of the deadly lift in time. Steed finally halts the lift inches from the detonator, using his umbrella. Having saved Pinter's department store from the biggest closing-down sale of all time, Emma and Steed depart on bicycles.

An early Emma Peel fight sequence from Death at Bargain Prices, using a choreographed technique pioneered by Cathy Gale.

CASTLE DE'ATH

In which Steed becomes a strapping Jock – and Emma lays a ghost

By John Lucarotti

John Steed	Patrick Macnee
Emma Peel	Diana Rigg
Ian	Gordon Jackson
Angus	Robert Urquhart
McNab	Jack Lambert
Roberton	James Copeland
Controller	Russell Waters

Directed by James Hill

EMMA ARRIVES at Castle De'ath in Scotland as a member of Aborcashata (Advisory Bureau on Refurbishing Castles and Stately Homes as Tourist Attractions). She is ill-received by Ian, the 35th Laird, and McNab, the head gillie, even though Ian's cousin, Angus, has invited her. Another guest is Mr John McSteed, researching a book on the 13th Laird, Black Jamie. Steed enquires about the fishing but Angus warns him about the loch. The previous week, an amateur frogman's body was washed up on the banks. Steed tells Emma that the frogman was four inches taller dead than when he was alive. It seems he had been put on the rack and stretched. . . . Steed leaves to walk around the loch, but is followed by McNab and another gillie, Roberton. Emma investigates the dungeons, where she discovers various instruments of torture. There, a seaman attacks her and another seaman crashes a blackjack over her head. She recovers and makes her way back to the main hall where she meets Steed and Ian. Emma says she slipped on the stairs. At dinner, Ian tells them the story of Black Jamie, who was walled up in the East Tower. Often, his ghost walks playing the Lament of Glen De'ath. Steed, however, is more interested in the vibrations shuddering through his brandy glass. Steed goes to his room, only to find Roberton has moved his things to the Lord Darnley Room, where the howling west wind will not bother him. Steed admires the magnificent canopy bed in the room and prepares to sleep. Silently, the canopy over the bed moves down on an enormous threaded screw, gathering momentum as it sinks lower until it crushes everything in the bed. . . . Emma, meanwhile, has heard the sound of pipes and gone to investigate. She is going down the dungeon steps when the heavy door slams behind her. Next morning, Emma is drowsing on the steps when the door opens to reveal Steed, who tells her what happened the previous night. Steed goes fishing in the moat – watched by Roberton through binoculars – and Emma returns to the dungeon again, armed with a map she has found. McNab is just about to descend, too, when Roberton calls him. Emma steps into an iron maiden, to hide. As she does so, the back opens to reveal a long corridor, which in turn leads to a room full of complicated electrical equipment. McNab goes to the moat but only finds Steed's clothes draped over a pole. Nearby are spare frogmen's clothes and oxygen tanks. When Emma returns, Ian tells her he has decided not to open the castle to the public, so Emma leaves. Meanwhile Steed surfaces from the moat, is seized by two men and taken to the control room beneath the castle. There, a controller sits before a fantastic complex, including a television screen, on which can be seen three midget submarines in a pen. McNab confronts Steed and tells him how they intend to corner the market in fish by driving them into their underground base with the submarines. Throughout the conversation, McNab is constantly interrupted by the phone and talks to someone he calls Chief. Steed manages to escape. That night, Emma returns to the castle to search for Steed. She is crawling across the battlements when she meets the ghost (McNab), blowing the pipes to deaden the sound of the turbine below. After a brief skirmish, Emma throws him over the battlements. Steed arrives in the main hall to do battle and is joined by Emma. Angus now reveals himself as the Chief and grabs a claymore to finish off Steed. Seizing a dirk from the wall, Steed soon disarms Angus who runs into the dungeon to escape. He enters the iron maiden, but the door jams and the maiden's spikes pierce into his body. Driving back to London along a remote Highland road, Steed, much to his partner's chagrin, drives into a Scottish loch. But when you're an Avenger, anything can happen – including the car sprouting 'fins' and floating away!

Mysterious goings-on in Castle De'ath *lead Steed into a rousing fight with shield and claymore.*

THE MASTER MINDS

In which Steed becomes a genius – and Emma loses her mind

By Robert Banks Stewart

John Steed	**Patrick Macnee**
Emma Peel	**Diana Rigg**
Sir Clive Todd	**Laurence Hardy**
Holly Trent	**Patricia Haines**
Sir Fergus Campbell	**Ian McNaughton**
Davinia Todd	**Georgina Ward**

Directed by Peter Graham Scott

AN EMINENT government official, Sir Clive Todd, is suspected of treason. Heavily guarded, he lies at home badly wounded after his surprise role in a raid on top-secret files. Emma is brought in to act as his nurse and Steed learns from Sir Clive's daughter, Davinia, that her father was a member of Ransack, a club for intellectuals. When Sir Clive begins to respond to questioning, Emma urgently calls Steed to his bedside. But before they can make further headway, Sir Clive's doctor, Fergus Campbell, gives his patient a fatal injection. Appearing to come out of a trance, Dr Campbell is as appalled by his action as those around him. He reveals that he, too, is a member of Ransack. Steed joins the mysterious Ransack Club, and goes to the country boarding school where the club conducts special courses. Emma arrives there, too, as a secretary. Giving an archery class in the grounds is Holly Trent, who speaks to Steed somewhat scornfully about Ransack and its members. The hub of Ransack's activities is the gymnasium, where its members exercise on the equipment and work on highly intellectual papers. Steed manages to gain a high IQ rating with a little help from Emma. That night, Steed discovers Emma in a trance, watching military training films and going out on some form of combat training. When he mentions it to her, she at first denies all knowledge of it, but then realises that she and the Ransack members were obviously victims of mass hypnosis, induced by a voice over the radio speakers in each bedroom. This also explains Sir Clive's unusual behaviour and his murder by Campbell. Steed has escaped hypnosis because the speaker in his bedroom was disconnected. Steed decides to feign hypnosis and attend the next indoctrinations, but the Ransack officials see through his hoax and order his disposal. A seemingly entranced Emma volunteers to do it, but when she reports Steed is dead, they realise her complicity and a fight breaks out. Steed rescues her, and using the gym equipment as weapons, they defeat the Ransack members. At the climax of the fray, Holly Trent is revealed to be the mastermind, and Emma knocks her out. Steed and Emma leave Holly Trent's school in a standard mode of transport – Steed's gleaming Bentley.

Steed watches Emma trying out the trampoline in the Ransack gymnasium. A scene from The Master Minds.

THE MURDER MARKET

In which Steed seeks a wife – and Emma gets buried

By Tony Williamson

John Steed	**Patrick Macnee**
Emma Peel	**Diana Rigg**
Mr Lovejoy	**Patrick Cargill**
Dinsford	**Peter Bayliss**
Barbara Wakefield	**Suzanne Lloyd**
Mrs Stone	**Naomi Chance**
Robert Stone	**John Woodvine**

Directed by Peter Graham Scott

WHEN AN outbreak of baffling murders commands the attention of The Avengers, Emma visits the widow of the last victim, Jessica Stone, while Steed, posing as a potential husband, visits the Togetherness Marriage Bureau. Emma successfully finds a number-one suspect, Robert Stone, the widow's brother-in-law; and, in the sickly sweet atmosphere of Togetherness, Steed overhears a client called Henshaw in a sinister encounter with the management. Fearing that Henshaw may prove to be the next victim, Steed asks Emma to go to his flat. As Emma arrives at Henshaw's, she bumps into a woman called Barbara Wakefield, making a rapid departure. Emma enters the flat and finds she is too late – Henshaw is floating dead in his bath. The first partner

the two partners recognise her as an enemy. Togetherness now tell Steed that he must murder Emma Peel. Emma plays 'dead' for Steed's benefit and is shown laid out in her coffin. Pleased with Steed's apparent efficiency, the match-makers offer him more work, but he insists on first meeting the organisation's boss. Togetherness now receive a tip making them doubt Steed's word, so they make him watch Emma's coffin being buried. Steed looks on unflinchingly. Having passed the test, Steed now meets the boss – Jessica Stone. The widow had used the bureau against her own husband when he became too interested in its female clients. Meanwhile, Emma, having escaped burial alive, discovers that Robert Stone is innocent and only wants to find his brother's killer. At that moment, the gang arrive and corner Emma and Robert. But Steed soon arrives and together they tear Togetherness apart, before departing in a hearse!

Togetherness may be the password, but Steed seems to be carrying friendship too far in this scene from The Murder Market.

In The Murder Market, *Mrs Peel gave the Togetherness ladies a much-needed lesson in etiquette.*

Togetherness suggest for Steed turns out to be Barbara Wakefield. Steed hints that only a cousin stands in the way of his acquiring a massive inheritance. The bait is taken and the Togetherness match-makers Lovejoy and Dinsford reveal that their bureau runs a murder racket on the side. If Steed will do a murder for them, they will kill his cousin. Meanwhile, Emma's investigation of Robert Stone has led her to the marriage bureau, where

A SURFEIT OF H₂O

In which Steed plans a boat trip – and Emma gets very wet

By Colin Finbow

John Steed	**Patrick Macnee**
Emma Peel	**Diana Rigg**
Jonah Barnard	**Noel Purcell**
Dr Sturm	**Albert Lieven**
Joyce Jason	**Sue Lloyd**
Eli Barker	**Talfryn Thomas**
Sir Arnold Kelly	**John Kidd**

Directed by Sidney Hayers

WHEN A village poacher is drowned in the middle of a field during a freak thunderstorm, his strange death seems to support the belief of local eccentrics that the Great Flood is coming again to Earth. Steed, however, looks for a more feasible explanation. Steed calls on Jonah Barnard, the village carpenter, who is building an ark. He points to a cloud hanging motionless in the sky which visibly increases in size every day. The cloud is in the vicinity of Grannie Gregson's wine-making factory. When Emma tries to enter the factory, as a reporter, she is rebuffed by Dr Sturm, but she later persuades Eli, the dead poacher's brother, to let her into the factory that night. When Emma arrives at the rendezvous she finds Eli is another victim of the mysterious rain. Posing as a vintner, Steed manages to gain admission to the factory. He learns from Joyce, the receptionist, that Dr Sturm has installed a lot of new equipment in his two years at the factory. When Joyce shows Steed around the cellars, she suddenly becomes alarmed when he hears the sound of heavy rain falling from somewhere in the premises. She hurries Steed away and he is astounded to discover that it is a fine day outside. Emma, meanwhile, alarmed by the weird readings she has had on her portable weather equipment, calls in Sir Arnold Kelly, a meteorological expert. He is working alone in a field, when the torrents suddenly begin and he is washed into the ground. Later Sturm's henchmen carry off his body. Realising that Emma called in Sir Arnold, Sturm decides to put an end to her. He invites her to look over the plant, and Emma is forced to accept – at gunpoint. Sturm straps her under the giant pulping press, hoping to force a confession as he steadily increases the pressure. Having told her that he intends to sell his deadly rain-making device as a military weapon, able to bog down whole armies, Sturm leaves Emma strapped on the press and only fractions of an inch from death. Meanwhile, Steed has convinced Jonah that the freak storms were man-made and he agrees to go with him to the factory. They enter by a secret tunnel and free Emma, then find the rain-making machine, but are confronted by Sturm and his henchmen. A fight breaks out in the rain, which steadily increases in merciless intensity. They quickly finish off the gang and Sturm's diabolical scheme is washed away, leaving The Avengers to depart the scene in a mini-buggy.

Water water everywhere, but only wine to drink. Steed finds A Surfeit of H₂O and a 'sturm' warning almost too much to handle.

THE HOUR THAT NEVER WAS

In which Steed has to face the music – and Emma disappears

By John Lucarotti

John Steed	**Patrick Macnee**
Emma Peel	**Diana Rigg**
Geoffrey Ridsdale	**Gerald Harper**
Philip Leas	**Dudley Foster**
Hickey	**Roy Kinnear**
Porky Purser	**Roger Booth**
Corporal Barman	**Daniel Moynihan**
Driver	**David Morrell**
Wiggins	**Fred Haggerty**

Directed by James Hill

STEED IS invited to the closing-down party of RAF Camp 472 – Hamelin, a camp at which Steed saw service during the war. He takes Emma as a guest. Nearing the camp by car, they are involved in an accident when a dog rushes blindly across the road. The dashboard clock stops at 11 o'clock. Recovering, they walk to the camp. In the distance they can hear the sound of a tinkling piano, but when they arrive at the camp, the place is deserted. The camp clocks have stopped at 11 o'clock. In the bakery they find a cake bearing the unfinished inscription 'Goodbye Hamelin'. They hear the sound of a milk float being started up and decide to climb the camp control tower to gain a better view. On the runway they see a man, dressed as a milkman, running for his life. A rifle shot rings out and the man falls. They edge over to the hangar from which the shot came and once again hear the sound of the milk float, which then stops. They can see it, and bundled on the rear platform is the body of the milkman. As they cross the now disused children's playground, Steed begins to stagger like a drunken man. The chains of the swings begin to rattle and vibrate loudly – the sound is terrifying. As the noise diminishes, Steed recovers his balance and hurries on to find that the milk float, the body and Emma have disappeared. He desperately searches the camp and finds a filthy man called Hickey.

He tells Steed of the strange sound that made him feel drunk. Deciding the man is harmless, Steed sets off for the main gate where he has seen a uniformed figure. The sentry-box is empty except for a uniform hanging from a peg. As Steed leaves, the striped barrier pole across the entrance falls and knocks him unconscious. Recovering, he finds that he is sitting in his car on the grass verge where it crashed. There is no sign of Emma! He sets off for the camp and once again hears the sound of a tinkling piano being played in the Officers' Mess. He bursts inside to find the place jammed with his wartime comrades – Ridsdale, Wiggins, Porky Purser, and the new camp dentist, Leas. The time is three minutes past 12. Baffled, Steed goes outside for some air. He sees the dog that caused the accident whimpering by a dustbin. Stuffed among the rubbish by the bin is the dead body of Hickey. Once again he hears the milk float and following it, he sees a powerful man carrying the body of a Sergeant into the bakery. He crosses to the window and is amazed to see the Sergeant busy icing the cake. Dumbfounded, Steed hurries after the milk float in time to see the powerful man put the body of an Officer on the milk float, before driving off. Steed arrives at the medical centre, goes inside and sees a guard. They fight, and, taking off the man's helmet, Steed finds that the guard is wearing an elaborate pair of earmuffs. He hears muffled sounds from the dentist's surgery, where he finds Emma, bound and gagged. He releases her and together they search the surgery. In a locked room they find an oscilloscope, which, when pitched correctly, would affect the brain and render people unconscious. They also find the drug C11, used in brainwashing. Obviously, the camp personnel are made unconscious, then taken to the surgery, where their secrets are divulged. As Steed and Emma leave, they are confronted by Leas, and the giant who drove the milk float. In the ensuing fight Steed knocks over a cannister of laughing gas, and he and Emma guffaw their way to victory. Outside, they get in the milk float and drive off to a new adventure.

Where is Mrs Peel? Searching Camp Hamelin, Steed meets Hickey who explains The Hour That Never Was.

DIAL A DEADLY NUMBER

In which Steed plays Bulls and Bears – and Emma has no option

By Roger Marshall

John Steed	**Patrick Macnee**
Emma Peel	**Diana Rigg**
Henry Boardman	**Clifford Evans**
Ruth Boardman	**Jan Holden**
Ben Jago	**Anthony Newlands**
Fitch	**John Carson**
John Harvey	**Peter Bowles**
Frederick Yuill	**Gerald Sim**

Directed by Don Leaver

SUDDEN DEATH strikes big business executive, Todhunter, during a board meeting – the sixth recent fatality in the financial world. Suspecting more than just coincidence, The Avengers decide to play the stock market. Steed calls on Henry Boardman, banker to all the deceased executives, and says he has £2,000,000 to invest. On Boardman's advice, Steed visits a broker, Frederick Yuill, who explains how money could have been made out of the sudden deaths. He also deduces that one of those to cash in was an investor called Jago.

Meanwhile, Emma is following another lead. Todhunter's bleeper, which meant he could always be reached, is missing. It was operated by remote control through an answering service. Emma calls at his office to investigate. Steed learns that the key mechanic on the bleep operation is Fitch, a nasty man who immediately arouses his suspicion. At a dinner party, Boardman introduces Steed to his wife, Ruth, whom Steed knows is involved with Jago. Returning home that night, Steed is attacked in his underground garage by two men wearing motorcycling outfits. Steed wins and recognises one of the men as being Yuill's butler. When Steed and Emma call on Yuill for an explanation, he is dead, with evidence that he, too, had a bleep device in his pocket. At a wine-tasting party in the cellar of Boardman's bank, Steed is unaware that he and Emma are being filmed by a hidden camera – enabling Fitch to make a pocket-watch identical to Steed's. At their next meeting, Ruth Boardman plants the lethal watch in Steed's pocket. An enlightened Emma is about to warn him when she is detained at gunpoint by Fitch. The maniacal mechanic now reveals that he was responsible for the bleep deaths. Steed detects the watch device and hurries to Fitch's workshop in time to rescue Emma, and, in the struggle, the evil Fitch is killed by one of his own devices. Emma examines the bleepers and discovers that each has been loaded with a capillary needle, which a call through the answering service would trigger off. The murder method now explained, Steed plants harmless bleep devices on all the suspects he has met, including Boardman, Jago and Boardman's partner, Harvey. In the ensuing mayhem, Boardman proves his innocence and his wife Ruth exposes herself as the guilty party. Jago shoots Boardman, and hurries down to the bank's cellar to join Harvey. However, Steed and Emma are waiting for them and soon stop the villains in typical Avengers style. The case complete, Emma joins Steed in a London taxi as he uncorks a bottle of claret to toast their success.

Steed and Emma discover the dead body of Yuill in Dial a Deadly Number.

MAN-EATER OF SURREY GREEN

In which Steed kills a climber – and Emma becomes a vegetable

By Philip Levene

John Steed	**Patrick Macnee**
Emma Peel	**Diana Rigg**
Sir Lyle Peterson	**Derek Farr**
Dr Sheldon	**Athene Seyler**
Laura Burford	**Gillian Lewis**
Alan Carter	**William Job**

Directed by Sidney Hayers

STEED AND EMMA set out to help botanist Alan Carter when his fiancée Laura Burford goes missing, thereby joining the ranks of several eminent horticulturists who have recently disappeared in Surrey. Steed discovers that all the missing scientists are working at an establishment run by Sir Lyle Peterson, a plant specialist who likes exotic insect-eating plants. Peterson tells him that all the scientists are working on a new flowering shrub. Rather surprisingly, Laura Burford is introduced to Steed. She seems happy enough, but casual about the forsaken Alan. Leaving the premises, Steed spots a giant oil derrick in the grounds. He later learns that Peterson has ordered a second derrick to be delivered to his farm. Steed and Emma investigate the farm and find the charred remains of a manned space craft. They are later told by the authorities that it was a space-shot which failed, and the craft, after a year in orbit, must have returned to earth, undetected, several months before – the very time when the first scientist went missing. Found attached to the space craft is a giant vegetable seed, and Steed asks a friend, Dr Cynthia Sheldon, to investigate. She says that not only has the plant got a brain and the capacity to grow to enormous size, but it is man-eating. Steed and Emma are horrified and set off with Dr Sheldon for Peterson's estate, equipped with an acid plant-killer. Steed fears that another space seed is being germinated there under the mysterious derrick. By now, Steed has realised that the few Surrey scientists to have resisted the call to Peterson's establishment all wear hearing aids. Conjecturing that the aids must be protection against the plant's unearthly hypnotic influences, he gets a set of aids for himself. When Steed and Emma reach the estate, they find pandemonium has broken out. The plant is growing rapidly and summoning local inhabitants with its hypnotic call to satisfy its hunger. They search for the control room. By now, the plant is covering the whole house. In the control room is Peterson, who tries to stop them. Emma overpowers him and Steed gives him a hearing aid, which immediately frees him from the plant's influence. While Steed and Peterson battle to save Dr Sheldon from the plant, Emma goes to collect the acid plant-killer, but the plant surrounds her and in the struggle she loses her hearing aid. Now the plant's slave, Emma battles with Steed to stop the plant's destruction. After a tense struggle, the acid is thrown onto the plant, which dies, releasing Emma from its deadly spell. Emma and Steed depart atop a hay cart, she placing a daisy in Steed's bowler band.

Horrified to learn that a man-eating plant is on the loose, Emma, Steed and Dr Sheldon, armed with an acid plant-killer, set out to find the Man-Eater of Surrey Green.

TWO'S A CROWD

In which Steed is single minded – and Emma sees double

By Philip Levene

John Steed	**Patrick Macnee**
Emma Peel	**Diana Rigg**
Brodny	**Warren Mitchell**
Alicia Elena	**Maria Machado**
Shvedloff	**Alec Mango**
Pudeshkin	**Wolfe Morris**
Vogel	**Julian Glover**
Ivenko	**John Bluthal**

Directed by Roy Baker

STEED BELIEVES that a notorious spy, Colonel Psev, will attempt to infiltrate a conference of defence chiefs in London. They are alerted to Psev's presence by the sudden arrival of four agents known to work for him. The quartet establish themselves at the national Embassy, where they use Brodny, the Ambassador, as a general runabout. While out on an errand for them, Brodny spots a man who is the double of John Steed. Brodny realises that the agents could use him – a seedy male model named Webster – to impersonate Steed and gain access to the conference. Emma sees the agents setting up a deal with Webster at the Embassy, and guesses what is afoot. She tells Steed about his double, but he does not seem to take her warning seriously. After being schooled in Steed's speech, dress and mannerisms, Webster goes to a cocktail party dressed as Steed, where it is arranged that he sees Emma. She soon sees through him, and the agents forcibly detain her. One of the Embassy staff, Ivenko, is blamed for the failure of the plan and, in desperation, he phones Steed with the offer of vital information in exchange for political asylum. A rendezvous is arranged in the Embassy grounds. However, the agents have wired Steed's apartment for sound and when Ivenko appears for the meeting, the agents send out a radio-controlled midget submarine which shoots him dead just before Steed arrives. Lethal model machines are a macabre hobby of Colonel Psev. Trussed up in the corner of a room, Emma believes she is about to be rescued when she sees the familiar face of Steed at the window, but instead of freeing her he declares himself to be the impostor, Webster. The agents are now satisfied that their man can pass the test and order him to dispose of the real Steed at his flat, and then go to the conference and secure on microfilm some top-secret documents. They hear Steed's death over the transmitter planted in his apartment, and soon Webster returns with the vital microfilm. Emma breaks free and demands the microfilm at gun point. Webster, however, disarms her and stresses that he will only give the film to Colonel Psev. The agents now reveal that there is no Colonel Psev. The elusive spy is in fact all four of them, and the name made up of all their initials. Webster now hands over the film and hurries Emma away. Once outside, Webster reveals himself to be the real Steed, who turned the tables on Webster earlier. The agents, however, discover the truth before Steed and Emma can leave, and using a complex panel board, they send a model Spitfire after the couple. Steed manages to bring it down with his revolver. Undaunted, the agents release a model bomber. Now out of ammunition, Steed discovers that the portable radio transmitter in the Bentley is tuned to the same frequency as the agents' control device. He diverts the bomber's path and brings it round on the Embassy. The agents themselves now fall victim to their own miniature bomb. In the closer, Steed, waiting beside his white mount as Emma trots up to him astride a superb grey, is foxed when his partner refuses to acknowledge him until, as she rides by, she calls him by name and the two ride off into the sunset.

Masquerading as Webster, Steed does his party piece to convince Brodny and Ivenko that Two's a Crowd.

TOO MANY CHRISTMAS TREES

In which Steed hangs up his stocking – and Emma asks for more

By Tony Williamson

John Steed	**Patrick Macnee**
Emma Peel	**Diana Rigg**
Brandon Storey	**Mervyn Johns**
Dr Felix Teasel	**Edwin Richfield**
Janice Crane	**Jeannette Sterke**
Martin Trasker	**Alex Scott**
Jenkins	**Robert James**
Jeremy Wade	**Barry Warren**

Directed by Roy Baker

STEED IS plagued by a vivid recurring nightmare. Featured as a corpse in this frightening dream is a one-time colleague, Freddy Marshall, with whom Steed shared exclusive knowledge of top-secret information. Steed's dream becomes reality when he learns of Freddy's sudden death in mysterious circumstances, his mind having collapsed from too much strain. To cheer him up, Emma invites Steed to a festive house party given by eccentric publisher Brandon Storey, a man obsessed with Dickens. But at Brandon's home Steed finds himself in identical surroundings to those of his dream. Unwittingly, Emma has led Steed into a trap; it is revealed that two other house guests, Trasker and Wade, are exerting dangerous, telepathic influences on Steed's mind. Their previous experiment with Freddy Marshall has misfired. Apparently unaware of the plot, Steed is induced into a deep sleep by the mind-benders, and into a *Tale of Two Cities* nightmare in which Steed is Sydney Carton, taunted at the guillotine by a dark, mysterious woman. As the blade crashes down, Steed awakens in a state of shock – heightened by the arrival of another guest, Janice Crane, the dark beauty of his dream. Storey holds a Dickensian-style Christmas Eve party in fancy dress. Emma is given an Oliver Twist outfit, while Steed gets the Sydney Carton clothes of his dream. At the height of the celebrations, Storey announces that Janice will do a mind-reading act, and she selects Steed as her assistant. However, it is really one last attempt by the mind-benders to extract the secret information from Steed's mind. As the game progresses, Emma becomes increasingly alarmed by Steed's strange behaviour and deliberately drops a glass of wine to shatter the spell. Wade, full of misgivings about his part in the experiment, is on the point of talking to Emma when he is murdered. Emma, believing that Steed is fast approaching a mental collapse, turns in desperation to another guest, Dr Teasel. She begins to suspect that Teasel is also involved, but no sooner has she knocked him out than she learns that Steed has been a willing victim all along, and that Teasel was working with him. Together, they had hoped to learn the motives behind the mind-benders and the identity of the mastermind. Now Steed – once again his debonair self – and Emma must stand alone against the sinister trio. They hunt down the mind-benders and after an all-out fight in a hall of distorting mirrors, Brandon Storey himself is revealed as the brain behind the plot. His nightmare laid to rest, Steed drives Mrs Peel away in an open-topped Surrey.

In this scene from **Too Many Christmas Trees**, *Emma, dressed as Oliver Twist, has a difference of opinion with Dr Teasel.*

SILENT DUST

In which Steed watches birds –
and Emma goes hunting

By Roger Marshall

John Steed	**Patrick Macnee**
Emma Peel	**Diana Rigg**
Omrod	**William Franklyn**
Juggins	**Jack Watson**
Mellors	**Conrad Phillips**
Croft	**Norman Bird**
Miss Snow	**Joanna Wake**
Clare Prendergast	**Isobel Black**
Sir Manfred Fellows	**Charles Lloyd Pack**
Quince	**Aubrey Morris**

Directed by Roy Baker

WHEN WHOLE areas of the countryside are laid to waste, and birds and beasts die by the hundred, Steed and Emma are called in to investigate. Steed is taken to an area of desolation at Manderley which is under War Department control, and a Minister tells him it was caused by Silent Dust, an organochlorine fertiliser which went wrong – killing instead of replenishing. Emma meanwhile meets a birdwatcher named Quince and she questions him as they walk along the country lanes. A gamekeeper, Mellors, orders them away from the area with a double-barrelled shotgun. Omrod, the owner of the land, appears on horseback and sends Mellors about his business. Eyeing Emma admiringly he invites her to join him at the next hunt. Steed is introduced to Sir Manfred Fellows, and learns that the man in charge of the Silent Dust project, Prendergast, was sacked years ago. Fellows tells Steed that the man had a daughter, Clare, who may be able to help. Steed visits her and finds that she is bitter about the treatment her dead father received. When Steed has left, Clare is joined by Omrod, who has been eavesdropping. Emma is having a drink at the local inn with a rose-grower, Croft, when she notices Quince beckoning her from outside. He arranges to meet Emma that night and leaves. Standing near the bar, listening, is Mellors. That night, Emma arrives to find no sign of Quince – only his broken spectacles suspended on a bush. Returning to the inn, Emma meets Steed. They are discussing the event when a horse trots into the yard. They look out to see the local beauty, Miss Snow, dismounting. She is obviously disturbed because her horse is sick. Steed invites her inside for a drink, but when Omrod and Croft appear she makes an excuse and leaves with the men. Miss Snow, Croft and another man named Juggins, all meet in Omrod's home. They decide to continue to destroy Britain county by county, until the government deposits £40,000,000 in a Swiss bank. Later, while strolling through the countryside, Steed is confronted by Mellors, still carrying his shotgun. Steed pretends to leave but later returns and breaks into a farmhouse. There he finds a padlocked cupboard and on the floor traces of powder. He puts a sample into an envelope and is about to leave when he hears a gun being cocked. Instinctively he jumps to the side but a shot from Mellors' gun hits him in the shoulder. Concerned at Steed's disappearance, Emma goes to the farmhouse. Forcing open the cupboard she finds the dead body of Quince behind a pile of apples. And lurching towards her is the blood-stained body of Steed. Having recovered, Steed is now invited by Omrod to join the hunt, and Emma is also invited. During the hunt, Miss Snow lures Steed into a corner of the stable-yard and, before galloping off, leaves him to face Croft, who is wielding a vicious-looking scythe. After a few wild slashes, Croft is left floundering in a horse trough. Emma manages to unseat Miss Snow and takes her horse. She follows Omrod and Juggins into a barn where they are piling Silent Dust into containers. Emma holds them at gunpoint but Mellors arrives and jumps her. Emma whips him over her shoulder and makes a run for it – pursued by Omrod and Juggins on horseback. Cornered by Omrod, she throws him to the ground and turns to face Juggins, who is carrying a long horse-whip. But then Steed appears, riding a horse and carrying a For Sale sign nailed to a sturdy wooden post. With a swish of the post, Steed sweeps Juggins into the duckpond. Steed and Emma exchange glances, then Steed picks up Omrod's fallen hunting horn and blows a long, triumphant call on it. Having served the villains their just desserts, Steed and Emma depart skywards in a hot-air balloon.

Hi Yo Silver, Away. Steed on foot is enough to scare the pants off any villain. Mounted on a horse, as in Silent Dust, *it's a case of baddies beware!*

ROOM WITHOUT A VIEW

In which Steed becomes a Gourmet –
and Emma awakes in Manchuria

By Roger Marshall

John Steed	**Patrick Macnee**
Emma Peel	**Diana Rigg**
Chessman	**Paul Whitsun-Jones**
Varnals	**Peter Jeffrey**
Dr Cullen	**Richard Bebb**
Carter	**Philip Latham**
Pascold	**Peter Arne**
Pushkin	**Vernon Dobtcheff**
Dr Wadkin	**Peter Madden**
Anna Wadkin	**Jeanne Roland**

Directed by Roy Baker

WHEN HE suddenly reappears after two years' unexplained absence, scientist John Wadkin is a mental wreck from intensive brainwashing. A government official, Varnals, tells Emma and Steed that Wadkin's state of mind suggests he has been held prisoner in a Manchurian concentration camp. In an attempt to restore Wadkin to his senses, Steed and Emma confront him with his one-time colleague, Dr Cullen, but without success. Wadkin babbles on nonsensically, obsessed by the number 621. Any further progress is thwarted when a gang of toughs make off with Wadkin in a Chinese laundry van, despite a desperate bid by Emma to stop them. The focus now turns on Dr Cullen. A mystery man, Len Pascold, begins making enquiries about him, and this leads Steed and Emma to suspect that Cullen may be kidnapped when he visits London for a conference. Steed and Varnals are in the background when Cullen books into Chessman's Hotel.

In Room Without a View, *Emma found herself imprisoned in a concentration camp – situated in London's West End!*

Significantly, he is given Room 621. Unknown to Steed, when Cullen reaches his room, he is confronted by the mysterious Pascold. The following morning, the man who checks out as Dr Cullen is obviously an impostor. Emma then gets a job at the hotel to help with the mystery. Steed meanwhile learns that Pascold had been attempting to secure Dr Cullen's services on behalf of an American chemical corporation. Pascold, however, suddenly exonerates himself by pestering the hotel management with enquiries about Cullen's sudden disappearance. In fact, Cullen now lies in a concentration camp cell, where he listens in horror to the staccato commands of the Chinese guards outside – and the demented ramblings of Wadkin in the next cell. Emma investigates a Chinese laundry in the basement of the hotel. She finds Pascold dead, in a laundry basket, but suspicion falls on her when she is seen leaving, and she is sent on an errand to Room 621. There, she is soon overcome by gas fumes. She comes to in the concentration camp, where an interrogator menaces her. Meanwhile in his penthouse above the hotel, sits the owner, Max Chessman, who, because of thin blood, has to live in a super-heated atmosphere, and lives on a severely restricted diet, because of his immense size. He hears that the renowned Monsieur Gourmet is a guest in his hotel, and orders a special epicure's dinner for him. Gourmet is, in fact, Steed, who has adopted the pose in order to avert suspicion. It now becomes apparent to Emma that Chessman is using kidnapped scientists as objects of barter to help him realise his plans for an unbroken chain of luxury hotels around the world. All the scientists were booked into Room 621 and thence transported to the prison camp. Wadkin's temporary escape had been a mistake. Finding Emma missing, Steed breaks into Chessman's penthouse and turns off the heat to freeze the information out of the delicate man. He soon learns that Emma is being held in a room on a disused floor of the hotel. Entering the room, Steed finds it is a perfect replica of Room 621, and the one to which the missing scientists had been deliberately misdirected. Steed discovers a false wall behind a wardrobe. Behind the wall is a passage leading to a block of cells. The concentration camp is actually in the hotel. Various tricks were used to simulate Manchuria and to deceive the inmates. He finds and releases Emma and they combine forces to defeat Chessman's vile plot. Exit the Avengers with Steed pulling a rickshaw while Emma advises him to 'Slow down, Steed – there's a 30 mph speed limit in force!'

SMALL GAME FOR BIG HUNTERS

In which Steed joins the natives –
and Emma gets the evil eye

By Philip Levene

John Steed	**Patrick Macnee**
Emma Peel	**Diana Rigg**
Col Rawlings	**Bill Fraser**
Simon Trent	**James Villiers**
Professor Swain	**Liam Redmond**
Dr Gibson	**A J Brown**
Fleming	**Peter Burton**
Razafi	**Paul Danquah**
Tropical outfitter	**Tom Gill**
Lala	**Esther Anderson**
Kendrick	**Peter Thomas**

Directed by Gerry O'Hara

STEED AND EMMA are called to a country cottage near London where a man named Kendrick is suffering from sleeping sickness. He was found, wearing a tropical kit, by a Dr Gibson, who is in attendance as Steed examines the man. Steed shows Emma the native arrow found in Kendrick's back. As they examine it tribal drums begin to throb away across the country. Professor Swain, an expert on primitive tribes, is brought to the cottage and he tells Emma about Shirenzai, a cult peculiar to the land of Kalaya. Shirenzai in Kalayan means The Curse of Sleep. Swain tries to cast a spell to revive Kendrick, but Gibson scoffs at it. Later, Gibson is found in a coma, and round his wrist is the mark of Shirenzai. Steed decides to investigate the Kalayan Ex-Serviceman's Association, run by a Colonel Rawlings. As he leaves the cottage, he is attacked by Razafi, a native, and is saved when the vicious knife he wields sinks into Steed's bowler hat. At Rawlings' home, Steed encounters the native a second time but manages to subdue him. But Steed, in the garden, steps into a spring-type animal trap. Recovering, he finds himself in Rawlings' study, where a lovely Eurasian girl, Lala, is beckoning to him. Reaching out he finds himself at the end of a hunting rifle, held by Simon Trent, who makes Steed change into tropical kit before taking him into an intensely-heated jungle area. The blimp-like Colonel Rawlings arrives and is introduced to Steed. The Colonel, his mind gone, believes he is still in Kalaya. After dinner Trent is visited by Fleming, who, not seeing Steed, begins to tell Trent that the two men are still sleeping. When Trent indicates Steed's presence Fleming leaves. Meanwhile, Emma, still keeping watch on the two sleeping men, begins to

read a book on Black Magic and dozes off. Back at Rawlings' home, Steed notices two natives arrive carrying a litter. He tries to leave, but Trent orders him to stay at gunpoint. Next morning, he rises early and manages to phone Emma. She tells him that Swain has disappeared as well as the two patients. Razafi creeps into the house and tells Steed to meet him in the garden at midnight. There, Steed is startled to find that Razafi has a perfect Oxford accent and is a member of the Kalayan Intelligence Service. He tells Steed that Trent and Fleming have grudges against his country. Razafi then takes Steed to a hut where Kendrick and Gibson are sleeping. Suddenly Lala springs out and stabs him, before running off. Trent appears, takes some papers out of Razafi's pocket and congratulates Steed on killing a spy. He then takes Steed to a laboratory and explains how he and Fleming have bred a new kind of tsetse fly immune to all known insecticides. They will take thousands of them to Kalaya, where they will breed in their millions and desolate the land. He and Fleming will then take over the country. Trent hears Lala and calls to her. Steed prepares to run, but Lala turns out to be Emma in a sarong. Steed fights with Trent and Emma runs off with the canister of tsetse flies but is cornered by Fleming and Swain – the brain behind the plan. Emma is saved by Steed swinging through the trees Tarzan-style to her rescue. In the cold, drizzly English day outside they open the canister and let the rain fall onto the flies – washing away the deadly plans of Swain and his henchmen. Having poured cold water on their enemy, Steed and Emma leave the scene in a rowing boat – Emma at the oars!

THE GIRL FROM AUNTIE

In which Steed almost outbids himself – and Emma is a bird in a gilded cage

By Roger Marshall

John Steed	**Patrick Macnee**
Emma Peel	**Diana Rigg**
Georgie Price-Jones	**Liz Frazer**
Gregorio Auntie	**Alfred Burke**
Arkwright	**Bernard Cribbins**
Ivanov	**David Bauer**
Aunt Hetty	**Sylvia Coleridge**

Directed by Roy Baker

STEED RETURNS from holiday to find a shapely blonde impersonating Emma. He follows her to a theatrical agency and, when questioned, she explains her real name is Georgie Price-Jones, and she got the job after answering a newspaper advertisement. They search the agency, and find the body of the agent – with a large knitting needle protruding from his back. Two other men were present when Georgie got the job, but when Steed tracks them down, they have also been killed with knitting needles. A cheque – part payment of Georgie's fee – with three signatures leads to three more bodies and three more knitting needles. Georgie now recalls that her Emma Peel outfit came from a theatrical costumiers, Jacques Brothers. They find three of the brothers dead, but the fourth manages to gasp, 'Auntie . . . Auntie did it,' before dying. At that moment, an old lady arrives carrying a bag of knitting. She says that she is Auntie Hetty, favourite auntie of the brothers. She then tells Steed that the needles could only have come from the Arkwright Knitting Circle, and she takes him to the circle where Steed meets Mr Arkwright, who complains that the needles were stolen from his storeroom. On the way out, Steed meets Colonel Ivanov, a Russian agent, coming out of Art Incorporated – the next office. Steed waits until he has left, then returns to the Circle, where through a ventilation shaft he hears a voice order the elimination of Mrs Peel. Meanwhile at her apartment, reading a book on self-defence, Georgie doesn't see the heavily-veiled old woman enter carrying the now familiar knitting needles. When attacked, Georgie puts the book to good use, before escaping into the kitchen.

Posing as an art connoisseur, Steed visits Art Incorporated, saying that he was recommended by Colonel Ivanov, but he cannot see the boss. The boss, however, has observed Steed, and orders his investigation. Later that day, Steed returns and breaks into the storeroom. He is discovered by the owner, Gregorio Auntie, who says that his organisation can get hold of anything – for a price. Steed offers to buy Mrs Peel, but Auntie tells him that her sale is already contracted. Steed and Georgie lay a trap for Ivanov, and once cornered, he admits he is Mrs Peel's purchaser. Steed arranges for his expulsion and once again offers to buy Mrs Peel. Auntie, however, still refuses to sell to Steed directly and arranges an auction instead. The bidding is fierce, but Steed's offer outbids them all. As Steed and Georgie are about to leave, the veiled old lady arrives with proof of Steed's real identity, and only quick action from Georgie prevents Steed from receiving one of the deadly knitting needles. As Steed battles with Gregorio Auntie, the old woman rushes off to kill the real Emma. Dispatching Gregorio, Steed follows. He finds her at the Knitting Circle and reveals her to be a man. The killer now tells Steed how to get to Emma. Steed, with Georgie in tow, arrives in time to see Emma struggling with the receptionist to get the keys to the cage in which she is a prisoner. Emma finally wins. Released from the cage, Steed now introduces Mrs Peel (Georgie) to the real Mrs Peel. The Avengers leave the scene in a cramped bubble-car and are soon overtaken by Georgie at the wheel of Steed's Bentley!

THE 13TH HOLE

In which Steed finds a bogey – and Emma gets a birdie

By Tony Williamson

John Steed	**Patrick Macnee**
Emma Peel	**Diana Rigg**
Reed	**Patrick Allen**
Colonel Watson	**Hugh Manning**
Adams	**Peter Jones**
Jackson	**Victor Maddern**
Collins	**Francis Matthews**
Professor Minley	**Norman Wynne**
Man on TV screen	**Richard Marner**

Directed by Roy Baker

STEED AND EMMA'S investigations into the murder of a colleague lead them to the Craigleigh Golf Club. There they decide the people they will have to watch are scientist Dr Adams, Collins the club pro, Jackson the caddy master and two members named Reed and Colonel Watson. Emma plays solo behind Reed and Adams up to the 13th hole. While they are playing on the green, she waits below. Suddenly a driverless caddy car plunges down the hill towards her and she just escapes. But Reed and Adams have completely disappeared. Steed meanwhile searches the club office and finds Reed's bag, containing a .303 rifle covered like a club, and a box of ammunition. Steed meets Emma in the bar and then Adams and Reed appear. Suddenly the lights begin to flicker, before going out. When they come on Adams and Reed have gone. Steed and Emma search independently for them on the course, even though it is dark. Emma is attacked by Collins, whom she subdues. As they are talking, a golf ball strikes Collins on the forehead and kills him. As she crawls away, Emma notices that she is on the 13th green. Across the course she sees the outline of a strange vehicle with what appears to be a gun turret jutting from the front. She eventually finds the vehicle in the staff office. It is a caddy car with a large telescope mounted in the front. Inside the cart are charts and maps of stars and constellations. Reed and Jackson enter and she hides behind a desk. Reed says he has been drawn against Steed in the club tournament and he tells Jackson that he must win, by fair means or foul. Jackson produces a gun which fires golf balls by compressed air and Emma realises that this is how Collins was killed. During the tournament, Emma hides on the course and helps Steed to win. Reed stalks off the green in disgust. Emma now joins Steed and as they talk, a golf ball strikes Steed, who falls to the ground. A specially-padded golf cap saves his life, and undeterred, he arranges to play the next round of the tournament – this time his opponent is Adams. Emma rings the Royal Observatory to check on the photographs she has taken of the astral charts. One chart shows a spaceship, Vostok 3, orbiting the earth. It is timed to be over England at four o'clock that afternoon. She goes to tell Steed but is captured by Reed. He then takes her to the 13th green where he moves a switch hidden in the grass, which parts to reveal a chamber below. Underground, the Colonel is watching a screen, on which thousands of miles away, men are seen waiting for Adams to arrive and pass on his scientific secrets by satellite. Steed and Adams meanwhile arrive at the 12th hole, where Adams asks Steed to hole out while he looks for a lost ball. Suspicious, Steed leaves his ball on the lip of the hole and sends another ball across the green to knock it in. There is a tremendous explosion, watched with glee through a periscope by the occupants of the underground shelter. The door opens and Adams walks in – followed by Steed. After a furious fight, Steed and Emma soon round up the gang, but in the ensuing mayhem, the Colonel escapes – only to be brought down by a beautifully-driven ball from Steed. Steed and Mrs Peel depart in a golf buggy.

QUICK-QUICK-SLOW DEATH

In which Steed has two left feet –
and Emma dances with danger

By Robert Banks Stewart

John Steed	**Patrick Macnee**
Emma Peel	**Diana Rigg**
Lucille Banks	**Eunice Gayson**
Ivor Bracewell	**Maurice Kaufmann**
Chester Read	**Larry Cross**
Peever	**James Belchamber**
Bernard	**Colin Ellis**
Willi Fehr	**Michael Peake**

Directed by James Hill

WHEN WILLI FEHR, a foreign agent, is involved in a road accident, the body of a man is hidden in the pram he was pushing. Having gained nothing from interrogating Fehr, Steed and Emma have to rely on two small clues they find on the body. Emma goes to check out a tattooist's, while Steed, convinced that the man's evening suit was hired, finds the hire company. Emma learns that the dead man's name was Peever. Steed finds the costumiers, but the assistant is murdered as he searches for the information in the back room of his shop. In the meantime, Willi Fehr has been shot while trying to escape. Steed goes to an address provided by the manager of Peever's bank, and narrowly escapes death when he opens the door – it is false and above a building site. Following up another clue, Emma visits the Terpsichorean Training Techniques – a dancing school run by Lucille Banks, and gets a job as an instructress. One of the first students she meets is introduced as Mr Peever. Emma decides to find out if he is genuine, and leaves a pair of the dead man's shoes in his locker. When Lucille sees Peever trying on the shoes she hurriedly takes them from him. Steed meanwhile visits the tattooist's shop, but he arrives too late to save the man, who has been shot. Before dying, the man tattooed a message on the skin of a large garlic sausage, reading 'The killer has a rose tattoo on his right wrist'. Emma is trying to become friends with Peever, but he says he will soon be graduating. Knowing him to be an atrocious dancer, Emma asks a fellow instructress what's happening. She is told that certain students are chosen for graduation, they receive a diploma, then disappear. Believing that he will get a lead at the dancing school, Steed enrols as a student. He tells Lucille that he is quite alone in the world, and she decides that he warrants her own personal attention. Emma learns that a man called Bernard has given all the students dancing shoes. Before she can visit him, however, he is given a face-lift – with a bowl of quick-setting plaster. At the school, Lucille tells an accomplice to inform someone called The Commander that Steed will be their next victim. At the Gala Dance, Steed tells Emma that he suspects the school is being used to infiltrate foreign agents into the country. Each agent, he says, assumes the identity of a lonely student who is then disposed of by Lucille and her friends. Lucille announces a dancing competition, and tells everyone to don masks. She insists on partnering

Steed, and slowly guides him towards a large display unit, behind which is an agent waiting to take his place. Steed realises what's happening and manages to signal to Emma – whose partner, Bracewell, has a rose tattoo on his right wrist. Working in perfect unison, they manoeuvre their partners until Emma manages to get Bracewell behind the display unit. She emerges with a different partner. In a game of change-your-partners, Steed joins up with Emma and together they make for the door. They find their way blocked by Lucille, Peever and The Commander – alias Read, the school music director. With a quick-quick left and right, The Avengers soon overcome the group and dance out of the school in true terpsichorean manner, to a Viennese waltz.

Steed opens a door to nowhere in Quick-Quick-Slow Death.

THE DANGER MAKERS

In which Steed joins a secret society – and Emma walks the plank

By Roger Marshall

John Steed	**Patrick Macnee**
Emma Peel	**Diana Rigg**
Major Robertson	**Nigel Davenport**
Dr Harold Long	**Douglas Wilmer**
Col Adams	**Fabia Drake**
Peters	**Moray Watson**
Lieut Stanhope	**Adrian Ropes**
RAF officer	**Richard Coleman**
Gordon Lamble	**John Gatrell**

Directed by Charles Crichton

WHEN GENERAL Woody Groves is killed in a crash, after apparently taking part in a chicken-run, and Gordon Lamble, Head of the Chemical Warfare Establishment, is injured while trying to scale St Paul's, Steed and Emma are briefed to find out what's going on. They visit Harold Long, consultant to the Psychological Warfare Department, who says that there have been a number of such inexplicable cases recently. Leaving Emma to keep an eye on the injured Lamble, Steed visits General Groves' Battalion Headquarters. There he meets Major Robertson who tells him he cannot understand why the General should have taken part in such a dangerous stunt. At the hospital, Emma and Long discover Lamble on the narrow ledge outside his window. Long stops Emma from helping Lamble, and soon he returns to his bed unaided. Later, a noise from Lamble's room attracts Steed's and Emma's attention. They enter the room and find Lamble dead. Following another clue, Steed visits Wing Commander Watson of the RAF but arrives in time to see him put a high-speed jet through a series of crazy stunts. One of them goes wrong, and the plane plummets to the ground. On Steed's instructions, Emma introduces herself to Major Robertson. She convinces him that she wants a more exciting life. Steed's suspicions are soon justified when Robertson acts favourably to Emma. Steed receives a phone call from a Lieutenant Stanhope of Groves' Battalion, who claims he has important information. When Steed arrives he finds Stanhope dead. He also finds a postcard of an army museum called Manton House. He goes there and meets the owner, Colonel Adams – an elderly ex-women's army officer whose only interest is military history. He also meets the sinister Peters, who talks to Steed as if he expects him to know all about the secret society of which he claims membership. Major Robertson tells Emma that he knows of a place where she will find the excitement she craves – Manton. Believing Steed to be a member of the organisation, Robertson tells Emma that the society is called The Danger Makers, and that members only live for the excitement of mortal danger. He adds that he will arrange for Emma to be initiated. For her test, Emma has to negotiate a metallic ring along live electrical poles – one slip spells instant death. It is no sooner over when the principal of the society appears – it is Harold Long. Steed is unmasked and he and Emma are thrown into a cell where Long tells them that he formed the society when he discovered that many ex-servicemen craved danger as a drug addict craves a fix. With such men, he says, he will fulfil Operation Grand Slam – the theft of the Crown Jewels. Steed and Emma manage to break free and Steed challenges Long to a fight. Long, however, tries to escape through the test room, but becomes entangled in the complex of wires and poles and is electrocuted. Another case successfully completed, Steed and Emma zoom into the sunset in go-carts.

A TOUCH OF BRIMSTONE

In which Steed joins the Hellfire Club – and Emma becomes the Queen of Sin

By Brian Clemens

John Steed	**Patrick Macnee**
Emma Peel	**Diana Rigg**
John Cartney	**Peter Wyngarde**
Lord Darcy	**Colin Jeavons**
Sara	**Carol Cleveland**
Horace	**Robert Cawdron**
Willy Frant	**Jeremy Young**

Directed by James Hill

AN IMPORTANT diplomat from the Eastern bloc is held up to ridicule before a television audience of millions and a massive oil deal is cancelled when the Sheik is made to look like a monkey. National prestige, not to mention big business, is in danger and The Avengers are ordered to take a closer look. Steed tells Emma that other hoaxes, such as plastic spiders in the Ambassador's soup, and something quite outrageous in a diplomat's bed, have been played. The only suspect is the Honourable John Cleverly Cartney, and Steed tells Emma to investigate. From the outset, Cartney is attracted to Emma. Believing her story about collecting for charity, he immediately donates a thousand guineas, and invites her to dinner. At dinner, their conversation is interrupted by the arrival of Lord Darcy and while the men are talking quietly, Emma searches Cartney's desk. All she can find is a diary with the entry 'Today – 4.30 – Friendship'. In the meantime, Steed searches Lord Darcy's office, and finds several pairs of scissors – all made of rubber. As he is leaving, he is interrupted by Horace, Darcy's manservant, but Steed overpowers him and makes his escape. Steed is puzzled by the rubber scissors, until Emma tells him of the entry in Cartney's diary. Steed and Emma tear across London to the newly built Hall of Friendship, but arrive too late – another hoax has been played, this time with more serious consequences. While performing the opening ceremony a VIP has been electrocuted by a current passing through the ribbon. Emma goes to see Cartney again, while Steed goes in search of Lord Darcy. He finds him drunk, and sets to work on him. He soon confesses to his part in the hoax, but insists he didn't know that murder was intended. Apparently, such jokes are part of the rules of the Hellfire Club. Emma attends the next meeting of the Hellfire Club at Cartney's home, and sees that it is an exact replica of the infamous 18th-century organisation, and all the members wear Regency costume. In the company of her host, she is forced to watch as two men fight before the members. Suddenly an agitated Lord Darcy arrives, and accuses Cartney of duplicity and murder. Cartney calmly orders a meeting of the 'Superior' members and they, with Darcy, withdraw. Later, as they stand over the coffin containing Darcy's mortal remains, Emma tells Steed that she is sure that he was murdered by the 'Superior' members of the Hellfire Club. Steed makes immediate arrangements to join the club. At the next meeting, Steed is introduced to Cartney, who is suspicious of Steed, and makes him take a number of tests. Afterwards Steed pretends to leave but eavesdrops, and hears Cartney tell the others that their next coup will be so outrageous that the whole country will be up in arms. It will occur during the next evening's Gala meeting. At the meeting, Steed sees two members carrying a sedan chair. Emma follows them deep into the catacombs beneath the house, where they unload a box of high explosives. Hurrying away to find Steed, she meets Cartney who tells her that he has something special planned for her. Meanwhile, Sara, Cartney's ex-girlfriend, tells Steed of a number of secret underground passages beneath the house. One, she says, leads directly to the government-owned Calverstone House. Their conversation is interrupted by the arrival of Cartney who introduces 'The Queen of Sin'. It is Emma, dressed in a corset and boots, and carrying a live snake! Dancing with her, Steed suggests that Cartney is going to blow up Calverstone House, where three foreign Prime Ministers are staying. His fears become greater when Emma reminds him that the original Hell Raisers were dedicated to overthrowing the government. Steed is suddenly exposed when Horace, Darcy's manservant, recognises him. A member called Frant challenges him to a duel, and as they fight, Emma slips away, followed by Cartney. In the catacombs Emma makes short work of the men guarding the explosives, but she is confronted by her host carrying a whip. Suddenly she hurls the rapier she is holding at him. As she stands over Cartney's dead body, Steed races in. Together they board an 18th-century coach and exit laughing.

WHAT THE BUTLER SAW

In which Steed becomes a Gentleman's Gentleman – and Emma faces a fate worse than death

By Brian Clemens

John Steed	**Patrick Macnee**
Emma Peel	**Diana Rigg**
Hemming	**Thorley Walters**
Benson	**John Le Mesurier**
Group Capt Miles	**Dennis Quilley**
Maj Gen Goddard	**Kynaston Reeve**
Brig Goddard	**Howard Marion Crawford**
Vice Admiral Willows	**Humphrey Lestocq**
Sgt Moran	**Ewan Hooper**
Barber	**David Swift**
Reeves	**Norman Scace**

Directed by Bill Bain

IN SEARCH of information, Steed visits his barber, a known double agent. The man says that one of three men – Admiral Willows, Brigadier Ponsonby-Goddard or Group Captain Miles – is selling secret defence plans. Steed settles back while the barber sees to another customer. His peace is soon shattered when the barber's body slumps beside him, a pair of scissors sticking out of his back. The rest of the shop is empty. Dressed in full naval rig and sporting a beard, Steed visits Admiral Willows, who is obsessed with horse racing. At Brigadier Ponsonby-Goddard's home, Steed, now in army uniform, meets the Brigadier's semi-senile father, Major General Goddard, who accuses his son of treachery. Before Steed can substantiate the old man's charge, the Brigadier himself arrives. When Steed mentions the accusations, the Brigadier says the charge is a result of his failure to join the cavalry regiment as all his forebears had done. As Steed leaves he overhears Reeves, Goddard's butler, arranging on the telephone to meet someone in the Brigadier's study that night. From one of Group Captain Miles' aides, Steed learns that the officer is dedicated to his work. Only one thing shares his attention – girls! After arranging for Emma to meet Miles, Steed returns to the Brigadier's home but arrives too late. The butler is dead. Steed manages to withstand a savage attack by Reeves' killer, but cannot prevent the murderer's escape. Operation Fascination is begun by Emma. She arranges for photographs of herself to be planted all over Miles' house and office. Everywhere he goes, Emma's likeness is staring at him. Soon Miles is fascinated to the point of desperation! When they finally meet, Miles invites Emma to dinner. When Steed hears that the replacement for the dead Reeves has come from the Butler's and Gentleman's Gentlemen Association, he enrols as a student. The principal is Hemming – butler to Group Captain Miles – who says his work at the Association is part-time. Hemming is pleased with Steed's progress, but another instructor – Benson, butler to Admiral Willows – isn't so happy. He has seen Steed somewhere, but cannot think when it was. Steed learns that Hemming has refused a handsome offer to leave Miles' staff. Later Benson catches Steed searching the laundry, where he has found Hemming taking a bath – in an electric washing machine! Benson tells Steed he knows he is a fake, but offers him the chance of making a great deal of money as Hemming's replacement on Miles' staff. Steed accepts and starts work in time to welcome Emma to dinner. Emma needs all her wits about her to deal with the amorous officer, but with Steed's help – he repeatedly interrupts – she manages to hold Miles at bay. At the same time, she discovers that Miles is actually very honest, and is bored playing the gay lover. While Miles is away at a conference, Steed is told to spill wine over Miles' uniform as soon as he returns. Mystified, Steed follows his instructions, and taking the uniform to the kitchen, he is met by Benson who orders him to hand it over. With Emma's help, Steed follows Benson to the B&GG Assocation. After a search, they find three torn uniforms – one naval, one army and one RAF – and three tiny tape recorders. They realise that the missing tapes must contain the defence secrets. They continue to search, but are caught by Benson and Sergeant Moran – an army barman from the Three Services Club – who admits to being the ringleader. As Benson is about to kill them, a bugle call rings through the building, and they hear General Goddard's order to charge. In the confusion that follows, Steed disarms Benson while Emma takes care of Moran. After the battle, the General explains that he became suspicious when he saw Benson with his son's uniform. A job well done, Steed and Emma take off in an army helicopter, with Steed teasing Emma, 'You're dying to say it – the Butler did it!'

Emma disposes of a villain in **What the Butler Saw**

THE HOUSE THAT JACK BUILT

In which Steed takes a wrong turning – and Emma holds the key to all

By Brian Clemens

John Steed	**Patrick Macnee**
Emma Peel	**Diana Rigg**
Professor Keller	**Michael Goodliffe**
Burton	**Griffith Davies**
Withers	**Michael Wynne**

Directed by Don Leaver

WHEN EMMA is told that a mysterious Uncle Jack has died and left her his country house, she goes to inspect her new estate. Puzzled by her good fortune, Steed calls Mrs Peel's solicitor. His fears are confirmed – the man denies all knowledge of Emma's Uncle Jack or any legacy. Quickly Steed makes a second call to his friends. Emma's journey is interrupted by a strange character called Withers, who is dressed in a scout-master's uniform and begs a lift, saying that he will be satisfied with Emma's destination. Mrs Peel finds the house dark and empty. Papers are strewn over a desk in the study. They are sheets of her solicitor's writing paper, and bear evidence of forged signatures. A telephone rings, but when she answers it all she hears is asthmatic breathing, before the line goes dead. As she hurries from the study, she is terrified to see that the hall has disappeared. In its place is a kind of perpetual motion machine with corridors leading off in several directions. Turning back to the study, she finds that it, too, has been replaced by corridors. Meanwhile, Steed decides to follow Emma to the house. Emma is now finding that whichever way she turns, she ends up in front of the perpetual motion machine. When she finds a scout's shoulder patch, she is convinced that Withers is her captor, and tries to escape. Suddenly the silence is broken by strange noises – a sinister laugh, the shuffling of feet, the tinkling of a music box. Desperate now, Emma starts to run, and finds herself back in the study. Lying on the floor is Withers, dead. Emma examines the door, and finds a small plug in the frame. She presses it and the whole room starts to spin. When it stops, she is in another room, and sees a huge photograph of herself. Under it is a sign reading 'Welcome to an exhibition of the late Emma Peel'. A strange voice tells Emma that she will find the answer to the riddle in the exhibition. Searching, she finds newspaper coverage of her life – her take-over of her father's empire after his death, her success, and the dismissal of Professor Keller, the company's automation expert, with whose plans for the replacement of men by machines Emma had disagreed. Suddenly Emma recognises the voice. It is Keller's! He tells Emma that she is prisoner within a house that is a huge machine. It is, says Keller, the justification of his theories. Trying to escape, Emma breaks into what appears to be a machine room, and sees a man she thinks

is Keller. After a ferocious fight, she finds that he is another prisoner – terrified, emaciated, and completely mad. She attempts to interrogate him but learns nothing. Suddenly he attacks her with a shotgun. She manages to divert the shot, and knocks him out. Then she sees that where the shot has damaged the wall the outline of a door is revealed. Quickly, she breaks into what is apparently the central control room, to be greeted by Keller's voice, and his face on a large screen. The voice tells her that her discovery will do her no good – the voice she hears is a recording, and Keller is dead. Breaking through the screen, she finds the body of Keller inside a large glass case. The voice tells her that the house is a vast indestructible machine from which she can't escape – a machine that will tend to her every need and still be functioning when she herself is quite mad. Release will only come when she uses the key provided to gain access to a special suicide box. After a brief hysterical outburst, Emma forces herself to think logically and goes in search of the madman. He gives her shotgun shells, from which she makes a bomb. Then the man makes another attack, but is killed when he falls into the suicide box prepared by Keller for Emma. Using the bomb, Emma stops the giant computer that controls the machine. A door quietly opens and Emma leaves the room to find a worried Steed waiting in the hall. As they ride away on a tandem, Steed explains that Withers was a friend of his, sent to keep an eye on her.

From **The House That Jack Built.**

A SENSE OF HISTORY

In which Steed dons a gown – and Emma becomes a Don

By Martin Woodhouse

John Steed	**Patrick Macnee**
Emma Peel	**Diana Rigg**
Richard Carlyon	**Nigel Stock**
Dr Henge	**John Barron**
Grindley	**John Glyn-Jones**
Professor Acheson	**John Ringham**
Duboys	**Patrick Mower**
John Pettit	**Robin Phillips**
Millerson	**Peter Blythe**
Allen	**Peter Bourne**
Marianne	**Jacqueline Pearce**

Directed by Peter Graham Scott

WHEN JAMES BROOM is found slumped across the front seat of his car on a lonely forest road with an arrow in his back, John Steed is sent to investigate. Broom, an economist, was author of the visionary Europa Plan to eliminate world poverty. When Steed arrives, he finds Richard Carlyon, Broom's right-hand man, rummaging through the boot of Broom's car. He emerges with Broom's briefcase. Carlyon tells Steed that Broom was on his way to a university when he was murdered. The briefcase offers no more clues, except that it is full of papers, all headed 'St Bodes'. Steed decides to call in Emma. He wants her to lecture at St Bodes. Emma soon establishes herself and after hearing a history lecture given by Dr Henge, she notices a group of students led by the insolent and cynical Duboys. Enquiring among the staff, she learns that Duboys is a brilliant student, and his insolence is put down to Rag Week high spirits. Emma is unconvinced, and her first meeting with Duboys and his gang strengthens her suspicions. Among the papers in Broom's briefcase, Steed discovers a thesis entitled Economics and a Sense of History, bearing the college crest but no author's name. A neo-fascist argument, it is diametrically opposed to all Broom stood for. Broom was on his way to see an enemy, not a friend. In the hope of discovering the author, Steed arrives at St Bodes and meets the friendly university archivist, Grindley. Dr Henge has discovered that Steed is not a member of the faculty and has no right to be there – a fact that has gone unnoticed by Duboys. Steed's investigations are hampered further when Grindley is found dead. That night Steed visits Carlyon, who lives in a caravan on the edge of a wood, and whom Steed believes will be the next target. He is right – they are soon attacked. Arrows whizz by the caravan they are hiding under. Steed draws his gun and the assailants flee. But they leave a clue – a photograph of Marianne, the girlfriend of a member of Duboys' clique. Next day, Steed corners Marianne and her boyfriend, Pettit, who agrees to help unmask the real leader of the group, the man who gives Duboys his orders. That night, Pettit dies when some heavy library shelves fall on him. The following day Carlyon, Emma and Steed are invited to the Rag Night Ball. It is in fancy dress and the theme is Robin Hood. At the ball, Marianne, disillusioned by Pettit's death, reveals that an attempt will be made on Carlyon that evening. Their leader will arrive as Friar Tuck, then they will dispose of Carlyon quietly. Once he is dead, the Europa Plan is finished and Friar Tuck and his Merrie Men will have changed the destiny of Europe. Steed's plans are thrown into chaos when three Friar Tucks arrive. However, Steed and Emma discover the author, and their real protagonist. It is Grindley, who feigned his death in order to avert suspicion. A furious battle breaks out from which Steed and Emma emerge the victors, then the successful pair ride merrily into the sunset on a motorcycle and sidecar.

HOW TO SUCCEED ... AT MURDER

In which Steed becomes a perfect boss – and Emma goes seeking charm

By Brian Clemens

John Steed	**Patrick Macnee**
Emma Peel	**Diana Rigg**
Mary Merryweather	**Sarah Lawson**
Sara Penny	**Angela Browne**
Gladys Murkle	**Anna Cunningham**
Henry Throgbottom	**Artto Norris**
Joshua Rudge	**Jerome Willis**
J J Hooter	**Christopher Benjamin**
Sir George Morton	**Kevin Brennan**
Jack Finlay	**Robert Dean**

Directed by Don Leaver

WHEN TEN top city executives are murdered within a few days, Steed is puzzled. The only link is the prominence of the victims in commerce, but that alone could hardly be the motive. Embezzlement is ruled out after the murder of Sir George Morton when Steed checks with Morton's accountant, Joshua Rudge, that everything is in order. The murder of executive Jack Finlay gives The Avengers a lead. In the car in which Finlay's corpse was discovered, there is a heavy scent of perfume that reminds Steed of Rudge's office. He searches the office that night, but is attacked and knocked out. Meanwhile, Emma collects a sample of the perfume in a footpump and takes it to the perfumier J J Hooter. He identifies it as one of his exclusive lines and promises to prepare a list of customers for Emma that afternoon. When she returns, Hooter is dead and his secretary, Gladys Murkle, has taken charge of the business. She refuses to help Emma. Steed now discovers that each of the victims had a complex office system only understood by their secretaries. In each case, the executive's death meant promotion for the secretary.

Once again, Steed calls at Rudge's office. His secretary, Sara, explains that Rudge is away on holiday and she is in charge in his absence. Steed introduces himself as a millionaire who is looking for a part-time secretary to help him set up a new business. Sara accepts the bait. Meanwhile, Emma becomes a secretary to Mary, formerly Sir George Morton's secretary. Following her one night, Emma discovers that Mary attends a keep-fit class run by Henry and Henrietta Throgbottom. Emma tells Steed and next day joins the class, while Steed unearths an interesting fact – Henrietta Throgbottom died in 1939. Emma soon impresses Mary with her efficiency, and is invited to attend the advanced classes. She soon discovers that the keep-fit school is a cover for a group of modern-day suffragettes intent on the elmination of all men. The group meets in a room at the gymnasium. Henrietta is the leader but never actually attends the meetings. Instead, she is represented by photographs of her when she was a ballerina, and a life-size doll sitting in an alcove. The doll speaks, and the voice seems to come from the alcove. Henry is present, but the women treat him as a menial. Just as Emma is about to be accepted into the group, Gladys Murkle enters and recognises her. The group now have a new problem – they have never killed a woman before. Meanwhile, Sara makes an unsuccessful attempt on Steed's life, but through his expertise in the art of tickling Steed forces her to reveal all about the group. He hurries to the gymnasium and arrives in time to rescue Emma, liberate Rudge – who had been held by the women because of his accountancy skills – and expose Henrietta as Henry. He formed the group in the bitter memory of the way businessmen ruined his late wife's career. The illusion of her voice had been simple ventriloquism. The closer finds The Avengers swotting up on the ventriloquial art, then falling over backwards as the caravan in which they sit is towed away at speed.

Mrs Peel and Steed stave off the threat of modern-day suffragettes bent on the elimination of all men in How To Succeed . . . at Murder.

HONEY FOR THE PRINCE

In which Steed becomes a Genie – and Emma joins a harem

By Brian Clemens

John Steed	Patrick Macnee
Emma Peel	Diana Rigg
Ponsonby-Hopkirk	Ron Moody
Prince Ali	Zia Mohyeddin
Arkadi	George Pastell
Vincent	Roland Curram
Grand Vizier	Bruno Barnabe
B Bumble	Ken Parry
Ronny Wescott	Jon Laurimore
Postman	Reg Pritchard
Bernie	Peter Diamond
Eurasian girl	Carmen Dene
George Reed	Richard Graydon

Directed by James Hill

RONNY WESCOTT – a colleague of Steed's, dies of gun-shot wounds in Steed's flat. Before dying, he tells Steed that the files on the case are in George Reed's flat, and that Reed, a fellow agent, is also dead. Steed visits the flat, but it has been broken into and Steed, caught unawares, is attacked. He fights with the intruder, who flees. The intruder has burnt all the files. Searching the flat further, Steed finds a jar of honey in cupboard. Back at his apartment, Steed discovers a present from Reed, posted before his death. It is a jar of honey from B Bumble & Company. Dispatching Emma to Bumble's, Steed returns to Reed's flat, where he discovers that Reed was a member of QQF. Quite Quite Fantastic Inc is run by one Ponsonby-Hopkirk. Its purpose is to create people's fantasies, with the aid of theatrical devices, which they can then live. From further enquiries Steed discovers that Ronny Wescott was also a client of QQF. His fantasy was to be chief eunuch in a harem. Meanwhile, Emma learns from B Bumble, a honey specialist, that the Bahrainian Embassy is a major customer. After leaving the shop, however, an attempt is made to kill her. She soon dispatches her assailant and returns to the shop. She finds Bumble dead, but his killer has left a clue – an application form to QQF. Steed has now discovered that Wescott's current assignment was to protect a Bahrainian Prince Ali, together with his full entourage, on a visit to London to sign over oil concessions in return for military protection. Obviously his assassination would give the contract to rivals! They hurry to QQF, only to find that Ponsonby-Hopkirk has been shot while staging the fantasy of the assassination of the Prince. Knowing that an assassination is being planned, but with no details, Steed decides to visit Prince Ali. Striking up an immediate friendship with him, Steed discovers that all the Prince's wives love honey and, as a favour, he has ordered forty man-size jars of it for them. Steed cannot examine the jars because the honey is in the Prince's harem and no man can enter. Steed is invited to dine with the Prince that night. Suspecting that the attempt on his life is to be made that evening, Steed takes Emma along, dressed as a Middle Eastern dancing girl. The Prince is well pleased with her dancing and when Steed offers Emma for his harem, the Prince gladly accepts and she is led away. Once there, she immediately begins to search for the assassin. Meanwhile, Prince Ali, excited by the thought of Emma, decides to retire early that night. Steed tries desperately to stall him, but fails. As the Prince enters the harem, Emma spots the assassin about to plunge a dagger into the Prince's back. She throws her new husband to one side and attacks the assassin. The noise of the fighting alerts the harem guards and they rush in to protect the Prince. In gratitude, he offers to grant Steed anything he wishes. He chooses Mrs Peel and he and Emma ride happily away on a magic carpet – precariously perched on the roof of a speeding van!

Steed versus masked assailant in Honey for the Prince.

This is all that remains of a sequence made on the set of Honey for the Prince, *never shown in the UK, to alert American viewers that* The Avengers – *in colour – would soon return!*

THE AVENGERS IN COLOUR

BY NOW, *The Avengers* had a worldwide audience of over 30 million viewers in 40 countries. However, it had still not sold to the vitally important American market, although two American networks had seen a number of episodes and expressed their interest. One of these, NBC, liked what they had seen but stated that they were not yet ready for such an extreme series, with its very British flavour. The most serious difficulty, they felt, was the inability of the great American audience to understand and appreciate the light, flippant, throwaway dialogue between Steed and Mrs Peel. They thought, however that Diana Rigg was 'remarkably good', and perhaps the biggest selling point in the series, both in the conception of her character and the way she was playing it. Another consideration was that *The Avengers* was in monochrome. (Partly because Britain and other countries were still transmitting in black and white, and partly to save money, ABC had decided to produce the first filmed series in monochrome.) The American networks, however, were moving rapidly to colour and, as NBC had announced their intention to go entirely to colour, the other networks, ABC and CBS, would clearly have to follow suit.

It was then that ABC Television made the biggest and most far-reaching deal ever made for a single British television series. Concerned that their product would be left out in the cold with little chance of recovering its production costs, they decided to take over the sales effort themselves, and their managing director, Howard Thomas, together with another director, Bob Norris, flew to New York for discussions with the two networks which had earlier shown interest. They were offering two things. Either, if a network would buy the first 13 episodes in monochrome, they would immediately order the second 13 to be made in colour; or, if a network would buy the first series, ABC would give them an option on a second, colour, series, which would go into production immediately after the completion of the first 26 episodes.

After meetings in London and New York, Bob Norris secured a sale on the second proposal to the American Broadcasting Company, which would bring four-and-a-half million dollars to Britain over an 18-month period and guaranteed *The Avengers* a peak-time US network, coast-to-coast transmission slot starting in January (which meant that the programme would be seen on US television screens continuously for over 18 months). A simultaneous Canadian renewal for *The Avengers* was also arranged by Mr Norris during his trip – ensuring that the whole of North America would see the programme more or less simultaneously with British audiences.

'The news from America confirms our confidence in the show, and Julian Wintle and his team,' said Howard Thomas at the time. 'It gives particular pleasure to us all, because the really significant factor in the success of *The Avengers* is that the series is one hundred percent British in conception, content, casting and style.'

While these negotiations were taking place, other problems beset ABC and associated producer and script editor, Brian Clemens.

Rediffusion, the company transmitting *The Avengers* in the London area, were demanding cuts in the story called *A Touch of Brimstone*. One of the highlights was a scene where Emma Peel, posing as the Queen of Sin, is whipped by the leader of a modern-day Hellfire Club. Deciding that as the programme would be seen by a family audience before 9 p.m., the whipping scene had to go, Rediffusion called for the scene to be cut. Quite happy with the original version, ABC nevertheless removed the sequence, but flatly refused to make further cuts. (Apparently even hardened studio technicians shared Rediffusion's concern over the skimpy costume worn – and designed by – Diana Rigg in the story; a tightly-laced, figure-hugging, black Edwardian corset, worn with knee-high leather boots and an iron collar with 3-inch spikes bristling from it!) The same scene caused a furore when the story was screened in America. 'The scene where Diana Rigg was attacked four times by a man wielding a whip had to be cut down to one crack of the whip,' said Clemens.

Emma Peel trapped in the catacombs below the **Hellfire Club,** *in* **A Touch of Brimstone.**

Meanwhile, Brian Clemens was fighting a battle of his own. Having initiated the use of the, by this time, world famous *Avengers* 'teaser' and 'tag' scenes, he was now being asked to remove these from all completed episodes and edit all references to them from further scripts. ABC found them unsuitable. Reminding the company that they had agreed that the tag scenes would be regarded as a separate entity – almost a mini-series on their own, a build-up joke, designed to keep the viewer tuned in to the very end, a trade mark, in fact – Clemens fought for the right to retain them and place them where they logically belonged, as part and parcel of the closing credits; the ultimate seal on *The Avengers'* style. Adding that the popularity of the previous series had been achieved *because* it had something no other series had; *because* it had bent (and sometimes broken) the rules and had its own unique style, he advised them 'to not be frightened of extending that style'. History shows that he won his case.

The Avengers. Two chips off the old block. Teaser to The Fear Merchants.

The success of the previous series had shown that the qualities which endeared *The Avengers* to its audience were its essential Englishness (no concession was ever made to mid-Atlantic compromise), its stylised off-beat, way-out humour and its preoccupation with a distorted view of the world. The producers kept these elements in mind when planning the colour series, but this time they added more danger, leaving Steed and Emma exposed to

every hazard that ingenuity could devise. New twists were added to allow the implacable spycatcher to react to danger with jocularity, while his partner whammed baddies senseless with a wallop of her delicate little fist and a cascade of chestnut hair. At the time ABC believed that the spy cycle was on the wane, so, in the new series, *The Avengers* fought the private sector of villainy. Dangerous madmen with delusions of power outnumbered agents of a foreign power. The villains became more diabolical and the show continued its unique blend of black humour, imaginative direction and polished bonhomie.

While plans for the new series were being formulated, Diana Rigg was finding that some of the rewards of being a celebrity were actually penalties to her: being approached in public by strangers, signing autographs, making personal appearances, coping with fanmail. Publicity sessions worried her: she found it difficult to talk about herself or her work unless the interviewer was on her wavelength, or to relax with photographers unless there was a rapport between them. Although a superbly mettled film actress, who worked fast and expertly on the studio floor, she was never at her best in the early morning. Understandable really, considering that her working day began at 6 a.m. when a car arrived to take her to the studio, where she'd work until 6 p.m. (or later) and was often so tired when she returned home that she was in bed by 9 o'clock. The monastic life which intensive film work demanded was thus a considerable sacrifice to her. So it's little wonder that, during the summer recess, Diana, who had been earning £150 a week from the show, declared 'I'm worth at least three times that,' and issued an ultimatum to ABC that unless she received more money, she would not return to the series. Her demands were met and she returned at £450 a week. (In fairness to Diana Rigg, however, it should be pointed out that she did not return simply for the financial benefits, but more from her loyalty to Patrick Macnee, the show and all those who were involved in it. She did make it quite clear, however, that this would be her last series.)

Emma tries on a handkerchief to discover how she looks in a yashmak in this scene from Honey for the Prince.

On hearing of her decision, Patrick Macnee said, 'I'm glad that Diana is staying. She is wonderful to work with and we share a mutual obsession for detail. We deliberately set out to contrive new and different ways of playing two-handed scenes for comedy. We put Emma and Steed in routine situations, like having a meal or playing a game of chess. Then, while serving the soup, we would casually discuss some mastermind's ploy to rule the world.'

Viewers of the previous series seemed to prefer the episodes with a science-fiction theme, so many of the new stories were slanted in that direction. Brian Clemens was reported as saying, 'When you're dealing with a make-believe world populated by larger-than-life villains, it is difficult not to get into bizarre situations. The science fiction thing was unintentional. Ideas were easy. It was more difficult finding writers with an *Avengers* mind.'

I asked him if there were any specifics that had to be adhered to when writing for the show. 'A new plot, or twist – that unique *Avengers* twist – or an old one. We became fond of inverting the cliché. . . . Mother became a *man*, father a *woman*. The Sherlock Holmes character didn't *find* clues, he *planted* them. I also required at least three high spots per story – action or an intriguing scene – an up-front teaser, and then I was ready to put the jigsaw together.' Along with Clemens, the most prolific writer on the new series was Philip Levene, who actually appeared in the story *Who's Who?* as Tulip, an agent employed by Major B. Between them, they supplied 20 of the 24 stories.

A popular feature of the previous series had been the closing sequence which showed Steed and Emma driving away in various forms of transport. This time around Steed would summon Emma to duty with the words 'Mrs Peel – we're needed!' The scenes formed part of the opening credits and usually took place in Emma's apartment, as did the closing tag sequences, in which the story was brought to an end with an appropriate flourish. There was still no indication, of course, of *who* needed The Avengers. Unlike most of the world's favourite thriller heroes and heroines, the duo had no 'M' figures, 'Uncles' or other visible or invisible means of support to control their activities; at least, not until the arrival of 'Mother' in the Thorson series. Steed and Emma fitted into no known category and continued to be a law unto themselves.

Could old Etonian Macnee be serenading his partner with 'The Eton Boating Song'?

As previously, the programme continued to present first-class actors in guest roles, and the audience were kept guessing as to which of them were on the side of the angels. Of these, two actors returned to appear in roles they'd played in the monochrome series: Warren Mitchell as Brodny, the Iron Curtain Ambassador in London (*Two's a Crowd*) and Frederick Jaeger, as Benson, Dr Armstrong's assistant in *The Cybernauts*.

*Brodny sees the joke but Emma is not so amused by the dubious
activities of* The See-Through Man.

*Patrick Macnee and Twiggy, pictured during the Avengerpack
fashion show in August 1965.*

Once again, ABC decided to change both the fighting
and fashion formats. This time Emma would be using
Kung Fu – a 50,000 year old Chinese art of self-defence,
based on relaxation rather than the brute strength
required for karate, or the complicated throws and holds
of judo. Diana Rigg was coached by stunt arranger Ray
Austin for the second time. Austin taught her the basics
of Tai Chi, a series of balletic-type movements which
improved her posture, relaxation and breathing.

The (by now obligatory) fashion changes were this
time in the capable hands of Alun Hughes. It was Diana
herself who suggested him to ABC. 'I felt the leather gear
had to go,' she told the Press. 'It wasn't me. It belonged
to Cathy Gale. Although I don't design Emma Peel's
clothes, I do talk them over with the designers and this
time I get to wear the sort of clothes I like. They are
based on my physique which is larger than people
imagine from the screen.' Although British viewers were
still awaiting the arrival of colour, countries that already
had it, such as the USA, were able to see the new
Avengers fashions in colour – a privilege denied British
viewers. Against sets specially designed to show off the
clothes – set designers Wilfrid Shingleton and Bob Jones
were told to spray the sets to show off Steed and Emma's
clothes to best advantage – both stars had gorgeously
hued plumage. The guiding principle of the brief given
to Mr Hughes was to make Emma elegant and feminine,
but dangerous. Alun Hughes interpreted this as Feminine and Feline: his Emma in day or evening clothes
looked beguilingly innocent and charming, but was
capable of delivering a knockout blow to any unsuspect-
ing villain. His 'action suits' (which he called
'Emmapeelers') were in stretch Crimplene and jersey,
with a recurring motif of buckles, links, thigh watches
and braiding, and differed from Emma's previous
Avengers fighting gear by having bootees of the same
material to give an all-in-one effect from throat to toe.

'In her Emmapeelers,' said Hughes, 'Emma is like a
cat in the night, prowling silently on her secret
assignments, ready to strike at anyone who challenges
her.' To enhance the feline effect, Mr Hughes also
designed several fur coats, including one with a tiger
motif. Emma wore boots only with her trouser suits or in
a blatantly theatrical manner at highwayman length.
She wore very little leather, but lots of glove-soft suede in
coats, trouser suits and co-ordinates which alternated
with Bermuda shorts.

The slim lines and physical elegance of Emma's new
wardrobe were echoed by the new Pierre Cardin
collection for John Steed. Cardin designed all Patrick
Macnee's clothes for the series, and intoduced two new
ideas for him – breast pockets with handkerchiefs, and
trousers with a parallel line from knee to ankle to give a
slightly more flared effect. Macnee, however, found that
his usual Chelsea boots didn't complement the trousers
and Alun Hughes designed some new shoes to go with
the Cardin suits. Steed's familiar bowler and umbrella
were also changed and they now came in assorted
colours to match the new wardrobe.

In order to take full advantage of the new colour
process, the producers decided to change the series' title
credits. In place of the stylised animated opener of the
previous series was a live-action vignette in which Steed,
finding difficulty in opening a bottle of champagne, has
the task made that much easier for him by the entrance

of Emma who, pistol at the ready, pops the cork with a well-aimed shot. The couple cross to a table, raise their glasses and drink. Cue *The Avengers* main title logo (superimposed over a table bearing Steed's bowler and umbrella, Emma's gold-plated pistol and two empty glasses). Unsheathing his umbrella's swordstick, Steed selects a single red flower from a vase of carnations, then deftly whisks it across to Mrs Peel, who in turn proceeds to place the bloom in her partner's buttonhole. In silhouette, the stars perform a choreographed display of umbrella thrusts and kung-fu moves, and cut to that week's story title.

Pop goes the champagne cork. Mrs Peel displays her shooting skill during the title credits sequence for the fifth series.

Steed's apartment at 5 Westminster Mews, near to London's Houses of Parliament, had now been given a face lift. Having been able to buy the freehold of the property, he had done it over in pine panelling with buttoned red leather upholstery and a gorgeous red 18th-century porter's chair by the hall door.

Emma, too, had moved. She no longer lived in her penthouse apartment in London's Primrose Hill, and had taken up residence in an L-shaped studio nearby, which had an artist's north light window, an antique stove in a tiled alcove, a scarlet baby grand piano in a matching alcove, and an early Victorian sofa and chairs in white and gold.

Filming began on 5 September 1966 and continued for 28 weeks. After completion of episode 13, the production took a short recess and resumed filming in March 1967. The production was completed in August that year.

Author's note:
Although *The Forget-Me-Knot* story introduced Linda Thorson as Tara King, making it the *first* Thorson story, it was actually a partly completed Rigg episode. Therefore it is the *last* to feature Diana Rigg as Emma Peel, and is credited as such in the studio files. I have divided the episode into two parts, with the cross-over scene and Diana Rigg's farewell as the introductory passage to the beginning of the Thorson series, but have given the episode its own spread.

FROM VENUS WITH LOVE

In which Steed is shot full of holes –
and Emma sees stars

By Philip Levene

John Steed	**Patrick Macnee**
Emma Peel	**Diana Rigg**
Venus	**Barbara Shelley**
Primble	**Philip Locke**
Brigadier Whitehead	**Jon Pertwee**
Crawford	**Derek Newark**
Bertram Smith	**Jeremy Lloyd**
Jennings	**Adrian Ropes**
Clarke	**Arthur Cox**
Cosgrove	**Paul Gillard**
Hadley	**Michael Lynch**
Mansford	**Kenneth Benda**

Designed by Wilfrid Shingleton

Directed by Robert Day

ASTRONOMER COSGROVE, observing the planet Venus, concentrates so much that he does not notice a nearby glass of beer begin to bubble furiously. A strange high-pitched sound is heard and as the now-hot Cosgrove stares at the glass, there is a blinding flash of light and he falls lifeless to the floor – his hair bleached white as snow. Cosgrove is followed by a second victim, Sir Fredrick Hadley. Found lying beside his body are his astro-camera and a note from a friend, Smith. Emma visits Smith, a chimney sweep, who tells her that he and Hadley both belonged to the British Venusian Society. She telephones this information to Steed who is busy developing the film found in Hadley's camera. While they are speaking there is a sudden high-pitched noise. Emma runs into Smith's room, to find his body in the fireplace, his hair and body bleached white. Steed joins the BVS, and meets the secretary, Venus Browne, and her assistant, Crawford. Venus says that with a grant, and contributions from its members, the society hopes to land a satellite on Venus. Although he is accepted as a member, Steed is told that he must have his eyes tested by their optician, Primble. As he leaves, Steed notices a list of members' names on the table – Cosgrove, Hadley, Smith, Lord Mansford and Brigadier Whitehead. Primble tests Steed's eyes. He also claims that invasion from

Venus is imminent, and when Steed shows him the photographs from Hadley's camera of a huge fireball, Primble declares this is further evidence. Emma visits Lord Mansford. She arrives to find that he is locked in his vault by a time mechanism. When his secretary, Jennings, opens the door, the dead Mansford lies inside, his body as white as snow. There still remains Brigadier Whitehead who is writing his wartime memoirs. Venus Browne visits him to ask for more money but he refuses to help. Between her leaving and Steed arriving, Whitehead is also given the bleaching treatment. Steed notices a tape recorder beside the body and when he plays it back, hears a strange, high-pitched hum. The tape is taken to the BVS, together with Hadley's photographs. Venus asks Crawford to look at them, and while she and Emma are waiting, an attempt is made on Venus' life too – a statue shatters and the curtains burst into flames. The twinkling light again flashes in the driveway outside. Steed meanwhile decides it is time to observe Venus himself and instals a tailor's dummy, dressed in his own suit, behind Cosgrove's telescope. There is a sudden flash of light and the dummy becomes a mass of bleached and molten wax. Primble then rushes in to say he has seen a strange light coming from the graveyard. Going there, Steed narrowly escapes the light by jumping into an open grave. Primble, meanwhile, is babbling that the Venusians have invaded the Earth. Clarke, a military official, says that the earth in the cemetery is carbonised. This, together with the ultra-sonic hum, indicates a laser beam. Emma searches Primble's home and finds the glittering object – a silver sports car, with a laser hidden in the bonnet. But Primble arrives with his assistant, Martin, and captures her. They tie her to a chair in Primble's surgery, and focus the laser at her. Steed bursts into the room, knocks out Martin and, using a mirror to deflect the laser rays, tricks Primble into killing himself with the laser. Steed and Emma leave behind their only casualty – Steed's bowler, bleached white by the deadly ray. *Teaser*: Emma, practicing fencing in her flat by lunging at a sack figure pinned to the inside of her front door gives a wry smile as Steed enters and pops a card bearing the legend 'Mrs Peel – We're Needed' to the tip of her epee. *Tag Scene*: Steed hurries Mrs Peel along by suggesting that they are 'invited to have dinner on Venus' – the Venus Browne society, that is.

In From Venus With Love, *Emma, searching Primble's garage, finds a silver sports car with unusual accessories.*

THE FEAR MERCHANTS

In which Steed puts out a light – and Emma takes fright

By Philip Levene

John Steed	Patrick Macnee
Emma Peel	Diana Rigg
Pemberton	Patrick Cargill
Raven	Brian Wilde
Dr Voss	Annette Carell
Gilbert	Garfield Morgan
Crawley	Andrew Keir
Gordon White	Jeremy Burnham
Meadows	Edward Burnham
Fox	Bernard Horsfall
Dr Hill	Ruth Trouncer
Saunders	Declan Mulholland
Hospital attendant	Philip Ross

Designed by Wilfrid Shingleton

Directed by Gordon Flemyng

BUSINESSMAN Richard Meadows awakes to find himself on the grass in the middle of a football stadium. It is completely deserted; he is surrounded by endless tiers of empty seats. Meadows gives way to hysteria and collapses, sobbing like a child. Meadows, along with two companions, both of whom are mental wrecks, is taken to hospital. They are soon joined by Fox, an athlete who has gone berserk at the sight of a mouse in a gymnasium. Steed discovers that all four men were directors of ceramic concerns, and visits Fox's partners, White and Crawley. Crawley can only spare Steed a minute before he is driven away for a business appointment. As the car leaves, Steed stumbles over the body of Crawley's chauffeur and immediately hurries after the departing vehicle. He is too late, however, for the driver jams his foot on the accelerator, and Crawley, who is terrified of fast cars, faints with fear, his mind shattered. A search of Crawley's car reveals a letter from Jeremy Raven, director of a rival company, British Porcelain, suggesting a merger between himself and Fox, White and Crawley – the other sick industrialists. Emma visits White, and overhears White saying he has been approached by a market research organisation, the Business Efficiency Bureau, with a strange questionnaire. Steed meanwhile visits Jeremy Raven. Unfortunately, says Raven, his rivals refused his merger offer, so he has found methods to eliminate their competition. The methods seem to work, for White falls from his office window, frightened by a huge bird which has been placed in his office. Steed visits Raven again and notices a brochure from the BEB in a drawer. Raven explains that he employed them quite innocently, and is horrified to learn that they have been using criminal methods to eliminate his rivals. Raven then visits the BEB, which is headed by Pemberton, whose assistants are Dr Voss and Gilbert, and tells Pemberton that he wishes to break his contract with the Bureau. Pemberton attemps to black-mail him, but Raven leaves and phones Steed with a message to contact him as soon as possible. Raven, waiting for Steed, sees the hairy legs of a spider crawling towards him. There is a terrifying scream and Steed and Emma enter to find the demented Raven surrounded by smashed china. Beside his body is a BEB brochure promising a unique way of building your business up. Steed tells Emma it is time they paid the BEB a visit. Next day Steed tells Pemberton that he is a travel agent wishing to improve his business. He has one rival, a Mrs Peel. What Steed does not know, however, is that his chair incorporates a lie-detector operated by Voss. Pemberton, knowing that Steed was lying, orders Gilbert to follow him. At the hospital, Steed notices that Raven is agitated by a tattoo of a spider on an attendant's arm, and realises what caused his condition. The doctor confirms that the other men had been subjected to things they feared, making them sick with shock. Gilbert tricks Steed into stopping near a deserted quarry, where Steed is almost buried alive by a bulldozer which tips earth on him. Finally Gilbert himself is killed when the machine crushes him. When Gilbert does not return, Pemberton decides to visit Emma and question her – with a gun. Steed finds Emma's apartment empty, save for a BEB card with the message 'Help' scrawled on the back. Meanwhile, having been unable to discover Emma's secret fear, Pemberton decides to torture her with surgical instruments. Steed arrives to find Emma struggling to escape from the chair in which she is bound. Steed then switches off the lights, and it becomes obvious that Pemberton's secret fear is darkness, for he is soon howling and crying like a baby. Steed releases Emma and she dispatches Dr Voss. *Teaser*: Emma, finding a box of chocolates, isn't too surprised when the accompanying card reads 'Mrs Peel – We're Needed'. *Tag*:Returning to her apartment, it takes Emma a few minutes only to discover Steed's secret fear – the idea that Emma has run out of champagne!

The Fear Merchants *signal Steed's early demise by burying the undercover agent in a gravel pit.*

ESCAPE IN TIME

In which Steed visits the barber – and Emma has a close shave

By Philip Levene

John Steed	Patrick Macnee
Emma Peel	Diana Rigg
Thyssen	Peter Bowles
Clapham	Geoffrey Bayldon
Vesta	Judy Parfitt
Anjali	Imogen Hassall
Sweeney	Edward Caddick
Parker	Nicholas Smith
Tubby Vincent	Roger Booth
Josino	Richard Montez
Paxton	Clifford Earl
Mitchell	Rocky Taylor

Designed by Wilfrid Shingleton

Directed by John Krish

SECRET AGENT Paxton is hurriedly searching an opulent country house. The furnishings are modern, apart from five death masks of the Thyssen family through the ages, all remarkably similar. Paxton goes through a door into a corridor which suddenly whirls round – and unconsciousness overtakes him. He wakes to find himself in the same room, now furnished in Elizabethan style. Only one mask remains, and while Paxton stares at it, he is shot from behind. His assassin is the Thyssen of the Elizabethan period. Steed and Emma arrive at Paxton's house, wondering how he came to be floating in the Thames, shot by a 16th-century bullet, when a visitor calls – with a Jacobean dagger in his back! He is holding a scrap of paper containing the message 'Josino – contact in Mackidockie Mews – Monday 12.30 pm' and a drawing of a black crocodile. Both Paxton and Vincent, the second victim, had been trying to discover an escape route through which notorious criminals had been vanishing into thin air. Josino, a ruthless dictator who has recently arrived in Britain, is obviously involved and Steed and Emma decide to keep the rendezvous in the mews. Josino arrives carrying a large toy crocodile. He contacts a girl, Vesta, and exchanges the crocodile for a giraffe. At a nearby toy stall the giraffe is exchanged for a kangaroo with a note in its pocket. After reading the note, Josino visits a barber's shop presided over by T Sweeney and leaves with an elephant, and a large piece of sticking plaster on his cheek. From the barber's shop he goes to an Indian art gallery, and when he leaves, Steed quickly realises that he is following a double! Emma, meanwhile, has been trailing Vesta, and is led into a country field where a man on a motorcycle attemps to run her down, but he crashes, and the machine bursts into flames. Steed decides to try his hand at escaping and bluffs his way through the mews and into the art gallery. There he meets a beautiful Indian girl, Anjali, who tells him that with the organisation's help, he can vanish from the face of the earth. He leaves the gallery and is escorted, blindfolded, into a waiting car.

Emma, standing outside, misses him and follows a double. Steed is taken to Thyssen's home, where Thyssen explains that he has perfected the perfect escape route – a time machine, which enables criminals to escape into the past. He lets Steed try, and he chooses the 18th century and enters the time corridor, while Thyssen's machine registers 1790. Steed wakes up on a couch in what appears to be the same room – with three death masks instead of five, and Georgian furniture. He then awakes to find himself back in the 20th century. He tells Thyssen to book him a one-way ticket into the past. Emma, having discovered that she is following a false trail, eliminates the double and decides that she, too, should sample the escape route. Armed with a toy she has made, she bluffs her way through Mackidockie Mews, but is recognised by Vesta, kidnapped, and taken to Thyssen's home. There, she is offered a visit to 1790. She enters the time corridor and falls asleep. While she lies unconscious, Vesta tells Thyssen who Emma really is and he decides to divert her to another era. She wakes in a Tudor room, searches it and finds Josino's body. Thyssen, dressed as his Tudor ancestor – a notorious sadist – enters the room, followed by a masked executioner. They then prepare to torture Emma by strapping her to the stocks in front of an open fire. Enter Steed, who uses medieval weapons in his fight with the torturers. He releases Emma and explains to her that the time machine was really a series of perfectly furnished rooms in which the victims, having been put to sleep, awakened to apparently find themselves in another era. *Teaser*: A trail of discarded items of clothing leads Emma to a card inviting her to attend the Grand Hunt Ball – and the added legend 'Mrs Peel – We're Needed'. *Tag*: A trail of arrows printed on the floor of her apartment leads Emma to Steed, who is there to take her to a party. Outside they find a veteran taxi, which Steed cranks into action before, black faced from the exhaust, he joins his partner to depart in style.

THE SEE-THROUGH MAN

In which Steed makes a bomb –
and Emma is put to sleep

By Philip Levene

John Steed	**Patrick Macnee**
Emma Peel	**Diana Rigg**
Elena	**Moira Lister**
Brodny	**Warren Mitchell**
Quilby	**Roy Kinnear**
Ackroyd	**Jonathan Elsom**
Sir Andrew Ford	**John Nettleton**
Ulric	**Harvey Hall**
Wilton	**David Glover**

Designed by Wilfrid Shingleton

Directed by Robert Asher

WILTON, A clerk in the Ministry's records office, is amazed to see doors apparently opening by themselves, filing cabinets sliding out, and hearing strange footsteps in the corridor. Then he is knocked unconscious by a blow – apparently from nowhere! When they find a file has been stolen from Wilton's office, Steed and Emma visit Sir Andrew Ford, at his Ministry office. But a mysterious – and apparently invisible – guest, has stolen a secret file from his office. Discovering that both the files dealt with Quilby, an inventor who had been sending useless ideas to the Ministry, Steed visits Quilby, while Emma drives to see Lord Daviot, a retired Ministry official who had previously dealt with the inventor. Quilby and his assistant, Ackroyd, welcome Steed, and he learns that Quilby has invented a formula for invisibility, and when it was rejected by the Ministry, he sold it to The Eastern Drug Corporation for $250,000. Quilby explains that he has lost the formula, but promises he will try to recall it. Emma, having found Lord Daviot taking a bath – in his lily pond – returns home, where Steed tells her of his discovery – and also that top enemy agents Alexandre and Elena Vazin are in town. Their cover is The Eastern Drug Company! Vazin and Elena are staying at the Embassy, and a not very bright Ambassador Brodny is shocked to discover that they have withdrawn $250,000 from the Embassy account. Elena tells him they have acquired a formula for making men invisible, and that Major Vazin has used it. When Brodny is addressed by the invisible Vazin he faints from fright. Elena receives a phone call from Quilby's assistant, Ackroyd, attemppting to blackmail her into silence. She agrees to meet him to talk, and leaves, carrying a gun. Steed arrives at the Embassy and the disturbed Brodny, well aware of Steed's capabilities since their last encounter during the *Two's a Crowd* affair, has to speak to him with the invisible Vazin in the room. When Steed mentions the formula, Brodny hotly denies knowledge of it and Steed leaves, having planted a bugging device. Outside the Embassy, Steed hears Vazin's voice ordering Brodny to destroy the bug, thus confirming his suspicions that Vazin was in the Embassy, heard, if not seen. Meanwhile, Emma has followed Elena, who fails in her attempt to kill Ackroyd. Elena escapes, and while Emma is driving home, she is almost run off the road by a car with an apparently headless driver! Emma picks up the driver's hat, which bears the name Major Vazin. Ackroyd now attempts to blackmail Steed, and arranges a rendezvous. But Vazin gets there first and Steed finds Ackroyd's dead body on a revolving child's roundabout. Steed receives a phone call from Quilby to say that the formula has been found, but when he arrives at Quilby's workshop, he finds the inventor's body on the floor. Then Steed, too, is knocked unconscious – by a headless man! Meanwhile, Vazin decides to put the second phase of his plan into action – the kidnapping of Emma Peel. She is taken to the Embassy, where Elena tells her that they have bought the formula, and Emma is confronted by the invisible Major Vazin. Steed, meanwhile, escapes from Quilby's workshop by mixing some chemicals together and blowing the door off its hinges. Emma escapes from the Embassy, but soon realises that her freedom was planned. She knocks Elena out and is about to search the room when she hears Steed's voice, but there is no one there – Steed is apparently invisible! Chairs move, doors and windows open . . . Steed, in a special room hidden behind the Embassy walls, now explains to Emma how the invisible man worked his miracles. The room contains microphones and television screens that enabled the invisible man to vanish at the touch of a button! Vazin, wearing a specially built-up suit to make him appear headless, enters, and is knocked out by Steed. There still remains Brodny. As he genuinely believes in the invisible man, Steed and Emma feel it would be hard to disillusion him. So the Ambassador is treated to a drenching, from the see-through man, of course, while apologising for allowing Emma to escape. *Teaser*: With Steed at her side, Emma slips a slide onto the culture plate of a microscope, then reacts with a smile as she reads 'Mrs Peel – We're Needed'. *Tag*: Emma and Steed arrive in the former's apartment. After some banter about 'invisible' men, Emma draws Steed's attention to a microscope. Peering through it he reads the words 'I'm hungry'. Outside Emma climbs into Steed's Rolls – fresh out of mothballs for the occasion – and smiles as Steed fails to start the engine. Exit The Avengers, pushing the vehicle!

THE BIRD WHO KNEW TO MUCH

In which Steed fancies pigeons – and Emma gets the bird

By Brian Clemens

Based on a story by Alan Pattillo

John Steed	Patrick Macnee
Emma Peel	Diana Rigg
Jordan	Ron Moody
Samantha Slade	Ilona Rodgers
Tom Savage	Kenneth Cope
Verret	Michael Coles
Twitter	John Wood
Cunliffe	Anthony Valentine
Robin	Clive Colin-Bowler
Mark Pearson	John Lee

Designed by Wilfrid Shingleton

Directed by Roy Rossotti

Steed has a 'little talk' with Samantha, girlfriend of the late Pearson in The Bird Who Knew Too Much.

DANVERS, A secret agent, is pursued by a young thug, Robin, and makes his way to a field telephone box. As Danvers desperately tries to contact Steed, Robin fires and Danvers falls dead. Beside his body lies a pile of bird seed from a bag in his pocket. Steed decides that a message may be hidden among the seeds and begins a search. A second agent, George Elrick, is killed when he tumbles into a tub of concrete on a building site where he had been chased by Robin and his partner Verret. Found in Elrick's pocket are photographs of a top-secret missile base, taken from the air, so Steed decides to visit Elrick's partner Pearson, but finds him dying of gunshot wounds. He is only able to whisper that the information about the base is being taken East by a Captain Crusoe. Emma finds an address, Heathcliff Hall, on Pearson's desk. Steed remains at the flat and after a search, finds some photographs of a girl. A moment later she enters the room, and introduces herself as Samantha Slade, Pearson's girlfriend, and Steed persuades her to have dinner with him. Meanwhile, Emma finds that Heathcliff Hall houses an international exhibition of caged birds, organised by one Edgar Twitter and his assistant Cunliffe. They agree to intoduce Emma to Captain Crusoe – who is a parrot! But the bird has flown, and its cage is empty. Steed accompanies Samantha to work. She is a model and poses for photographer Tom Savage. Steed, too, does a little modelling – and a little interrogation. While he questions Samantha, Verret arrives, and unseen, slips an impact grenade into Steed's umbrella. Fortunately, Steed discovers the grenade in time, and narrowly escapes death. Deciding that the photographs found in Elrick's pocket could have been taken by a bird, maybe a carrier pigeon, Steed keeps watch at Pearson's pigeon loft, while Emma stays to pose for Tom Savage. Steed's hunch proves correct, for Verret and Robin are soon releasing carrier pigeons which fly over the missile base – all except one, which flies back to Pearson's loft. The pigeon has a miniature camera strapped to its leg, but before Steed can investigate further, Robin arrives and

knocks him out. Tom Savage, meanwhile, poses Emma with some very old props, including a parrot in a cage, provided by Samantha. She asks Tom for a copy of the photograph of her and the bird, and takes it to Heathcliff Hall. Twitter and Cunliffe are unable to identify the bird from a photograph, so Emma decides to borrow the bird from the studio. But Verret and Robin are there, and Emma is tied to a chair, facing a loaded gun triggered to go off when Steed arrives. Only quick thinking by Steed saves his life and he rescues Emma in the nick of time. Emma again visits Heathcliff Hall where Twitter tells her that the parrot's real owner is a man called Jordan. Emma sets off to see him, closely followed by Robin. Jordan explains that his hobby is teaching birds to talk. Captain Crusoe is his prize pupil – a parrot with a remarkable memory, but trained to talk only from a given signal, which is a note on Jordan's special triangle. As Jordan finds the triangle, Robin begins shooting at them from the diving board of a nearby swimming pool. Emma overpowers him, and learns that the parrot has been returned. Steed and Emma return to Heathcliff Hall to search for the missing Captain Crusoe. Emma knocks Twitter out but finds she has the wrong man, when Cunliffe and Verret appear and hold her and Steed at gunpoint. A brief skirmish follows and Verret and Cunliffe are soon overpowered. As Steed and Emma depart, Captain Crusoe cries out loudly – demanding political asylum. *Teaser*: As Emma draws back her apartment window curtains, an arrow bearing the legend 'Mrs Peel – We're Needed' thuds into her living-room wall. *Tag*: Once again the curtains are drawn, and a second arrow announces Steed's arrival, this time to invite Emma to meet a bird – basted in wine and turned on a spit. Leaving through the window, Emma gestures towards a handsome 1906 limousine – before using the driver's compartment as a short cut to climb into a veteran bone shaker!

THE WINGED AVENGER

In which Steed goes bird watching – and Emma does a comic strip

By Richard Harris

John Steed	Patrick Macnee
Emma Peel	Diana Rigg
Sir Lexius Cray	Nigel Green
Professor Poole	Jack MacGowan
Arnie Packer	Neil Hallett
Stanton	Colin Jeavons
Julian	Roy Patrick
Tay-Ling	John Garrie
Peter Roberts	Donald Pickering
Simon Roberts	William Fox
Dawson	A J Brown
Damayn	Hilary Wontner
Fothers	John Crocker
Gerda	Ann Sydney

Designed by Wilfrid Shingleton

Directed by Gordon Flemyng and Peter Duffell

A live comic book character who claws its victims to death is a worthy opponent for Steed in The Winged Avenger.

PUBLISHING TYCOON Simon Roberts, and his son Peter, sit in their office late one night talking business. After his son has left, Simon pours himself a drink. A few minutes later, the window shatters, there is the sound of beating wings and a huge shadow envelops the man as he falls dead to the floor. The Avengers are called in and they find strange marks on Roberts' body, as though he had been clawed to death by a large bird. Steed explains to Emma that this is the fourth such death recently, and soon there is a fifth, for Peter Roberts dies in the same circumstances as his father. Steed finds a letter Peter was dictating into his tape recorder, mentioning an author, Sir Lexius Cray. Emma visits Cray, who is also a famous mountaineer. He offers her tea, served by his Tibetan servant, Tay-Ling, who seems strangely interested in newspaper cartoons. Cray tells Emma that one of his books was published by Roberts and that he had tried to cheat him. After Emma leaves, Sir Lexius blows a small whistle and a huge falcon perches on his hand. Emma's enquiries lead her to believe that Tay-Ling is blackmailing someone, so she decides to visit Sir Lexius' home again. When she arrives, however, she is met by Cray, who shows her into the study. There, lying on the floor, is Tay-Ling's body. He also has been clawed to death by some large bird. Sir Lexius discovers that a file is missing from his desk, containing correspondence from a Professor Poole who claims to have invented a special pair of mountaineering boots. Steed and Emma visit Poole, who is dedicated to birds and proving that man can fly. He refuses to talk about his boots however and locks himself in his study. When Emma peers through the transom, she is amazed to see the Professor hanging upside down, bat-like, from the ceiling. Certain that the next victim will be Damayn, a factory owner who has just sacked thousands of workers, Steed and Emma pay him a visit. But the man has been clawed to death while out shooting. Emma points out that all the victims had been evil, ruthless men. Whatever killed them is selecting its victims carefully,

like a winged avenger. She notices a scrap of newspaper lying beside the dead man which shows a cartoon strip called The Winged Avenger – a Batman-like creature which is seen attacking a man in hunting apparel, who looks identical to Damayn. They discover that the cartoon is produced by a cartoonist, Arnie, and a writer, Stanton. Emma visits Poole again and discovers how he is able to hang from the ceiling – a pair of climbing boots with magnetic soles, identical to those worn by the cartoon Winged Avenger. Steed realises that all the deaths so far had been predicted in the Winged Avenger strip cartoon and a search of the cartoonist's office reveals a sketch of Professor Poole – obviously the next person to be murdered. He also finds a second sketch showing Emma walking towards Poole's house. Meanwhile, as predicted, Emma is walking towards Poole's house in response to an urgent call. She enters Poole's study and finds herself confronted by Arnie, dressed in the Winged Avenger costume and wearing the magnetic boots. He has already murdered Poole. Emma hurriedly removes the dead Professor's boots and climbs onto the ceiling, followed by Arnie – now completely mad and believing himself to be the real Winged Avenger. They are struggling on the ceiling when Steed arrives, carrying writer Stanton's story boards under his arm. Steed hits Arnie on the head with the heavy boards (they read 'Pow' and 'Splat'), then with one final lunge, Emma throws him out of the window. *Teaser*: Emma, adding a final dab of paint to a canvas and about to add her signature, notices the words 'Mrs Peel' . . . Enter Steed to complete the legend '. . We're Needed.' *Tag*: Arriving home, Emma pops a champagne cork as Steed, in the background, busies himself by sketching a canvas. When revealed, it is a *drawing* of the feast Steed has promised her. Leaving the room, Steed returns with a food trolley containing a gourmet's delight. To the PING of cymbals the meal is served.

THE LIVING DEAD

In which Steed finds a mine of information –
and Emma goes underground

By Brian Clemens

Based on a story by Anthony Marriott

John Steed	Patrick Macnee
Emma Peel	Diana Rigg
Masgard	Julian Glover
Mandy	Pamela Ann Davy
Geoffrey	Howard Marion Crawford
Hermit	Jack Woolgar
Hopper	Jack Watson
Rupert	Edward Underdown
Olliphant	John Cater
Spencer	Vernon Dobtcheff
Tom	Alister Williamson

Designed by Robert Jones

Directed by John Krish

Before she can rescue Steed from execution by The Living Dead, *Emma must overcome the challenge of the treacherous Mandy.*

STEED AND EMMA go to the country, to investigate rumours that a ghost has been seen in the private chapel of the Duke of Benedict. Two other investigators also appear – Mandy McKay of FOG (Friends of Ghosts) and Spencer, of SMOG (Scientific Measurement of Ghosts). They are perplexed to find that the local hermit who claimed to have seen the ghost, now denies it, although the local inn-keeper, Hopper, corroborates a story of chapel bells ringing at midnight. The chapel is near the private estate of Geoffrey, 16th Duke of Benedict, a weak character who seems strongly influenced by his estate manager, Masgard. Geoffrey became the 16th Duke when his cousin Rupert was killed, with 30 companions, in the Benedict mine disaster five years before. When Steed seeks permission to shoot on the estate, Masgard says it is impossible, and Steed gets the distinct impression that his presence is not wanted. From a chance remark of Masgard's, he suspects that something is hidden in the Duke's wine cellar. Spencer decides to spend the night in the chapel, having first prepared a great deal of equipment to record any noises. Later, his body is discovered by Steed and Emma – he has been stabbed to death with a sword from a nearby statue. The next night, Emma and Mandy decide to keep watch in the chapel. Soon the hysterical Mandy tells Steed that Emma has been kidnapped – by a ghost! An unsuccessful search is made, and the hermit tells Steed the best place to find Mrs Peel is in the mine, where, he swears, the entombed men are still alive. Before he can say anything more, he is shot. Steed decides to check the mine, and persuades the inn-keeper, Hopper, an ex-miner, to help him. A third accomplice is Mandy, who insists on tagging along. Together they begin their search in the mine. At the pit-head, the waiting Hopper is attacked by Masgard and his men, who then cut through the cables of the mine lift. In the mine, Steed hears the sound of tapping and discovers a door cut into the rock. Passing through, he is amazed to find a complete street. As he stares at the scene, five chained prisoners appear, led by Rupert, the 15th Duke of Benedict – the man supposedly killed five years before. Before Steed can comment further, however, Mandy, gun in hand, cautions him to move away . . . Meanwhile, Emma is being held prisoner in a nearby cell. Rupert brings her food, and explains that she is in an underground city, and that he and his friends are the sole survivors of the pit disaster. Masgard enters and tells her the city has been built by slave labour and will shortly hold 20,000 men and their families, who will be brought in by submarine. It is a vast nuclear shelter, built to house an army which will take over after Masgard's country has dropped a bomb on Britain. Masgard had organised the whole thing, living underground. He would never have come up if Rupert hadn't escaped and caused the ghost scare in the village. As Emma listens to his story, she sees Steed, escorted by guards, pass her cell window. She realises that he is about to face a firing squad. She overpowers Masgard and fights her way back out of the cell, to find her way blocked by Mandy. Emma soon subdues the ghost huntress, and rescues Steed by turning Mandy's machine gun on the firing squad. Rupert arrives, and tells Steed that there are only two escape routes – the pit-head and the main exit, which has a specially-built lift. They crowd into the lift, and when safely aloft, put the lift out of action. Below, Masgard and Mandy are horrified to realise they are trapped in the mine . . . Above, the 16th Duke of Benedict is horrified to see his so-called dead cousin once again rising from the depths. *Teaser*: Mrs Peel, stopping at a set of traffic lights, pulls up as the light turns to red – STOP. Then amber 'Mrs Peel' . . . and finally green ' . . .We're Needed!' *Tag*: Steed, inspecting his parked Bentley, listens with interest as the 'mechanic' ferreting around beneath its bulk, states, 'Just as I thought. There's the trouble . It's a ghost, sir. You've got a ghost in your engine.' Identifying the voice as that of his partner, Steed smiles as Mrs Peel slides into view to share a glass of the proverbial champagne.

THE HIDDEN TIGER

In which Steed hunts a big cat – and Emma is badly scratched

By Philip Levene

John Steed	Patrick Macnee
Emma Peel	Diana Rigg
Cheshire	Ronnie Barker
Dr Manx	Lyndon Brook
Angora	Gabrielle Drake
Nesbitt	John Phillips
Peters	Michael Forrest
Erskine	Stanley Meadows
David Harper	Jack Gwillim
Dawson	Frederick Treves
Samuel Jones	Brian Haines
Williams	John Moore
Bellamy	Reg Pritchard

Designed by Robert Jones

Directed by Sidney Hayers

Something evil is afoot, so Steed has no time to pussy-foot around with the fiendish society behind The Hidden Tiger.

WHEN GENTLEMAN farmer Sir David Harper and his butler are mauled to death, apparently by a member of the cat family, Steed and Emma are called in. They are helped by a neighbour of Harper's, ex-big-game hunter Major Nesbitt, who confirms that there is no big cat loose in the area. At Harper's farm, devoted to research into new farming methods, Emma is met by the assistant, Erskine. As he shows Emma around, Peters runs in to announce that the prize bull has been killed by a large animal. Erskine is surprised and tells Emma that security on the farm is strict – the whole place is rigged with traps. Steed, Emma and Nesbitt decide to organise a safari to trap the animal, but the only thing they find is the mauled body of Erskine, so they decide to organise a second hunt. While Nesbitt prepares a strong-smelling liquid, guaranteed to attract big cats, Steed and Emma rig up a walkie-talkie set, having first planted miniature microphones around the farm. While they keep watch in the farm grounds, Nesbitt, securely locked inside a cage, watches with his rifle. Hearing a sound on the headphones, Steed follows it to Nesbitt's house, but arrives too late. The big-game hunter is dead, inside the cage! Beside his body Steed finds a small medallion, inscribed with the initials PURRR. Steed discovers that PURRR is in fact the Philanthropic Union for Rescue, Relief and Recuperation of Cats – an organisation providing a shelter for lost cats. It is managed by Cheshire, and his assistants Angora and Dr Manx, a veterinary surgeon. Steed is amazed to find that the committee of PURRR consists of the dead men, Harper, Nesbitt and Erskine. Two other members are Bellamy and Jones. Steed visits Bellamy, but finds him lying dead beside his cottage door, his clothes torn to shreds by some enormous animal. While Steed searches the telephone directory for Jones' address, Emma visits PURRR, claiming she has lost her cat. She is shown around the building by Cheshire, who is especially proud of the psycat-therapy, a new form of treatment devised by Dr Manx. As Emma leaves, she spots Peters, from the Harper farm, leaving a van in the courtyard. Investigating, she finds it is equipped like a small caravan, full of food, and secured against possible intruders. Peters and Angora see her searching the van and decide she must be eliminated. Steed meanwhile drives to Jones' home, but again he is too late. He finds the man lying dead on the floor, accompanied only by his pet cat. The cat is wearing a PURRR medallion, and as it leaps from Steed's arms, the medallion falls to the floor. Steed notices that it contains a complicated miniature circuit. Emma is rather taken aback to receive a visit from Cheshire, who brings her a Siamese cat to replace the one she has supposedly lost. It is also wearing a PURRR medallion which, she discovers, is a miniature receiver, containing an electrophone which can transmit brain waves capable of turning an ordinary cat into a ferocious killer. Steed decides to search PURRR but, having dispatched Peters and Cheshire on entry, he is captured by Angora and Manx. Manx tells him that they intend to overthrow the entire country. Each cat wearing a medallion will attack at a given signal, while Manx and Angora stay secure in the van. They decide to leave, and tie Steed to a chair, surrounded by the deadly cats! Emma, meanwhile, visits PURRR, taking the Siamese cat with her. She arrives in time to rescue the struggling Steed and switch off the transmitter relaying the deadly brain waves. Manx and Angora, unaware of what has happened and still believing that their cats are potential killers, notice Emma's Siamese cat in the van with them. Manx is so terrified that he drives the van off the road and into a tree. The only survivor is the cat, which emerges from the van without a scratch. *Teaser*: Emma, redecorating her apartment walls, tears off a long strip of paper to reveal the legend 'Mrs Peel . . .' Enter her partner who follows suit by revealing the words '. . . We're Needed' beneath another. *Tag*: Discussing their successful mission, Steed and Emma are doodling pictures on the wall of Emma's apartment until, as Steed puts his foot in a tray of paint, Mrs Peel remarks 'A *cat*-astrophe!'

THE CORRECT WAY TO KILL

In which Steed changes partners – and Emma joins the enemy

By Brian Clemens

John Steed	Patrick Macnee
Emma Peel	Diana Rigg
Olga	Anna Quayle
Nutski	Michael Gough
Ivan	Philip Madoc
Ponsonby	Terence Alexander
Percy	Peter Barkworth
Algy	Graham Armitage
Merryweather	Timothy Bateson
Hilda	Joanna Jones
Winters	Edwin Apps
Grotski	John G Heller

Designed by Robert Jones

Directed by Charles Crichton

Discovered by Ponsonby and his followers, Steed and temporary assistant Olga debate The Correct Way to Kill *the opposition.*

WHEN TWO top enemy agents are found dead, suspicion falls on John Steed and Emma Peel. Steed manages to convince Nutski and Ivan, representatives of the other side, that he and Emma are not to blame and they decide to join forcessss to discover the murderer. Then, a third agent is murdered. Steed, accompanied by Nutski's assistant Olga, leaves for an address which Grotski (one of the dead men) is known to have visited. Ivan and Emma, following another clue, arrive at the surgery of a chiropodist called Merryweather who, with his assistant Hilda, examines Emma's feet. When she leaves the surgery, Ivan has vanished. Steed and Olga find themselves at a shop which sells umbrellas and raincoats. Winters, the owner, denies Steed's accusation that he sold an umbrella to the dead Grotski, but then Steed notices Ivan's body in a packing case. The case is carried away by four bowler-hatted gentlemen – all perfect replicas of Steed. He and Olga follow them to an establishment called Snob, a finishing school which teaches young men how to become complete English gentlemen. The proprietor, Ponsonby, says he has never heard of Grotski, and the packing case which Steed followed now contains only umbrellas! Olga, however, remembers seeing a second, identical, packing case in the umbrella shop, addressed to Merryweather, the chiropodist. Meanwhile, Merryweather and Hilda are examining an umbrella which is really a complicated radio. The four bowler-hatted thugs enter with the packing case containing Ivan's body, and while they are arguing about its disposal, Steed and Olga arrive outside

the surgery. Olga enters and is captured by the thugs. Emma now joins Steed but they find the surgery empty, save for the bare-footed body of Merryweather. Olga is taken to Winters' umbrella shop and bundled inside a packing case. Nearby lies the dead body of Winters. Emma goes to summon Nutski, while Steed returns to the umbrella shop. He arrives just in time to see the bowler-hatted men about to remove the packing case. Swiftly he changes places with one of the men. They reach Snob and Steed manages to release Olga. But they cannot escape, for Ponsonby and his pupils are outside in the corridor. Meanwhile, Nutski refuses to leave for Snob with Emma, so she sets off by herself. By the time she arrives, Steed and Olga have been discovered and are being held at gunpoint by Ponsonby and his thugs. Emma overpowers Hilda and, donning a fencing mask, prepares to fight her way to Steed and Olga. As she enters the room, the boss arrives. It is Nutski, who has been selling the secrets to the highest bidder – a profitable business until Grotski discovered the truth. With Emma's help, Steed and Olga are released and together they round up the gang, then leave for a celebration drink – vodka of course. *Teaser*: Emma, stopping at a news vendor's to buy the evening paper, discovers an unusual headline – 'Mrs Peel – We're Needed'. *Tag*: Entering Steed's apartment, Mrs Peel finds her colleague decked out in Cossack attire, his hat pulled tightly round his ears. After some wordplay about bourgeois decadence, they link arms and depart.

NEVER, NEVER SAY DIE

In which Steed meets a dead man – and Emma fights the corpse

By Philip Levene

John Steed	**Patrick Macnee**
Emma Peel	**Diana Rigg**
Professor Stone	**Christopher Lee**
Dr Penrose	**Jeremy Young**
Dr James	**Patricia English**
Eccles	**David Kernan**
Whittle	**Christopher Benjamin**
Sergeant	**John Junkin**
Private	**Peter Dennis**
Carter	**Geoffrey Reed**
Selby	**Alan Chuntz**
Elderly gent	**Arnold Ridley**
Young man	**David Gregory**
Nurse	**Karen Ford**

Designed by Robert Jones

Directed by Robert Day

WHEN A corpse walks out of a mortuary, Steed and Emma investigate. They meet a man named Whittle, who claims to have given the dead man a lift in his car and later, Steed and Emma are astonished to witness the corpse involved in a second accident with Whittle's car. This time, however, they are certain that the man is well and truly dead, but Emma realises that there is no sign of blood. An ambulance arrives, and takes the body away but the dead man comes alive and, smashing open the ambulance doors, escapes into the countryside. Emma and Steed visit a local pub where a workman tells them of a man who miraculously survived the shock from a 100,000-volt pylon. They are later joined by an army sergeant, who tells of a stranger who walked onto the nearby army firing range and appeared to be unaffected by machine-gun fire. Believing that the events are linked in some way to the missing man, Steed and Emma set off to search for him. Emma arrives at a lonely cottage. She is searching the premises and fails to see the man arrive. He attacks her, and although she fires at him from point-blank range, the bullets seem to have no effect on his tough skin. He is about to strangle her when the driver of the ambulance, Dr Penrose, arrives with two assistants. They throw a net over the man and carry him away, leaving Emma unconscious on the floor. Later, the still-dazed Emma finds a diary on the floor. It belongs to a Professor Stone and on one of the pages are the words George Eccles – Ariel Cottage. Steed locates Dr Penrose and follows him to the Neoteric Research Unit, which is engaged in top-secret government work, under Professor Stone. Posing as a security officer, Steed bluffs his way into Stone's office and is astonished to find that Professor Stone is, in fact, the man for whom they have been searching. Emma meanwhile visits Ariel Cottage and meets George Eccles, an amateur radio enthusiast. He tells her that Stone has accused him of interfering with the research unit's radio equipment. He demonstrates the method used to tune into the unit's frequency. At the same moment, Stone is suddenly taken ill and rushed into the experimental section of the unit. Leaving the cottage,

Emma hears a crash and, dashing back to investigate, finds Eccles has been strangled. His radio equipment lies smashed on the floor. Meanwhile, Steed is shown plans of the research unit by Professor Stone. Steed asks about a section on the plan unmentioned by Stone. He is told that it houses the unit's experimental section, which is top secret. Even Steed would need special clearance to enter it. Later, Steed returns and convinces Stone that he has obtained the necessary clearance. Under protest, Stone offers to allow Steed into the experimental section. He leads Steed through a series of sliding doors into a special chamber, where Steed is astounded to find two Professor Stones – one human, one a replica! Stone informs him that the replica is a duplicate – not a robot, but a computerised double capable of thinking by itself. Stone says great minds need never die: they could be stored inside a duplicate's brain and used for the benefit of future generations. Returning to the pub, Steed meets Penrose and, suspicious of his strange mannerisms, follows him back to the research unit. They are met by Stone who tells him he has been following another double – Penrose, too, is a duplicate man. Steed is taken into the experimental section, where he finds Mrs Peel locked in a cell with the real Professor Stone and the real Dr Penrose. Steed has been led into a trap! Confronted by the duplicate men, The Avengers are faced with a battle to the death. Steed produces a small transistor radio and quickly tunes it to the frequency which gives the duplicates their power. Before he can use the radio, however, Stone knocks it from his hands. The two duplicates now try to strangle the agents, but Emma retrieves the radio in time to overload and stop the duplicate men. Then a sliding panel suddenly springs open to reveal – Emma and Steed. As they stare at the doubles, Emma lifts the bowler on the duplicate Steed. The word 'reject' is stamped on its forehead. *Teaser*: Emma, sitting watching an earlier *Avengers* episode 'The Cybernauts' on her TV set, rises as the sound fades and static breaks up the picture. As she adjusts the receiver, Steed appears on screen to announce 'Mrs Peel – We're Needed'. *Tag*: Steed watches with glee as Mrs Peel tugs the ribbon from a package he's brought her. When unwrapped, the package reveals another box, then another and another until Emma withdraws a brand new transistor radio. Smiling at her partner, Emma turns on the TV and The Avengers settle down to watch a party political broadcast.

EPIC

In which Steed catches a falling star – and Emma makes a movie

By Brian Clemens

John Steed	**Patrick Macnee**
Emma Peel	**Diana Rigg**
Stewart Kirby	**Peter Wyngarde**
Damita Syn	**Isa Miranda**
Z Z Von Schnerk	**Kenneth J Warren**
Policeman	**David Lodge**
Actor	**Anthony Dawes**

Designed by Robert Jones

Directed by James Hill

A YOUNG ACTOR is interviewed for a film part by three Hollywood veterans – director Z Z Von Schnerk and his two stars Damita Syn and Stewart Kirby. Damita decides the actor is perfect, so Kirby shoots him – with a gun, not a camera! In response to an anonymous call, Emma and Steed drive to the countryside. The road is deserted except for an elderly vicar. As they drive past him, the vicar (actually Kirby, a master of disguise) photographs them with a camera concealed in his bicycle. The journey is fruitless and, back in his flat, Steed replays the tape recording of the anonymous caller, but fails to recognise the voice. Kirby shows Von Schnerk and Damita his photographs of Emma and the director insists that she must star in his next epic. Emma is kidnapped by Kirby and taken to a deserted film studio which is surrounded by a high, electrified fence. When she wakes up she thinks she is in her own flat until, opening the door, she finds herself in a mews. Venturing further, she comes to a vast studio floor snaked with cables and huge arc lamps. She sees a limousine parked nearby, containing a bridal head-dress with an invitation to the wedding of – Emma Peel! Church bells ring and Kirby appears, again dressed as a vicar. She chases him away and arrives at another set with a hearse and a coffin, which bears her own name. A headstone in a nearby graveyard is also inscribed Emma Peel. Suddenly, all the lights are switched on, and then she sees a figure sitting on a chair. To her relief, it is Steed. She goes up to him then realises, to her horror, that it is the corpse of the young actor, dressed in Steed's clothes. Kirby reappears, now dressed as an undertaker, and tries to strangle her. She fights him off but is knocked unconscious. As she lies on the floor, Von Schnerk arrives ready to film another scene for his new epic, *The Destruction of Emma Peel*. Emma recovers consciousness to find herself in a cinematic nightmare, in which she is attacked and shot by a cowboy in a Western saloon; fired at with a machine gun during a First World War setting; and shot at by a Red Indian. Then an elderly extra, in policeman's uniform, arrives. He visits the studio to relive old memories. Before he can help Emma, however, he is shot down by a Chicago gangster. Meanwhile, Steed has recognised the voice on the tape

recording as that of Kirby and dashes to the studio. He arrives in time to find Emma has been tied up by Kirby and Damita, and placed on a platform that is moving slowly but relentlessly towards a huge circular saw. Steed overpowers Kirby and Damita and rescues the helpless Emma, saving her by inches. Von Schnerk, having witnessed the scene, and the destruction of his own plans, shoots himself. *Teaser*: Steed, having entered Emma's apartment in a hurry, is about to utter the words 'Mrs Peel . . .' when his partner retorts '. . . Sorry Steed, I'm needed elsewhere!' *Tag*: Watching a film show in Emma's apartment, Steed reminds Mrs Peel that an old Stewart Kirby movie is showing at the Plaza – a movie with unbridled passion as its theme. But The Avengers decide to stay home.

Watched by Damita, Emma overpowers Kirby, whose attempts to film her life – and death – have reached Epic *proportions.*

THE SUPERLATIVE SEVEN

In which Steed flies to nowhere – and Emma does her party piece

By Brian Clemens

John Steed	Patrick Macnee
Emma Peel	Diana Rigg
Hana	Charlotte Rampling
Mark Dayton	Brian Blessed
Jason Wade	James Maxwell
Max Hardy	Hugh Manning
Freddy Richards	Leon Greene
Joe Smith	Gary Hope
Jessel	Donald Sutherland
Kanwitch	John Hollis
Stewardess	Margaret Neale
Toy Sung	Terry Plummer

Designed by Robert Jones

Directed by Sidney Hayers

THE SCENE is a huge, bare gymnasium. Ranged along one wall is a line of men and women. Enter Kanwitch, Jessel and Toy Sung, a huge oriental wrestler. At a given signal, Toy Sung and one of the young men begin to fight. The young man soon overcomes his huge opponent, and as the wrestler remains on his knees, coughing, a girl steps forward. They fight, and again Toy Sung loses. This time, however he is killed with a sword. But Kanwitch is not satisfied and insists on one final test. Steed receives an invitation to attend a fancy dress party, held by the explorer, Sir George Robertson. Dressed as one of Wellington's officers, he sets off to find that the party is being held on board a private aeroplane! Steed meets his fellow guests, and the plane takes off. They are soon horrified to discover that there is no pilot. The controls are operated automatically and cannot be turned off. Talking amongst themselves, they discover that they have each been sent a false invitation. They have been brought together for a purpose – but what is it? Each of them is an expert in some field. As well as Steed, there is Freddy Richards, a professional strongman; a bullfighter, Joe Smith; fencer, Max Hardy; big-game hunter, Jason Wade; war hero, Mark Dayton; and Hana Wilde, a pretty girl who is an expert shot. The aircraft lands and they find themselves on a small deserted island. Not entirely deserted, however, for Kanwitch and Jessel, well hidden, watch their every move. The seven make their way to a crumbling house. Inside, they find a table set for a meal, and at each place a weapon. At the back of the room are six coffins, and as they stare at the empty caskets, Kanwitch's voice is heard through a loudspeaker. He tells them they are part of an experiment. One of them has been trained to be a lethal unbeatable opponent and in order to pass the test, he, or she, will have to kill the others. Hana taps a nearby suit of armour and the body of Toy Sung falls to the floor. They decide to search the island, while Steed remains at the house. Suddenly, a cry is heard and they return to find Richards' body in a coffin, his neck broken. They realise that Smith is not with them – at the same time, Smith is killed with a pitchfork hidden in an old wagon. They set out again and search the undergrowth. Jessel is pleased with his protégé's progress, but Kanwitch insists on the test being fully completed. Before his country will finance Jessel's methods, they must have complete proof. The next victim is Hardy. Steed finds him lying at the bottom of a ravine, with a sword in his chest. Dayton and Hana appear, and Dayton thinks Steed may be the killer. Back at the house, they find the bodies of Hardy and Wade, in two coffins. Dayton knocks Steed unconscious, and he and Hana leave for the aircraft. But while he is working on the controls, Dayton is garotted by an unseen attacker. Hana and Steed are now the sole survivors, it seems, but suddenly a third person arrives. It is Emma, who has landed by parachute from a fighter plane which followed Steed's plane by radar. Emma explains to Hana that Steed knew the invitation was forged, as his host was in South America. Steed, recovering from the knockout blow, is pouring himself a drink when one of the bodies steps out of the coffin! It is Wade, who confesses that he is the killer. They fight, Steed with a spear, Wade with a rapier. Eventually Steed throws the spear into Wade's chest, and he stumbles off. Emma and Hana return to the house, but then Steed and Hana are both knocked out by Wade. Just as he is about to shoot Steed, Emma knocks the gun from his hand and makes him unconscious with a kung fu hold. They now realise that Wade was two identical twins, both playing the same deadly game. Kanwitch, too, realises that he has been double-crossed, but Jessel shoots him and prepares to escape. As he leaves, a shot rings out. It is Hana, who has recovered, and as Jessel reaches for weapon after weapon from the table, Hana shoots them from his hands. Jessel is eventually handcuffed by Steed – much to the dismay of Hana, who admits that she was just beginning to enjoy herself. *Teaser*: Steed, out shooting, brings down a plastic duck on which is printed 'Steed'. Hearing a noise behind him, he turns as Mrs Peel shoves aside the greenery to add 'You're needed'! *Tag*: This time Emma is the one duck hunting. Pointing skywards, she fires – and brings down two toy teddy bears – one of which contains a bottle of bubbly secreted in its tummy. But where are the glasses? Shoving Steed aside, Emma fires again and two champagne glasses fall into their hands!

A FUNNY THING HAPPENED ON THE WAY TO THE STATION

In which Steed goes off the rails – and Emma finds her station in life

By Bryan Sherriff

John Steed	Patrick Macnee
Emma Peel	Diana Rigg
Ticket collector	James Hayter
Crewe	John Laurie
Groom	Drewe Henley
Bride	Isla Blair
Salt	Tim Barrett
Admiral	Richard Caldicot
Warren	Dyson Lovell
Attendant	Peter J Elliott
Lucas	Michael Nightingale
Secretary	Noel Davis

Designed by Robert Jones

Directed by John Krish

STEED AND EMMA arrange to meet another agent, Lucas, at Norborough station. While they are waiting, Steed explains that Lucas had been tracking down a gang of troublemakers. The train arrives, but Lucas does not appear, and although they search the compartments, they find no trace of him. They do not know that he got off the train some miles back down the track, at a derelict station which he was led to believe was the one he wanted. A search of Lucas' cottage reveals two things: his body (with a note 4.4.67 in the pocket) and a photograph, which Emma recognises as that of a passenger on the train. Steed recognises him, too – it is

Salt, a clerk at the Admiralty. Posing as a journalist, Emma visits the Admiralty and interviews Salt's boss. She thinks Salt may be passing on top-secret information, and they decide to test her theory by passing on a false story. Steed has been checking the train timetables, and realises that the 8.10 to Norborough stopped down the line at one point. He and Emma visit the derelict station, Chase Halt, and meet railway enthusiast, Crewe, who has bought the station and intends to live there. They also find a station name-plate reading Norborough. Steed decides to travel on the next 8.10 to Norborough. Among his fellow passengers are Salt and a honeymoon couple. Steed notices the dining-car attendant pass Salt a note, which he intercepts. It reads 4.1.67. This turns out to be a reserved seat, which Salt takes. But although Steed watches him, Salt makes no suspicious move, and when they reach Norborough, Salt takes the next train to London. The information that Emma has leaked is passed on, but when it is discovered to be false, Salt is killed. His murderer is the young bridegroom from the 8.10 train. Beside Salt's body, Steed finds a pile of railway tickets, all first-class returns from London to Norborough. Each of them has a hole punched through the middle, the size of a micro dot. Steed also discovers a tape recording, which is apparently that of a train. Emma takes the tape to Crewe, who cannot recognise it as being any train he knows. But, he tells her, some trains do have a strange sound – particularly the 8.10, which always interferes with his radio. Once again the honeymoon couple travel on the 8.10. Aided by the ticket collector, they are busy installing a bomb in one of the carriages – a carriage that will be used by the Prime Minister on his visit to Norborough the next day. Crewe's observation that the tape recording cannot possibly be that of a train, leads Steed and Emma to suspect a code, and they set out to break it. They discover that it spells out a name, Durbridge. It is a station on the Norborough line. That night, the 8.10 carries two extra passengers. Emma sits opposite the young bride who is in seat number 4.1.67. Steed drinks coffee in the restaurant car. At the rear of the train, the car attendant and the ticket collector sit in a special control carriage, filled with electrical apparatus and radio computers. They are checking every minute detail of the Prime Minister's progress. Steed is recognised by the ticket collector, who captures him and takes him to the special carriage. There, he is told of the bomb, set to explode in 15 minutes' time, as the train reaches Durbridge. Emma has also been recognised by the bride, but after an intense struggle, she manages to evade the girl, by making her way along the outside of the train to the guard's van. She arrives just in time to save Steed from being shot. Together they round up the gang and try to shut down the computer, but fail. Steed eventually saves the day by ripping the leads from the equipment. *Teaser*: Entering her living room, Mrs Peel espies an electric train set circling her apartment floor. Attached to its carriages is a card bearing the legend 'Mrs Peel – We're Needed'. *Tag*: Steed and Emma, awaiting the arrival of the Prime Minister, discuss the honours they expect him to bestow: 'Dame Emma', 'Sir John', etc., then get cold feet and depart before the PM arrives.

Emma fights her way out of a tight corner on the 8.10 in A Funny Thing Happened on the Way to the Station.

SOMETHING NASTY IN THE NURSERY

In which Steed acquires a nanny – and Emma shops for toys

By Philip Levene

John Steed	Patrick Macnee
Emma Peel	Diana Rigg
Mr Goat	Dudley Foster
Miss Lister	Yootha Joyce
Beaumont	Paul Eddington
Webster	Paul Hardwick
Sir George Collins	Patrick Newell
Gen Wilmot	Geoffrey Sumner
Gordon	Trevor Bannister
Martin	Clive Dunn
James	George Merritt
Nanny Roberts	Enid Lorimer
Nanny Smith	Louise Ramsay
Nanny Brown	Penelope Keith
Dobson	Dennis Chinnery

Designed by Robert Jones

Directed by James Hill

WHEN AGENT Dobson is found dead in the home of General Wilmot, Chief of Defence, The Avengers are called in. Wilmot explains that vital defence secrets have been stolen, and that these secrets had been entrusted to only three men, apart from himself – Sir George Collins, son of the Attorney General, Viscount Frederick Webster, DSO, and Lord William Beaumont. All of them come from the noblest of British families. Steed and Emma decide to visit Beaumont first, and ask Collins and Webster to be there too. But when they arrive, Beaumont is acting like a two-year-old. Disgruntled, Webster leaves, followed by Emma. Later Beaumont recovers to tell Steed that he had a strange dream in which he was back in his childhood. He remembers his old Nanny Roberts, and a bouncing ball. He produces a photograph of himself as a child, with Nanny Roberts, and a rubber ball at their feet. Meanwhile, at home, Webster thinks back to his own youth, and looks out some old photographs. His nanny was also Roberts. Emma arrives to find Webster hallucinating, clutching a rubber ball marked Martin's Toyshop. Emma discovers the butler's body in the cellar, and an unseen attacker tries to kill her with a pike from a nearby statue. When she returns to the drawing-room, Webster is fast asleep and the ball has gone. They now have two leads. Emma follows one to Martin's Toyshop and Steed visits a school for nannies, run by one Nanny Roberts. Martin, the toy shop owner, refuses to sell Emma a ball, when she spots a box of them in the shop. He tells her they are produced specially for GONN – The Guild of Noble Nannies. Meanwhile, at GONN, Steed meets Miss Lister, Nanny Roberts' assistant, who says the old lady is too ill to receive visitors. Steed poses as an old charge of hers, but when he eventually sees her, it is only for a few seconds in a darkened room. Miss Lister tells her partner, Gordon, that it is time to deal

with Sir George. At the same time, Emma realises he is in danger and hurries to his home. She is seen by Gordon who attempts to run her over, but although she escapes, she is not in time to prevent Sir George from becoming mesmerised. Miss Lister and Gordon check their records and find that Nanny Roberts never had a charge called Steed. Accordingly, Steed finds a bomb in his kitchen. Emma meanwhile returns to the toy shop, but finds that Martin has been killed by a lethal jack-in-the-box. Steed discovers that Nanny Roberts also brought up General Wilmot, and he leaves for the General's home. He soon realises that he is being followed. Emma searches the GONN offices and finds Nanny Roberts a weak, helpless prisoner. She also finds Gordon, and knocks him unconscious. She next sees a box of rubber balls and, examining one, is immediately transported into a strange, dreamlike nursery world. At the General's home, Steed is explaining that he believes that the General will be the next victim on Nanny's list, when a rubber ball bounces through the window. Wilmot picks it up and immediately begins to act like a child. Miss Lister and Goat, one of her tutors, enter. He is disguised as a nanny. Assuring Miss Lister that his special drug, which is absorbed by the skin, never fails, Goat produces a map of the British Isles, and makes Wilmot mark off the names of secret missile bases. Steed, who has picked up the rubber ball, pretends that he, too, is drugged, but then they notice that he is wearing gloves. Goat tells Wilmot to kill Steed and Emma, for by this time she has recovered and joined them. But in the ensuing fight, Goat loses his blonde wig and Wilmot, still a child in his mind, and realising Goat is not his real nanny, shoots the impostor. *Teaser*: Emma, dozing in an armchair, awakens to find a toy carousel revolving on her dresser. As it turns, she notices the message it carries, 'Mrs Peel – We're Needed'. *Tag*: Steed and Emma are gazing into a crystal ball, he agog at what his partner sees. After some verbal banter, Emma tires of the game and drapes a black velvet cloth over the orb – leaving Steed in the dark as to what his future holds.

Steed pays a visit to the premises of toyshop proprietor Martin in **Something Nasty in the Nursery.**

THE JOKER

In which Steed trumps an ace – and Emma plays a lone hand

By Brian Clemens

John Steed	**Patrick Macnee**
Emma Peel	**Diana Rigg**
Prendergast	**Peter Jeffrey**
Ola	**Sally Nesbitt**
Strange young man	**Ronald Lacey**
Major George Fancy	**John Stone**

Designed by Robert Jones

Directed by Sidney Hayers

WHEN EMMA publishes a successful book on bridge, she is invited to spend a weekend in Devonshire with a fellow-player, Sir Cavalier Rousicana. Steed stays at home, with a badly bruised leg from a fall. He does not want to ruin Emma's weekend by being an invalid – or by telling her that Prendergast, a vicious criminal who was jailed on Emma's evidence, has broken out and is in London. When Emma arrives at Sir Cavalier's home, she is welcomed by his ward, Ola, a fey young woman with strange ways, who says her host has been delayed in London and will return later. The old rambling house contains antiques, and many decorations showing playing cards, including a huge card serving as a door to an upper storey. After Emma has dined in a huge candle-lit room and surrounded by life-size playing cards, Ola is suddenly called away to a friend who has been taken ill in the village. She borrows Emma's car, and drives off, leaving Emma alone – or so she thinks. A search of her room reveals little but a pile of old gramophone records, all in German, all the same tune, *My Love, My Tender, Beautiful Rose*. As she begins idly wandering through the rest of the house, she hears the doorbell ring and answers it. The caller is a young man who tries to scare Emma, and will not reveal the purpose of his call. But he does point out that the telephone wires have been cut. Meanwhile Steed has discovered that his fall was no accident, and finds a trip device hidden on the staircase. He also finds out that Sir Cavalier has been out of the country for some time. When a friend of Steed's picks up a playing card from the floor, and is killed by a poisoned blade attached to it, Steed is certain that someone – Prendergast? – is out to kill The Avengers. He leaves for Devon at once. Emma, alone in the house, begins to suspect that there is someone else there. She finds her room full of roses, the phone rings although the wires are cut, and then she hears a blood-curdling scream. She rushes outside and finds a dummy, dressed as a man, inside the young man's car. When she returns to the house, someone has turned off the gas under the kettle. Suddenly she hears voices calling her in a whisper, then the gramophone record begins playing upstairs. She begins searching the house, and finds the young man in a rocking chair. He is dead – and she is locked in the house with his murderer, who continues to call her in a soft, coaxing voice. She finds him in the dining room, seated beneath a huge reproduction of the joker card. When she reaches for the candle she recognises him as Prendergast. He is completely insane. He tells Emma that he intends to kill her, for he once loved her but she handed him over to the police. Prendergast has Ola as an ally, and she wants to see Emma killed. Finding her gun is loaded with blanks, Emma throws it at the girl, they fight, and Emma knocks Ola out. But Prendergast has enormous strength and Emma finds she is powerless against him. Suddenly, though, they hear the German song ring out again, and Prendergast is horrified to see the huge joker card move menacingly towards them. Terrified, he collapses onto the ground. Emma looks enquiringly at the card, which turns out to reveal Steed. He has come to offer her a lift home! *Teaser*: Steed, descending the stairs to open the door to his partner, stumbles and injures himself. Breaking into the apartment, Emma finds her colleague prostrate at her feet as Steed gasps, 'Mrs Peel – You're Needed'. *Tag*: Emma, finding Steed playing solitaire and aware that he has missed placing a red eight on a black nine – plus other moves, proceeds to show her partner a card trick. Not to be outdone, Steed replies with one of his own: a trick that produces a bottle of bubbly – and two Joker cards from Emma!

WHO'S WHO???

In which Steed goes out of his mind –
and Emma is beside herself

By Philip Levene

John Steed	**Patrick Macnee**
Emma Peel	**Diana Rigg**
Lola	**Patricia Haines**
Basil	**Freddie Jones**
Major 'B'	**Campbell Singer**
Tulip	**Peter Reynolds**
Krelmar	**Arnold Diamond**
Daffodil	**Philip Levene**
Hooper	**Malcolm Taylor**

Designed by Robert Jones

Directed by John Moxey

HOOPER, AN agent of Floral (a secret department of British agents run by Major B, a green-fingered flower expert, who codenames his agents after types of flowers), strolls through a deserted warehouse to keep a rendezvous with John Steed. Suddenly, two figures emerge from their hiding place and shoot the agent dead. They leave the body propped up high above the ground, but with his feet on the floor – his legs are elongated by a pair of wooden stilts! Hooper's body is discovered in this ludicrous position by Steed and Mrs Peel, who notices the manufacturer's name, Hi-Limba, pinned to the side of the stilts. Steed tells her that Hooper's codename was Rose, and immediately sets out to locate the Hi-Limba address. Steed's search is made that much easier, when the two assassins, Basil and Lola, erect a sign bearing the name Hi-Limba Products Ltd outside the building in which they lie in wait for him. When Steed arrives, he is knocked unconscious and carried into a back room where Krelmar, an enemy agent, waits beside his new invention – a machine which can transfer the mind, soul and psyche from one person to another. The agents intend to use the machine to transfer Basil and Lola's personalities into the bodies of Steed and Emma. They will then be the perfect double agents, able to infiltrate any government department without suspicion. Steed and Basil are placed side by side under the machine and Krelmar begins the transfer. The remarkable result is that Steed (now with Basil's personality) rises from the machine to plant a loving kiss on Lola's lips! Emma undergoes the same process with Lola, leaving the two assassins (now outwardly Steed and Emma) to set out to begin their reign of havoc and mayhem on Britain's spy network. The bodies of Basil and Lola – now with the personalities of Steed and Emma – are chained to a supporting post and left under Krelmar's guard. In rapid succession, agents Daffodil, Poppy and Bluebell are all killed by the new and deadly Steed. (Their behaviour gives a novel twist to this Avengers story, as the formerly imperturbable Steed smokes cigars and nuzzles Emma's neck, while the cool and untouchable Emma chews gum and swings her hips to beat music.) In a desperate bid to stop the mayhem caused by their clones, Steed and Emma escape – only to be trapped by agent Tulip, and taken to Major B. Though continuing to protest their innocence throughout the interrogation, Major B is convinced that, though their briefing was thorough, it was only a cover, and they are placed under arrest pending trial! They soon escape and, finding a clue to the assassins' whereabouts – a small box of migraine pills, given to Basil by Krelmar – they race to the premises. Emma knocks out Lola, and both are put under the machine. Though Steed attempts to reverse the process, he cannot recall how to operate the machine, and leaves to search Krelmar's office for the instructions. He is spotted by Krelmar, who having knocked Steed unconscious, enters the machine room and finds Emma and Lola. Believing that Steed has managed to reverse the transformation, he reverses the process. After a few seconds, a smiling Emma, now fully restored, rises from the machine and hits Krelmar in the jaw. At that moment, Basil arrives and attempts to kill Mrs Peel but Steed, having recovered consciousness, bursts into the room. After a hectic battle, Basil and Steed are placed beneath the machine and their personalities reversed. A few moments later, when the Floral agents, led by Major B arrive, they are astonished to find the three agents bemused, and trussed up in a corner. Exit a smiling Steed who, when passing through the door in advance of Emma, has to be reminded 'Manners, Steed'. *Teaser*: As Emma tidies her dress in a mirror, her reflection is replaced by that of Steed who states, 'Mrs Peel – We're Needed'. *Tag*: Arriving at Emma's apartment and astonished to see flowers in every corner, Steed frustrates Emma by pretending to know nothing of her 'special occasion'. Then, coming clean and inviting her to join him on a flight to Paris, she repays him in kind by stating that she is already packed!

Emma fights Steed as State enemies and Avengers switch
personalities in Who's Who???

RETURN OF THE CYBERNAUTS

In which Steed pulls some strings – and Emma becomes a puppet

By Philip Levene

John Steed	**Patrick Macnee**
Emma Peel	**Diana Rigg**
Paul Beresford	**Peter Cushing**
Benson	**Frederick Jaeger**
Dr Neville	**Charles Tingwell**
Professor Chadwick	**Fulton Mackay**
Dr Russell	**Roger Hammond**
Dr Garnett	**Anthony Dutton**
Conroy	**Noel Coleman**
Rosie	**Aimi MacDonald**
Hunt	**Redmond Phillip**
Cybernaut	**Terry Richard**

Designed by Robert Jones

Directed by Robert Day

EMMA AND STEED are invited to the home of Paul Beresford, a rich art dilettante. There, Steed receives a telephone call saying that a scientist, Dr Russell, has disappeared, shortly after Professor Chadwick vanished. Steed and Emma make their apologies and leave, and as they do so, Beresford presses a button hidden beneath his desk, which opens a sliding panel in the wall. In walks a cybernaut, carrying the latest victim, Dr Russell, on its back. The scientist is taken to an underground cell, where shortly afterwards, Beresford and his aide, Benson, visit him and the other captive scientist, and we learn that they now plan to kidnap electronics expert, Dr Neville. Together they programme the robot with Neville's cardiograph, and the cybernaut goes off to fetch him. Neville is waylaid outside his office and brought back to Beresford's home. Emma and Steed return to Beresford's house, and Benson is worried that the cybernaut, due back any minute, will be seen by them. However, just as Steed is about to enter Beresford's home, he hears of Neville's disappearance on his car telephone, and he and Emma drive away – missing the cybernaut's return by seconds. Beresford now informs the three captives of his plan to get rid of Steed and Mrs Peel by the most gruesome and protracted means possible. Their part in the plan will be to devise the means of doing so, and he offers them £100,000 in cash as part payment for their task. Russell is revolted by the idea and tries to escape, but he finds his way is blocked by the cybernaut which, with one deadly swing of its arm, kills him. Dr Garnett is the next to go, his door being smashed down by the cybernaut's fist. His scatter-brained blonde secretary, Rosie, is struck too, after she has mistaken it for a male visitor. She tells Steed 'His eyes were all misty with desire'. Later that day, Benson makes Dr Garnett and the other scientist watch Emma paying another visit to Paul Beresford, through a two-way mirror. Beresford and Benson listen-in when Steed receives a telephone call from Conroy giving him the address of Hunt, Dr Clement Armstrong's lawyer when he was alive. Armstrong had been responsible for unleashing the cybernauts two years earlier, and had met his death during an attempt on Steed and Mrs Peel's

lives. Fearing that Hunt may reveal him as Armstrong's brother, Beresford dispatches Benson and the cybernaut to dispose of Hunt. Steed arrives at Hunt's home, but discovers that the cybernaut has got there first. It is still in the room and knocks Steed unconscious. Meanwhile, Beresford is making advances to Emma, and tries to persuade her to stay overnight, but she declines and leaves. We next see her trying to help Steed recover from the cybernaut blow. Dr Garnett now presents Beresford with a bomb he has made. It unexpectedly goes off in Beresford's face and Garnett escapes. Beresford soon recovers and sends the cybernaut to bring the scientist back. It finds him in Steed's flat, where Emma is tending Garnett's wounds. She is thrust aside like a toy and the robot leaves with the dazed Garnett over his shoulder. Chadwick and Neville, meanwhile, have discovered an ideal way of getting rid of Emma and Steed, for which they need information about their victims' skins. They obtain the required information from a bronze bust which Steed and Emma handled in Beresford's flat. They also photograph Steed's clip-on watch and then duplicate it in the workshop. Inside the watch they install a mechanism which will make Steed Beresford's puppet when he wears it. Chadwick is forced by Beresford to test the watch device on Dr Garnett. It works perfectly, although Garnett is killed when Beresford meddles with the controls. Delighted by the results, Beresford now makes the scientists install a second device in a jewelled bracelet-watch, which he later gives to Emma, asking her to wear it at their next meeting.

Benson breaks into Steed's flat and manages to exchange the watch device with Steed's watch. Arriving home, Steed and Emma find the place ransacked. Steed is disturbed, but fails to connect the break-in with Beresford. They then prepare for the evening date at Beresford's home. Beresford, awaiting his guests, now puts the control mechanism into action, before Steed has put his watch on. Emma, wearing the jewelled watch, now becomes Beresford's puppet. She jumps into her car and almost runs Steed down as she drives away. He follows her in the Bentley, unaffected by Beresford since he has left his watch at home. Emma now arrives at Beresford's home, completely under his control. He decides to use her like a cybernaut to knock out Steed. Later, however, when Beresford tries to make Steed wear a watch containing a control device, Steed manages to get it onto the wrist of the cybernaut, whereupon the robot runs amok, finally killing Beresford. Emma is released when Steed smashes the watch she is wearing, and together they soon handle Benson and the scientists. Steed adjusts the watch control to immobilise the robot and, as Emma had the privilege last time, he takes pleasure in pushing over the enemy. *Teaser:* None. *Tag:* Repairing an electric toaster, Steed triumphantly declares the repair complete. Warily, Emma pops two slices of bread in the device – then stands back as the toaster explodes and zooms towards the ceiling.

Top: The cybernaut holds Dr Garnett, while the villainous Paul Beresford straps a killing device to his wrist in Return of the Cybernauts. *Time almost runs out, too, for The Avengers before Steed smashes the deadly watches.*

Left: Steed encounters his most dangerous enemy in the guise of the cybernaut, played by Terry Richard, posing a renewed threat in Return of the Cybernauts.

DEATH'S DOOR

In which Steed relives a nightmare – and Emma sees daylight

By Philip Levene

John Steed	**Patrick Macnee**
Emma Peel	**Diana Rigg**
Boyd	**Clifford Evans**
Stapley	**William Lucas**
Lord Melford	**Allan Cuthbertson**
Becker	**Marne Maitland**
Dr Evans	**Paul Dawkins**
Pavret	**Michael Faure**
Saunders	**Peter Thomas**
Dalby	**William Lyon Brown**
Haynes	**Terry Yorke**
Jepson	**Terry Maidment**

Designed by Robert Jones

Directed by Sidney Hayers

A CROWD OF reporters burst into a conference ante-chamber and face Stapley and Pavret, two government men, who are waiting the arrival of Sir Andrew Boyd, chairman of the conference and head of the British delegation. Pavret speaks of a rumour that the British may withdraw from the talks. Sir Andrew Boyd arrives, but he stops short at the door to the conference room and refuses to enter. Lord Melford, Steed and Emma meet in Boyd's study, and Steed learns from Stapley that he has covered up Boyd's lapse by saying he had a sudden attack of migraine. Steed promises to collect Boyd that evening and make sure that he attends the next conference. Boyd's doctor gives him some pills, and the highly-disturbed Boyd is left alone. As Dr Evans leaves the study, he begins to rub his neck and soon falls into a deep sleep. In his bedroom, Boyd also rubs his neck and falls asleep. Steed arrives to take Boyd to the conference, and as they leave, Boyd looks for a button missing from the coat of Dalby, his butler. Travelling to the conference in Steed's Bentley, Boyd talks about an escaped lion – 'The last thing I saw before I died'. At the conference hall he really *does* die, by leaping in front of a moving car. Over the entrance to the hall, Steed notices a large stone lion, reminiscent of the one Boyd had mentioned. Steed meets Emma in his flat and they discuss Boyd's strange death. Later, Steed reassures Melford, who tells him he is confident that he will be able to attend the conference in Boyd's place. That evening, Melford gets a sudden irritation at the back of his neck, which he rubs. He asks Stapley for a morning call, and dozes off – it is then that his nightmare begins. He is taken to the conference with menacing incidents dogging him as he goes. Faceless men torment him, Stapley appears in his dream with his face slashed, and the sequence ends with the conference room chandelier crashing down on him. Later, Stapley wakes Melford, wearing a piece of sticking-plaster on his face, and when Steed arrives and tears off a sheet on his office calendar, revealing Friday 13th – the date in Melford's dream – Melford is in a highly-disturbed state. However, Melford is clearly relieved to find there is no out-of-order sign on

the lift door – another item of his dream. But on the way to the conference, several more of the dream's details *are* confirmed. Becker opens the door exactly as he had done in the nightmare, at which point Melford cracks, and will not enter the conference chamber. Steed and Emma tackle Melford and Dr Evans respectively about the Minister's dream. Steed can only discover that Melford thinks he is having genuine premonitions of death. Emma learns nothing from Dr Evans. That night, Steed keeps watch in the room next to Melford and Emma waits outside in her car, keeping in touch by radio. In his room, Melford once again rubs his neck and falls into a deep sleep, and another nightmare follows. Emma is slow to react to Steed's summons – she appears to be recovering from a drugged condition – but Steed is relieved when she finally arrives. They decide to go over the route to the conference together, and find that various items from Melford's dream are revealed even to them. From photographs given him by Steed, Melford identifies the man at the door in his dream as Alfred Becker, an observer from the Eastern bloc. Meanwhile Emma is seen discovering the lift being put out of action, as required in Melford's dream. Her observer informs Jepson, one of the conference wreckers. Later, Jepson waylays Emma in Steed's flat, and after a fight, he is killed on a sword. From his body, Emma removes a

Yale key to the Temporary Storage Company in W4. Steed meanwhile waylays Becker, who is practising on a private shooting range in his house. Steed manages to kill Becker by making some holes in the wooden target, and lodges a bullet in them, which he fires by hitting the percussion cap with a stone. Steed also finds a Temporary Storage tag on the body. Emma visits the Storage Company and discovers an air-gun with which the conference wreckers have drugged Boyd, Melford, Steed, Emma and Dr Evans, so they can carry out their deception undisturbed – carrying off Boyd and Melford's bodies to the warehouse, then rigging reality to fit their dreams. Steed meets Emma in the conference room and together they confront Stapley with his guilt, and rip off his plaster to show he has feigned the cut on his face. Emma throws Haynes, an assistant attaché also in the plot, and Stapley dies when a stray bullet slices through the cord holding the chandelier, bringing it smashing down on his head, as in Melford's dream. *Teaser:* None. *Tag:* Steed is seen dozing on a couch, an expression of ecstasy on his face. Emma's entrance wakens him and he explains his dream of being in a harem. Emma, too, has a dream – to go to the theatre and occupy Row D, Seats 11 and 12. An extraordinary coincidence as Steed has purchased seats for that very row. But he can't find them. How could he, Emma already has them in her hand!

Steed and Emma foil Stapley and Haynes in Death's Door.

THE £50,000 BREAKFAST

In which Steed dabbles in Tycoonery – and Emma in Chicanery

By Roger Marshall

John Steed	Patrick Macnee
Emma Peel	Diana Rigg
Glover	Cecil Parker
Miss Pegram	Yolande Turner
Sir James Arnell	David Langton
Mrs Rhodes	Pauline Delaney
Judy	Anneke Wills
Minister	Cardew Robinson
First assistant	Eric Woofe
Second assistant	Phillippe Monnet
Rhodes	Richard Curnock

Designed by Robert Jones

Directed by Robert Day

RHODES IS driving along a country road, chatting amicably to a ventriloquist's dummy by his side. Operating the dummy, Rhodes makes it ask him where they are going this time! Charlie, the dummy, answers that they are bound for Zurich. Suddenly Rhodes is forced to swerve to avoid hitting a haycart ahead of him. He crashes the car and ends up in hospital, where the X-rays reveal that he has a stomach full of diamonds worth £50,000. Steed and Emma pick up the dummy from the wreck and return it to Rhodes' wife, who keeps a shop that sells dummies. Mrs Rhodes tells them that her husband has recently been flying to Switzerland every few days to perform at the Alex Litoff Homes there. She is unconcerned about her husband's serious injuries, and will not visit him in hospital. When Steed and Emma have left, Mrs Rhodes turns to her white Borzoi dog, Bellhound, and murmurs 'Visit Dusty! I should laugh!' The scene changes to a funeral for a black Borzoi dog called Dancer, held in the Happy Valley Resting Place, a pet cemetery. The chief mourner, Glover, tells the officiating cleric that Alex Litoff is paying for the funeral. Emma meanwhile learns from a Treasury official that Litoff is a wealthy industrialist and financier who came to London from Armenia in the 1930s, and is now a shy little man who is alleged to have his heart set on a knighthood. If he left London, many would go with him, and the pound would be in difficulty because of the outflow of cash. Steed decides to visit Litoff at his penthouse, and is received by Glover who has the black Borzoi with him. He is then introduced to Miss Pegram, Litoff's formidable assistant, who supervises two junior assistants, both hard at work in the business section. She tells Steed that Rhodes has simply stolen the diamonds, and that he is just an employee, as she is. She will have nothing to do with Steed's offer of £5000 for the diamonds, but says she will put it to her chief, and asks him to call back the next day. That night, Miss Pegram's first assistant enters the hospital, disguised as a doctor, and gives Rhodes a fatal injection of poison. The only lead Steed can get at the hospital is that blonde Borzoi hairs have been found on

Rhodes' suit. Later, the first assistant steals Rhodes' car from a garage, and has it crushed in a breaker's yard. Steed now shows Emma some old newsreel film of the mysterious Alex Litoff, but she is unable to pinpoint him. He shuns the public eye and never grants interviews – a fact which irritates Miss Pegram, for she would like some credit for her achievements. Steed returns to Litoff's penthouse and Miss Pegram says that her chief says he can have £4000 for the diamonds, which Steed accepts. On his way out, he meets Sir James Arnell, Litoff's doctor, and also Glover, whom he questions about Rhodes' death. He asks if Rhodes had anything to do with the dog Dancer, and Glover discloses that as well as the black one, there is a blonde dog called Bellhound. We next see Miss Pegram talking to Mrs Rhodes. She tells her that her husband, a dog lover, did not get rid of Bellhound as he was supposed to.

Steed is out on a limb in The £50,000 Breakfast.

Later, as a result of the information being passed on, the first assistant visits Mrs Rhodes, kills her, and removes the dog. Dr Arnell has told Steed that Litoff is suffering from heart trouble, but Emma has learned from his niece, Judy, that he has kidney disease. Emma searches Arnell's car but is attacked by the first assistant, who has passed Bellhound on to Glover. Emma throws the man, who falls awkwardly and dies. Steed joins her and learns that, according to the doctor's files, Litoff has heart trouble. Steed also finds more blonde Borzoi hairs on the dead man's body. Later he finds Mrs Rhodes dead in her shop, and when a kennel man calls for Bellhound, Steed pays him to go away. Steed breaks into Litoff's bedroom via the window, and tears away the newspaper covering his face. It is Glover – with Sir James Arnell at his side holding a gun. Meanwhile Emma is told by the minister at the dog cemetery that a dog named Bellhound was buried there recently, though the dog was black, not blonde. Back at Litoff's penthouse, Steed learns from Glover how the plotters propose to benefit from concealing the financier's death. Glover stands to make £11,000,000 but will not accept that Litoff has been murdered. When Steed accuses them of plotting the deaths of Rhodes and his wife, both Glover and Sir James deny complicity in this. At the dog cemetery, Emma learns that it is Litoff who is buried there, not Bellhound. Glover, paying his last respects, sees her and when she arrives at the penthouse dressed as a kennel-maid to collect the dogs, she is tied up with Steed. Miss Pegram, hearing that Litoff's body has been found, plans her escape in the financier's private plane. She decides to kill Emma and Steed before she leaves, but Glover and Sir James are opposed to this. As they are arguing, Steed and Emma manage to escape and Emma soon takes care of the murderess, while Glover and Sir James decide to come quietly. *Teaser*: None. *Tag*: Back in Steed's flat, Emma sets her partner a quandary. What to do with the two Borzois she's found – and the dalmatian-spotted tie she's given him as a gift!

Director Robert Day and stars on set of The £50,000 Breakfast.

DEAD MAN'S TREASURE

In which Steed rallies around – and Emma drives for her life

By Michael Winder

John Steed	**Patrick Macnee**
Emma Peel	**Diana Rigg**
Mike	**Norman Bowler**
Penny	**Valerie Van Ost**
Alex	**Edwin Richfield**
Carl	**Neil McCarthy**
Benstead	**Arthur Lowe**
Bates	**Ivor Dean**
Danvers	**Rio Fanning**
Miss Peabody	**Penny Bird**
First guest	**Gerry Crampton**
Second guest	**Peter J Elliott**

Designed by Robert Jones

Directed by Sidney Hayers

A CAR DRIVEN by agent Bobby Danvers is pursued in a night chase by another car, that of Carl and Alex. Danvers shakes off his pursuers by turning into the grounds of Benstead's open driveway, and he enters the house by the French windows. He then puts the small metal despatch box he is carrying into a red treasure chest he finds in the room, addresses one of the invitation cards he finds on a desk to John Steed, Esquire, and departs. He drives past Carl and Alex again, who have turned back after realising they have lost him. Emma joins Steed in his flat. He is worried because Danvers is already an hour late. The mortally-wounded agent finally arrives and before he dies, tells them he has hidden the despatch box in a red treasure chest. He does not say where. Carl and Alex, who have trailed Danvers to Steed's flat, listen at the window. They also overhear Steed telling Emma of an invitation he has received to attend Sir George Benstead's car rally. Steed and Emma go to the rally, and discover that Benstead is a car maniac, who practises car-racing on a Brands Hatch simulator he has rigged up in his home. Steed takes Benstead off to have a drink, leaving Mrs Peel to search alone. In the study she distracts Carl, who is looking for an invitation for himself and Alex. She fights the masked intruder, but is unable to prevent his escape, armed with an invitation to the rally. Next day, Carl and Alex are amongst the guests attending the function. Steed mentions the treasure chest to Benstead, not realising that this is the trophy in the car treasure hunt, which Benstead won't show to anyone. Steed continues to ask about the chest while Benstead plays with the simulator. Suddenly, he receives an electric shock from his apparatus and dies. Steed has only one clue – Bates was at the voltage control in the next room but, when questioned, the man can reveal nothing of value. Carl finds the dead Benstead, and later discovers from Alex that neither of them are responsible for his death. Even they are puzzled by this strange turn in events. Steed orders Bates to begin the treasure hunt as if nothing had happened, telling the guests that Benstead is unwell upstairs. Alex knocks out Mrs Elston, the partner

to whom he has been assigned, and grabs the envelope containing the first clue, 'The vaults at Mithering'. Carl tackles his partner, Miss Peabody, and joins Alex in their red Jaguar, to be the first away. The cars roar off. The race is complicated by the contestants changing the directions of the signposts, adding sugar to petrol tanks and scattering spikes on the road. Mike, with Emma as his passenger, reaches the house first and forces her to drive faster and faster in the racing car simulator, increasing the voltage in order to force her to give away a clue to the treasure. Meanwhile, Carl and Alex come to grief, their car spinning off the road, through a gate and into a tree. Steed drives on to the house, getting there in time to save Emma from Mike, whom he knocks out after a prolonged fight. He disconnects the shock equipment before Emma is aware that she is safe, giving her a few anxious moments. They then solve the last clue, 'What a shocking place to hide treasure', and find the missing chest – under Emma's driving seat in the racing car. *Teaser:* None. *Tag:* Entering Steed's apartment, Emma is shocked to hear the roar of a powerful motor. The puzzle is solved when Steed appears. He is shaving with 'the latest thing in electric razors, a new model with an exceedingly-powerful motor – and reverse speed!' She, investigating what happens when the reverse speed is used, soon finds the answer. The process in reverse leaves Emma sporting a droopy long moustache!

Steed and Penny discuss strategy in Dead Man's Treasure.

YOU HAVE JUST BEEN MURDERED

In which Steed chases a million – and Emma runs off with it

By Philip Levene

John Steed	Patrick Macnee
Emma Peel	Diana Rigg
Unwin	Barrie Ingham
Lord Maxted	Robert Flemying
Needle	George Murcell
Rathbone	Leslie French
Jarvis	Geoffrey Chater
Shelton	Simon Oates
Chalmers	Clifford Cox
Hallam	John Baker
Morgan	Les Crawford
Nicholls	Frank Maher
Williams	Peter J Elliott

Designed by Robert Jones

Directed by Robert Asher

TWO MOCK attempts are made on the life of millionaire Gilbert Jarvis, but each time the handsome blond assailant does not go through with the assassination. First he fires an unloaded gun at Jarvis, then attacks him with a dummy dagger. Each time he leaves a visiting card reading 'You have just been murdered'. Jarvis contacts Steed and says he will talk about the matter at a party held in the home of George Unwin, another millionaire. Jarvis, however, does not turn up at the party and Steed phones him at home, where we see that Jarvis is *really* being murdered, by Shelton, the good-looking assassin. Jarvis answers the phone but does not speak to Steed, who leaves the party to investigate. Steed finds Jarvis shot, and evidence that he had been trying to protect himself with elaborate locks on his doors. While Steed is away from the party, Lord Maxted, a banker, tells Emma that Jarvis has recently asked him for £1,000,000 in cash from his account. When Rathbone, another millionaire, hears that Jarvis has been murdered, he reacts with apparent fright and leaves the party, followed closely by Emma. She finally reaches him through an array of guard dogs, armed men and locked doors. She tries to discover why he is so afraid, without success. Later we discover that Rathbone has also been terrified by four mock attempts on his life. The last was a mock poisoning, which his tormentors managed to stage despite his elaborate precautions. The next millionaire to receive the treatment is George Unwin, whom Shelton terrifies with a pantomime of murder by shooting, again leaving the visiting card. Maxted, the banker, learns that Rathbone wants £1,000,000 in cash to pay off his blackmailers, and tells Emma. She then follows the man to a stream where he drops the case of money into the water. Here Emma meets Nicholls, another good-looking hireling of the (as yet) unseen mastermind. She finally impales him on a scythe. Shelton now increases the pressure on Unwin. First he nearly runs him down against a wall, and then stabs him with a harmless knife. Finally he fires an arrow at him – with a rubber sticker on the end. Then, a telephone caller tells Unwin to watch his television set that night. On screen as promised, the mastermind (a man called Needle) tells Unwin how he must take the £1,000,000 to Bridge Farm and what to do with it. Unwin contacts Maxted about the money. Steed follows Unwin to the farm, using a bleeping device attached to the case. At the farm Emma is waiting under the bridge and manages to catch Unwin's case before it hits the water. She then traps Morgan, another of Needle's henchmen, by floating the case to him. Emma then overpowers him and forces him to take her to Needle's headquarters. But Morgan misdirects her to a caravan, where Shelton fells her with a karate chop. She is then taken to Needle's headquarters, which are hidden beneath a haystack. Meanwhile Steed catches up with Unwin, who tells him he has put a bomb inside the case. Steed manages to track the case via the bleep device, and the men find themselves at the haystack. While they search for an entrance, Unwin is knocked out by one of Needle's henchmen, who in turn is flattened by Steed. Shelton investigates the disturbance, and Steed drops on him from the top of the haystack, and gets into the headquarters. He releases Emma and together they round up the gang. But they are unable to prevent Needle from escaping with the case in a van. Needle's plans are finally thwarted when the bomb goes off and the van is blown up. *Teaser:* None. *Tag:* Steed is seen at home piling box after box of his savings into a pyramid in the centre of his living-room – each box of halfpennies containing 10,000 worth of Steed's future. Emma, totting-up the amount as the boxes grow higher, comments that she never knew Steed was so wealthy. Suddenly she stops in her tracks. 'That's 9,999. You're just short of a million', she tells him. Steed is fraught with despair: who ever heard of a nine-thousand, nine-hundred and ninety-nine-anaire? It's Emma to the rescue as, handing Steed a half-penny piece, she comments 'You are now a self-made, fully-fledged, halfpenny millionaire!'

In You Have Just Been Murdered, *Steed bursts in on Unwin, the blackmailing millionaire.*

THE POSITIVE-NEGATIVE MAN

In which Steed makes the sparks fly – and Emma gets switched on

By Tony Williamson

John Steed	Patrick Macnee
Emma Peel	Diana Rigg
Cresswell	Ray McAnally
Haworth	Michael Latimer
Cynthia Wentworth-Howe	Caroline Blakiston
Mankin	Peter Blythe
Maurice Jubert	Sandor Eles
Miss Clarke	Joanne Dainton
Charles Grey	Bill Wallis
Receptionist	Ann Hamilton

Designed by Robert Jones

Directed by Robert Day

GREY, AN electronics expert, is working at his drawing board in the Ministry of Science when an intruder in a pin-stripe suit and wellington boots enters, points a finger at him, and blasts him into the back wall. When the body is found embedded in the wall, Steed and Emma are called in. They discover that Grey's papers, though securely locked in a safe, have been burnt to a crisp. From Cynthia, Grey's private secretary, Steed learns that the papers related to the lately abandoned Project 90, on which Grey had been working with Bryant, Mankin, Jubert and Cresswell. The intruder, Haworth, next arrives at Jubert's electronics company, and on his way in to Jubert, gives Miss Clarke, his secretary, a bad shock from the filing cabinet. She falls to the floor unconscious. Emma discovers both the unconscious secretary and the dead Jubert. He has been hurled back with prodigious force through both a door and a wooden cupboard. Miss Clarke tells Emma of the strange electronic crackling that accompanied the intruder, and as Emma leaves the office she sees a van that has brought Haworth departing. Meanwhile, Steed visits Risely Dale, where the scientists worked on Project 90, and investigates a small black van he finds there. It has a small generator working inside, and when he grips the door handle, he receives a violent electric shock and is thrown to the ground. Emma, who also visits Risely Dale, finds Steed dazed, and the van gone. They bump into Cresswell, the leader of Project 90, who arrives bearing a shotgun. Steed stops Emma from fighting with him, and suggests that they go to his house to discuss what has happened. Emma stays behind to have a closer look at Risely Dale. Cresswell tells Steed that the research team had been working on broadcasting electricity by radio waves, when the project was shelved and Cresswell retired. Suddenly the French windows crash open, and all the lights are dimmed. The light in the room increases in intensity, and Cresswell says unconvincingly that it must have been a fireball. Steed, however, discovers a boot print outside, and Emma appears, saying she has seen a blue light approaching the house through the trees, and heard the sound of faint electrical

crackling. They also discover a handprint, buried deep in the back of a tree. Steed returns to the Ministry of Science and persuades Cynthia to show him the rest of the files on Project 90, but they discover that these, too, are charred to ashes. Steed next visits Mankin, who tells him about the possibilities of broadcast power. As he leaves, the driver of a black van focuses the sights of an electric broadcasting apparatus, hooked to a generator in the van, on Steed's car. The car is given a charge of electricity and Steed is forced to crash it to escape. Mankin goes to Risely Dale, and discovers the black van. He telephones Steed to, say that something strange is going on, but no sooner has he hung up than the man in rubber boots traps and electrocutes him along a metal wire fence, simply by touching it! Emma arrives and discovers Mankin's body. The murderer, after administering the shock treatment to Emma, escapes in the van. Emma is left unconscious beside the body of Mankin. Steed visits Cresswell, who is taken aback because he is expecting someone else. Haworth arrives and, having first removed the rubber boots, joins them. He thinks he has left Mrs Peel dead at Risely Dale and receives a surprise when she soon joins them. As they leave, Emma falls to the ground. The fall, however, was feigned, and Emma now has a trace of the make-up from Haworth's collar. They later discover that the make-up is a mixture of non-conducting oil and aluminium dust and acts as an insulating barrier. Haworth later raids Emma's flat, and she is shocked into unconsciousness and taken to Risely Dale. There she is forced to record her voice, making it appear to Steed on the phone that she is summoning him. Cresswell then encases her in silver foil from head to foot, so that they can charge her with electricity from which she is insulated, like Haworth. Cresswell hopes to electrocute Steed when he attempts to rescue Emma. However, when Steed arrives, he is wearing rubber galoshes. In the ensuing mayhem, Haworth and Cresswell both die, Haworth when one of his earthing boots is removed. Cresswell by falling through a window. *Teaser:* None. *Tag:* Outside Risely Dale, Steed and Emma pay the penalty of their contact with electricity. He becomes magnetised to his Bentley, as does Mrs Peel when she goes to help him. As Steed remarks, 'Don't fight it, Mrs Peel. We're inseparable!'

In The Positive-Negative Man, *Mrs Peel, charged with electricity, plants her rubber boot in Haworth's chest.*

MURDERSVILLE

In which Emma marries Steed – and Steed becomes a father

By Brian Clemens

John Steed	**Patrick Macnee**
Emma Peel	**Diana Rigg**
Mickle	**Colin Blakeley**
Hubert	**John Ronane**
Dr Haynes	**Ronald Hines**
Prewitt	**John Sharp**
Jenny	**Sheila Fearn**
Croft	**Eric Flynn**
Forbes	**Norman Chappell**
Banks	**Roger Cawdren**
Miss Avril	**Marika Mann**
Maggie	**Irene Bradshaw**
Higgins	**Joseph Greig**
Jeremy Purser	**Geoffrey Colville**
Chapman	**Langton Jones**
Miller	**Tony Caunter**
Morgan	**John Chandos**
Williams	**Andrew Laurence**

Designed by Robert Jones

Directed by Robert Asher

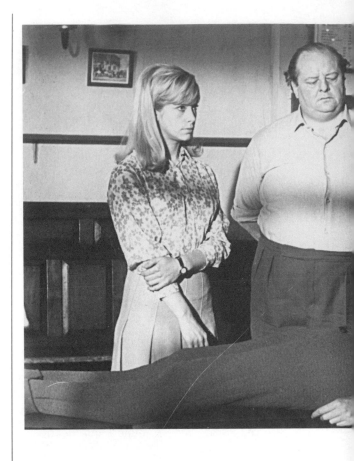

OUTSIDE A pub at the sleepy village of Little Storping-in-the-Swuff, Hubert and Mickle, two local rustics, are playing dominoes and quaffing ale, when suddenly a man bursts onto the scene, pursued by another man, who shoots him dead. The rustics continue their game, and the village sleeps on. Emma introduces Major Paul Croft, whom she has known since she was a little girl, to Steed. Back from his overseas posting, Croft has bought a house at Little Storping, and his batman, Forbes, has gone on ahead to tidy things up. Forbes is staying at the local inn, and is told by Jenny Prewitt, the landlord's daughter, that some kind of event will happen soon, at twelve o'clock. Forbes wants to leave, but the locals insist that he has another drink with them. Minutes later, a man arrives and is given a package, containing a shotgun, by Prewitt, the landlord. The man goes outside and apparent gunshots are heard. The man returns and gives the package back to Prewitt. Mickle and Hubert pass off the incident as a car back-firing. The next strange event occurs when Forbes enlists the aid of Mickle and Hubert to unload things at Croft's new home. The pair unaccountably begin to destroy valuable china and furniture. Emma insists on driving Croft to his house, and on the way they pass a limousine driven by Samuel Morgan. At the village, Croft identifies a local man, Frederick Williams, to Emma as they pass the pub. Williams was once an important financier, whose crash was caused by the man they had passed earlier, Samuel Morgan. Croft says it seems strange to see both men on the same day. Croft is furious when he finds his possessions smashed and sets off for the pub to find Forbes. He is not there, and the

locals say they have never seen him. Croft next goes to the library, supervised by the attractive Miss Avril, who is arguing with Morgan. As he enters, Croft pots Williams with an unsilenced gun trained on Morgan from behind the bookshelves. Miss Avril points to the 'Silence' signs, and Williams produces a silencer before calmly shooting Morgan dead. As Croft backs to the door, he turns and finds himself confronted by Mickle, with a gun, and Hubert, holding a sickle. Emma, searching the grounds of Croft's house, finds a sickle lying in the grass. Searching further, she finds the dead body of Forbes, with what looks like a sickle wound in his back. Then someone throws a large block of wood at her, knocking her out. She comes to in the pub, where she is in the care of Dr Haynes, with Prewitt and his daughter Jenny in attendance. They try to convince her that her car has skidded, and indicate the car resting on the grass verge, but Emma insists that Dr Haynes goes with her to the house where she has found Forbes' body. At the house, the mess has been removed, and Forbes' body has gone. There instead is the gardener, Higgins, who claims that he has been there all the time, and has no knowledge of Croft buying the house! Emma goes to collect her car but finds Mickle leaning on the bonnet. She notices that he is wearing Croft's wristwatch and, now suspicious, returns to Dr Haynes and says she will take up his offer of pills to help with her delusions. At his surgery, Emma gives up her pretence that something is wrong with her, and threatens to summon the police. Banks, the local policeman, arrives in a squad car, but as Emma is about to tell him of the strange events, she notices that he is wearing bright, un-policeman-like

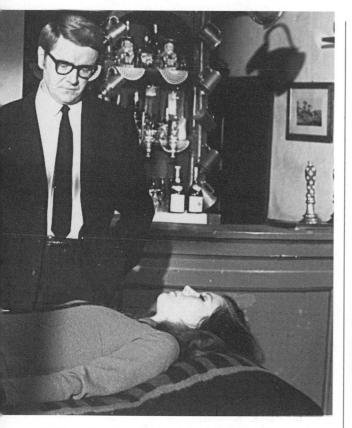

Dr Hayes, Prewitt and Jenny wait for Emma to regain consciousness in Croft's house in **Murdersville.**

Peel'. They are startled and Steed knocks them out. He then moves on to the museum and is freeing Emma, when Haynes, Mickle, Hubert and Prewitt arrive. In the fast and furious fight that follows Emma and Steed soon put paid to the villains – Emma by grabbing and wearing a medieval helmet throughout the fight, and Steed by wielding a broad sword and smiting the poor unfortunates over the head with it. In the final scene, Steed and Emma enter the library and, with custard pies from the craft exhibition, pelt the rest of the townsfolk into submission. *Teaser:* None. *Tag:* In Steed's flat, Emma, drinking champagne through a straw, is finding difficulty in removing the medieval helmet from her head. After several attempts, Steed manages to remove it. Commenting that she hadn't adjusted it properly, then showing her how it should be worn, he too finds it stuck firmly around his ears. At last he's become Emma's knight in shining armour!

Steed helps Mrs Peel to clean off the custard pies used in a fight sequence in **Murdersville.**

socks. Banks leaves, and Emma tells Haynes that the policeman is bogus, but he threatens to commit her to hospital. He then pulls a gun on her as she attempts to escape. While he calls the exchange operator, Maggie, and orders her to call an emergency meeting, Emma knocks him unconscious. As she is leaving, she notices a private room off the hall. Inside are the bodies of Forbes and Croft. Finding the village deserted, she goes into the pub and breaks open a cupboard to find millions of pounds in cash bundled in there. Meanwhile, the townsfolk are attending a meeting in the library. Haynes bursts in with the news that Emma has escaped and they rush off to find her. They spot Emma leaving the pub and give chase. Pursued by the whole village, she escapes into the fields. Mickle pursues her in a helicopter, and she is knocked out by the machine's skids. When she comes to, she is confined and chained in the village museum, along with the village's former vicar, police sergeant, local magistrate and the telephone exchange girl. They tell Emma how the village got into its present state. When a murder was once committed there in broad daylight, the rich murderer bought the town's silence for £1,000,000. Since then, the townsfolk have become greedy, and have let it be known that they would kill people discreetly and silently in the privacy of their village for a fee! The four now imprisoned with Emma were the only dissenters. Emma is discovered and taken to the witch's ducking pool where she eventually agrees to reveal who else knows of their plans. She is allowed to ring the other person, her husband John. This is obviously Steed, who drives to the village and tests the reaction of Prewitt and Jenny by shouting out 'Emma

MISSION HIGHLY IMPROBABLE

In which Steed falls into enemy heads – and Emma is cut down to size

By Philip Levene

John Steed	**Patrick Macnee**
Emma Peel	**Diana Rigg**
Shaffer	**Ronald Radd**
Susan	**Jane Merrow**
Prof Rushton	**Noel Howlett**
Chivers	**Francis Matthews**
Col Drew	**Richard Leech**
Josef	**Stefan Gryff**
Gifford	**Nicholas Courtney**
Sir Gerald Bancroft	**Kevin Stoney**
Sergeant	**Peter Clay**
Corp Johnson	**Nigel Rideout**
Blonde	**Cynthia Bizeray**
Brunette	**Nicole Shelby**
Henrick	**Nosher Powell**
Karl	**Denny Powell**

Designed by Robert Jones

Directed by Robert Day

A ROLLS-ROYCE, registration number GB1, disappears while being escorted into a Ministry testing area. The passenger is Sir Gerald Bancroft, a Treasury official, who is to investigate apparent overspending by the research workers. The car passed the perimeter post and had a motorcycle escort in front and security officer behind, and yet vanished. Steed finds a miniature Rolls there, but Gifford ignores this. While they are talking, they fail to notice that Sir Gerald is in the grass not far away from them, and he is soon scooped up in a net by Dr Chivers. They next discover the tracks of a truck with a worn offside tyre. Steed confirms that the tracks are those of a MT4 military truck, and later we see Chivers getting down from just such a truck. He puts the box he is carrying – containing the miniaturised Sir Gerald – into a dustbin among the rubbish. Chivers then tells Professor Rushton that Sir Gerald will be delayed. Rushton has been overspending on an invention of his, urged on by Chivers. He wants to show it to Sir Gerald, but Chivers insists that the time is not yet ripe. Steed arrives at the administration block and stops to check on a truck parked outside. He is nearly hit by Chivers, who quickly regains his composure, and takes Steed to meet Rushton and his daughter Susan, who is also worried about her father's overspending. Steed asks her for an inventory, so he can find the truck with the worn tyre, but Susan lies and says that the inventory is missing. Gifford, meanwhile, finds the truck in the shed with the Champion MK 39 armoured car. He takes the tiny Rolls with him and realises that the registration number matches that of the missing Rolls. He rushes to phone Steed, but Chivers enters and turns a reducing device, installed in a truck, on him. Gifford is now also miniaturised – and left looking at a giant telephone. Chivers then turns on the water hose and washes him down a grating. Susan now confronts her father. She says she has lied for him, and insists on knowing why he is overspending on the research grant. She, too, is given a working demonstration of the reducing device. Meanwhile, Chivers tells Shaffer, the head of the East European delegation which have arrived to see the Champion MK 39 demonstration, that he can deliver the vehicle. At the demonstration, Steed becomes suspicious when he identifies Shaffer as a Head of Intelligence he has met before – that time the man was dressed as an Admiral! The visitors are impressed with the MK 39, which emerges unscathed after being fired at by heavy artillery. Leaving the test area, Steed finds the miniature Rolls-Royce lodged in the mudguard of the MK 39. Later, he visits the experimental shed, and when he hears someone coming, hides in the MK 39. Chivers enters and trains the reducing ray on to the MK 39. Pocketing the now tiny MK 39 – and the equally miniature Steed – he drives out of the establishment. Chivers takes the MK 39 to Shaffer, who says he is even more interested in the greater prize of the reducing machine. He tells Chivers that he intends to kidnap Susan Rushton to make her father bring the machine to him. Steed, unnoticed by Shaffer and Chivers, crawls out of the MK 39 and manages to telephone Emma,

It's a **Mission Highly Improbable** *for a miniaturised Steed to telephone his partner Mrs Peel . . .*

. . . but he gets through to her successfully.

despite his reduced size. He tells her to stay with Susan as she is in danger. Emma then goes to Susan's home, but two of Shaffer's henchmen kidnap her instead of Susan when she is inspecting the latter's car. Shaffer soon realises the mistake. He locks Emma in his study, bound hand and foot, and there she is surprised to find the miniaturised Steed. He helps her to get free, and pushes the key of the study to her under the door, allowing Emma to escape. Steed then jabs the dozing Henrick with a pen-point, and Emma knocks him out. She also manages to throw Karl when he is harpooned by Steed with the same pen. Meanwhile, Rushton has burned his papers on the reducing machine, and he and Susan are forced by Chivers to take the truck out of the testing area. At the house, Emma notices the arrival of the truck as it enters Shaffer's grounds. Shaffer demands a demonstration of the machine, and they select a nearby pavilion to be reduced. When Emma overhears them saying they will bring it back to its normal size, she decides to put Steed inside it. This she does, but is seen, and Chivers reduces Emma herself. Chivers now collects Emma in the butterfly net, and pulls a gun on Steed. He tells Josef to take Steed back to the house while he brings Mrs Peel. But Emma makes Chivers slip on a loose stone and he falls dead, face down into an ornamental pool. Emma now makes her way to the house, where Susan, Rushton and Steed are tied up on the floor. She frees Steed's hands, and he hits Henrick. Rushton, freed by Steed, then restores Emma to normal size. They then turn the reducing ray on the truck, in which Shaffer and Josef are trying to escape, and Steed is able to trap them in his bowler. *Teaser:* None. *Tag:* Watched by Steed, Emma adjusts the furniture in her apartment. Commenting that they could have used Rushton's reducer ray to make things easier to move, Steed adds, 'Never mind, we'll console ourselves with a gigantic feast.' When Emma notes that a storm is brewing outside, Steed cautions her not to worry – and hands her his *miniaturised* brolly!

THE FORGET-ME-KNOT

The Forget-Me-Knot was the only one of the 161 episodes of The Avengers to be bridged. For this reason, the episode has been given this spread to itself, and is divided into two halves. The main part of the story falls on this page, and the tag scene is on the opposite page.

By Brian Clemens

John Steed	**Patrick Macnee**
Emma Peel	**Diana Rigg**
Tara King	**Linda Thorson**
Sean Mortimer	**Patrick Kavanagh**
George Burton	**Jeremy Young**
Mother	**Patrick Newell**
Karl	**Alan Lake**

Designed by Robert Jones

Directed by James Hill

SEAN MORTIMER, a fellow agent of Steed's who has been missing for two weeks, staggers into the forecourt below Steed's flat. Emma Peel, sitting by the window, spots him as he wanders around aimlessly in the street below. She mentions 'a tall, well-built man, wearing an overcoat' to Steed who, seeing Mortimer wandering below, rushes outside and brings the agent back to his flat. It soon becomes apparent that Mortimer is suffering from loss of memory – he does not even recognise Steed. After continual questioning by Steed, Mortimer manages to gasp 'The organisation – a traitor in the organisation'. Worried, Steed leaves to contact Mother, his superior at Headquarters – a large mansion set in spacious grounds. While he is wandering through the garden, he is attacked and knocked down by a trainee agent, 69, who is undergoing a training session at the house. Her tutor, a military man called George Burton, apologises profusely, saying she has mistaken Steed for someone else. Meanwhile, Karl and Brad, two thugs who have trailed Mortimer to Steed's flat, attack Emma and Mortimer. They fire a memory-killing dart at Emma and leave her unconscious, then carry Mortimer's body to the sidecar of their waiting motorcycle. Back at Headquarters, Steed, waiting for Mother to arrive, is somewhat surprised to see a tall, well-built, auburn-haired girl in a mini-suit enter the room through the French windows. She introduces herself as Tara, and seems surprised when Steed doesn't add a 'Ra-boom-di-ay' to her name. Steed then realises that she is the same trainee agent 69 who had earlier knocked him down. She goes on to inform Steed that she recognises him, and that his name crops up everywhere in training. She gives him her address and telephone number on a piece of paper, which he stores in his shoe. Their conversation is interrupted by the arrival of Filson, another agent, who then directs Steed into Mother's office. Mother suggests that Steed returns to his apartment and brings back Mortimer who, because he has been missing for more than two weeks, is now on Mother's wanted list. When Steed arrives, he finds that Emma has no recollection of ever having met Mortimer. Disturbed by her condition, Steed decides to take her back to Headquarters. On the way they are waylaid by Karl and Brad, who ambush Steed's car and kidnap Emma. Steed is left lying in a ditch, with several memory-killing darts

in him. Before he passes out, he overhears one of the thugs mention The Heights, a familiar place to Steed. Having lost his memory, Steed wakes up in hospital, but some sense of urgency makes him break out of the place and, finding Tara's address in his shoe, he drives to her flat. She helps to restore his memory by giving him the address of his own flat. Steed, now fully recovered, heads for Mother's headquarters, and arrives to find that his name has been added to Mother's wanted list. He also finds George Burton, the man in charge of Tara's training, waiting with a gun! Steed manages to persuade him to drive him to The Heights, where he expects to find the hideout of Karl, Brad and the rest of the opposition. Arriving at The Heights, Burton pulls a gun on Steed and reveals that he is the traitor in Mother's section. The quick-thinking Steed manages to overcome him, however, and with the help of Emma and Sean Mortimer – who have been battling the villains inside the hideout – and Tara King, who has by this time found her way to the showdown, they round up the thugs in a fast and furious finale of flying fists and karate kicks.

Memory-killing darts lay Steed low in
The Forget-Me-Knot.

Mrs Peel
meets Tara King
on the staircase outside
Steed's apartment and hands over
responsibilities to the new girl . . .

THE NEWSPAPER headline reads 'Peter Peel Alive. Air ace found in Amazonian jungle . . . Wife Emma waits.' Steed is on the telephone, saying he has seen the newspapers and will need a replacement as soon as possible. Sadness lines his face. The door to his apartment is suddenly flung open by an excited Mrs Peel, resplendent in a yellow trouser suit. They discuss the newspaper story, and Emma says that her husband will be arriving in the mews in a few minutes. Emma crosses to Steed and places her hand on his chest. Memories of past adventures fill her mind and with a half-smile she says 'Always keep your bowler on in times of stress – and a watchful eye open for diabolical masterminds!' She leans towards him and kisses his cheek, then silently turns and heads for the door. Steed gazes at the retreating figure. 'Emma!' he softly calls. A quizzical look crosses her face as she realises that he has used her first name. 'Thanks!' Mrs Peel looks sadly at him, gives one last smile, and leaves. On the staircase outside Steed's apartment she notices Tara King coming through the front entrance. Tara spots Emma and asks, 'Excuse me, Apartment 3?' With a coy smile, Mrs Peel points upwards. 'At the top of the stairs,' she says. 'Thanks,' says Tara, as the two pass each other. Mrs Peel pauses and looks back at her. 'Ahem,' she calls. 'He likes his tea stirred anti-clockwise.' With her index finger she mimes a stirring motion. Tara, looking confused, mimics the stirring motion. 'Yes,' says Emma, nodding. Steed, upstairs, is gazing sadly out of his window. In the mews, he sees Mrs Peel cross to a waiting car, beside which stands – *Steed?* Bowler-hatted, impeccably dressed. Steed stares in amazement at the resemblance. He watches Mrs Peel climb into the car. She looks lovingly at her husband then, with one final look in Steed's direction, the couple drive away. Steed's thoughts are broken when Tara walks in. 'Mother sent me,' she begins. 'Tara–.' 'Ra-boom-di-ay,' smiles Steed.

. . . but not before she reminds
Tara that Steed likes
his tea stirred
anti-clockwise!

ENTER TARA

Patrick Macnee/Linda Thorson   1969

THE COLOUR series proved to be a big money earner worldwide. Foreign sales were in excess of £5,000,000 and the show was being screened in over 70 countries. In May 1967, the show was put forward as a candidate for the best foreign dramatic series of the year by ABC in America. Diana Rigg was nominated for an American Emmy (television's equivalent of the Oscar) – it was eventually won by Barbara Bain of *Mission Impossible* – and voted Actress of the Year by the 16 European countries screening *The Avengers*.

The success of the show had once again led to discussions about making a feature-length film of *The Avengers*. Sadly, as with earlier plans, it never materialised.

After filming of the colour series was completed, Diana Rigg left the show and returned to Shakespeare, as the female lead in the filmed version of A *Midsummer Night's Dream*. (In true *Avengers* spirit, her departure from the set was greeted by the clink of champagne glasses – the bubbly being provided by herself – as she drank one final toast to her co-star and production staff.) Soon afterwards she said, 'Television is so immediate. Within a week of appearing in my first *Avengers* story I was recognised by 90 per cent of the viewing public. A week after I'd left, I was unrecognised by 90 per cent of the public.'

After screening the colour series, the ITV network repeated the 26 Rigg monochrome episodes. (Ironically, until Channel 4 began to rerun them at the end of 1982, British viewers had only seen the Rigg colour episodes once in colour. That was in 1970, only a few months after its introduction, when very few people had colour sets.)

At this time ABC (having become Thames Television) felt that, though the show had been highly successful and had style, it was becoming more extreme. They believed that a backward move to reality would help prolong the show's success, and this needed to be achieved mainly in the writing. John Bryce (formerly story editor and then producer of the Blackman series) was appointed producer of the new series, and, after a dispute over the direction the series was going, Brian Clemens and Albert Fennell left the production team.

Unfortunately, for a number of reasons, this arrangement did not work out and, as ABC were committed to deliver the series for American and British telecast dates, Clemens and Fennell were asked to return as joint producers, with almost total control.

One thing they had no control over, however, was the choice of Steed's new Avenger girl. During their absence, Linda Thorson had been signed to play Tara King.

Oddly enough, renowned film director John Huston was partly responsible for Linda getting the role. Having seen the young actress at RADA (the Royal Academy of Dramatic Arts), he had promised her a lead part in his next firm, *Sinful Davey*. When circumstances forced Huston to change his mind, the director sent Linda to see Robert Lennard, the casting director of ABC, who told her that they were casting the female lead in *The Avengers*, (a programme which, due to the fact that Linda didn't have a television set at the time, she'd heard about, but never seen!). Linda told me, 'I was one of 200 girls, which soon became 100, then 50, then 25 and eventually 8. Three of us, Tracey Reed, Mary Peach and myself were given screen tests and the tapes were sent to Don Boyle, then head of the ABC network in America. He liked what he saw and I was sent to Henlow Grange Beauty Farm to lose weight.' After eight days on hot water and lemon, she received a telegram from ABC telling her that she had the part. She signed for her *Avengers* role in October 1967.

Linda was formally 'launched' as Tara King at a Press Reception held at Thames TV on 19 October. She remembers a far from amusing anecdote. 'I remember going to Thames, to attend a luncheon. And they asked me to play a short scene in which I was to pretend that I was a secretary applying for the post of John Steed's secretary. That is to say, if John Steed was my boss, how would I treat him? Would I mother him? Baby him, etc? And they had this hidden camera and were filming the entire proceedings – which made me very uncomfortable, to say the least. I didn't take kindly to that.'

Neither Clemens nor Fennell believed that Linda was the right choice. As Clemens said later, 'She was fresh out of drama school, and didn't have the necessary experience to handle a star role in a major series. But the show had been pre-sold to the American market, and there was no time to recast the part.' Interviewed recently, he told me, 'Linda did the best she could – bearing in mind her total inexperience. Of course she got better. Who wouldn't, filming five days a week for so many months? The main problem was that she never really had a definitely prescribed attitude to Steed. One never quite knew what she was doing there.' Linda agreed. As she told me, 'The problem arose because the one thing that RADA didn't do – couldn't do – was to teach you camera technique. I'd never been in front of a camera before. So I'm there making episodes of a

well-known television series, with no experience whatsoever. I had to learn as I went along. The most difficult thing was shooting it for a year before it went on the air. I didn't know if people would take to me. I didn't know if I was any good. Frankly I was terrified of what the outcome would be. Then as soon as the show went on the air and everybody said "She's great", and I picked up good reviews, I felt better about it.'

Pictured left to right, at a Thames TV party to 'launch' Tara King: Brian Clemens, Linda Thorson, Patrick Macnee and the late Albert Fennell.

The first thing that Clemens and Fennell did upon returning to the show was to scrap the episodes filmed in their absence. John Bryce had produced two stories, *Invitation to a Killing* and *The Great Great Britain Crime*. Both were thrown out as unsuitable by the team. The former was refilmed as *Have Guns, Will Haggle* (using several scenes from the first story – in particular those in which Linda is sporting a blonde wig) and scenes from the latter made up the 'framing device' for Mother's birthday party story in *Homicide and Old Lace*. Linda believes that John Bryce wasn't supported enough. 'I was still learning, and there was a lot of tension on the set,' she told me. 'I was very sorry when John Bryce had to go – and toyed with the idea of leaving with him. But Patrick and two of my colleagues, including John himself, said "You can't do it". By then Patrick had become very supportive and was always taking the time to find out if everything was all right. He was marvellous. So I stayed.'

The name Tara was Linda's own choice. 'Because *Gone with the Wind* was my favourite movie at the time and that was the name of the estate. And "King" for King and Country, which I felt was a nice touch.'

Tara was the daughter of a prosperous farmer, and had all the skills associated with the outdoor life. At her expensive finishing school, she had learned how to glide, ski and fly, and had acquired the sophistication of the young international set. She was a warm, feminine and sexy woman, with an exuberant and jaunty approach to her adventures with Steed.

There was a bond between the two principals not previously in evidence. Whereas the hallmark of Steed's relationships, both with Cathy Gale and Emma Peel, was haughty, well-hidden respect, the bond of friendship with Tara was frequently sealed with a kiss and a cuddle.

Unlike Steed's earlier partners, Tara was single.

'It was my idea,' Linda told me. 'They suggested it might seem indecent for a single girl to be shown in his flat and perhaps having stayed overnight. I thought it was highly indecent for a *married* woman to be staying with him. So I persuaded them that it was much better for Tara to be single. Before my series, you had never really seen a girl making a fuss of Steed. But I saw Tara as being in love with him – absolutely, unquestionably in love. Let's face it. Here was this young girl who had been trained to do this job and tripped around at his "Ra-boom-di-ay" beck and call. No one could have worked that closely with Steed and not been in love with him. Originally she was flying by the seat of her pants quite a lot of the time, so she had this image of Steed looking after her. Patrick would be there and I'd throw my arms around him in a gesture that implied love – but without saying the words. We took the sex relationship for granted and Tara, like Emma before her, did sometimes stay overnight – but it was all very civilised.'

Patrick told the media at the time, 'As a younger girl, Linda will be more defenceless. I'll be able to put my arms around her; look after her more. I want us to share the same easy, friendly relationship I had with Ian Hendry and then Honor Blackman and Diana Rigg. We're going to spend a large part of our working lives together and I'd like it to be happy for both our sakes.'

Before Linda herself could find happiness, however, she had first to overcome the damage done to her hair when a studio executive issued orders that Tara King should be a blonde. Linda takes up the story: 'They were so afraid that I was going to be just like Diana, that everything was done to go against that image; blonde instead of dark; fluffy and pink instead of black leather. Being a natural brunette, they decided to give me a day-to-day, weekly treatment of ninety-volume peroxide. As a consequence, my hair became brittle – and eventually fell out! I was left with a short stubble of patchy growth on my head. So during the first half-dozen episodes, I camouflaged this by wearing a selection of colourful wigs and hid from the public gaze for about six months until my own hair had regrown and I could show my face in public.'

There were to be no new fighting techniques for Tara. No judo, karate or kung-fu. Instead, she would rely more on feminine guile than muscular skill. Tara would hit her opponents with a straight right-hander, her handbag, or whatever was at hand that might be used as a weapon. She would even give the occasional scream for help! (This idea slipped away as the series progressed. Tara would soon be throwing baddies over her shoulder in true Cathy Gale style. Linda would also find herself doing lots of her own stuntwork; leaps from tall buildings, etc. – but not any of the driving scenes. Having failed her driving test five times, and crashed Tara's sports car into a wall during the second day's

1. On their way to the ordnance factory, Steed tests the FF70 rifle. (In HGWH Tara travelled alone to the establishment and test-fired the gun on a rifle range.)

Five scenes from the unscreened Invitation to a Killing. *(Note how they differ from the scenes that appeared in the* Have Guns . . . Will Haggle *remake.)*

2. Conrad forces Tara to drive him to Adrianna's house. (In HGWH Conrad held a brunette Tara at gunpoint in her flat.)

3. Note Tara's blonde wig and lamé suit – not to mention her weight! (In HGWH she was brunette and wore a tartan mini-skirt.)

4. In HGWH Conrad was on the losing end. Here the roles are reversed.

5. Who is the guy holding Steed at gunpoint? This scene never appeared in the remake.

shooting, Linda's double handled all the motoring sequences.)

Ray Austin, stunt arranger on the two previous Diana Rigg series, would soon leave the show to work on ITC's *The Champions*. This time around, Joe Dunne, who had worked as *The Avengers*' fight coordinator with Austin on the previous series, took over the role of guiding Linda Thorson through the rough stuff she would encounter during the stories. Together with Cyd Child, who had been Diana Rigg's stunt double throughout the entire Emma Peel series, Dunne coached Linda in basic moves until her on-screen action scenes looked convincing.

Avengers fight coordinator and stunt double, Cyd Child.

Two men were responsible for designing Linda Thorson's Avenger outfits: Harvey Gould and Alun Hughes. Harvey Gould was a successful coat and suit designer. In fact, he was so successful that he only had time to create the clothes for the first six stories, making a total of about 30–40 garments. Clothes for the remaining 27 stories were created by Alun Hughes, the man who had designed Diana Rigg's second screen wardrobe. Asked what special considerations there were when designing clothes for a series such as *The Avengers*, Hughes replied, 'The key word is movement. It's basically an active series, so the clothes have to be active, too. Yet for this particular heroine, Tara King, with her essentially feminine character, the clothes must not be harsh. I think a good example of the combination of action with femininity comes in my design for the brown gaberdine poncho-culotte outfit. Of course, the series is shot in colour, so I must think in terms of this at all times. Not just the avoidance of horrible clashes with such flamboyant sets as Tara's flat, but also in the manner in which colour is transmitted to the television set. I have to know how much colour actually comes over on the screen. And sometimes colours can appear differently during interior scenes shot under strong studio lighting than in scenes set outdoors.'

Linda Thorson in relaxed mood.

It wasn't only Tara's coats and dresses that Hughes designed. His job was a full-time one, designing hats, scarves, gloves, handbags, shoes – even stockings. 'I must create an outfit as a whole,' he said. 'Not a hodge-podge of separate units. Every single colour and shade has to blend perfectly.'

As he recently told my colleague Chris Clazie, he designed about 24 outfits during the transition stage of the early Tara of, say, *Have Guns, Will Travel* to the sex-bomb Tara that followed in *My Wildest Dream*. By the summer of 1968, the producers had completely changed the role around. Linda's hair had regrown, she was slimmer and was beginning to get to grips with her character. Alun Hughes designed outfits that were more in keeping with the dual personality that was emerging; part soft, feminine and vulnerable, yet adventurous, resourceful and assertive when she had to be. When the credit titles were refilmed to mark the beginning of the new season, although Tara is introduced wearing a long, backless, black crepe evening gown and pearls, she soon changes into a new-style fighting suit of brightly coloured shirt, waistcoat and trousers, to replace her earlier brown gaberdine culotte fighting gear. (Incidentally, the original credit titles, the 'target-alley' motif, followed by Linda appearing in a light tan, figure-hugging two-piece suit, with gun at the ready, were produced during the first two weeks of production.) The new 'tough' look was adopted for many of Linda's costumes – suggesting hidden complexities of character that Linda's experience (at that time) could only hint at. A bright yellow suit teamed with a navy shirt, spotted cravat and trilby; a poppy red trouser suit worn with a white shirt and red-spotted tie; a specially treated cord Levi suit for her new-style all-action fight scenes in *All Done with Mirrors* (the earliest episode with Linda sporting her own hair); an emerald green jersey battle jacket worn with Navy skirt, trousers and spotted cravat; and several new fighting suits consisting of trousers with matching waistcoats worn with shirts of contrasting colour. Linda confessed that she was 'terribly overweight at the time. I had a huge bust and went on this massive crash diet. After I'd lost a lot of weight, they saw that I had good legs so they put me into mini-skirts and sleeker gear.'

During the summer break, Patrick Macnee gave a press interview in which he said, 'I thought of leaving after Diana went, but as I've always believed that once you start something, you should see it through to the end, I stayed. I was feeling pretty jaded and beginning to look like Methuselah. I had a double-chin and' (indicating his waist-line) 'my stomach was out here. Well, I ask you, how could I carry on with the show looking like that? I cut down on smoking and visited my doctor, who gave me some pills to help me to cut down on food, and now I'm down from 14 stone to 12.'

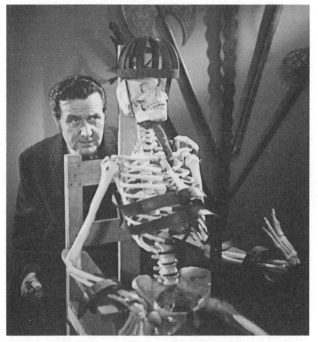

Patrick Macnee and fleshless friend, in Fog.

The weight loss meant that all Patrick's Avenger suits had to be taken in at the seams to suit his sprightly figure.

Macnee's weight problem was not shared by the second newcomer to the show, Patrick Newell. His vital statistics were 50–50–50. Newell had been signed to play Mother, John Steed's superior.

The introduction of Mother to the series was almost by accident. In January, producer Brian Clemens asked Patrick Newell to play John Steed's chief as a small cameo part, in the episode *The Forget-Me-Knot*.

The first episode of the Thorson series was shown in America on 20 March 1968, and the character of Mother was so successful that ABC telephoned Clemens the next day and demanded that Newell be put under contract.

Interviewed recently, Patrick Newell gave me his own hilarious version of events. 'I was sitting in the home of an actor friend of mine, when this taxi arrived with a script from *The Avengers* people. Having thumbed through its pages I said to my friend, "Why this is absurd. There's no part in this for me – none at all. There's this *woman's* part called Mother, but I don't see any other." He suggested that they had perhaps sent along the wrong script. So I telephoned the studio and

said "What's all this then? Where is my part?" That's when they replied "It's Mother – Mother is a *man!*" Oh lummy, I thought. So I went along and did the part and when I'd finished they said "Thanks very much, old boy. We may be bringing the character back again, so if you're free . . ." That was the last I heard of it until, during a party being given by Johnny Mortimer, I bumped into James Hill, the director I'd worked with on *The Avengers*. He said "Congratulations. Isn't it wonderful? You must be very pleased. It will do you a lot of good all over the world." As the evening crept on and other friends passed similar comments, I cornered James Hill to ask him what they were talking about. "*The Avengers,*" he said, "haven't you heard?" So the following morning I rang the studio and they said "Oh, we were going to tell you. It's the Americans. They seem to like your character, so we'd like you to come into the show permanently." So that's how it came about. The Americans picked up the phone and said "Get the FAT guy!" Everyone had known apart from me!'

Mother was crippled when he was blown-up in the prime of his Secret Service career. Unable to walk without the aid of special straps and ladders suspended from the ceiling, and in constant pain from his injuries, he was not the kindest of men to work for. He often carried a stick, which he used as much to strike his colleagues as to support himself. Patrick Newell added, 'In the first one we did, *The Forget-Me-Knot*, I moved around the room swinging on these straps. But unfortunately, not knowing that it was going to be a permanent set, they'd broken it up and it would have cost too much to rebuild. So they came up with the idea of the wheelchair. It's a pity. I would have liked to have swung around more. That would have made the character more lively.' Mother was forever turning up in the strangest of places. In one story, *False Witness*, Steed boards a London bus and finds the upper level has been transformed into Mother's office. In another, he comes across the huge man and his telephones in the middle of a field of buttercups, and in a later story, Mother and his office equipment are floating in the middle of a swimming pool!

In The Forget-Me-Knot, *Mother swung along on straps. Thereafter he was wheelchair-bound.*

Patrick Newell told me, 'It was probably the best break of my career. I actually had a studio chair with "Mother" written on it – instead of my own name. It didn't bother me – I thought it was wonderful. To this very day taxi drivers in London shout out of their windows "Morning Mother". That happens all over the world. Like Steed, Mother was terribly British. He spent most of his time drinking champagne out of silver tankards and saying things like "Good show, old boy". In addition, he was irascible, ruthless and had a dislike bordering on hatred for organisations like MI12 and MI15. He was a real character – the best I've ever played.'

Another semi-regular character (she didn't arrive until a third of the way through the series) was Rhonda, Mother's statuesque assistant. Her role also came about by accident. Twenty-one-year old Rhonda Parker, a 6 ft-tall Amazon with a 39–25–37 figure, was booked as an extra. Her role called for her to walk onto the set in the scene where Steed finds his chief sitting in the swimming pool.

The scene was set up, and Rhonda (wearing a white swimsuit) walked onto the set. As she arrived, Patrick Macnee and Patrick Newell stopped what they were doing and just gaped at her.

Patrick Newell told me, 'I remember that I was finding it extremely difficult to manipulate the wheelchair. I'd pick up these drinks and telephones and move around on fixed marks, which was proving very difficult – I'm a lousy driver. It was then that Rhonda arrived on the set, so I said "Mother should have a servant of sorts, a housekeeper or something. Well there you are, she's different from the other girls, let's have her," and she was put under contract that day. So poor old Rhonda had to push me around for the next year or so.'

There were no fashion problems for her, though, as she was mostly seen wearing white boxer shorts or tight-fitting sweaters!

Mother was often pushed around by his nurse-cum-confidant, Rhonda.

One other member of the Secret Service department that Steed worked for was introduced in the episode *Stay Tuned*. This was Father. (Well, *someone* has got to look after the department during Mother's absence.) Father was a middle-aged, blind colleague of Mother's. She was more gentle than her opposite number, but just as perceptive – she only had to feel the lapel of Steed's jacket to know he was still using the same tailor. Father appeared only once, and was played by actress Iris Russell.

Steed's address in this series was changed to 3 Stable Mews, but, with slight changes of decor, remained the same. With the arrival of Tara, however, the production team really went to town on her flat.

In his flat, Steed pours a champagne fountain into a tower of glasses to mark the successful conclusion of another case.

Set designer Kenneth Tait gave her a brand new apartment. The flat, 9 Primrose Crescent, was a mixture of modern and antique fashion design. It contained two primitive paintings, two Chinese pendant lanterns and a collection of shop signs; spectacles from an optician's; a giant boot from a bootmaker's; a padlock from a locksmith's (that hid a spy-hole in her front door); a bearded bust of a Turk from a snuff and tobacco shop; a wooden horse's head, from a French meat shop; plus two giant gold-plated letters, TK on one wall, and NO on another. A fireman's pole enabled her to get from her upper landing to the ground floor at top speed.

The rooms were furnished with shocking-pink carpets; blue, grey, mauve and Imperial Chinese yellow panels; a couch in orange, green and yellow, with curtains to match; and scatter cushions in a mass of colours. There were a dozen period telephones – through which Tara had to search when one of them rang. A wooden postbox was converted into a drinks cabinet. There was even a glass-panelled door with a stained-glass bird in it from an old pub.

Terry Nation, creator of the Daleks for the popular *Doctor Who* series, joined the writing team and was later to become script supervisor. A man who had contributed to every major filmed television series in the country, Terry Nation said of the programme, 'Although an *Avengers* script is such a distinctive thing, it still covers a wide range of stories, from the straightforward detection tale, by way of the horror variety, to the most zany comedy thriller. Yet at the end of the day, the programme takes itself very seriously. Our villains and heroes are never sent up, and remain serious.'

Once again, the title theme music was revamped. It now started with a frenetic staccato drumbeat and progressed to a more exuberant version of the familiar *Avengers* theme. Laurie Johnson explained the need for the change: 'We thought the new series ought to reflect the times we live in a bit more. So we generally jazzed it up, adding the sound of gunfire and a lot more percussion and brass. When Tara King came into the series I decided to superimpose a counter melody over the existing title music at the point at which the face of the new character appeared on the main titles. This counter melody I then used and developed in the incidental score where appropriate. Unlike many television series, *The Avengers* does not contain the same music throughout. In fact it is doubtful that anyone was even noticed the music that accents the action. If it has been noticed, then I haven't done my job well. Good scoring should be unobtrusive.' He also composed a new tag theme, called, appropriately enough, *Tag Theme*, for the closing segments of each episode, in which Steed and Tara were seen in a short, self-contained vignette, which, following the pattern set by Patrick Macnee and Diana Rigg, Linda and Patrick were allowed to ad-lib.

The producers asked Diana Rigg to appear in the first Thorson story, and after spending a week vetting the script, Diana, who still 'owed' the company one episode (her 1967 contract called for her to film 26 episodes for the second season colour series) consented to film *The Forget-Me-Knot*, in which she would tender her resignation and hand the role over to Linda. Contrary to what has been reported elsewhere, it appears that this story was specially written in order to say goodbye to one girl and hello to another. Linda Thorson recalls that the producers had no idea how to get rid of Emma Peel. 'I think Diana herself wanted Emma to be killed, but they didn't like that idea. So they dreamed up the idea of her husband coming back – which was really quite witty, because the character looked just like Steed. In the hand-over scene, I remember that they had originally just wanted us to pass on the stairs without saying anything beyond Diana giving me a wink. But then they decided we should say something, so Brian Clemens whipped up the dialogue about Steed preferring his tea to

be stirred anti-clockwise.' The cross-over scene, filmed on 19 January 1968, was restricted to a 30-second encounter on the staircase leading to Steed's flat, making this the *only* bridged series.

Shooting began on the series at Elstree Studios, using Add-a-Vision, a video-aid to film production pioneered by ABC at Elstree, which allowed the director to see, via a monitor screen marked with a frame outline that showed the limits of the picture that would be received on a home television set, exactly what was in frame during shooting. The process had previously been used on the second 13 Rigg colour episodes.

Although the Thorson series was well received in Britain, and international sales had grossed over £18,000,000 – with Paris awarding the Macnee/Thorson partnership *Le Prix Triomphe* in 1970 – the show's success was still dependent on it being accepted in America.

For some inexplicable reason, ABC/TV (America) decided to screen the series in direct opposition to the immensely popular *Rowan and Martin's Laugh-In* shows, and for the first time, *The Avengers* met an unbeatable opponent – the American television audience ratings. Faced with such opposition, the show only managed to reach 69th position in the top 100 ratings. Soon after, ABC telephoned Clemens to say they wouldn't require any further episodes of *The Avengers* after the 33 Thorson shows.

I asked Linda Thorson why *she* thought the show had failed. 'That's it exactly,' she replied. 'We found ourselves in a no-win situation. The *Laugh-In* series was the biggest thing on American television at the time and we just didn't get the ratings. The spy thing was on the wane by then – although I believe that we could have gone on for say, another year, but the money wasn't there.' After the series had ended, Linda went into rep at the Bristol Old Vic. She is only slightly rueful that, like previous *Avengers* girls, Honor Blackman and Diana Rigg, she *wasn't* offered a role in a Bond movie (she was asked to appear in a Hammer horror movie – which she turned down). She then went to America to promote a record she'd made, which was consequently issued on a Motown album, *New Faces of the Seventies*, and actually went to number one in the French top twenty, after which she returned to America to become a star name on Broadway.

Although *The Avengers* went on to become the single biggest foreign currency earner of any television series (a record it still holds today), Thames Television couldn't afford the cost of producing the show alone. The final story went before the cameras on 16 February 1969. The studio lights were switched off and *The Avengers* came to an (abrupt) end.

However, though the series was gone, it was never forgotten. Thanks to syndication, the reruns just keep going on, with *The Avengers* seldom off TV screens throughout the world; and, as we shall see, interest in reviving the series would continue unabated.

GAME

By Richard Harris

John Steed	**Patrick Macnee**
Tara King	**Linda Thorson**
Bristow	**Peter Jeffrey**
Manservant	**Garfield Morgan**
Professor Witney	**Aubrey Richards**
Brig Wishforth-Browne	**Anthony Newlands**
Averman	**Alex Scott**
Dexter	**Geoffrey Russell**
Student	**Achilles Georgiou**
Manager	**Desmond Walter-Ellis**

Designed by Robert Jones

Directed by Robert Fuest

IN THE home of a man called Bristow, a strange game of snakes and ladders is in progress. Bristow throws a six, moves his marker, and then we see Dexter, the victim of the deadly game. He climbs a ladder to a trap door marked 'Reward', opens it, and is bitten by a snake. He falls to the floor, dead. Bristow's man-servant idly watches, then calmly serves tea. Later, Steed discovers Dexter's body on a children's roundabout. He tells Tara he is an old army comrade. Strangely, the dead man is clutching a handful of jigsaw pieces. Steed explains to Tara that it is the second death of this type in recent weeks. Another of his army colleagues, racing driver 'Cootie' Williams, was found in identical circumstances the week before. Tara takes the jigsaw pieces to a games shop but the manager is unable to help. She doesn't see Bristow's man-servant in the shop, keeping an eye on her. The next victim is the financier Henry Averman, who is chloroformed in his flat and taken to Bristow's home. Averman is forced to play a mad game of 'Stock Market', which he loses. He then dies when Bristow won't let him take his heart pills. The financier also ends up on the roundabout, jigsaw pieces in hand. Adding the latest pieces to her puzzle, Tara has now assembled the picture of a house. It seems as though the killer is giving them a clue, and playing a kind of game. Steed recalls another army friend, Brigadier Wishforth-Browne, and visits him. But he can't think of anyone who served with them and now bears a grudge. Wishforth-Browne is the next participant in Bristow's deadly game, and is invited to Bristow's house for dinner. Now, for the first time, we see Bristow's face, which has had plastic surgery. He makes Wishforth-Browne play a game of toy soldiers, at which he does very well – until Bristow shoots him with a toy cannon. When Steed and Tara keep a dawn appointment with the Brigadier on a military parade ground, they are startled to see Wishforth-Browne's body advancing towards them, propped upright in a field car. Steed now realises that the four dead men were all part of a tribunal which court-martialled one Sergeant Daniel Edmund in 1946, for black market activities in Germany. Edmund was believed killed while trying to escape from detention. Ex-Major Witney is the fifth member of the tribunal, but Steed and Tara are unable to contact him. He is already in the clutches of Bristow, who devises a word game for him, which he fails to solve. Witney, like the others, ends up in the children's playground. Steed now realises that he was the sixth, and last, member of the tribunal. Bristow now sends his man-servant, to kidnap Tara. She is abducted after being chloroformed in her flat. Steed later discovers the signs of the fight and pursues his enquiries with more urgency. The manager of the games shop is now able to identify Tara's completed jigsaw puzzle as being a picture of the home of games king Bristow, a leading jigsaw manufacturer. Steed goes to Bristow's home, and is astonished to find that he is expected. Bristow has actually been playing a macabre game with Steed, of which the deaths and jigsaw pieces were a part. He now sets Steed his game, which he calls 'Super Agent'. Steed is given only six minutes to beat a number of obstacles and save Tara, who is now a captive in a giant hour-glass. She will suffocate unless he completes the course. He first defeats a Japanese wrestler, then opens a safe in 60 seconds. He gets safely out of a six-sided room – five of the doors are booby trapped – and then negotiates a tunnel in which a steel blade slices through his bowler. He is rewarded with a gun and six cartridges, only one of which is live. He then has to take on six assailants. Steed quickly solves the problem of finding the live bullet by repeatedly firing at Tara's hour-glass. She is then free to help him defeat his adversaries. Armed with his half-bowler, Steed prevents Bristow's next obstacle, which is a razor-edged card. Steed deflects it with the steel-lined bowler brim back at Bristow, who is killed. Tara, meanwhile, takes care of the man-servant. In the last scene, Steed stacks the odds against Tara in a dice game he has invented, called 'Steedopoly'.

Given six minutes to run Bristow's 'Super Agent' obstacle course and save Tara's life, Steed requires only sixty seconds to open a safe in **Game.**

THE SUPER SECRET CYPHER SNATCH

By Tony Williamson

John Steed	Patrick Macnee
Tara King	Linda Thorson
Peters	John Carlisle
Maskin	Simon Oates
First Guard	Alec Ross
Jarret	Clifford Earl
Vickers	Donald Gee
Ferret	Ivor Dean
Betty	Anne Rutter
Myra	Angela Scoular
Second Guard	Lionel Wheeler
Davis	Anthony Blackshaw
Lather	Nicholas Smith
Webster	Allan Cuthbertson

Designed by Robert Jones

Directed by John Hough

JARRET, AN agent, runs for his life from the Cypher headquarters building, pursued by an armed man dressed in white overalls, gas mask and bowler. Other men in overalls block Jarret's way as he desperately tries to escape, but finally he is gunned down. The guards at the establishment pay no heed to what has happened and Jarret's body is bundled into a van bearing the sign Classy Glass Cleaners and driven away. Mother tells Steed that MI12 have lost Jarret, and their department has been asked to find him. Steed's enquiries begin with Webster, the director of the Cypher HQ, whom we have seen briefly in the opening scene, witnessing Jarret's death. But when Steed shows him a photograph of Jarret, Webster denies all knowledge of him. Tara is sent to Jarret's flat with Ferret of MI12, and they find the agent's body lying in a window seat. They also find, hidden in a pen, a rolled-up page torn from a calendar, bearing the date of Jarret's death. As they search the flat, they fail to notice Maskin, dressed as a window cleaner, watching them from across the street. Meanwhile, Webster continues to deny that Jarret was ever at his establishment, and Steed, suspecting he is lying, picks up Jarret's lighter-cum-camera from a desk. Steed, together with photographer Peters, joins Tara and Ferret at Jarret's flat. Peters says he will develop the apparently ordinary pictures the agent took of the Cypher establishment. When he is in his darkroom, Maskin, the window cleaner, shoots him from outside the window. Steed and Tara are quickly on the scene. They find the charred remains of the photographs, but Steed has the negatives from which to prepare more prints. From these they see the Classy Glass Cleaners van, which they immediately connect with Peters' murder – the assassin must have used a ladder. Ferret decides that after the murders they must have someone inside the Cypher building and Tara is nominated. Steed, meanwhile, visits the Classy Glass Cleaners. Charles Lather, in charge of Classy Glass, tells Steed that his firm has not visited the Cypher establishment for months. They used to have the concession, but gave it up as uneconomical. When Steed leaves, he is followed by Maskin, in one of the firm's vans. Maskin uses a ladder to smash Steed's windscreen and the car is driven off the road. Steed, however, escapes uninjured and when he regains consciousness, he tells Mother to send Ferret to help Tara, whom he now believes is in danger. At the Cypher building, Webster sends Tara to fetch the 'Q' Cypher file. As she finds it Tara is alarmed to see a Classy Glass van pull up outside. When Ferret arrives, he is amazed to see there are no guards at the gate. Driving to the main entrance, he is attacked by one of the Classy Glass men, and suffocated with a cleaning leather. Tara, watching from the window, can see the body of Ferret, but she just stares blankly. In the next scene, the Cypher establishment is back to normal. Ferret's body has been removed and the guards are working normally. Tara, however, is puzzled that she forgot to fetch the file for Webster. When Steed arrives, she is sure that Ferret has not been there. In fact, she feels that the day did not happen at all. Together they visit the Classy Glass Cleaners yard, where they discover Ferret's body. They also see Jarvis and Vickers, two of the staff, as they take the body away in a van and dump it at Ferret's home. Next day, Tara returns to Cypher, keeping in touch with Steed by walkie-talkie. Later, Steed discovers something strange in one of the photographs taken by Jarret. Meanwhile, Vickers and Jarvis are leading another raid on Cypher. They cut the telephone lines, and knock out the guards with vapour sprays they carry with them. They also introduce the knock-out vapour into the ventilation shafts of the building, and a voice – on a dictaphone – tells the staff it is a perfectly normal working day, while the raiders photograph all the documents in sight. From the picture of Myra, taken by Jarret, Steed notices that the girl is holding a match which is burning down to her fingers. Puzzled, Steed goes to Classy Glass, and bursts in on Jarvis and Vickers at their work. Tara eventually joins him in a hectic fight, at the end of which Steed meets Lather, the boss of Classy Glass, at gunpoint in Webster's office. Tara saves him by impaling Lather to the wall with a ladder. Later on, Steed decides to try his hypnotic powers on Tara, but sends himself to sleep instead. Tara orders her hypnotised partner to take her for an expensive dinner.

In order to rescue Tara from Cypher headquarters. Steed has to run a gauntlet of none-too-friendly villains in The Super Secret Cypher Snatch.

YOU'LL CATCH YOUR DEATH

By Jeremy Burnham

John Steed	Patrick Macnee
Tara King	Linda Thorson
Colonel Timothy	Ronald Culver
Butler	Valentine Dyall
Glover	Fulton Mackay
Matron	Sylvia Kay
Mother	Patrick Newell
Dexter	Dudley Sutton
Preece	Peter Bourne
Dr Fawcett	Charles Lloyd Pack
Maidwell	Henry McGee
Camrose	Hamilton Dyce
Farrar	Bruno Barnabe
Janice	Fiona Hartford
Seaton	Geoffrey Chater
Georgina	Jennifer Clulow
Melanie	Emma Cochrane
Padley	Willoughby Gray
Herrick	Andrew Laurence
Postman	Douglas Blackwell

Designed by Robert Jones

Directed by Paul Dickson

A cautious Steed dons a face mask to open a deadly envelope in You'll Catch Your Breath.

RALPH CAMROSE, FRCS, is attending to a patient when Preece arrives, travelling in a Rolls-Royce but dressed as a postman, to deliver a letter. As the patient leaves, Janice, the receptionist, gives Camrose the envelope. It is empty, but makes Camrose sneeze violently and he finally chokes to death. Receiving the news of Camrose's demise, Mother tells Steed and Tara of the deaths of other ear, nose and throat specialists, and asks them to investigate. Steed visits the scene of the crime, while Tara is sent to see Padley, an ENT man who is a friend of Steed's. Steed finds the empty envelope and wonders why it contained no letter. At Padley's, Preece, the fake postman, delivers another apparently empty envelope, which sets Padley sneezing, and he soon chokes to death. Tara, sitting in the waiting room, is powerless to prevent his death. Steed finds out from the envelope manufacturers, Maidwell and Pugh, that the envelopes left with Camrose and Padley are of their cream-wove bond, and that a nursing academy recently bought 10,000 in a single order. Tara visits Seaton, another ENT man, but he is unable to explain his colleague's deaths and soon, he too, encounters one of Preece's envelopes. This time, however, Tara spots the Rolls departing and gives chase, but she loses the car in a country lane. Dexter, the driver of the Rolls, and Preece, decide to follow Tara back to Steed's flat, where they chloroform her with a perfume spray. Steed, posing as a moneyed philanthropist, visits the Anastasia Nursing Academy, which bought the envelopes. He learns from the Matron that the academy send out about 50 letters a week. Arriving back at his flat, Steed finds Dr Fawcett, of the Institute of Allergic Diseases, waiting for him. Fawcett explains that Tara made an appointment to talk to him about the deaths of Padley and Seaton. They find the empty perfume spray, suggesting what has happened to Tara. Steed returns to the nursing academy and discovers a suspicious letter from Colonel Timothy of

Walsingham House. Steed also sees a room full of girls busily typing addresses on envelopes. He pays Colonel Timothy a visit, and finds that he runs a private clinic with an assistant, Dr Glover. Steed tells them he is looking for advice for the Steed Foundation, which is considering endowing the Anastasia Academy with funds. Timothy says he has nothing to do with them, although Steed notices there are Anastasia nurses working in Timothy's cold-cure clinic. Steed is concerned when Timothy admits he has written to Padley and Seaton for their co-operation on cold-cure research, without success. And he leaves quickly when he discovers a notice on Timothy's desk to contact Herrick, another ENT man at Padley and Seaton's consulting rooms. Unknown to Steed, Tara is now confined in the cold-cure clinic. Preece and Dexter are already on their way to kill Herrick, who is in his car, and sneezes himself off the road to his death. One of the envelopes is now posted to Steed. However, Steed opens it wearing a face-mask as a precaution. Dr Fawcett examines the envelope and explains that the tiny quantity of powder in the envelopes is concentrated cold virus, sufficient to kill anyone exposed to it. He also tells Steed that all the dead ENT men had been working on an anti-allergy drug, which would make them the rivals of anyone able to produce the powder. Meanwhile, Tara explodes her way out of her deep-frozen prison and into a tunnel, which leads to the main area of the clinic, dominated by a huge replica of a nose. Tara is listening to Matron, Preece and Dexter inside the nose when she sneezes and gives

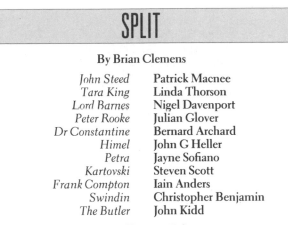

SPLIT

By Brian Clemens

John Steed	Patrick Macnee
Tara King	Linda Thorson
Lord Barnes	Nigel Davenport
Peter Rooke	Julian Glover
Dr Constantine	Bernard Archard
Himel	John G Heller
Petra	Jayne Sofiano
Kartovski	Steven Scott
Frank Compton	Iain Anders
Swindin	Christopher Benjamin
The Butler	John Kidd

Directed by Roy Baker

Designed by Robert Jones

herself away. She is recaptured and told by the gang that they intended to use her as a guinea pig in one last, dangerous, experiment. That night, Steed is also captured by Colonel Timothy and his butler, when he makes a second visit to Walsingham House. Although Steed is held at gunpoint by the Colonel and his butler he soon discovers that the Colonel is not responsible for the lethal envelopes. This is confirmed when the Colonel himself receives one of them. He does not open it, however, because of what Steed has told him. Steed now enlists the aid of the Colonel and his butler in finding the real culprits. At this moment, Tara is being prepared for a test of Dr Glover's new lethal serum, capable, she is told, of killing millions. Glover means to gain power by selling to the highest bidder. Steed and the Colonel arrive in time to free the distraught Tara, but Glover escapes down the tunnel behind the huge nose to the deep-freeze room. He is about to throw the deadly phial of virus at Steed, when Steed forestalls him by throwing the deadly envelope of powder sent to the Colonel. It hits Glover in the face, and he immediately begins to sneeze and then chokes to death, falling out of the nose. Tara catches a terrible cold, but Steed preens himself on not having one. He does, however, suddenly develop one, and ends up producing a foot-bath just like Tara's.

THE STRINGENT security of the Ministry of Top-Secret Information is badly shaken when agent Frank Compton is suddenly murdered in the executive rest area of the Ministry's rural retreat. It seems impossible that anyone could have penetrated the security screens, and in fact the murderer is agent Harry Mercer, who also works at the establishment. He shoots Compton after a voice on the telephone asks for someone called Boris – an enquiry which causes a sudden change in Mercer's personality. The handwriting on his report changes suddenly to an extrovert scrawl, his hand gnarls and his left shoulder slopes. But after the murder he appears to resume his own personality, and he himself raises the alarm, as if he has really forgotten what he has just done. When Steed and Tara arrive at the Ministry, they are joined by Lord Barnes at the scene of the crime. Tara picks up the report that Mercer was writing, and notices the sudden scrawl. Steed takes another call for Boris and Mercer reacts as before. Steed notices the gnarling of the hand, but Mercer explains it away as the result of an accident during the Berlin episode of 1963. This gives him away, as Steed knows full well that Mercer was not involved in this. Steed and Tara consult a graphologist called Swindin, who tells them that Mercer's report indicates two distinct personalities at work; one is a brutal, hard-living extrovert, and the other a reliable agent. The former sounds to Steed like a man who was involved in the Berlin episode of 1963, an enemy agent called Boris Kartovski. Steed asks Colonel Rooke, in charge of security at the Ministry, to find him a sample of Kartovski's handwriting. Mercer, overhearing Rooke mentioning Boris' name again, immediately begins his personality change, and when Rooke leaves the room, Mercer is so much invaded by the other personality that he even does a wild Cossack dance. Mercer now telephones Dr Constantine at Nullington Hospital, asking for help. Dr Constantine and his colleague, Himel, confer, and agree that their experiment has gone wrong. They decide that they will now have to use another subject, and they ring Lord Barnes, asking if Boris is there. The same personality split begins to affect Barnes. In this condition, Lord Barnes goes to the Ministry and shoots Mercer. The only clue is that Mercer has left a note reading 'Help Me', with the 'Me' in the extrovert scrawl. Steed also discovers that Mercer has recently admitted to Nullington Private Hospital. Steed visits Nullington, and Dr Constantine tells him that Mercer was a routine minor accident case. Steed then discovers a link with Lord Barnes, who had also been admitted to Nullington recently. He visits Barnes, who is still in the other personality, and he attacks Steed with a knife. Steed escapes death, but he has not seen the face of his attacker, who quickly leaves the room. Moments later, Lord Barnes rushes in and he, like Mercer, seems to have forgotten what he has done, and has reverted to his normal personality. Tara discovers from Swindin that the 'Me' section of the note is similar to Kartovski's handwriting, given to Steed by Rooke. It is also like a specimen of Lord Barnes' writing stolen by Rooke during his investigations. Tara and Rooke are now convinced that Barnes is involved, and therefore Steed is in danger, because he is on the way to see Barnes, who has called him for help. Torn by his personality split, Barnes handcuffs himself to an object in his room, but even this does not prevent him eventually leaving to visit the hospital. Once there, however, he reverts once again, and returns home. By this time, Rooke and Tara have got there, and before Steed can intervene, Rooke shoots Barnes, claiming that he is Kartovski. This Steed strenuously denies, saying that he himself shot Kartovski in the heart, in Berlin in 1963. Kartovski is lying in the Nullington Hospital surrounded by heart and lung machines. Constantine and Himel have kept him alive because no other agent has such a good mind. They can transfer his personality to another man's brain, using the ten per cent of the brain that lies dormant. Steed's bullet from 1963 lodged in the Russian agent's left side, causing those given his mind to limp and develop a gnarled hand. They next try to use Tara as Kartovski's mind-carrier. They fake an accident, and take her to the hospital for the fusion with Kartovski's brain. But Steed is on their trail and manages to get into the hospital, free Tara, and send her to fetch Rooke. But he is another victim of the transferred mind, and although he struggles between his two personalities, he attacks Tara when she enters the Ministry. Steed dashes in to save them both, just in time. The last scene shows Steed with a limp and an injured hand, making Tara suspect him of having the treatment. But, Steed has just taken one knock too many in his recent fight.

Steed manages to rescue Tara just in time, before her brain is fused with that of Kartovski, in Split.

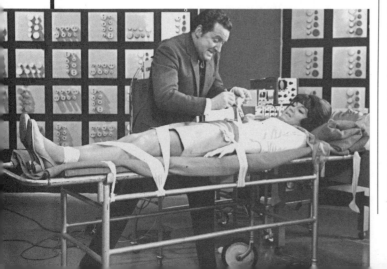

WHOEVER SHOT POOR GEORGE OBLIQUE STROKE XR40

By Tony Williamson

John Steed	Patrick Macnee
Tara King	Linda Thorson
Jason	Dennis Price
Pelley	Clifford Evans
Loris	Judy Parfitt
Ardmore	Anthony Nicholls
Tobin	Frank Windsor
Baines	Adrian Ropes
Anaesthetist	Arthur Cox
Keller	Tony Wright
Jacobs	John Porter-Davison
Jill	Jacky Allouis
Betty	Valerie Leon

Designed by Robert Jones

Directed by Cyril Frankel

COMPUTER RESEARCH worker Baines calls in his colleague, Tobin, when George/XR40, a computer, suddenly goes wrong at a Ministry of Technology research establishment. Then Jacobs, an intruder, breaks in while they are away and shoots George, nearly finishing him off. Dr Ardmore, a cybernetic surgeon, is called in and he conducts an operation to save George. Steed stays for the operation and Tara goes with Baines to his flat to fetch the set of equations which, when fed into George, made him go wrong. But Jacobs has got there first and he shoots Baines. Back at the research establishment the operation progresses, and George coughs up some computer tape which appears to condemn Sir Wilfred Pelley, George's creator, as a traitor. Steed visits Pelley, and is received by Jason, his butler. Pelley, however, refuses to attend George. He is not even keen to talk and seems to be drunk. Tobin gives Steed a file on Sir Wilfred then, when left alone with George, he again sabotages him, this time by pouring acid into George's 'mouth'. Dr Ardmore decides to give George a 'brain' transplant from an earlier model of George named Fred MKIII. Steed visits Pelley and tells him of this, but Pelley still refuses to attend the operation. During his visit, Steed notices a woman's fur coat hanging in the hall. The coat belongs to Loris, who appears to dominate Pelley. She tells Jacobs to follow Steed to Baines' apartment and kill him there. Steed, however, has set this up, and he makes a dummy which the would-be killer shoots, and Jacobs dies in the ensuing fight with Steed. Steed next sends Tara to Sir Wilfred's home, disguised as his long-lost niece, Prunella, whom he has not seen since she was a child. Meanwhile, Loris and Pelley have learned that Jacobs' attempt on Steed's life was not successful. Tara visits Pelley's home, introducing herself as Prunella, and tells Jason, Pelley and Loris that she would like to stay for a few days. She discovers that Loris has a strange hold over Pelley, induced by drugs, and also that food is being taken to someone in the basement – perhaps the top man? Meanwhile, the 'brain' transplant on George proceeds. It is no sooner completed, when Tobin makes a last attempt to sabotage the operation, by snipping some electric cables. Steed notices and prevents Tobin from doing any serious damage. Tara is now revealed as an impostor by Jason, the butler, who then declares himself to be an impostor, too. He is, in fact, the ring-leader of the plot to get secrets from Pelley. Meanwhile George has been repaired, and out of his 'mouth' come the words which Pelley has been trying to convey to them – that he is being drugged and interrogated daily against his will. This proves that he is not the traitor. Steed rushes to Pelley's home, where he knows Tara will be in danger. He told her to trust Jason, whom George has now revealed as the real traitor. The gang tell Keller, one of their henchmen, to burn Tara alive in the summerhouse, but when he gets there, Steed is waiting. Tara and Steed then return to the house and rout the opposition. Steed later tries out a recipe supplied by George for the world's most devastating cocktail. Finally the mixture explodes, and Steed decides it should remain on the secret list.

Whoever Shot Poor George Oblique Stroke XR40? That's the question facing Steed and Tara when called in to put the byte on computer thieves.

FALSE WITNESS

By Jeremy Burnham

John Steed	Patrick Macnee
Tara King	Linda Thorson
Lane	Rio Fanning
Melville	Barry Warren
Brayshaw	John Atkinson
Penman	Peter Jesson
Lord Edgefield	William Job
Mother	Patrick Newell
Rhonda	Rhonda Parker
Dr Grant	Arthur Pentlow
Gould	Larry Burns
Little Man	Jimmy Gardner
Sloman	Dan Meaden
Sykes	John Bennett
Plummer	Michael Lees
Sir Joseph	Tony Steedman
Amanda	Terry Eliot
Nesbitt	Simon Lack

Designed by Robert Jones

Directed by Charles Crichton

STEED'S DEPARTMENT is in trouble. They are losing agents and suspect that one of their own men, Melville, may be working against them. Melville, keeping a lookout for his colleague, Penman, who is photographing a notebook in a Rolls-Royce in an underground garage, fails to warn him of the danger when the chauffeur arrives. Shot by the chauffeur, Penman staggers away. Steed keeps a rendezvous with Mother, on top of a double-decker bus which has been stripped and furnished as a sitting-room, with his secretary, Rhonda, in attendance. Mother tells Steed that they have lost two men trying to prove that a peer of the realm, Lord Edgefield, is blackmailing security and Foreign Office personnel. As they talk, Melville boards the bus. He does not report the shooting of Penman, and is sent with Steed to look after Plummer, the star witness in the case against Lord Edgefield. Meanwhile, the badly wounded Penman, after hiding the film he has taken in a dustbin, arrives at Steed's mews flat. Before he dies, he warns Tara that Melville is a traitor, and tells her the whereabouts of his film. Steed and Melville arrive at Plummer's flat, too late to assist him in a brush with an intruder. They look over the flat but nothing seems to have been disturbed except the fridge door, which is open. Plummer is only too willing to testify against Edgefield, who was responsible for his brother's suicide. All three have coffee, Steed taking his black, the other two white, and leave for the office of Sir Joseph, who is compiling the case. Lord Edgefield, who has been summoned to be confronted by the witness, is ushered into the room by Amanda, Sir Joseph's secretary. But Plummer, under questioning, completely contradicts everything he has said before. Edgefield leaves, gloating. When Steed returns home, he finds the contents of several dustbins piled high in the room. But Tara has found the film, and passes Penman's final message on to Steed. They inform Mother, who sends Tara to question Plummer and discover why he changed his evidence. Steed's mission is more hazardous. He must go with

Melville and discover, the hard way, whether he is a traitor. Leaving Melville to keep guard outside a nearby telephone box, Steed enters Lord Edgefield's flat. Occasionally calling to Melville on a portable transmitter, he begins to probe Edgefield's wall safe. Steed manages to escape approaching danger by seconds when Melville fails to warn him that an intruder has entered the flat. He then rushes outside and knocks Melville to the ground. But Melville is adamant that he warned Steed, and denies that he is a traitor. Steed takes Melville to Mother, and the suspected traitor is strapped to a lie-detector by Dr Grant. Steed and Mother question the agent and are astonished when Melville tells apparent lies, because the graph indicates that he is not lying. The real test comes when Steed asks Melville if he worked with him that evening. Melville replies in the negative. Yet according to the graph he is telling the truth! Tara finds her assignment equally puzzling. While searching through Plummer's flat in his absence, she knocks over a bottle of milk, which is lapped up by Plummer's pet dog. Afterwards, even the dog lies, by barking at a non-existent intruder! Tara later hides from a real intruder, Lane, dressed as a milkman, who, after placing a bottle of milk in the fridge, leaves on a milk float bearing the sign Peter Pan Dairies. Tara follows in her car. At the dairy, Lord Edgefield is paying off Sykes, who has manufactured and arranged the deliveries of the strange milk. Sykes is then given a new customer for the milk round. Using an intercom, Sykes tells the bogus milkman, now returning with Tara in pursuit, to make a detour. The new customer is Sir Joseph. Tara watches

the delivery to Sir Joseph, then continues to follow the milk float. Steed gives Sir Joseph the list of blackmail names he stole from Edgefield's safe. Sir Joseph then telephones each of them, and the last one, Nesbitt, agrees to testify. He is brought to Sir Joseph's office and tells him what he knows. But before the confrontation with Edgefield, Sir Joseph asks his secretary to serve three coffees. Tara investigates the dairy, but is cornered by the bogus milkman. After a fight, she finds the milk vat room, where she sees an employee, Sloman, mixing a colourless liquid with the milk. As he leaves, Tara checks the milk vat, but Sloman reappears with Sykes. In the ensuing fight, Tara and Sloman end up in the vat of milk. She manages to knock him out but, in the process of doing so, her head is pushed under and she swallows some milk. Covered with milk, she escapes to a nearby telephone where she conveys a strange message to Sir Joseph – 'This is very important. I *don't* want to warn you . . .' Sir Joseph, Steed and their witness discuss the strange message over coffee. When Lord Edgefield arrives, both Nesbitt and Sir Joseph reverse their testimony and exonerate Lord Edgefield . . . Only Steed makes sense, but he has been drinking black coffee. Steed is the next to receive a delivery from the bogus milkman. But Tara recognises him, and rushes out to the milk float to stop the man, only to be thrown to the ground. She immediately runs back to the apartment and knocks a glass of milk out of Steed's hand. Strangely, she does not know why. Tara, unable to warn of the dangers in the milk, goes to the dairy and begins to smash all the bottles she finds there. But she is caught by Sloman and Sykes and forced into a butter-making machine. Steed has the milk analysed and, discovering it contains an hallucinatory drug, sets off for the dairy. The butter machine is about to churn when he arrives, and he is astonished to find Tara with milk oozing around her waist. He subdues Sykes and Sloman with cartons of yoghurt, and then opens the butter machine to rescue Tara. A large slab of butter pops out with a smile on its face. Later on, Tara is showing Steed her new outfit. He is rude – then she notices the half-empty glass of milk beside him.

Doubling for Linda Thorson, stuntwoman Cyd Child finds it hard to accept the milk of human kindness in False Witness.

ALL DONE WITH MIRRORS

By Leigh Vance

John Steed	**Patrick Macnee**
Tara King	**Linda Thorson**
Watney	**Dinsdale Landen**
Sparshott	**Peter Copley**
Barlow	**Edwin Richfield**
Col Withers	**Michael Trubshawe**
Mother	**Patrick Newell**
Pandora	**Joanna Jones**
Miss Emily	**Nora Nicholson**
Carswell	**Tenniel Evans**
Miss Tiddiman	**Liane Aukin**

Designed by Robert Jones

Directed by Ray Austin

STEED IS under house arrest at Mother's headquarters, because Steed has been spending time recently at Carmadoc Research Establishment, and secrets have been leaked from there. Mother has sent Tara to investigate, together with a very serious trainee agent named Watney. There, they meet the establishment's security chief, Major Sparshott, who sits in the security area surrounded by strips of silver foil. A flare of light hits the foil as they go, with Sparshott, to the main part of the building, where the establishment's research is revealed to be connected with harnessing the power of the sun. The flaring light is associated with the ability of Markin, a radio operator, to overhear their conversation as Sparshott tells them of the death of a local resident named Guthrie. Markin overhears Tara say that she would like to visit Guthrie's home. From Miss Emily, Guthrie's housekeeper, Tara learns that Guthrie was interested in astronomy, and was friendly with radio-astronomer Williams. He had also, recently, told her to smash everything shiny in the cottage, including the mirrors. Markin again overhears their conversation. Tara arrives at Williams' home, and finds the man dead. He has been strangled by Gozzo, a huge man who is still there and whom Tara fights. After a furious brawl, Gozzo is left impaled on a scythe. As Tara leaves, she picks up an envelope on which Williams has written a complex equation before he died. Returning to the research establishment, Tara enlists the help of Professor Carswell to decipher the figures on the envelope. He tells her that they are a table of light intensities. Watney meanwhile is investigating the research team. Seligman arranges to meet him outside in the clearing, and Sparshott follows Watney as he goes to keep the rendezvous. Both are too late to prevent Seligman from being shot. The voice of Markin calls Seligman to a shaving mirror hanging from a tree. This is then shattered by the bullet which kills Seligman. As he dies, he tells Watney 'It was all done with mirrors'. Tara now investigates a lighthouse owned by Colonel Withers. He says he did not know Guthrie or Williams. Through Withers' telescope, Tara sees the arrival of Pandora Marshall, a pretty young woman, at the lighthouse. Yet Withers does not know who she is, and asks his secretary, Barlow, and Kettridge, another of his staff, to find out. As she leaves, Tara just misses seeing Markin (the window in the stair wall hides his secret radio room). She does, however, notice his smouldering cigarette in the stairway. Barlow behaves strangely as he receives Pandora, who has come to the lighthouse to interview Colonel Withers. She has arranged her accommodation with Barlow, but he does not seem to know about it. Pandora knows the man to be an impostor, for she has met Barlow before. She creeps out of her room and up to the lamp-room, where she discovers that the telescope hides a device which can both transmit and receive sound over vast distances. The sound travels on a beam of light which flares over the object at which the telescope is aimed. Before she can tell Tara, however, she is taken prisoner by Kettridge and Barlow. Tara is examining the cliff edge where Guthrie fell to his death, and they force Pandora to lure her to the cliff face. Then Kettridge drives his motor-cycle at her. Tara falls into the sea below, and when Watney and Sparshott arrive, they assume she is lost. They telephone the news to Mother, who reluctantly tells Steed of Tara's death ... Tara, however, is not dead. She crawls on to the rocks and then makes her way to the lighthouse. She then disposes of Kettridge and discovers the secret of Markin's telescope device and knocks him out, after discovering the secret radio room. There, she finds Pandora, the real Colonel Withers, and the real Barlow, all bound and gagged. Pandora explains that the telescope is a retro-meter and the Colonel confirms that the impostors have been using it to steal information from the research establishment. The fake Barlow finds the unconscious Kettridge as Tara surprises and knocks cold the fake Colonel in the lamp-room. Downstairs they overhear Tara using the speaking tube on the retro-meter to contact Watney. She just manages to make contact before she is attacked by two more heavies who have come up from below. One of the thugs is killed by his own gun, and the other falls down the stairs after being thrown through the door by Tara. She then disposes of Markin and Kettridge. Barlow, however, corners Tara in the lamp-room, but she is saved when Watney arrives and slams the lamp door into Barlow's back. Moments later, Steed arrives, only to find that Tara has handled the heavies in her own special game of 'Solo'. Afterwards, Steed drives Tara for a meal with a difference. This time he's arranged a magnificent spread on a table for two, set in the middle of a field of buttercups. With steaks cooked to perfection on the engine of Steed's gleaming Rolls Royce and a bottle of ice-cool champagne, its a beautiful day for, as Steed tells Tara, 'The simplest pleasures in life are the most enjoyable!'

Linda Thorson receives a surprise visit from Saint Roger Moore during the filming of All Done With Mirrors.

LEGACY OF DEATH

By Terry Nation

John Steed	Patrick Macnee
Tara King	Linda Thorson
Sidney	Stratford Johns
Humbert	Ronald Lacey
Baron Von Orlak	Ferdy Mayne
Dickens	Kynaston Reeves
Farrer	Richard Hurndall
Zoltan	John Hollis
Ho Lung	Leon Thau
Gorky	Tute Lemkow
Oppenheimer	Peter Swanwick
Slattery	Vic Wise
Winkler	Teddy Kiss
Dr Winter	Michael Bilton

Designed by Robert Jones

Directed by Don Chaffey

KILLERS ARE on their way to murder elderly Henley Farrer for the ornate dagger in his possession. But Farrer, who has lived his life surrounded by trappings of the Orient, has found a way to elude his assassins. He hands the precious dagger to his servant, Zoltan, telling him to take it to John Steed. Then Farrer steps into a prepared coffin, and within seconds his pulse has stopped. Sidney Street, a large fat man, and his colleague Humbert Green, a small sad-faced man, arrive to take possession of the dagger, which is engraved with a falcon's head. They find Farrer in his coffin, but no dagger. Zoltan is already on his way to Steed. He finds Steed at his home, trying to master a line-controlled model aeroplane. Zoltan hands the ornate dagger to him, refusing to give any information, save that it is a legacy. One of the many cut-throats seeking the dagger, Gorky, is eavesdropping. Another, Slattery, waits across the street as Tara drives up in her car. Wearing full evening dress, she has dropped in on Steed between parties. Before she leaves, Steed hands her the dagger and asks her to research into its background. As Steed intercepts Gorky at his letter-box, the cut-throats outside are joined by Oppenheimer, and a mysterious elevating truck. After drinking Steed's champagne, Gorky offers

Steed and Tara check the unconscious body of a villain for clues to the Legacy of Death.

him £1,000,000 for the dagger. Before he can add anything further, he is shot from the elevated truck outside the window. Steed calls a doctor. Meanwhile, Tara takes the dagger to a Chinese curio shop. The proprietor, Ho Lung, is strangely excited when Tara shows him the dagger, and when she leaves, he makes a hasty telephone call to his accomplice, Gregor, who soon joins the growing number of thugs after the dagger. At Steed's apartment, Oppenheimer has intercepted Doctor Winter, and takes his place to examine Gorky. At gunpoint, he attempts to force Steed to reveal the whereabouts of the dagger, but Slattery bursts in and they shoot each other. Street and Green are the next to call. Bemused by the pile of bodies, they fabricate a story of sentimental attachment to the dagger, but leave when Steed tells them he has given it to a friend. Meanwhile, Tara has used the dagger as a coat-hook on the wall of her apartment, and content that it is safe, decides to take a bath. She is surprised by Gregor and a fight breaks out. When Steed arrives, he is in time to see Gregor fall to his death on the dagger, which has been removed from the wall during the fight. As the two agents ponder the strange attraction of the dagger, cars arrive outside with more men after the dagger. Machine-gun bullets shatter the window as Street and Green eliminate their rivals with a well placed grenade. During all this, Steed and Tara have slipped out of the rear entrance and escape, rendering another villain unconscious as they go. In his pocket they find a slip of paper containing a solicitor's address. Now pursued by a vast number of cars and motorbikes, they drive off to hide the dagger in a secret place, known only to Steed. Tara then leaves to investigate the Chinese curio shop and Steed heads for the solicitors mentioned in the slip of paper. Before Dickens, the solicitor, can unearth the source of the dagger's bequest to Steed, he is also shot through the window from the elevated truck. The assassin is Zoltan, Farrer's assistant. Meanwhile, at the curio shop, Tara is captured and tortured by Von Orlak, a one-armed Prussian in a wheelchair, and his midget henchman, Winkler, while Ho Lung looks on. Street and Green take over the torture, which is a feather duster on Tara's feet. Unable to withstand the dreadful torture, Tara agrees to disclose the whereabouts of the dagger. She manages to turn the tables, however, and under similar torture, the two villains reveal that the dagger is the key to a secret treasure. At the solicitor's, Steed has made the same discovery. Driving to Farrer's home he meets Tara accidentally, and they discover that the reflected pattern from the shaft of the dagger matches the mosaic on the floor. The blade itself fits into a slot on the floor. The lights come on and they find themselves surrounded by all those wanting the dagger, who have now decided to form a consortium. Green reveals that they are all after a priceless black pearl, which is the largest in the world. But it is not under the floor. Henley Farrer (still alive, having only taken a drug to simulate death) steps from his coffin and reveals that he has the pearl. The legacy to Steed was just a trick to ensure that he could possess the pearl in peace. All Farrer's enemies are now under one roof, and Zoltan steps forward to mow them all down with a machine gun. In the mêlée that follows, Farrer is killed and the pearl falls into a glass of wine. It dissolves, leaving the villains to go sadly on their way and Steed and Tara to drink the world's most expensive glass of wine.

NOON-DOOMSDAY

By Terry Nation

John Steed	**Patrick Macnee**
Tara King	**Linda Thorson**
Farrington	**Ray Brooks**
Grant	**T P McKenna**
Baines	**Griffith Jones**
Lyall	**Lyndon Brook**
Kafta	**Peter Bromilow**
Mother	**Patrick Newell**
Rhonda	**Rhonda Parker**
Perrier	**Peter Halliday**
Sunley	**Anthony Ainley**
Hyde	**John Glyn-Jones**
Carson	**David Glover**
Cornwall	**Lawrence James**

Designed by Robert Jones

Directed by Peter Sykes

STEED IS recovering from injuries sustained during a recent case. His leg is in plaster and, needing crutches, he is recuperating at a special convalescent home for agents. Tara decides to visit him, and the taxi-driver is astonished when she asks to be dropped in the middle of nowhere. But Tara, armed with a large bunch of flowers, pushes her way through hedgerows, barbed wire, an electrified fence and a minefield (both turned off for her visit) and finally arrives at the secret sanatorium. She is greeted, and vetted, by a guard, Cornwall, who then reactivates the defences by turning a key in a device like a parking meter. Steed is delighted by Tara's visit, especially as the flowers conceal a bottle of vintage champagne. As they chat, Cornwall is ambushed by two hired guns, Kyle-Farrington and Norman Grant, and killed with a farming implement. Tara gives Steed his post, and he explains that his leg injury was caused by stepping into a cucumber frame while pursuing a suspected saboteur. Tara also meets Dr Hyde, and Sir Rodney Woodham-Baines, another patient, who has both his arms and neck in plaster. Steed opens a letter containing a ticket for the opera, dated 19 June 1961. The date, seven years ago to the day, is familiar. Steed puzzles over it for a moment, then realises that on that date he sent Gerald Kafta, head of Murder International, to prison at noon. Now he is out and bent on revenge! Tara tries to contact Mother's headquarters, but finds the telephone lines are dead. Farrington and Grant have cut the wires. Roger Lyall, another patient, takes Tara to use the radio transmitter, only to find that it, too, is wrecked. They decide to separate and search for Cornwall. Tara enters the hospital grounds and is only inches away from stepping on a land mine, when a French patient, Jules Perrier, with an eye-patch and his arm in a sling, saves her. The sundial in the grounds moves slowly towards noon. Tara discovers the dead body of Cornwall hanging from a rope, in the barn. As she turns to leave, a mysterious intruder knocks her down. Recovering, she goes outside to find Perrier in the grounds. Meanwhile, at a nearby deserted railway station, Farrington and Grant are practising their skills with knife and gun. Tara and Steed discuss their plight and she remembers that Cornwall had a key to activate the defence system. Who

has it now? Hearing shots, Tara runs into the gardens to a well, at the bottom of which lies the dead body of Dr Hyde. His assistant, Carson, obviously works for the other side, and proves his guilt by trying to gun her down in the garden. But Tara grapples with him, and he is accidentally shot with his gun. Before he dies he tells her that he threw the system key away. As the sundial approaches noon, the two hired killers prepare to meet their leader, Kafta. Tara meanwhile questions the four patients in the sanatorium and three of them give their reasons for not helping in the defence of the crippled Steed. The Frenchman says he works only for France, Sir Rodney claims he is a pacifist, and Lyall is obviously suffering too badly from battle fatigue. The only one who offers to help is Edward Sunley, who is so incapacitated by bandages that he is only able to act as lookout. As Farrington and Grant meet their leader's helicopter, Steed tries to lock Tara in a cupboard for her own safety. But she knocks him out with the vintage champagne bottle. As the clock strikes 12, Tara sets out to do battle for Steed. Kafta, Farrington and Grant arrive for the kill in classic Western style on horseback. Tara soon finds herself cornered by Grant in the barn. She outwits him with a bale of hay on the end of a rope, and then shoots him. Sunley, keeping a lookout, saves Tara from Farrington's knife by dropping a flower vase on him. Tara then uses his knife with deadly effect. With one bullet left in her gun, she and Kafta pin each other down and it is checkmate. But the mortally-wounded Farrington recovers enough to knife Tara's sleeve to a wall, giving Kafta the upper hand. Steed, having regained consciousness, staggers out on crutches and shoots Kafta with a spear gun concealed in a crutch. Steed, now fully recovered, takes Tara a present – his plaster cast. It is full of presents: champagne, pearls, a hat, parasol – and a sundial.

This one-eyed villain will challenge Tara to a showdown at **Noon-Doomsday.**

LOOK (STOP ME IF YOU'VE HEARD THIS ONE) BUT THERE WERE THESE TWO FELLOWS

By Dennis Spooner

John Steed	Patrick Macnee
Tara King	Linda Thorson
Maxie Martin	Jimmy Jewel
Jennings	Julian Chagrin
Bradley Marler	Bernard Cribbins
Marcus Pugman	John Cleese
Lord Bessington	William Kendall
Seagrave	John Woodvine
Brig Wiltshire	Garry Marsh
Miss Charles	Gaby Vargas
Cleghorn	Bill Shine
Sir Jeremy Broadfoot	Richard Young
Merlin	Robert James
Fiery Frederick	Talfryn Thomas
Tenor	Jay Denver
Escapologist	Johnny Vyvyan
Ventriloquist	Len Belmont

Designed by Robert Jones

Directed by James Hill

SIR JEREMY Broadfoot, head of the Land and Development Company, is alone, working late in his office. Two men, 'Merry' Maxie Martin and Jennings, move through the building towards him, stopping to change into music-hall entertainers' dress as they go. Maxie Martin shoots him with a silenced gun, then he and Jennings make a crazy music-hall dancing exit. Steed and Tara are called in. Tara finds a magician's wand and Steed a footprint of enormous size made by the clown shoes of Maxie Martin. The killers are inmates of Greasepaint Grange, a variety artistes' rest home, and there they receive their instructions to kill from Mr Punch in a Punch and Judy theatre. Mr Punch praises their successful killing of Sir Jeremy and urges them on to their next victim, another director of the Capital Land and Development Company, Thomas Randolph Cleghorn. Martin and Jennings kill him with an iron bar when he is duck-shooting, and this time they leave a red ping-pong ball false nose at the scene. This makes Tara suspect that the killer could be a vaudeville clown. She asks Marcus Pugman, who keeps a register of copyrighted clown make-ups, to help her find the red-nosed comedian. Steed meanwhile tells the board of the company (who are building the government's new underground seat, for Ministers to use in a wartime emergency) the line they are taking. Strangely, this information seems to get to Mr Punch. He reprimands Maxie and Jennings for leaving pieces of their make-up behind, and gives them their next victim, Pugman, who has Maxie's make-up on file. He is killed just as he is about to tell Steed and Tara on the phone that he has found the clown make-up they are after. They arrive to find him dead in his office, but, fortunately, he is holding an egg painted with Maxie's make-up. Brigadier Wiltshire is the next director to die, meeting a grotesque-ly funny end when he detonates a comical-looking bomb, labelled 'bomb' in his car. The Brigadier is killed when it really does blow up. Lord Bessington, however, the next victim, escapes from a custard pie of suffocating gluey material thrown at him by Maxie in his board-room. Miss Charles, his secretary, arrives in time to help Bessington to recover. From Bradley Marler, Maxie's gag-writer, Steed discovers that Maxie was a vaudeville star of the now-closed Gladchester Palladium. Lord Bessington says that the theatre was taken over and closed down by the Capital Land and Development Company. Marler is the next to go, knifed by Maxie on the instructions of Mr Punch. He is left dying, but manages to phone Steed and say that he has written down Maxie's present address. When Steed arrives at Marler's office, however, he finds the place piled high with screwed-up pieces of joke scripts. After a long search, he eventually finds a piece of paper bearing the address of Greasepaint Grange. Tara, meanwhile, is sticking close to Lord Bessington, but this does not prevent Maxie from killing him in broad daylight. He is disguised as a tree, and when Tara is investigating what she rightly thought was a tree moving, Maxie strangles him. Tara gives chase, but she is tricked and captured by Maxie when he does another quick change and arrives dressed as a policeman. Under arrest, she is taken to Greasepaint Grange. Steed decides to visit the rest room dressed as 'Gentleman Jack, a smile, a song, and an umbrella'. Meanwhile, Tara is in the process of becoming the first woman to be burnt in half, by ex-vaudeville magician, 'Fiery' Frederick. Steed arrives, but finds the place closed, so he breaks in and finds 'Fiery' Frederick in the throes of warming up Tara. He disposes of the magician in typical style and releases Tara. They then dress up as two halves of a pantomime horse and join the meeting Mr Punch is holding in the main hall. Eventually, the meeting ends and a panto-mime fight breaks out, which The Avengers win, revealing Mr Punch to be Seagrave, the last of the directors of the company. Later on, Steed does a fast quick change, like 'Merry' Maxie, when Tara turns up in a lovely evening gown, ready to go to the opera. However, it takes him three attempts to find the right attire.

Arrested by false policeman Maxie Martin, Tara faces a fiery fate in Look (Stop Me . . .).

HAVE GUNS . . . WILL HAGGLE

By Donald James

John Steed	Patrick Macnee
Tara King	Linda Thorson
Col Nsonga	Johnny Sekka
Adrianna	Nicola Pagett
Conrad	Jonathan Burn
Spencer	Timothy Bateson
Crayford	Michael Turner
Lift Attendant	Robert Gillespie
Giles	Roy Stewart
Brad	Peter J Elliott

Designed by Robert Jones

Directed by Ray Austin

FOUR MEN carry out a raid on a Government Ordnance Factory. They leap over the perimeter fence with a trampoline they have brought with them, then they signal with a knock on the warehouse door to Crayford, their contact inside the factory. Crayford lets them in, then encourages them to fake a struggle with him. They knock him unconscious, and leave with several crates of FN rifles of a new top-secret type, the FF70. Tara King goes to the scene of the break-in, and bounces on the trampoline. She and Steed have come to investigate the raid, which means that 3000 of the new rifles are now off the secret list. Meanwhile, in the garden of English-rose Adrianna's house, Conrad, her brother, stalks and kills Smith in a weird rifle testing duel which ends with Adrianna coolly inviting her victorious brother Conrad to come in for tea. Smith's body is dumped in a reservoir, and Steed and Tara are on the scene when it is dredged up. Steed gets the bullet from the dead man's body, but needs the help of ballistics to prove whether it is fired by an FF70 or not. He sends Tara to find out, while he calls on Colonel Nsonga, an African military man newly arrived in the country. He is well-known to Steed, who believes, rightly, he may have come in search of the rifles to back up his struggle for the Presidency of a newly independent African state. Adrianna visits Nsonga in his room, but does not yet name a price for the rifles. Steed, hiding in the hotel phone booth, sees Adrianna, Conrad and Nsonga leave, and when they are gone, he bribes the lift-operator to take him up to Nsonga's room. Picking the lock with a credit card, he searches the room and finds some money in Nsonga's safe. As he leaves, he accidentally knocks over a tailor's dummy wearing military uniform. But he gets away just as Nsonga and Giles, his servant, return. Tara, disguised as a blonde, visits the ballistics establishment, and there Crayford sees her give Spencer the bullet, taken from the dead Smith for testing. Crayford phones Conrad who asks him to deal with Tara, and she is ambushed as she leaves. The thug tries to retrieve the bullet, but Tara escapes after a fast and furious car duel. Tara, now back to a brunette, tells Steed that the bullet was fired from an FF70. Steed tells her about the money he found in Nsonga's safe and that he is having a uniform with presidential insignia made, which shows his ambitions. Handing her a blonde wig, Steed suggests that she take a closer look at the Ordnance Factory.

Meanwhile, Steed visits Nsonga again, this time meeting him as he knocks Giles out. Steed confuses Nsonga by telling him that he, too, is a gun-runner, for the Colonel's own President. When Tara reaches the factory, she interrupts a second raid – this time for ammunition – by Conrad's men, but she escapes. Conrad, however, kills Crayford, then pursues Tara back to her apartment. There, he attacks her and takes her off in his car to Stokely House. Steed visits Tara's flat, and finds the signs of a struggle. He returns home and discovers from his answering service that Adrianna has invited him to Stokely House. Nsonga has told her that Steed is in the market for guns. As Steed arrives at the house, he just misses being killed by a shot from Giles. Conrad, noticing the servant, shoots Giles before he can fire a second shot at Steed. Before the gun auction begins, Adrianna holds a demonstration, in which two men duel with the FF70s. One finally kills the other. Then she surprises Steed by bringing in Tara, to duel with Conrad. Steed manages to hold up the proceedings during the auction, but his bid is beaten by Colonel Nsonga's. Nsonga then orders the duel to commence. Steed moves off from the group to try to help Tara with a friendly shot, but Tara, rather than going for her gun, sneaks up behind her opponent and knocks him cold. She and Steed then escape. Steed, following Tara, comes across a hut in which he finds the FF70 rifles. He lights a fuse to blow them up, not knowing that Conrad has captured Tara, tied her up and left her in the hut. Steed finds her in time, however, and after a struggle kills Conrad and frees Tara. The hut explodes and one of the FF70s falls on Nsonga's head, killing him. Afterwards, Steed, having anticipated the arrival of an exotic gift from the grateful President for sorting out the Nsonga business, is more than surprised when he finds a large jungle cat growling at his door.

In Have Guns . . . Will Haggle, *Tara knocks out Conrad before he can take a shot at her in their projected duel.*

THEY KEEP KILLING STEED

By Brian Clemens

John Steed	Patrick Macnee
Tara King	Linda Thorson
Baron Von Curt	Ian Ogilvy
Arcos	Ray McAnally
Zerson	Norman Jones
Captain Smythe	Bernard Horsfall
Mother	Patrick Newell
Verno	Arthur Howell
Golda	Bill Cummings
Smanoff	Frank Barringer
Bruno	William Ellis

and Hal Galili, Nicole Shelby, Rosemary Donnelly,
Gloria Connell, Michael Corcoran, Ross
Hutchinson, Reg Whitehead, Anthony Sheppard,
Angharad Rees, George Ghent

Designed by Robert Jones

Directed by Robert Fuest

A WRECKED car in a disused quarry conceals the entrance to an underground headquarters, where a group of men are hatching an imaginative plot. Using a scientific method, they intend to provide one of their agents with a replica of John Steed's face. Then, as Steed, the agent will infiltrate a peace conference with a bomb. However, when Arcos and Zerson finish their first experiment, it is not perfect. Arcos now decides that they must have the real Steed and make a mould from his face. Steed and Tara are asked to be official observers at the peace conference and they book into an hotel, thinking they can have a rest. They have a light-hearted incident when a Baron Von Curt knocks at their door and asks Tara to pose as his wife so that he can escape the advances of two young women. Steed receives a phone call from a Captain Smythe of Security, and is kidnapped as he climbs into a taxi. He is taken to the quarry headquarters and Arcos and Zerson explain their plan to make a cast of his face. Then, by injecting their agent's face with a special serum, the man will assume every detail of the mould. Steed is then strapped to a concrete base and the agents proceed to make the face mould. Arcos decides that Nadine, one of the five agents available, will impersonate Steed. A labelled mould and syringe are placed in a special case, ready to be delivered to him. But Steed escapes, locks the gang out of their headquarters, and before being recaptured, places four more labelled moulds in the case. Arcos then gives the case to another of the gang, Bruno, to deliver to Nadine. Bruno, reading the labels, innocently delivers the Steed kits to all five agents. Meanwhile, Tara finds a useful ally in the Baron. As they visit Mother in a bizarre underwater capsule he is testing for the Navy, the five agents inject themselves, put on their masks and become John Steeds. One dies in the process, but the other four make their way to the peace conference, where on seeing each other, they begin to fight. The sole survivor then places a percussion bomb under the gavel to be used by the chairman. Arriving at the conference hall, Tara and the Baron find – and keep on finding – dead Steeds. Only when their fingerprints don't match those of the real Steed is Tara reassured. Steed manages to escape and reach the conference just in time to snatch the deadly gavel from the chairman's hand and throw it through the window. In the garden, Tara accepts the fake Steed as her real partner and is narrowly saved from death at his hands by the Baron. Joining them, Steed sets off in his car to trap the villains in their quarry hideout, and Tara and the Baron follow him in hot pursuit. Steed arrives to find that Arcos has become another Steed double in an effort to escape. Steed attacks him and they fight over a gun. Meanwhile, above ground, Tara and Von Curt win a spectacular sword fight and rout the rest of the villains. One of them, Zerson, recovers before dying and returns to the underground shelter where he shoots Steed, who staggers from the fight into the waiting Tara's arms. But is it the real Steed, or the bogus one? As a second, smiling, Steed steps out of the shelter, Tara has the answer. Only the real Steed would smile under such circumstances. In the final scene, Steed and Tara are sunbathing in deckchairs with the sea in the background. The camera then pans back and reveals sunlamps and a travel poster on the wall. They are in Tara's apartment – Mother has cut short their holiday and sent them home. Outside, it starts to rain.

THE INTERROGATORS

By Richard Harris and Brian Clemens

John Steed	**Patrick Macnee**
Tara King	**Linda Thorson**
Col Mannering	**Christopher Lee**
Minnow	**David Sumner**
Caspar	**Philip Bond**
Mother	**Patrick Newell**
Blackie	**Glynn Edwards**
Rasker	**Neil McCarthy**
Mallard	**Neil Stacy**
Norton	**Neil Wilson**
Mr Puffin	**Cardew Robinson**
Captain Soo	**Cecil Cheng**
Naval officer	**Mark Elwes**
RAF officer	**David Richards**

Designed by Robert Jones

Directed by Charles Crichton

WHAT APPEARS to be an ordinary dentist's waiting-room is actually being used for torture and interrogation – part of a brilliantly conceived plan to extract information from secret agents. Lieutenant Roy Caspar is strong enough to withstand the torture imposed by Colonel Mannering, Blackie, Captain Soo, and their associates, yet they manage to extract the names of his two most important contacts, Wilson, an archer, and Izzy Pound, a one-man band. Both men are shot by Blackie. After interrogation, Caspar is released. Believing it is part of the test, he refuses to tell Mother and Steed what has happened to him, even when they confront him with the dead bodies of Wilson and Pound. Afterwards, Colonel Mannering has him shot when Caspar asks awkward questions. The next agent for interrogation is Minnow. He too is told by Mannering and associates that the interrogation is part of a test set by Mother's organisation to discover their breaking point under torture. Tara and Steed, following the trail of the missing agents – who always seem to take their toothbrushes with them – are too late to save Minnow's prime contact, Fillington. He is shot while playing football. Tara does, however, save the second contact, Puffin. Like Caspar, Minnow returns and acts as though nothing has happened. But Steed and Mother show him photographs of his dead contacts, and he finally realises that the interrogation was not part of a training course. Yet he still denies that he broke down while under pressure. Minnow does not know where the interrogation took place, but recalls that he was given a pigeon to release, should anything go wrong. Steed follows the pigeon in a helicopter. Just as well, because another agent, Mallard, is now under torture, and Tara – who has played a phoney taped message from Mother – has also gone willingly to undergo the interrogation course. In the bar at the interrogation establishment, where agents are allowed to relax, Tara gains some insight into how the agents unwittingly leak their secrets. When congratulated by Colonel Mannering on withstanding interrogation and passing the test, they are plied with drinks and eventually tell what they know. But not Tara. She overpowers Captain Soo after noticing that Mannering's cigarettes are the same brand as the butts she saw in the homes of the dead agents. When Steed arrives, Mannering tells the assembled agents that he is an intruder breaking into the building as a security test, and there will be merit points awarded to the one who shoots him with the pistols, loaded with blanks, he provides. Steed, however, soon overcomes two of Mannering's henchmen with his bowler, and then turns to face the agents. To protect him, Tara leaps in front of them, but she is unable to convince them that they have been duped, until she tells them to aim their guns at Mannering. His nerve breaks and he ducks – only to be hit over the head with a firm tap from Steed's steel-lined bowler. Later on, Steed is seen interrogating Tara, but it is simply to make her disclose the vital ingredient of her delicious soup.

Tara leapfrogs over Col Mannering's agents to save Steed from certain death in The Interrogators.

THE ROTTERS

By Dave Freeman

John Steed	**Patrick Macnee**
Tara King	**Linda Thorson**
Kenneth	**Gerald Sim**
George	**Jerome Willis**
Pym	**Eric Barker**
Palmer	**John Nettleton**
Mother	**Patrick Newell**
Rhonda	**Rhonda Parker**

Frank Middlemass, Dervis Ward, Harold Innocent, Toni Gilpin, Amy Dalby, John Stone, Charles Morgan, Harry Hutchinson, Noel Davis, John Scott

Designed by Robert Jones

Directed by Robert Fuest

AT THE Department of Forestry Research, Sir James Pendred is fleeing for his life from two gunmen. He finds sanctuary in his office, and throws the bolt on the heavy wooden door. Suddenly, the wood dissolves, leaving only the metal fittings. Two men, Kenneth and George, are framed in the doorway and without emotion, George shoots Pendred. Steed and Tara discuss the murder with Mother, in an office built completely of polythene. Sir James Pendred, it seems, had telephoned the Prime Minister before he was shot, claiming he had information of national importance. Mother sends Steed to Pendred's office, while Tara goes to the dead man's apartment. She arrives in time to see Kenneth and George about to shoot Pendred's man-servant, and although she stops them stealing a photograph, she is unable to prevent the servant's death. The photograph shows Pendred with four other boffins. Meanwhile, a pencil has dissolved in Steed's hands at Pendred's office.

In The Rotters, *Tara wields an axe with deadly effect to bring the plans of the wood-rotters crashing down.*

Puzzled, he decides to seek the advice of Reginald Pym, a leading expert on timber decay. He finds Pym, one of the men in the photograph, probing a woodworm-ridden beam in a church tower. When Steed shows him the remains of the decayed pencil, Pym is strangely silent and tells him he is busy. Tara visits Professor Palmer, who is nurturing young trees at the Institute of Timber Technology. He is able to identify the other men in the photo and reveals that they had recently made a startling discovery while researching fungi, but he has taken an oath not to reveal it. Before he can say more, he is killed by a knife thrown by Sandford, a gardener working nearby. Steed and Tara are also too late to save Pym's life. Kenneth and George arrive at the church and dissolve the woodwork in the bell-tower, bringing the giant bell crashing down on the timber expert. Tara and Steed discuss the three remaining men in the photograph. They are Mervyn Sawbow, an antique dealer, Forsythe, who is in Africa, and Wainwright, the managing director of Wainwright Timber Industries. Steed finds Sawbow faking antique furniture but the man is unable to help him and he leaves. Tara calls at Wainwright's timber yard, where she meets Sonia, his receptionist and Mrs Parbury, a solemn-looking colleague of Wainwright's. Together they lead her to a coffin. Inside lies Wainwright. They explain that he died of overwork. As Tara leaves, Sonia and Parbury are joined by Kenneth and George. Sonia then phones Sandford, the gardener, and orders him to kill Tara. He blocks the road with a large truck and stops her car, then tries to kill her with an axe. Tara outwits him, but to her astonishment, Sandford escapes by driving his car through a wooden farm gate – which suddenly disappears! Steed hears that Forsythe, the other man in the photo, is returning home, and he goes to his house to wait for him. Forsythe fails to arrive, but not so Kenneth and George who, to the amazement of Forsythe's mother, dissolve a piano which falls on Steed while they escape. Tara now follows Sawbow in her car, and is in time to see him killed – after digging his own grave – by Sandford and his huge friend, Jackson. The two thugs spot Tara and she hides in a nearby wooden hut – which suddenly dissolves around her! Jackson knocks her cold, and she is taken to Wainwright's timber yard and chained to a chair by Sonia and Sandford. Once alone, Tara manages to burn off her chains with acid. She disposes of Sandford, on guard outside the room, and is about to leave, when she is cornered by Wainwright, now very much alive, with a gun in his hand. Forsythe, back from Africa, manages to overcome Jackson, who has been sent to waylay him, and arriving home, meets Steed. He then reveals that he and the others had been working on a mutation of dry rot that was highly contagious. He also reveals that Wainwright cannot be dead, as he telephoned him offering a job. Wainwright, meanwhile, is telling Tara the details of his plan. He is going to rot the whole of Europe unless the main powers pay him £1,000,000,000. Armed with a spray-gun taken from the dead Jackson, Steed arrives in time to save Tara. Using the wood-dissolving spray with both deadly and comical effect, he overcomes the villains and brings the building crashing down around their ears. In the final scene, Tara is ticking off her shopping list as Steed prepares a gourmet meal – Steed's crushed omelette of mushroom. Alas, Tara has forgotten the mushrooms. Steed, fortunately, is able to produce a giant mushroom grown by Professor Palmer.

INVASION OF THE EARTHMEN

By Terry Nation

John Steed	Patrick Macnee
Tara King	Linda Thorson
Brett	William Lucas
Huxton	Christian Roberts
Emily	Lucy Fleming
Bassin	Christopher Chittell
Trump	Warren Clarke
Sarah	Wendy Allnutt
Grant	George Roubicek

Designed by Robert Jones

Directed by Don Sharp

B Y THE side of a remote English country road, agent Bernard Grant cuts his way through a high wire-mesh fence and finds himself looking at three teenagers in semi-military uniform in a disused quarry. Emily Wade is flashing a signal lamp at the sky, Rodney Trump is shooting stars with a sextant, and Huxton is operating a radio transmitter. Suddenly, a giant boa-constrictor grabs Grant. The three teenagers note his plight but instead of helping, they simply laugh out loud. Huxton and Trump are watching from their jeep as Steed and Tara arrive at a country hotel. In Grant's room, Steed finds a prospectus for the Alpha Academy, which he was investigating when he disappeared. Tara, looking through the window, notices that the insignia on the jeep outside is the same as the one on the prospectus. They decide to visit the Alpha Academy and the jeep follows them. From behind the closed gates, they notice groups of teenagers strolling around the grounds. They finally gain entrance, and are shown into the headmaster's room where, posing as parents interested in sending their 18-year-old son to the school, they meet Commander Brett, the headmaster. As they leave, Steed takes an interest in the classrooms and Tara even manages to get into one, where she sees a strange helmeted spaceman. As she does so, Huxton rabbit-punches her from behind and she falls to the floor unconscious. Huxton later explains to Steed, who has been brought back under escort, that Tara stumbled and hit her head. Back in their car, The Avengers give the jeep the slip and return to the school. Getting into the grounds via the wire fence used by Grant, they begin to search the quarry. When they are almost killed by a booby-trap of falling rocks, they decide to split up and investigate separately. In the quarry Tara finds a radio-active canister and a human skeleton. Then, she finds another of the helmeted space creatures, and has a narrow escape when a scorpion alights on her hand. Fortunately, she is able to knock it off. Steed meanwhile has penetrated the school buildings and enters the cryobiology store-room, where he finds dozens of cocooned bodies of young people. Back at the quarry, Tara saves Huxton from Bassin, another student, who is about to crush him from above with a huge boulder. All she gets in return for her warning cry, however, is an arrow from Huxton's bow – which fortunately sticks in her jacket sleeve. In the Academy, Steed enters another room and accidentally activates a powerful wind current, which swirls him up into the centre of the room. He manages to reach a switch and return to the floor of what appears to be a weightlessness-simulating room. As he leaves, he notices a dark tunnel at the far end of the passage outside. Tara, meanwhile, is in a state of anxiety for she is now faced with another of the space creatures – with a group of the Alpha teenagers in support. She loses consciousness, and they carry her away. As Steed leaves the Academy, he finds Bassin prowling in the grounds. He overpowers him and learns that the young students at the Academy are being trained by Commander Brett, for the conquest of outer-space, and will take over the new territories of space when inter-planetary travel becomes feasible. Tara learns exactly the same from Brett in his office, from which she is trying unsuccessfully to escape. Bassin tells Steed that the students have to run the gauntlet of the tunnel, to come face to face with their secret fears. Brett is so impressed with Tara's instinct for survival that he releases her – sending his students off in pursuit 60 seconds later as part of their survival training. Huxton now finds Bassin, left bound and gagged by Steed, but this time they do not attempt to kill each other. Huxton explains that there is a security condition red alert, and together they set out in search of their joint enemy, Steed. Tara soon finds herself trapped by a space creature and, knocking it to the ground, she removes the helmet to discover that there is an ordinary human being inside the suit. With the aid of a map he found earlier, Steed locates a bolted door in the quarry, and enters the darkness of the tunnel hidden behind it. Tara also finds herself in the tunnel. She enters it from the corridor hotly pursued by the group of students. But they pull up at the tunnel's entrance and refuse to follow her. Emily, the group leader, decides to report to Brett. In the tunnel, Tara is faced with one danger after another. First she has to ward off an attack by giant rats, then she is bitten by some leeches. Finally, she enters a narrow tube section in which she is sealed when large metal doors close ahead of and behind her, and spiders drop through a hole in the grating. Crushing spiders as she goes, she finally manages to break through the doors. Brett, meanwhile, is following her progress through the tunnel when he spots a second figure on his radar screen. It is Steed, making his way towards Tara from the quarry entrance. Brett orders the students to head them off and block their progress. Emily's group enter from one end, Trump's from the other. But Steed is facing dangers of his own. He just misses being caught in a man-trap when his umbrella tip is snapped off by it, then he has to negotiate a stretch of acid that looks like water, by jumping over it. He finally meets the distraught Tara, and when the students meet in the centre of the tunnel, Steed and Tara have vanished – into the ventilation shaft. When Steed and Tara get out, they seal off the shaft, and block both ends of the tunnel. Steed then puts Huxton and Bassin out of action with his bowler. Tara then knocks out Brett, who is leaving his office to deal with her and Steed personally, being disappointed with the performance of his troops. Later on, Steed shows Tara a hip-throw, which she, in return, uses on him. She then asks Steed what's next on the agenda. Dinner in the country? A ride in the park? Ogling his partner, he replies, 'Practice?!'

KILLER

By Tony Williamson

John Steed	**Patrick Macnee**
Tara King	**Linda Thorson**
Lady Diana	**Jennifer Croxton**
Merridon	**Grant Taylor**
Brinstead	**William Franklyn**
Clarke	**Richard Wattis**
Mother	**Patrick Newell**

and Harry Towb, John Bailey, Michael Ward,
James Bree, Michael McStay, Anthony Valentine,
Charles Houston, Jonathan Elsom, Clive Graham
and Oliver Macgreevy

Designed by Robert Jones

Directed by Cliff Owen

SOMEONE, OR something, is depleting the ranks of Steed's fellow agents. Trouncer, a double-agent, has found out that the killer is Remak (Remote Electro-Matic Agent Killer), a computer programmed for murder. And in Remak's lair, a factory from which there is no escape, Trouncer is fighting for his life. Steed, waiting for Trouncer to arrive at his apartment, receives a visit from Tara. She explains that she is taking a well-earned holiday and, kissing him on the cheek, leaves. Outside Steed's apartment, Merridon and Brinstead, two employees of the Remak organisation, lie in wait for Trouncer. As he arrives, they shoot him from their car and drive away. Trouncer's dying words to Steed, are "Remak . . . killer . . . Polly . . . tell Mother'.

In Killer, Steed enters the inner sanctum of Remak, a computer programmed to kill.

Steed arrives at Mother's headquarters, to find him giving a lecture in a room full of blackboards and maps. He sits in a rocking-chair, as do the rest of the agents in the class, save for one, a beautiful young woman called Lady Diana Forbes-Blakeney. Mother links the word Polly with a recently-discovered body, wrapped in *poly*thene, tied with ribbon, and found in a churchyard. He assigns Lady Diana, from Special Services, to help Steed. When the body of Wilkington, the architect of Remak, is found similarly wrapped in the same churchyard, Steed and Lady Diana go to investigate. Clarke, an expert from the forensic department, tells them that the man was clubbed, poisoned, shot, spiked, stabbed, strangled and suffocated to death. Steed discovers that his neck has also been broken! Wilkington's identity is revealed by his wrist-watch, but Merridon and Brinstead have watched the scene and reach Wilkington's house first. Lady Diana arrives in time to fight – in an unusual balletic style – with Brinstead. He escapes, leaving only charred remains of Wilkington's papers. Steed meanwhile tackles the source of the pink ribbon which tied the corpses. The proprietor of Fancy Frills and Packaging Limited tells him to return later, but when Steed has left, Merridon strangles the proprietor with one of his own ribbons. As Mother and Lady Diana piece together Wilkington's papers, three other agents are lured, one at a time, to a disused village, erected as a film set. There, another Remak man, Paxton, sends them on to a pub at Lower Storpington with his dying breath. (He feigns death – once with a knife in his back, then from an arrow in his chest, and finally with a sword in his stomach.) At the pub the agents are met by Brinstead and sent to the factory, to be murdered by Remak. Lady Diana gets a lead to the factory where she meets Ralph Bleech, partner of the dead Wilkington. He tells her that his partner was an electronics expert working on an advanced computer at Lower Storpington. Bleech, however, knows more than he reveals and immediately leaves to blackmail the men behind Remak. But at the factory he himself becomes another victim and is pushed into a murder room by Brinstead and Merridon. His gift-wrapped body is then dropped by helicopter into the same graveyard as before. Steed and Lady Diana close in on the factory, crushing Brinstead on the way with a large log which they roll down a hill. They enter the factory from different ways, and Steed runs the gauntlet of the murder rooms, pitting his wits against his computer adversary. He successfully avoids death by arrow, horizontal guillotine (which cleaves his bowler in two), crushing, garrotting and electrocution, before being joined by Lady Diana. He then feigns death at the hands of a remote-controlled gun, and as his jacket is whisked away to be gift-wrapped, he and Lady Diana follow it and find Merridon operating the computer. In the ensuing fight, Merridon meets his death in one of his own murder rooms, and before they leave Lady Diana sets the computer on a course of self-destruction. Steed arrives back at his apartment and has difficulty entering because Tara has sent him so many postcards. Tara is waiting for him, her arm in a sling. Writer's cramp, she explains. She also has a present for him, an inflatable dinghy concealed in a small box. When it is released . . .

THE MORNING AFTER

By Brian Clemens

John Steed	**Patrick Macnee**
Tara King	**Linda Thorson**
Merlin	**Peter Barkworth**
Jenny	**Penelope Horner**
Brigadier Hansing	**Joss Ackland**
Sgt Hearn	**Brian Blessed**
Major Parsons	**Donald Douglas**
Yates	**Philip Dunbar**
Cartney	**Jonathan Cartney**

Designed by Robert Jones

Directed by John Hough

IN THE hands of John Steed, a bowler and an umbrella can be as deadly as a machine gun. So he seldom carries a firearm. But as Steed hides in his apartment, waiting for a visitor to arrive, he startles Tara by producing a pistol. He explains that Merlin is one of the most cunning, dangerous and charming spies of them all. Steed has lured him to his flat to capture him before he can sell the newly developed sleep capsules he has stolen from a secret establishment. Merlin – actually a quadruple agent – lives up to his reputation. He bursts through the door, and in the resulting mêlée a gas capsule is smashed and all three fall to the floor unconscious. When Steed awakens, he discovers a whole day has passed. He tries to phone headquarters, but there is no answer. And when he goes out into the normally busy street, he finds it deserted. Returning to his apartment, he finds Tara still sound asleep, but Merlin is almost awake, so Steed decides to hand him over to the authorities alone. Handcuffed to each other they set off in the vintage Rolls until they find their way blocked by abandoned vehicles. Continuing their journey on foot, they arrive too late to save a man, Cartney, from being shot by military firing squad led by Sergeant Hearn. Steed and Merlin are nearly shot themselves, but escape when Steed grabs Sergeant Hearn, and uses him as a shield. From reporter Jenny Firston, and her photographer Yates, whom they discover hiding in a van, they learn the truth of the situation. Martial law has been declared, and the population evacuated because a nuclear bomb has been discovered beneath a trade commission building. With everyone on the streets being shot on sight, Steed is concerned that Tara may wake and go outside. So, placing Merlin on his honour not to escape, he unlocks the handcuffs and with Jenny and Yates sets off to warn Tara. Sergeant Hearn, however, has set a trap for them and in the resulting fight, Yates is killed, Merlin escapes, and Steed and Jenny are captured. Tara, meanwhile, wakes and sets out to find Steed and Merlin. She arrives in time to rescue Steed and Jenny from the firing squad they are now facing, but Merlin has come back to help too, and accidentally puts Tara back to sleep with one of the gas capsules. From the captured Hearn, Steed learns that Brigadier Hansing, who is supposed to be defusing the nuclear bomb, is in fact masterminding a scheme to hold the government to ransom. Disgusted at being made redundant by a computer, he invented the story about the bomb as an excuse to substitute bribed men for the real troops, and is now in the throes of placing a real nuclear bomb in the trade commission building! Steed and Merlin join forces to overcome the Brigadier, his adjutant Major Parsons, and their phoney troops. Using the gas capsules, they put the Brigadier's gang out of action. After a long, drawn-out fight, Steed puts Merlin on his best behaviour and allows him to go free. As Jenny leaves to file her story, Tara wakes and asks if anything exciting has happened. Later, Steed opens the door to his apartment to find Tara holding a box she has found on his doorstep. The box, from Merlin, is empty. Then Steed receives a phone call to say that Merlin has broken into a secret establishment and stolen some luminous dust. Realisation dawning, Steed switches out the lights – the empty box is glowing.

Steed and Merlin, handcuffed together, see a man being shot by firing squad in The Morning After.

THE CURIOUS CASE OF THE COUNTLESS CLUES

By Philip Levene

John Steed	Patrick Macnee
Tara King	Linda Thorson
Earle	Anthony Bate
Gardiner	Kenneth Cope
Stanley	Tony Selby
Doyle	Peter Jones
Janice	Tracy Reed
Flanders	Edward de Souza
Burgess	George A Cooper
Dawson	Reginald Jessup

Designed by Robert Jones

Directed by Don Sharp

TWO MEN are apparently investigating a murder which has been committed in the Dulwich flat of Herbert Dawson. A chalk outline indicates where the body would lie, but the body is missing! Suddenly, Dawson arrives home, and Earle, one of the two men, shoots him, firing his gun through a polythene bag. The two men depart, leaving Dawson's body lying in the chalk outline on the floor. Steed commiserates with Tara in her apartment. Her leg is in plaster following a mishap on holiday. He explains that he cannot stay long, since he has an appointment with Ministry sleuth, Sir Arthur Doyle, who sports a deer-stalker hat, smokes a meerchaum pipe, and has a (female) assistant called Watson. Doyle has picked up all the carefully-laid clues at the Dawson murder and he suspects a friend of Steed's, press tycoon Sir William Burgess. Doyle suspects that Burgess might be the owner of a Rolls-Royce seen leaving the scene of the crime, with the registration number partically identified as CLU. Steed is asked to check out Burgess' story. Steed questions his friend and is disturbed to see that Burgess has a button missing from his coat. A similar button was found in Dawson's flat. Also during the interview, the mention of Dulwich seems to shake the man so much that he miscues a shot on the billiards table. He smokes Havana cigars, and the butt of such a cigar was found at the scene of the crime. However, Burgess has a strong alibi when he mentions being helped out after a breakdown on the A4 by the Motor Rescue Service, at the time of the murder. (Later Steed discovers that the MRS have not recorded the breakdown and the matter will take some time to check.) As Steed leaves, Earle, Dawson's killer, enters and begins a game of billiards with the distraught Burgess. Earle and Gardiner, his partner in Dawson's murder, get into a lift with financier Robert Flanders, and manage to take his handkerchief and a button from his coat. Then, when Flanders goes for a drive in his white Jaguar, the two men pick up an identical car. Flanders' car soon breaks down on the road in the same way that Burgess' did. Earle then dresses in Flanders' clothes and allows a passing cyclist to see him. He then takes a rifle, which he and Gardiner have brought with them, to a nearby cottage where he shoots a man named Scott. This is to pin the Scott murder on Flanders, who is meanwhile

Tara lays out the villainous Earle in novel fashion in The Curious Case of the Countless Clues.

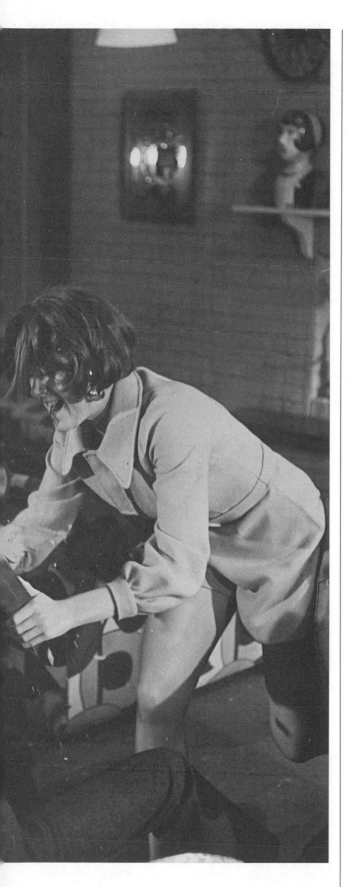

being helped after his breakdown on the A4 by a Motor Service Rescue patrolman. Doyle reports Scott's murder to Steed, and points out that the clues point to Flanders being the killer (as intended by Earle). Steed says he knows the financier through his sister, Janice, so Doyle asks him to check Flanders' alibi. Steed discovers that Flanders also had a breakdown on the A4 at the time of the murder, but when he finds a .275 calibre rifle missing from Flanders' cabinet, a rifle of the type used to kill Scott, he is suspicious. Flanders, however, tells him the rifle is at his hunting lodge. Steed leaves and just misses the arrival of Earle, who now shows Flanders how he has been set-up with Scott's murder. Even the Motor Rescue man, Stanley, who was part of the plot, will not establish his alibi for him. Earle then extorts a valuable Valesco painting from Flanders. As he leaves with the painting, Janice notices him and goes to her brother's study to find the Valesco missing. Gardiner now menaces Burgess and tries to extort a painting from him, but Burgess refuses. He phones Steed and says he lied about the Dawson murder, and now wants to make a clean breast of things. But before Steed can get to him, Earle menaces Burgess again, saying that the police, having found Dawson's murder weapon, are on the way to pick him up. Before Steed can intervene, Burgess is arrested and charged. Doyle is convinced that Burgess is guilty, but Steed believes that it is all too neat. And he is encouraged further when Janice calls to tell him that Scott was sacked from Flanders' firm for fiddling the books. Janice also tells him that a man has removed a valuable painting from her brother's collection. When questioned, however, Flanders won't discuss it. Earle now puts further pressure on Flanders for another painting, and Janice once again sees Earle and Gardiner removing the painting. She follows them to Earle's cottage, but as she is phoning Steed for help, Stanley, the MRS man, finds her. When Steed arrives, Earle and his entourage have flown, leaving a cross-bow trap for Steed to walk into. He foils it by wearing a breast-plate which he has taken from a suit of armour in the hall. Steed goes to Flanders' house and is astonished to see that the paintings have been restored. Janice backs up her brother's story that nothing is amiss. Only later when Steed returns to look at Flanders' rifle does the real story break. Flanders disturbs Steed as he removes the rifle, which Steed points out as being the wrong one. The real one has been removed in order to frame Flanders. Janice cracks first, then persuades her brother to tell Steed how the frame was worked. Earle now decides to use the framing technique on Steed himself. He and Gardiner remove a glove, umbrella and bowler from Steed's Rolls, then tamper with the car so that it will break down. Stanley arrives, but Steed knocks him out. He then discovers a photograph of Tara among Stanley's possessions, which suggests that she may be next for the framing technique. He phones Tara, but before he can warn her, the line goes dead. Earle is with Tara already, and cuts the wires. Steed rushes to Tara's apartment. Tara meanwhile, fighting for her life, squirts the contents of her hot-water bottle into Earle's face, then knocks him out with a pair of skis. Steed arrives in time to dispose of Gardiner, then, rather ignominiously, he trips over the furniture and hurts his leg. In the last scene, Steed is an invalid, with the fully-recovered Tara playing the ministering angel. She produces champagne – and for Steed, a yard of ale in a special elongated glass.

WISH YOU WERE HERE

By Tony Williamson

John Steed	Patrick Macnee
Tara King	Linda Thorson
Charles Merryvale	Liam Redmond
Maxwell	Robert Urquhart
Basil	Brook Williams
Parker	Dudley Foster
Mother	Patrick Newell
Kendrick	Gary Watson
Mellor	Richard Caldicot
Vickers	Derek Newark
Brevitt	David Garth
Miss Craven	Louise Pajo
Mr Maple	John Cazabon
Girl	Sandra Fehr
Rhonda	Rhonda Parker

Designed by Robert Jones

Directed by Don Chaffey

Tara goes missing on holiday and Steed and Mother have to find and rescue her in Wish You Were Here.

TARA'S UNCLE, Charles Merryvale, is being held prisoner in a holiday hotel, while his captors take over his vast business empire, It is a prison with no visible restraint, but Parker, the manager, and Mellor, the waiter, prove it is just as effective when Merryvale's friend, James Brevitt, attempts to walk out. He slips on a highly polished step and breaks his leg. Concerned that Charles has not returned from his holiday, Maple, the family retainer, calls on Tara King. He explains that Stephen Kendrick, the company secretary, has taken over the business. When Kendrick appears and produces a postcard reputed to come from Tara's uncle, Steed and Tara pretend to believe him and leave. But Tara visits her uncle at the hotel shown on the postcard – and finds that she too is a prisoner at the hotel. She sees Brevitt try to escape again but this time he is knocked down by a car. Trying to escape herself, Tara finds her car won't start, and then a window-cleaner drops a bucket of water on her. Her wet dress is taken away to be dried, but when it is returned it has a large burn mark on it. Steed meanwhile visits Mother, whom he finds suspended by a parachute harness in a room full of photographs of agents. Another agent, Basil Crighton-Latimer, Mother's nephew, is in attendance, practising with a golf club. After Basil chips a golf ball into Mother's drink, he is sent to assist Tara, while Steed is told to go in search of a missing agent. Meanwhile, at the hotel, Tara has stolen a chambermaid's dress and gone to look for Brevitt, the man knocked down while trying to escape. She finds him dead in his room, but when she and her uncle take a bonafide guest, Maxwell Greene, to see the body and prove they are being held prisoner, it lashes out at them. Vickers, one of the captors, has changed places with the corpse. Maxwell says he will go for help, but soon limps back with a story that he fell on a roller skate. Over a game of croquet, Tara, Maxwell and Uncle Charles discuss their plan of escape. Enter Basil, with a huge collection of luggage and holiday paraphernalia. He finds Tara's uncle bandaged in bed, after trying to escape in a visiting laundry van. He was unceremoniously returned through the laundry chute! At first Basil refuses to believe that they are being held prisoner. Then he tries to leave, but his car tyres are flat, and a pot of red paint is dropped on him. As Stephen Kendrick arrives to see Parker, the manager, Basil, now wearing a waiter's uniform, tries to escape while playing ball with Tara in the grounds. Once on the road, however, he is lured into a trap by a girl in a bikini. Mellor knocks him out. Basil is returned to the hotel, and he, Tara, Maxwell and Uncle Charles barricade themselves in the hotel kitchen and cut off all food, water and electricity supplies, to make the real hotel guests leave. Then, Maxwell produces a gun and reveals that he is the mastermind behind the hotel prison. Maxwell is knocked out by Basil with two large wooden butter-patters, and then Basil signals to the rest of the gang with a flashlight, making them believe that Maxwell has the upper hand. He then turns off all the hotel lights and, under cover of darkness, they render the rest of the gang unconscious, one by one, with frying pans. Maxwell, now recovered, is the last one to succumb. He escapes and runs to his car but finds the tyres are flat. As he passes the hotel, a pot of red paint is dropped on his head, and his demise is completed after he slips on a carefully-placed banana skin! Steed arrives at the hotel as Basil and Tara are shaking hands. Then Tara visits Steed. He whispers to her that he is being held in his flat against his will. Tara pledges herself to tackle the hidden culprit – and Steed goes off smiling. Leaving her holding a baby, which then starts to cry . . .

STAY TUNED

By Tony Williamson

John Steed	**Patrick Macnee**
Tara King	**Linda Thorson**
Proctor	**Gary Bond**
Lisa	**Kate O'Mara**
Mother	**Patrick Newell**
Father	**Iris Russell**
Wilks	**Duncan Lamont**
Collins	**Howard Marion-Crawford**
Sally	**Denise Buckley**
Kreer	**Roger Delgado**
Dr Meitner	**Harold Kasket**
Travers	**Ewan Roberts**
Taxi driver	**Patrick Westwood**

Designed by Robert Jones

Directed by Don Chaffey

STEED IS about to leave for a holiday. He puts a carnation in his button-hole and picks up his luggage. But as he opens the door he is confronted by Proctor, who then knocks him out. We come back to a scene identical to the first. Except that when Steed goes to take a carnation, the vase is full of withered flowers. This time, as he tries to leave the apartment, it is Tara King who confronts him. She convinces him, with some difficulty, that he has already had three weeks' holiday. And that he sent postcards and even phoned Mother from Paris and Rome. Opening his luggage, Steed finds that all his clothes have been used, and there is even a present for Tara. Dr Meitner, the Department's psychiatrist, tells him he is suffering from a form of amnesia, but Steed still has his doubts and decides to visit his chief. But Mother is away, and Father is looking after the Department. Father is a gentle, middle-aged, blind woman who surrounds herself with objects which are nice to touch. Everything in the room has an interesting texture, shape or smell – sculptures, ornate door knobs, collages and flowers. Steed persuades her to remove him from the active list and reduce his security rating to third class. Back in his apartment, an extremely worried Steed tries hard to recall the last three weeks, but can only remember the grinning face of an oriental. After driving around London in a taxi, Steed eventually comes to a street that seems vaguely familiar. Paying off the cab, he walks down the street until he is surprised by Proctor, who again knocks him out. Steed is again in his apartment, preparing for a holiday, until, with astonishment, he sees the vase of dead carnations and recalls what has passed. When Tara arrives, she finds Steed in a state of mental disintegration. Steed next goes to see Travers, a forensics expert, who is examining his car. Travers assures him that even if Steed did not take a holiday on the Continent, the car most certainly did – it even has French petrol in its tank! Steed returns, brooding, to his home. When the doorbell rings, he finds an attractive girl waiting for him. She introduces herself as Sally Unstrutter, and explains that she has called to apologise for colliding with his car a fortnight ago – in London! Sally restores Steed's faith in his sanity and when he goes to the street where the accident took place, he sees the smiling oriental face he recalled. It is a brass door knocker. Later, he drives Tara to the house, but the knocker has gone. Inside the house are Kreer, Proctor, Wilks, and Lisa, gloating over their successful plan. It appears that Kreer has hypnotised Steed and is conditioning him to kill Mother. Steed and Tara decide, separately, to break into the house and investigate its contents. Tara arrives first and after a fight, Kreer is impaled on his own sword-stick. Proctor and Lisa capture Tara, however, and through post-hypnotic suggestion, tell her that Proctor has been erased from Steed's mind and that he is unable to see him. When Steed breaks into the house, Tara accuses him of killing Kreer. What Steed does not see is Proctor standing with a gun at his head, in case Tara should disobey. Father sends one of her agents, Collins, to follow Steed when he goes back to the house. But Proctor shoots Collins. Steed, not seeing Proctor, imagines that he may have killed the agent himself. Taking a gun with him, Steed goes to see Mother, who has now returned. Tara, meanwhile, escapes after overpowering Lisa and Wilks, and sets off to stop Steed before he can kill Mother. Steed's finger is tightening on the trigger as she arrives. She knocks the gun from his hand, and then explains the whole mystery. Steed is now able to see Proctor, who has been shadowing him. With a blow that matches the ones he's received from the thug, he knocks Proctor cold. It is now Tara who is performing the pre-holiday ritual previously enacted by Steed. He arrives and at her apartment offers her a holiday in the sunshine, but Tara turns it down – only to discover that the job was in Bermuda!

TAKE ME TO YOUR LEADER

By Terry Nation

John Steed	**Patrick Macnee**
Tara King	**Linda Thorson**
Stonehouse	**Patrick Barr**
Mother	**Patrick Newell**
Captain Tim	**John Ronane**
Cavell	**Michael Robbins**
Major Glasgow	**Henry Stamper**

and Penelope Keith, Hugh Cross, Elisabeth
Robillard, Michael Hawkins, Sheila Hammons,
Bryan Kendrick, Raymond Adamson, Mathew
Long, Cliff Diggins, Wilfred Boyle

Designed by Robert Jones

Directed by Robert Fuest

FOR THE Avengers, it is a case with a difference. This case is an ingenious device, slightly larger than a briefcase, which is being used by the other side to carry stolen secrets. Steed and Tara must follow it, as it is passed on by a chain of enemy agents, and find out for whom it is intended. The case has a mechanism which enables it to talk, and this it uses to startling effect while it is in the hands of an agent named Shepherd. When Holland, one of Mother's men, breaks into Shepherd's room to steal it, the case cries 'Stop thief!' Shepherd emerges from the bathroom to shoot Holland, with a blade fired from a clarinet. Steed and Tara follow the next link in the chain, Howard Trent, to an airfield. Steed has filled the area with concealed agents – even one masquerading as a scarecrow – but the next contact surprises them all. It is an Alsatian dog! In the resulting confusion, Trent falls from his motorbike and is killed. Steed, however, manages to grab the case. He takes it to a warehouse where he finds Mother sitting in a fork-lift truck, driven by his secretary, Rhonda. Without the keys possessed by the agents in the chain, the case will self-destruct if opened. Major Glasgow, a forensics expert, X-rays it and declares it is a security expert's dream. Its contents include a tape recorder, an explosives charge, an elaborate key mechanism and £500,000 – the final pay-off for the mastermind. Tara finds a key hidden in one of the studs on the dead Trent's leather jacket. When she turns it in the case, a recorded voice tells them the next contact is at the Cremone Hotel. At the hotel the case tells Steed to place it in a wardrobe and wait. But he fails to realise the wardrobe has a false back, and as he lies on the bed, the case is stolen by its new envoy, Condon. Tara saves the day by hiding in the back of Condon's car and knocking him out after he has turned the key and triggered off the taped information about the next contact. Substituting herself for Condon, she takes the case to its next rendezvous, a ballet school. There she meets teacher Audrey Long, a child of six called Beryl, and her lollipop-sucking contact, a little girl in a fairy outfit, called Sally Graham. When Steed arrives and is hit on the head by Audrey, Tara fights with

her and finally knocks her out. They then bribe Sally for the key to the case, which is hidden in the star of her fairy wand. The case announces that their next contact will meet them at a telephone box. Mother meanwhile receives a visit from Colonel Stonehouse, head of a rival department. Mother, it seems, is suspected of leading the chain of agents who are stealing the secrets. At the telephone box Tara is met by Cavell, who is at first inclined to mix business with pleasure, until Steed steps in and overpowers him. Tara gains details of Cavell's next contact by pretending to escape, and they leave Cavell tied up as they take the case to Captain Tim, one of the world's leading karate experts, who they find practising at a judo school. Unfortunately, the agent Tara has replaced was reputed to be the only person in the world who could beat the Captain in a fight. And the karate expert decides to put her to the test. Steed ends the fierce fight by reaching through the door and hitting Captain Tim on the head with his steel-lined bowler. The Captain, believing Tara has dealt him a secret blow, gives her the key to the case. Shepherd, the killer with the clarinet, is the next contact. As he fights Steed, he reveals that this time there is no metal key – only a sonic note on a tuba. Shepherd is killed in the struggle, but Steed finds the key note, by sitting on a set of bagpipes! At the luggage-loading bay at Kings Cross station, The Avengers deposit the case, and are astonished to see two men arrive carrying similar cases. Tara follows one, Jackson, and buries him under a pile of timbers, only to find she has been following a decoy case. She is trapped in a church crypt as the case begins to emit poison gas, but escapes by using the case's self-destructing device to blow off the crypt door. Steed, who is following the other man, Williams, is astonished when he takes the case to Mother! But he refuses to believe that his chief is a traitor and overpowers Williams. Then he and Mother wait to see who comes to collect the case. It is Colonel Stonehouse. Tara arrives in time to place a booby-trapped case in the Colonel's car, and he is gassed. In the final scene, a dog carrying a talking case enters Tara's flat. As it does so, a taped message from Steed informs her that with no room in his apartment for Fang the Wonder Dog *and* himself, he's packed the dog's case and sent Fang to Tara for a holiday. His message falls on deaf ears: Tara has flown the nest to spend some time with her aunt. She has, however, left her own taped message which interjects with Steed's. Fade as both cases rattle on and Fang races to join his canine friends.

FOG

By Jeremy Burnham

John Steed	Patrick Macnee
Tara King	Linda Thorson
President	Nigel Green
Travers	Guy Rolfe
Mother	Patrick Newell
Carstairs	Terence Brady
Sanders	Paul Whitsun-Jones
Maskell	David Lodge
Fowler	Norman Chappell

and David Bird, Frank Sieman, Patsy Smart, Virginia Clay, John Garrie, Bernard Severn, Frederick Peisley, Stanley Jay, Arnold Diamond, William Lyon Brown, John Barrard

Designed by Robert Jones

Directed by John Hough

WHEN TWO foreign delegates at a disarmament conference are murdered as they walk through the foggy London streets, there is all the makings of an international incident. But the murderer seems to be re-creating the Gaslight Ghoul murders which took place in 1888. Wearing a top hat and cape, and carrying a sword-stick in a cricket bag, this modern Jack the Ripper even makes his escape in a hansom cab. Steed and Tara meet Mother, who is navigating his Rolls-Royce through the dense fog in nautical fashion, with Rhonda at the helm. They are assigned to investigate the murders and visit the scene of the crime in time to glimpse a man named Osgood, wearing a similar outfit to the murderer, leaving the scene. He escapes but leaves behind his cape and sword. Tara takes the cape to a theatrical costumiers, where Fowler, the proprietor, identifies the owner. Steed visits a master cutler, Maskell, with the sword to discover who owns it. Both agents then meet at the home of the owner of both – Osgood. The landlady, Mrs Golightly, tells them that Osgood is out, wearing his Gaslight Ghoul outfit. When he returns, Steed and Tara pounce on him. But he is not the killer. Opening his cricket bag they discover only a flask of coffee and sandwiches. Osgood turns out to be a member of the Gaslight Ghoul Club, formed to investigate the unsolved murders committed by the killer. As Steed and Tara leave and are about to get into their car, a blood-curdling scream is heard. They rush back to Osgood's flat, where they find him dead, an obvious victim of the Gaslight Ghoul. With a fake diary in which Steed's Great Aunt Florence recorded an eye-witness account of a hitherto undiscovered Gaslight Ghoul murder, Steed manages to gain membership of the exclusive club. The headquarters are an eerie Victorian mansion, set in an imitation Victorian street. In the clubroom Steed meets the President, Sir Geoffrey Armstrong, and five bearded members. Mark Travers, secretary of the club and the possessor of a warped sense

In Fog, *Steed joins the exclusive Gaslight Ghoul club to uncover a modern-day Jack the Ripper.*

of humour, takes him to see the club's Black Museum. The museum's curator, Wellbeloved, says that several knives are missing from the collection. Meanwhile, Tara, having broken into the club's rear entrance, is searching through Sir Geoffrey's office. She learns from papers that Sir Geoffrey was once a surgeon. And in a dimly-lit, fog-filled street, the Gaslight Ghoul strikes again. Valarti, another member of the conference, is the victim. Sir Geoffrey returns in time to discover Tara looking through his files and collection of scalpels. They fight, and Tara knocks him out with a chair and escapes. She returns to her flat and, opening the door, is confronted by the Gaslight Ghoul! It turns out to be Steed, wearing his new club uniform. Steed leaves to check on the safety of the three remaining members of the conference. But on arriving at their hotel he learns that one of them, Haller, has gone for a walk. Rushing out into the foggy street, Steed manages to save him from the Gaslight Ghoul. He leaves Haller at his apartment, armed with an arsenal of weapons, and under the protection of Carstairs, an agent from another department who is helping him on the case. Tara is checking on the hansom-cab that is always heard leaving the scene of the murders. She visits Sanders, proprietor of the only hansom-cab firm in London, but she is unable to prevent him from being murdered by the Ghoul, who escapes after bowling Tara over with a wheel. An invoice, bearing Sir Geoffrey's name, leads her to his home. Steed is already there, but before she can enter, however, they see someone leave in Sir Geoffrey's car. Tara follows in Steed's vintage Rolls, while Steed stays to search Sir Geoffrey's study. A figure suddenly lurches out of the dark at Steed. It is Sir Geoffrey. He has been stabbed by the real Ghoul, who has stolen a file containing the professions of the conference members. Steed now has a clue to the identity of the Ghoul, for he remembers that Travers has an armaments business, and it would be in his interest to sabotage the disarmament meeting. Hindered by the wheel of the hansom-cab, which threatens to fall off, Steed clatters his way to the Gaslight Ghoul Club to save Tara, who is already feeling the point of Travers' blade in the Black Museum. As Steed arrives, Travers uses swords from a showcase as spears and hurls them at him, but Steed deflects them with his sword. As he finally knocks Travers out, he discovers that the deflected swords have narrowly missed Tara and are embedded in the wall around her. The fog outside is clearing, and Mother and Rhonda, still navigating their car like a boat, are able at last to confirm their bearings. They have taken a wrong turn and are in a railway tunnel! Back at Tara's apartment, the fog has returned, both outside and inside. The air conditioning unit has gone wrong. As they stumble about the room, Tara wonders what has happened to Mother and Rhonda. They soon find out. There is a roar of an engine and Mother and his secretary whizz straight through the apartment in their car. It seems that Tara has left the front door open!

HOMICIDE AND OLD LACE

By Malcolm Hulke and Terrence Dicks

John Steed	Patrick Macnee
Tara King	Linda Thorson
Mother	Patrick Newell
Harriet	Joyce Carey
Georgina	Mary Merrall
Col Corf	Gerald Harper
Dunbar	Keith Baxter
Fuller	Edward Brayshaw
Rhonda	Rhonda Parker

Designed by Robert Jones

Directed by John Hough

IT'S MOTHER'S birthday. And to celebrate the occasion he pays a visit to his two ageing aunts, Harriet and Georgina, who present him with a brace of duelling pistols. As well as being his most ardent fans, they have also seen practically every spy film ever made, and are consequently familiar with the jargon of the underworld. So they beg him to tell them an inside story about the workings of his department. Mother embarks on the story to end all stories. Embellished by some of the best fights from the Avengers series, and by Mother's own vivid imagination, he tells his two aunts how Steed and Tara thwarted the crime of the century – The Great, Great Britain Crime. Intercrime, the opposite of Interpol with whom Steed had battled before (helped by Mrs Catherine Gale), is an alliance of the international underworld. And they are aiming high. In one swoop they are going to steal every single art treasure in Britain, including the Crown Jewels. It appears that in a national emergency, Colonel Corf, head of security, is given a

...

code word on his hot line from the Prime Minister, and immediately every art treasure in the country is secured in a hidden underground warehouse, and replicas substituted. Dunbar, head of Intercrime, plans to gain possession of the code word – changed every 24 hours – and use it to get all the art treasures in one place. Then he will move in with his men. Mother, however, gets wind of the plot and sends Steed and Tara to infiltrate the gang. This Steed achieves by robbing an Intercrime gang of £3,000,000 worth of diamonds that they have just stolen from a Bond Street jewellers. Thus gaining their respect, he introduces Tara, who proves her worth by beating the world's best safe-cracker in a safe-breaking contest. The double-agent Avengers then visit Colonel Corf, and under cover of a security check, Tara cracks his safe and photographs the code which will actuate the withdrawal of every item of Britain's heritage. Intercrime's Chinese operative, Osaka, taps Colonel Corf's hot line and enables Steed to pass on the codeword to Operation Rule Britannia, ostensibly run from the Prime Minister's office. Corf then calls in all the art treasures in Britain. Even the throne is removed from Buckingham Palace. Dunbar, however, suspects The Avengers and leaves Tara behind as a hostage when they go to raid the vaults where the treasures are stored. Tara escapes from her captors and tries to warn Colonel Corf of the imminent raid. But he will not believe her, and she is forced to hide when Dunbar's gang arrive. Between them, she and Steed overpower the whole gang. Steed and Tara are later having a drink with Mother, and Rhonda in attendance, when Steed says that he has never heard Rhonda speak. He persuades her to talk – only for Mother's voice to issue from her mouth, ventriloquist fashion!

A scene from The Great Great Britain Crime, *parts of which were used in* Homicide and Old Lace.

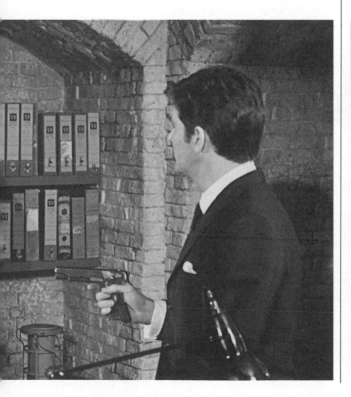

LOVE ALL

By Jeremy Burnham

John Steed	Patrick Macnee
Tara King	Linda Thorson
Martha	Veronica Strong
Bromfield	Terence Alexander
Sir Rodney	Robert Harris
Mother	Patrick Newell
Thelma	Patsy Rowlands

and Brian Oulton, Frank Gatliff, Ann Rye, Zulema Dene, Peter Stephens, Norman Pitt, John Cobner, Robin Tolhurst, Larry Taylor, David Baron

Designed by Robert Jones

Directed by Peter Sykes

FOUR IMPORTANT civil servants, Tait, Fryer, Roxby and Sir Rodney Kellogg, are attending a top-secret meeting in a Whitehall Ministry. All have one thing in common – they seem incredibly prone to love at first sight. This is unfortunate, for the first person they see is a frowsy-looking charlady scrubbing the corridor outside. And she is in the pay of the enemy. After the meeting, Sir Rodney embraces the charlady, Martha, and she extorts the secrets of the meeting from him. When Metcalfe, a young man from security, overhears them, Martha orders Sir Rodney to shoot him with her gun.

Tara, madly in love with Bromfield but spurned by him, elects to leap to her death in Love All.

Steed keeps a strange rendezvous with Mother at an underground cricket school. Nonchalantly walking along the road reading a newspaper, he falls down an open manhole, landing safely on a mattress. He finds his superior playing cricket, with Rhonda bowling and Tara looking on. They discuss the security leaks and Mother assigns the two agents to the case. Sir Rodney, meanwhile, is under arrest following the murder. But he escapes and makes his way to Martha's home. Without her charlady disguise, she is an attractive young woman. Sir Rodney persuades her to elope with him in his Rolls, but after they have driven a short distance, she shoots him and joins an accomplice, Bromfield, in another car. At the scene of the crime, Tara recognises the scent of a rare perfume in the Rolls-Royce and visits the manufacturers, Bellchamber Brothers. From them, Tara receives a list of the rich clients the perfume had been sold to, but Martha (in her charlady disguise) has been listening and makes Bromfield send one of his henchmen to get the list from Tara. In the ensuing fight at Tara's apartment, the man accidentally shoots himself and the list is charred to ashes. At the Ministry, it is Roxby's turn to succumb to Martha, soon after he receives a strange book. His colleague, Tait, gets a book, too – and immediately declares his passionate devotion to a policewoman who has come in to give him a parking ticket! An engraving on a ring taken from the dead thug in Tara's apartment leads Steed to the Casanova Ink Company, where he finds author Rosemary Z Glade, a man, dictating a book to his attractive secretary, Thelma. In the printing room he sees Bromfield, Martha and a large, tough woman called Athene. Steed distracts their attention and steals a copy of the books they are printing. Before he can read the book in his apartment, Steed is attacked by Fryer, the fourth civil servant, who is the latest to fall for the charlady. She has told him that Steed is a rival for her affections. After knocking him out, Steed looks at the book and finds a mechanism in the back which shines through a hypnotic pattern of microdots on the pages. Under magnification, they reveal the message 'You will fall in love with the next person you see'. Tara, alas, has been reading a similar book in Tait's office. And the next person she sees is Bromfield. He tells her their love has no future and orders her to leap through the window. Fortunately, Steed arrives in time to knock out Bromfield and save Tara, but she, in turn, wishing to avenge the man she loves, attacks Steed, who is forced to give her a gentle tap from his bowler. Steed then dismantles the mechanism from the books and sticks 12 of them on his jacket and waistcoat. As Athene, Bromfield and Martha advance menacingly with their guns, it is love at first sight. Tara, recovering from the bump, also catches sight of Steed's coat and joins the queue for his affections. As Steed's Rolls glides off into the darkness, it is full of admirers arguing their claims on him.

GET-A-WAY

By Philip Levene

John Steed	Patrick Macnee
Tara King	Linda Thorson
Col James	Andrew Keir
Rostov	Vincent Harding
Major Baxter	William Wilde
George Neville	Terence Langdon
Paul Ryder	Neil Hallett
Lubin	Robert Russell
Ezdorf	Peter Bowles
Professor Dodge	Peter Bayliss
Peters	John Hussey
Bryant	James Bellchamber
Magnus	Barry Lineman

Designed by Robert Jones

Directed by Don Sharp

In Get-a-Way, Steed visits Russian agent Ezdorf in his cell. The Russian promptly vanishes into thin air.

THREE RUSSIAN agents, Rostov, Lubin and Ezdorf, are sent by their bureau to kill three British agents. They are, however, caught by the British and confined in a tightly-guarded monastery, held by the British Army. Rostov escapes by knocking out one of the security personnel, Major Baxter, and bolting from his cell. Once recovered, Baxter searches, but finds no sign of the prisoner. Nor does anyone else, as Rostov makes his way to the East Wing, from which there is no escape. Although apparently cornered there, he appears to vanish completely and get clean away. Steed, Tara and a couple of agent friends are meanwhile enjoying a reunion dinner party at Steed's apartment. George Neville and Paul Ryder are the two guests. They were among the targets of the attempted Russian Great Assassination Plot. The party ends, and as Neville walks home, Rostov suddenly emerges as if from nowhere to kill him, and disappears just as quickly. Hearing the shots, Steed and Tara look out into the street, but they see nothing. Steed complains of the administration slip in not letting Neville know that Rostov was at large, but is told that Colonel James at the monastery was not apparently aware of the nature of the Great Assassination Plot. Steed decides to investigate the monastery, and while he is there, talking to Ezdorf, who has not yet divulged his target, Lubin suddenly escapes. He, like

Rostov, appears to vanish into thin air. Steed tells Tara to go to the flat of Paul Ryder, who is Lubin's target. But she is too late. Lubin shoots Ryder just before she gets there, and then apparently vanishes. All Tara finds is a trail of red footprints, caused by Lubin accidentally knocking over a tin of red paint during his escape. Steed and Tara check the contents of Lubin's cell, and Steed is puzzled by the Lizard brand vodka they find there, because he believed that Lubin was a teetotaller. Colonel James, however, confirms that Lubin started drinking while at the monastery. Checking the remaining agent, Ezdorf, he tells Steed that he is gratified that his friends have succeeded in their missions, and also that Steed will be his target when he escapes. Puzzled that the men have escaped from what seems to be an impregnable place, Steed goes to see Professor Dodge, the technologist who designed the monastery's security system. Dodge is concerned that his brainchild has failed and together they visit the monastery. After a check of the system, however, Dodge is flummoxed, and can offer no explanation for the escapes. Steed, however, finds a clue – a copy of Bryant's Natural History Magazine, like the one found in Lubin's cell. Page 25 of Rostov's copy is missing. Tara is sent to visit Peters, a civil servant, who shows her the files on the three Russians. All three agents had the Roman numerals CXVIIIVIIIV written on a piece of paper hidden in their shoes. Although the cypher man fail to crack the code, Tara by chance discovers that it means page 25 in a certain issue of Bryant's Natural History Magazine, a copy of which she has in Steed's apartment, taken from Lubin's cell. The issue number is CXVIIIVI, and the page is IIV, or 25. Tara phones Bryant for another copy of the issue, because Lubin's has page 25 missing. However, Lubin has got to Bryant before her and kills him. Then, with the aid of Magnus, a heavy, he makes his escape – apparently straight through a window, five storeys up. Tara, however, finds an intact copy in Bryant's office. On page 25 is an article on lizards, which seems to connect in some way to the Lizard trademark on the vodka bottle found in Lubin's cell. It also bears the name and address of the Magnus Importing Company, which matches the name on the van Tara saw leaving Bryant's premises. Steed pays the Magnus Importing Company a visit and finds crates of Lizard vodka in a warehouse. As Steed leaves, Magnus is preparing a bottle for special delivery to Ezdorf. Intercepting it, Steed himself delivers the package to Ezdorf, and lets it be known that he is hot on the trail. Tara, however, makes the real breakthrough. In conversation with Peters, he tells her about his pet chameleons, which change their colour to match their background. Meanwhile, in his cell, Ezdorf pours the contents of the Lizard vodka bottle down the sink, unscrews the top and removes some liquid. This he pours onto his tracksuit, and its colour changes to merge with the background. He then escapes, throwing the prison officers into confusion. Ezdorf then meets Magnus and arms himself to kill Steed. Meanwhile, Colonel James warns Tara that the Russian has escaped and is on his way to eliminate Steed. Tara drives to his flat. Steed, however, has discovered the secret of the vodka bottles, so when he gets home and finds Ezdorf waiting, he is able to make himself invisible and he takes the Russian, who has bound and gagged Tara, by surprise. In the last scene, an invisible Steed wreaks havoc on Tara as she desperately tries to fix the curtains.

THINGUMAJIG

By Terry Nation

John Steed	**Patrick Macnee**
Tara King	**Linda Thorson**
Inge	**Dora Reisser**
Teddy	**Jeremy Lloyd**
Kruger	**Iain Cuthbertson**
Truman	**Willoughby Goddard**
Major Star	**Hugh Manning**
Dr Grant	**John Horsley**
Brett	**Edward Burnham**
Stenson	**Vernon Dobcheff**
Pike	**Russell Waters**
Philips	**Michael McKevitt**
Williams	**Neville Hughes**
Greer	**John Moore**
Bill	**Harry Shacklock**

Designed by Robert Jones

Directed by Leslie Norman

AN ATTRACTIVE archaeologist, Inge Tilson, and her colleague Greer, are excavating some Stone Age remains beneath a village church that is being rebuilt, when they discover several passages. And in one of the passages is 'It'. Greer is working separately from Inge, when he hears a slithering sound, then a soft bleeping, that is both electronic and animal. Suddenly the organ upstairs mysteriously begins to play and there is a blinding flash of light. Inge finds Greer's body, with a small burn mark in the middle of his forehead. In the dust behind him, he has traced the word 'It'. The vicar of the church, the Rev Shelley, seeks the help of Steed, who was his wartime colleague. While Steed investigates the church grounds, Tara visits an electronics expert, Professor Truman, to get his opinion on Greer's lamp, which was badly damaged when he was killed. The Professor, a constantly-sneezing snuff-taker, tells Tara that the lamp has been subjected to a white-hot discharge of electrical energy. Two other finds from the tunnel – some sand which has fused into glass and a necklace which has become molten – seem to indicate the same thing. Meanwhile, Major Star, an officious and overbearing member of the excavation team, tries to track down the mysterious killer in the catacombs below. But he and an elderly deaf man, Reston, are both killed. Brett, a third member of the team, who witnessed their deaths, is in a trance when rescued. Later Brett is wakened from the trance by the sound of the church organ and dies when he goes to investigate. Steed is at the church when Pike, a local angler, rushes in to report that all the fish in the stream are floating dead on the surface. The stream is dredged and a mysterious sealed box discovered. Steed is unable to open it and decides to send it to Tara so it can be examined by Professor Truman. Before he can do so, however, he first has to foil an attempt to steal it by Kruger, a large man with a foreign accent. Kruger then reports to Stenson, a representative of a foreign power, that he has been unable to recover either of the two deadly boxes that he has developed for them. He apparently lost them after crashing his van into a quarry. Tara meanwhile has received the box and shown it to Professor Truman. But he can make nothing of it. Later, when an X-ray of the box is developed, he phones Tara to say that the box is lethal. But he is too late. The deadly black box is already slithering towards her. Tara now plays a deadly game of hide and seek, and by the time she gets back to the phone, nearly every piece of furniture in the apartment is scorched. On the phone, the Professor tells her the box recharges itself on the electricity in the room, so Tara throws off the mains switch, plunging the flat into darkness. She finally manages to halt the progress of the box by throwing every electrical appliance in the room at it. She then administers the coup-de-grâce with a cascade of foam from bottles of champagne. She rushes to the church to save Steed from the other box in the catacombs below. But Steed is already in the catacombs, doing battle with Kruger as well as his deadly invention. Kruger reveals that he intends to release thousands of the boxes all over the country to devour the electricity and wipe out the population. The megalomaniac is about to shoot Steed when the box makes its presence heard. But instead of destroying Steed, it attacks and kills its inventor, and Steed manages to overcome it with the help of an arc welder. In the closer, Steed, attempting to remove the black and white diagonal lines and fuzz from his colour television set, has sent Tara to the roof to adjust the aerial. Finally, as the reception improves, he calls to Tara to stay right where she is. She does so, and we see her hanging precariously from the roof by her feet!

PANDORA

By Brian Clemens

John Steed	Patrick Macnee
Tara King	Linda Thorson
Mother	Patrick Newell
Rupert Lasindall	Julian Glover
Henry Lasindall	James Cossins
Murray	Reginald Barrett
Juniper	John Laurie
Miss Faversham	Kathleen Byron
Hubert Pettigrew	Anthony Roye
Uncle Gregory	Peter Madden

Designed by Robert Jones

Directed by Robert Fuest

IT IS a bizarre scene from another era. In the corner of the room a phonograph blares out a rag-time tune of the 1914–18 period. And even the conversation between Rupert Lasindall, and his brother Henry, as they sit at the heavy Victorian dining table, is dated. Rupert is in the uniform of an Army Captain of the First World War, and he tells his brother that he will soon be recalled, as the Kaiser has launched an offensive on the Somme. 'But they cannot call me before tomorrow, so I shall not miss your wedding,' he says, turning to Pandora, who sits at the head of the table. Pandora stares back blankly. Pandora is a dummy! The elaborate charade is part of the brothers' plans to prise a hidden fortune from their insane and senile Uncle Gregory. They have re-created Pandora, the beautiful girl who jilted him in his youth. The next step is to capture Tara King and brainwash her into believing she is Pandora. Tara is lured to an antique shop to see a rare clock, and is chloroformed by Henry, while Rupert looks on. Steed, having invited Tara to lunch, is concerned when she does not arrive. He visits the antique shop, only to be told by Murray, the proprietor, that he was out to lunch when Tara was supposed to have called. The next occurrence is unprecedented. Instead of Steed visiting his chief, Mother actually calls on him! Mother explains that his latest office was in a balloon and communications had become difficult. Steed shows Mother a piece of paper which fell from Tara's assailant's pocket. It contains the words 'Fierce rabbit'. Mother is astonished. He explains that Fierce Rabbit was the code-name of the British agent in Armentières during the First World War! From the government file on Fierce Rabbit, Steed learns that the operative was named Simon Juniper, and goes to the clock shop where he now works. Juniper, however, tells him that the code-name was used twice before he inherited it. Later Juniper visits a previous Fierce Rabbit – the brothers' weird and sinister Uncle Gregory (who is heard but not seen). And in the Victorian house, a terrified Juniper dies mysteriously. The brothers and their grim servant, Miss Faversham, attempt to brainwash the captured Tara. But, although dressed in Pandora's clothes, heavily drugged, and continually told that she is Pandora, she tenuously clings to her real identity. In an attempt to sidetrack Steed, Rupert and Henry place a skeleton in Tara's car and set fire to it, then place Juniper's body nearby. Mother breaks the news of her death to Steed, who refuses an offer of compassionate leave and continues on the case with renewed fury. He receives a visit from another Fierce Rabbit, Hubert Pettigrew, who, after exhausting the contents of Steed's cocktail cabinet, tells him that the third Fierce Rabbit is Gregory Lasindall. Meanwhile, the brothers continue to brainwash Tara and she finally believes that she is Pandora. Wearing Pandora's wedding dress, she is taken by the brothers to meet their terrifying uncle. Faced by his lost love, Uncle Gregory tells them his fortune is hidden behind the picture of Pandora on the wall. In his haste, Rupert slashes away at the painting with a knife, only to discover that he has destroyed a priceless Rembrandt beneath Pandora's portrait. His furious brother, Henry, struggles with Rupert, and the strain is too much for their uncle, who has a heart attack and dies. Finally, Steed breaks into the house and, with his trusty steel bowler, finishes off the brothers and Miss Faversham. Later on, Steed has apparently got a headache. On the table nearby is the rare clock that Tara had been searching for in antique shops. It bears a label to Steed. But when Tara arrives, he pleads with her to take it back. She soon discovers why when it starts to chime – in tones that would rival those of Big Ben.

REQUIEM

By Brian Clemens

John Steed	**Patrick Macnee**
Tara King	**Linda Thorson**
Miranda	**Angela Douglas**
Firth	**John Cairney**
Wells	**John Paul**
Mother	**Patrick Newell**
Murray	**Denis Shaw**
Rista	**Terence Sewards**
Barrett	**Mike Lewin**
Jill	**Kathja Wyeth**
Bobby	**Harvey Ashby**
Vicar	**John Baker**
Rhonda	**Rhonda Parker**

Designed by Robert Jones

Directed by Don Chaffey

THE INSCRIPTION on the wreath, propped on the grave, reads 'In loving memory of our dear Mother – the finest chap we ever knew. Died suddenly – explosively – RIP'. Among the mourners sits Tara King in a wheelchair, both legs in plaster, sustained only by pain-killing drugs. John Steed's department, it seems, is at its lowest ebb. But back to the beginning. Two thugs, Rista, and Murray, are waiting in an underground car park for Miranda Loxton, key witness in a court case against Murder International. But Miss Loxton and her bodyguard have been to a fancy-dress party and when their car arrives they are dressed as a tramp and a bewigged dame. The thugs mistakenly shoot the bodyguard (dressed as the dame) and Miranda escapes in her car. Mother sends Steed to guard Miranda and he takes her to a house in the country until the hearing. Cleaver, another agent, acts as decoy by dressing as Steed and placing a dummy of Miranda beside him in the passenger seat of Steed's Rolls. At the house, Steed and Miranda spend the time by enacting famous Army and Naval battles. But Miranda inevitably defeats Steed, for most of her ancestors were famous military strategists. Steed suggests a game of chess – his uncle was a chess Grand Master. Alas, he is defeated again. Miranda's aunt was a Grand Mistress. Only when they turn to Ludo does Steed show signs of superiority. Meanwhile, Tara is kidnapped by Rista and Murray and overhears them planning a booby-trap for Mother in Steed's apartment. She escapes, but has been so heavily drugged that she arrives outside Steed's apartment too late to stop the tragedy. She recovers consciousness to find her legs covered by debris and two ambulance men carrying Mother's body away. Major Firth and Dr Wells tell her that her legs have received multiple fractures and they place her under sedation. She awakens in what appears to be a hospital, with her legs in plaster. A nurse called Jill, and Major Firth's assistant, Lieutenant Barrett, are in attendance. They tell her it is vital that they trace Steed, for he too is in danger. His gold pencil contains a bomb. But Tara cannot remember the whereabouts of the house. In the hope of jogging her memory, she asks Firth and Dr Wells to see agent Cleaver, but when they arrive he has been killed. Later she asks them to take her to Mother's funeral. They agree, but insist on tranquillising her to make the journey more comfortable. When they return, Tara wakes up and sees Murray, one of the two men who held her prisoner, at her bedside. She recognises a tattoo on his arm, and tells Major Firth, who shoots the man. The incident jogs Tara's memory, and she recalls that there is a cannon weather vane on top of Steed's childhood home – the house in question. After Firth and Barrett leave to look for the house, Tara notices that one of her plaster casts is cracked. Breaking it open, she finds her leg is unscathed. Outside her room, she discovers that the hospital is actually a house, and in it is a mock-up of Steed's apartment in which Mother was supposed to have been killed. Investigating further, she finds the room in which she was earlier held captive by Rista and Murray. Realising that all the people in the house are impostors, and that Steed is now in danger, she escapes, overpowering Wells and Jill on the way. She finds Mother alive and well in Steed's flat, and together they devise a plan to construct a replica of the house that Firth and Barrett are looking for. When the two men come across the house with a cannon weather vane, they enter and are soon disposed of by Rhonda, Mother's assistant. She shows, for the first time, a dazzling display of speed and precision fighting. Tara later visits Steed and find him busy studying his family tree. He discloses some startling facts. One of his ancestors, Steed-the-Ready, dominated three shires in the Dark Ages. Another, Sir Steedalot, was one of King Arthur's knights. Finally Steed finds what he has been looking for. 'As I've always suspected,' he tells an enthralled Tara, 'I have Royal blood!'

TAKE-OVER

By Terry Nation

John Steed	Patrick Macnee
Tara King	Linda Thorson
Grenville	Tom Adams
Laura	Elisabeth Sellars
Bill	Michael Gwynn
Circe	Hilary Pritchard
Sexton	Garfield Morgan
Lomax	Keith Buckley
Groom	John Comer
Clifford	Anthony Sagar

Designed by Robert Jones

Directed by Robert Fuest

AN ELEGANT limousine shudders to a halt on a lonely country road. It appears to have engine trouble, and two of the occupants alight to investigate, leaving a handcuffed man, apparently their prisoner, in the back of the car. But it is a put-up job and the men, Fenton Grenville and Lomax, exchange secret smiles as their prisoner slides out of the car and makes his escape. It is an ideal test for a secret weapon which will help them sabotage a peace conference of foreign ministers, to be held at nearby Critchley Manor. For as soon as the fleeing man is out of sight, Grenville lights a cigar with a lighter, and the fugitive drops dead with a cloud of smoke gushing from his throat. With the aid of their mysterious weapon Grenville, Lomax, Sexton, and the beautiful Circe, take over the country cottage of Bill Bassett, in order to train a long-range rocket gun on Critchley Manor. Bassett, his wife Laura, and their servant, Groom, are gassed. Circe performs an operation on their throats. Then, to ensure the co-operation of Bill and Laura, their captors allow Groom to escape and kill him from afar with the aid of the lighter. But the gang have not reckoned on John Steed. He and Bill were prisoners-of-war together and, because they lost track of time while in captivity, they later discovered that they had celebrated Christmas in February. As a result, Steed has visited Bill and Laura for a February Christmas ever since. When he arrives, Bill introduces his captors as business colleagues. He has no choice, for Grenville tells him that he and his wife both have phosphor-bombs implanted in their throats, which can be detonated with the specially adapted lighter! Steed, however, quickly suspects that something is wrong, and after beating Grenville in a record contest of 'Guess the musician', Grenville challenges him to a shooting match. The wager is a hundred guineas for the first kill of the day. Unfortunately, Grenville intends the first kill to be Steed, and in a duel of wits and guns next day, Steed is wounded in the temple and only escapes by convincing his enemies that he has died in some quicksand. Then he passes out. He is found by Hatch, one of the security men who has been drafted into the area for the peace conference, and is put on a London-bound ambulance for questioning. When he recovers consciousness and hears the men talking about the conference, he remembers everything. He knocks the men out and turns the ambulance back towards Critchley Manor. Meanwhile, Bassett receives another surprise visitor – Tara King. She is soon overpowered by Grenville and the gang, but breaks her bonds before Circe can operate and put a bomb in her throat. Grenville, however, forces Tara to drop her gun by threatening to detonate the bombs implanted in Bill and Laura's throats. Tara is then bound and gagged and left in a spare room while Lomax goes upstairs to fire the rocket gun at Critchley Manor. As Lomax is leaving, Steed arrives, and with an elastic-band catapult, he fires a phosphor bomb at Grenville, which sticks to his neck. Sexton, realising that he cannot detonate the bombs in the throats of Bill and Laura without killing Grenville too, falters – giving Steed the chance to overpower him and Circe. Steed then releases Tara and they dash upstairs reaching Lomax in time to swivel the rocket gun from its target, and knock him out. Some time later, Tara arrives at Steed's apartment to find him playing a round of invisible golf. But when Tara follows suit with an invisible club and an invisible ball, there is a resounding crash! Invisible maybe, but the ball has broken a window!

WHO WAS THAT MAN I SAW YOU WITH?

By Jeremy Burnham

John Steed	**Patrick Macnee**
Tara King	**Linda Thorson**
Fairfax	**William Marlowe**
General Hesketh	**Ralph Michael**
Zaroff	**Alan Browning**
Gilpin	**Alan MacNaughtan**
Mother	**Patrick Newell**
Dangerfield	**Alan Wheatley**
Phillipson	**Bryan Marshall**
Miss Culpepper	**Aimee Delamain**
Perowne	**Richard Owens**
Kate	**Nita Lorraine**
Hamilton	**Ralph Ball**
Powell	**Ken Haward**
Pye	**Neville Marten**

Designed by Robert Jones

Directed by Don Chaffey

FAIRFAX AND Perowne, two of Mother's agents, keep a rendezvous with enemy agent Gregor Zaroff, who has something to sell. Perowne finds Zaroff, who kills him, leaving his identity card in his hand. Afterwards, Zaroff reports to Dangerfield, who spends his time in a boxing ring receiving beauty treatment at the hands of his attractive secretary, Kate. As Zaroff gives his report, the mud-pack on Dangerfield's face cracks into a smile and together they drink a toast in champagne – to Tara King! At a secret Whitehall establishment, Tara, wearing a commando-style outfit, goes about her latest assignment – testing the security arrangements of the government's War Room. She breaks in through the back of a sentry-box and overpowers security guards, Powell and Hamilton, before taking a lift to the floor which houses the War Room. Inside the room, Gilpin and Pye, two boffins, are explaining to General Hesketh the function of the room's most vital piece of equipment – a black box nicknamed The Field Marshal. This can monitor the flight of every military aircraft in the world, and not only detect whether they are carrying nuclear weapons, but programme Britain's own anti-missile missiles to intercept them. Tara enters the room through a ventilation shaft and attempts to fire her pistol at the box. But a special magnetic field surrounding it locks her pistol solid, and she is overpowered by the guards. Gilpin and Hesketh congratulate her on nearly reaching the security box, and encourage her to keep trying. After all, if she can break the system, so can the enemy. Tara returns to her apartment and finds Steed waiting for her. He has passed the time away by building a house of cards. He reveals that he devised the security arrangements for the Field Marshal, and then lets her into another secret – he has glued the house of cards together! As Steed prepares to leave, Tara receives a gift of flowers and pearls in the post. Enclosed is a card bearing the initials GZ. She says she does not know the identity of her admirer. Tara's fellow agent, Fairfax, is beginning to suspect that she may be a double-agent, and as he keeps

Tara crawls through a ventilation shaft to discover the secret of the field Marshal in Who Was That Man I Saw You With?

her under surveillance with a cine-camera, he sees Gregor Zaroff waiting outside her flat. He then follows Tara when she goes to a telephone box and picks up a strange envelope. To test the security in the War Room, Tara is taking pictures of secret documents with a miniature camera concealed in her handkerchief. But as she is about to leave, a beam that is sensitive to the chemical components of film emulsion sets off an alarm, and she is once again arrested by the guards and the camera is taken from her. Unknown to the guards, Tara has a second camera concealed in her watch, and arriving back at her apartment, she develops the film. When Fairfax shows Mother the film he has taken of Tara, and adds that he has seen Zaroff, Mother reduces Tara's security rating to zero minus, and instigates an investigation into her loyalty. Returning to her apartment with Steed, Tara finds one of Mother's agents, Phillipson, going through her room. They fight, but the agent escapes. Later, when Steed next visits Mother, he recognises Phillipson and demands an explanation. Mother is forced to tell him that Tara is under suspicion of selling secrets to the enemy. More importantly, she has breached the War Room and its secrets. Her bank account has been checked – Gregor Zaroff has recently paid her £2000. Steed is given 24 hours to prove her innocence. But when he discovers the photos Tara took in the War Room, even he begins to have doubts about her loyalty. The case against her becomes even graver when Steed discovers her standing over the dead body of Fairfax with a gun in her hand. Tara is taken to Mother's, where Phillipson presents his case against her, while Steed tries vainly to defend her. But the evidence against her is too strong and Tara is placed in Phillipson's custody pending an official enquiry. Tara, however, escapes and Mother is forced to reduce her rating to zero minus three – she is to be shot on sight! An anxious Steed gets a call to go to a phone booth in the country, where he finds an envelope. When he returns home, he finds a crate of champagne in his sitting-room, with a note from Zaroff. Tara is lying dead in the next room. As Steed picks up the gun and kneels over her body, Tara sits up. She explains that she has planned the demonstration to show how easy it is to manufacture circumstantial evidence. As they leave the apartment, Steed is knocked out by Zaroff, who then takes Tara at gunpoint to Dangerfield, whom they find still sitting in the boxing ring and being fussed over by Kate. Dangerfield now reveals his plan. They have deliberately discredited Tara and allowed Mother's security to believe that she penetrated the War Room, in order to make it necessary to dismantle the black box and build in new circuits. In the 48 hours this will take, the country will be totally defenceless and foreign rockets will be launched. Meanwhile, a desperate Steed shows the film taken by Fairfax to a lipreader, Miss Culpepper, and from Zaroff's mouthings, she gives Steed a clue about the enemy's headquarters. Steed arrives there just as Zaroff is about to shoot Tara, and using the boxing ring to its full advantage, Steed delivers a knockout blow to Dangerfield's plans. Later on, Tara finds Steed looking over a complex blueprint. While she watches agog, he erects his latest invention – a tower of glasses. He pours champagne into the top glass until it overflows and fills all the other glasses. Steed then proposes a toast: 'To Tara King – whom I never suspected of funny business for one moment. Well, almost never.'

MY WILDEST DREAM

By Philip Levene

John Steed	**Patrick Macnee**
Tara King	**Linda Thorson**
Jagger	**Peter Vaughan**
Tobias	**Derek Godfrey**
Chilcott	**Edward Fox**
Nurse Owen	**Susan Travers**
Slater	**Philip Madoc**
Reece	**Michael David**
Paul Gibbons	**Murray Mayne**
Dyson	**Tom Kempinski**
Winthrop	**John Savident**
Peregrine	**Hugh Moxley**

Designed by Robert Jones

Directed by Robert Fuest

ALOYISIUS PEREGRINE, Vice-Chairman of the Acme Precision Combine Limited, is stabbed in his penthouse as he is working on his hobby, mending watches. His attacker is Paul Gibbons, also on the board of Acme. But the killing has taken place only in Gibbons' mind so far. Gibbons is actually shown stabbing a dummy in the office of Jagger, a psychiatrist. Peregrine is alive when Gibbons collects a card for his next appointment from Jagger's assistant, Nurse Owen, and then joins him in his chauffeur-driven car outside. At Gibbons' next appointment, Jagger incites him under sedation once again to kill Peregrine, getting him to stab at a dummy which has Peregrine's face. When he has been conditioned, Gibbons goes to Peregrine's penthouse and stabs him to death. Nurse Owen tells Steed and Tara on the telephone that the crime is about to happen. They arrive at the penthouse to find Peregrine dead, and see Gibbons stagger in shock back out of the window, to fall to his death. Steed visits Gibbons' office, but learns little of interest. Tobias, another board member, however, tells him that it seems strange that Gibbons does not appear to have left a diary. The next member of the board to die is Winthrop. Jagger again conditions one of his colleagues, Slater, to do the killing. Tobias, the fifth member of the board, is now under threat from Slater who, after the murder of Winthrop, is sedated and placed under the care of Dr Reece in hospital. Tara investigates Slater's office and finds his diary, but loses it when Dyson, an aide of Jagger's, attacks her and escapes. She tails Dyson but loses him in Marlin Street, where Jagger has his consulting rooms. Later, Steed calls to mind a Dr Jagger while under sedation in hospital, and Tara finds a Dr Jagger listed at 42 Marlin Street. Nurse Owen and Dyson arrive at the hospital and knock out Dr Reece. They then take Slater with them, and when they have conditioned him, Nurse Owen phones Steed and tells him that Tobias is in danger in Slater's office. Tara and Steed rush to the

Acme office but find Tobias alive. He has shot Slater, after the man went for him with a gun. Steed visits Jagger, who admits that Gibbons and Slater were indeed his patients, and that he taught them to act out their aggressive fantasies in the surgery. He claims, however, that both men came to him too late for him to prevent the real murders being committed. When Steed has left, Jagger decides that the game is up and he must get rid of Steed. He and Nurse Owen decide to use their technique on the agent and they select as Steed's enemy Lord Teddy Chilcott, who has been appearing in scenes throughout being rejected as a suitor by Tara. He has built up a real hostility against Steed, especially when he was caught in Tara's flat. Steed, believing that Tara was being molested by a stranger, hit Chilcott with his bowler. Chilcott is picked up as he is leaving Tara's flat and taken back to Jagger's consulting room, where he is given the conditioning treatment. Dyson meanwhile goes after Tara. But she knocks him out and pockets the key to 42 Marlin Street. Tobias and Nurse Owen are in league, for Tobias drugs Jagger, who is discovered by Tara when she reaches Marlin Street. She realises Steed is in danger when she sees a dummy with his face on it, used in the conditioning of Chilcott. Tara rushes to Steed's flat, and although Chilcott lies in wait for Steed, she manages to warn her colleague by throwing her shoe at the window. Steed quickly discovers and disposes of Chilcott, then he and Tara foil Tobias when he appears for the showdown in the flat. They tug the carpet from under his feet and knock him cold. In the closer, Steed bares his soul to Tara. It appears that he is 'tormented' by childhood memories of raiding his father's drinks cabinet – for soda water! 'Ah,' says Tara, producing a bottle of bubbly, 'then that explains your fondness for this.' Not so, says Steed. His insatiable craving, perpetual desire and uncontrollable urge to lay hands on a bottle of champagne is because – he likes it!

BIZARRE

By Brian Clemens

John Steed	**Patrick Macnee**
Tara King	**Linda Thorson**
Helen Pritchard	**Sally Nesbitt**
Captain Cordell	**James Kerry**
Jonathan Jupp	**John Sharp**
Happychap	**Roy Kinnear**
Tom	**Michael Balfour**
Bob	**Patrick Connor**
Mrs Jupp	**Sheila Burrell**
Shaw	**George Innes**
Charley	**Ron Pember**
The Master	**Fulton Mackay**

Designed by Robert Jones

Directed by Leslie Norman

HELEN PRITCHARD, an attractive London secretary, is found wandering in a daze, miles from civilisation. She is wearing only a nightdress. Captain Cordell, one of Mother's men, deduces that Helen fell, or was pushed, from a passing train. In hospital Helen rambles about a coffin on the train – and a man in it who wasn't dead! In a flashback we see what really happened.

During the night Helen went to the luggage van to feed her pet dog and was startled to see a man getting out of a coffin. In the ensuing struggle she fell from the train.

A distraught Tara joins Happy Meadows proprietor Happychap (the late Roy Kinnear) as Steed's coffin is exhumed in Bizarre.

Steed and Tara discover that the coffin on the train should have contained the body of a financier called Jonathan Jupp, who was later interred at the Happy Meadows Cemetery. When Tara foils an attempt on Helen's life by Morton, another financier, they discover another strange coincidence. Morton was interred at Happy Meadows Cemetery six months before. And both he and Jupp were on the verge of prosecution for fraud when they died. Visiting the cemetery, Steed and Tara receive another shock. It is commercialised in the worst possible taste, with signs such as 'Get in while the going's good' and 'People are dying to get into Happy Meadows'. The cemetery even gives trading stamps! But even worse, they discover that bodies have a habit of popping in and out of their coffins, even when they are buried – especially in the exclusive area called Paradise Plot. Steed obtains permission to exhume the bodies of Jupp and Morton and finds they are both missing. So too are the bodies of four other men, who all have good reasons for wanting to elude the law. The proprietor, 'Bagpipes' Happychap, and his two gravediggers, Tom and Bob, look on in ever-increasing consternation. Captain Cordell calls on Mrs Jupp, and learns that her husband spoke of taking a holiday with Mystic Tours, which he described as 'a trip to Paradise'. Investigating Mystic Tours, Cordell tells the proprietor, Shaw, that he is in business difficulties, and needs to get away. Shaw offers him their Paradise Holiday, and arranges for him to have a convenient road accident. As Steed and Tara survey his grave in Paradise Plot, Cordell is very much alive enjoying himself with wine, women and song, in an elaborate complex built beneath their feet. But he is recognised as a spy by Charley, one of Shaw's men, and by the time Steed and Tara have Cordell's grave exhumed, he really is dead! Steed follows in Cordell's footsteps. A visit to Mrs Jupp leads him to Mystic Tours, and a briefcase full of banknotes gains him an interview with the real boss of the tour company – The Master. He is a small wiry man, dressed as an Indian Fakir, who lies in suspended animation on a bed of nails. When Steed gains his confidence, he reveals there is a sheet of glass between his body and the nails! He is a charlatan in all save one thing – he really has found a way of simulating death. A road accident is arranged for Steed, and soon Happychap and the two gravediggers are gazing down at the agent's lifeless body in a coffin. By the time Tara arrives, he has been buried in Paradise Plot. Steed awakens to the sound of music and dancing. He is lying on cushions and being offered grapes by two pretty young women. It now becomes obvious what has happened to the missing financiers, for in the rock formation above his head there is a series of coffin-shaped doors. The bodies can leave and re-enter their graves at will! When a distraught Tara has Steed's coffin exhumed, he tries to attract her attention by sliding a knife through the lid of the coffin, but he is seen by Jupp, Charley Shaw and The Master. Tara, however, leaps through the coffin to his assistance and there is a short but amusing fight, which culminates in The Avengers leading a crocodile chain of prisoners from the open grave. For Happychap, the sight of all the dead bodies coming to life is too much – he faints!

In Bizarre, *Mother decides to record Steed's new toy – a home-assembled rocket ship – for posterity.*

'Can you get us down?' Tara asks Steed when their rocket leaves the launch pad in the tag scene from Bizarre.

And so the series ended. But not quite, for there remains the final tag sequence. As this was the last Avengers *episode, I have transcribed the whole sequence.*

Steed and Tara stand overlooking a control panel. Steed is adjusting various controls.

STEED: Like it?

TARA: Very complicated, isn't it?

MOTHER: (*Entering.*) Steed! Tara!

STEED: (*Aside, almost to himself.*) Boom! Boom! (*Then, aside to Tara.*) Bit of a squash. (*And directly to Mother.*) Mother!

MOTHER: I say! Splendid achievement, Steed. Splendid!

STEED: Well, thank you very much.

MOTHER: Hard to believe you assembled it yourself.

STEED: Well, the instruction booklet is very explicit.

MOTHER: Yes, but a thing like this . . . and in your own back yard.

STEED: (*Chuckling.*) Hmmm!

MOTHER: It must have been expensive?

STEED: Oh, I've saved up a bit. (*Then wistfully.*) I've always wanted one of these.

TARA: (*To Mother as he turns towards the door.*) Well, where're you going?

MOTHER: Outside.

STEED: Outside?

MOTHER: Yes . . . I want to take a snap of it . . . for my album.

STEED: Ah! (*Mother leaves, while Steed continues to adjust the control panel. Tara is watching curiously.*)

TARA: (*Flippantly.*) Where do you light the blue paper?

STEED: (*Chuckling.*) You don't. All you do is press that button there.

TARA: (*Nonchalantly.*) This one?

STEED: Yeah! (*Tara presses button. Set vibrates as sound of unleashed power drowns Steed's cry.*) No! (*Cut to shot of rocketship leaving a launch pad, beginning its ascent. Cut back to Steed and Tara at rocket's control panel, Tara looking bewildered at Steed.*)

TARA: How do you stop it?

STEED: Er . . . (*Chuckles.*) That part of the kit arrives next week. (*Mother's voice is heard over the intercom.*)

MOTHER: Steed! Steed! Steed, I demand that you bring that thing down at once!

STEED: (*Feigning indignation.*) Demand? (*A broad grin crosses his face.*)

TARA: *Can* you get us down?

STEED: Eventually, yes.

TARA: (*Coyly.*) Eventually?

STEED: There's no hurry . . . (*Long pause.*) Is there? (*Tag theme gently fades in.*)

TARA: (*Seductively.*) None at all. (*A knowing look passes between the two of them, and the tag theme continues to build. Cut to Mother, seated in his wheelchair in the middle of a field. He looks skyward.*)

MOTHER: (*Turning to camera and addressing the viewers.*) They'll be back . . . (*Then, realisation dawning.*) They're unchaperoned up there! (*Camera pans skyward, gives way to main title theme and End credits.*)

THE AVENGERS CHRONOLOGY

	Title	Production completed	Transmission date
1	Hot Snow	30/12/60*	7/1/61
2	Brought to Book	12/1/61*	14/1/61
3	Square Root of Evil	21/1/61	21/1/61
4	Nightmare	28/1/61	28/1/61
5	Crescent Moon	4/2/61	4/2/61
6	Girl on the Trapeze	11/2/61	11/2/61
7	Diamond Cut Diamond	18/2/61	18/2/61
8	The Radioactive Man	25/2/61	25/2/61
9	Ashes of Roses	4/3/61	4/3/61
10	Hunt the Man Down	12/3/61*	18/4/61
11	Please Don't Feed the Animals	30/3/61*	1/4/61
12	Dance with Death	13/4/61*	15/4/61
13	One for the Mortuary	26/4/61*	29/4/61
14	The Springers	11/5/61*	13/5/61
15	The Frighteners	25/5/61*	27/5/61
16	The Yellow Needle	8/6/61*	10/6/61
17	Death on the Slipway	22/6/61*	24/6/61
18	Double Danger	6/7/61*	8/7/61
19	Toy Trap	20/7/61*	22/7/61
20	Tunnel of Fear	3/8/61*	5/8/61
21	The Far-Distant Dead	14/8/61*	19/8/61
22	Kill the King	30/8/61*	2/9/61
23	Dead of Winter (aka The Case of the Happy Camper)	7/9/61*	9/12/61
24	The Deadly Air	20/9/61*	16/12/61
25	A Change of Bait	27/9/61*	23/12/61
26	Dragonsfield (aka The Un-Dead)	18/10/61*	30/12/61

* Note that episodes 1 & 2 and the last 17 stories were videotaped.

	Title	Production completed	Transmission date
1	Dead on Course	9/5/62	29/12/62
2	Mission to Montreal	12/5/62	27/10/62
3	The Sell Out	9/6/62	24/11/62
4	Death Dispatch *1	23/6/62	22/12/62
5	Warlock	7/7/62	26/1/63
6	Propellant 23	21/7/62	6/10/62
7	Mr Teddy Bear	4/8/62	29/9/62
8	The Decapod	12/8/62	13/10/62
9	Bullseye	20/9/62	20/10/62
10	The Removal Men (aka The Most Expensive Commodity)	4/10/62	3/11/62
11	The Mauritius Penny	18/10/62	10/11/62
12	Death of a Great Dane *2	1/11/62	17/11/62
13	Death on the Rocks	15/11/62	1/12/62
14	Traitor in Zebra	29/11/62	8/12/62
15	The Big Thinker	13/12/62	15/12/62
16	Intercrime	29/12/62	5/1/63
17	Immortal Clay	10/1/63	12/1/63
18	Box of Tricks *3	17/1/63	19/1/63
19	The Golden Eggs	31/1/63	2/2/63
20	School for Traitors	9/2/63	9/2/63
21	The White Dwarf	16/2/63	16/2/63
22	Man in the Mirror	22/2/63	23/2/63
23	A Conspiracy of Silence	1/3/63	2/3/63
24	A Chorus of Frogs	8/3/63	9/3/63
25	Six Hands Across the Table	15/3/63	16/3/63
26	Killerwhale	22/3/63	23/3/63

*1 This was the first televised episode starring Honor Blackman
*2 This story (with slight script changes) was later remade as *The £50,000 Breakfast* (Rigg colour series, episode 20.)
*3 This story was scripted to star Steed, Cathy and Venus Smith.

	Title	Production completed	Transmission date
1	Concerto	26/4/63	2/3/64
2	Brief for Murder	1/5/63	29/9/63
3	The Nutshell	10/5/63	19/10/63
4	The Golden Fleece	24/5/63	7/12/63
5	Death à la Carte	14/6/63	21/12/63
6	Man With Two Shadows	21/6/63	12/10/63
7	Don't Look Behind You *4	5/7/63	14/12/63
8	The Grandeur That Was Rome	19/7/63	30/11/63
9	The Undertakers	2/8/63	5/10/63
10	Death of a Batman	14/8/63	26/10/63
11	Build a Better Mousetrap	28/8/63	15/2/64
12	November Five	27/9/63	2/11/63

Patrick Macnee and Ian Hendry in a scene from the first season title credits.

13	Second Sight	11/10/63	16/11/63
14	The Secret's Broker	19/10/63	1/2/64
15	The Gilded Cage	25/10/63	9/11/63
16	The Medicine Men	8/11/63	23/11/63
17	The White Elephant	22/11/63	4/1/64
18	Dressed to Kill	6/12/63	28/12/63
19	The Wringer	20/12/63	18/1/63
20	The Little Wonders	3/1/64	11/1/64
21	Mandrake	16/1/64	25/1/64
22	The Trojan Horse	30/1/64	8/2/64
23	The Outside-In Man	12/2/64	22/2/64
24	The Charmers	27/2/64	29/2/64
25	Esprit de Corps	11/3/64	14/3/64
26	Lobster Quadrille	20/3/64	21/3/64

*⁴ This story also served as the plot for *The Joker* (Rigg colour series, episode 15).

Cathy Gale runs into trouble in **The Medicine Men.**

The Avengers pose for the camera in rehearsals for **The Undertakers.**

MACNEE/RIGG SEASON 4 (Monochrome)

	Title	Production completed	Transmission date
1	The Town of No Return	Not known	2/10/65
2	The Murder Market	n/k	13/11/65
3	The Master Minds	n/k	6/11/65
4	Dial a Deadly Number	n/k	4/12/65
5	Death at Bargain Prices	n/k	23/10/65
6	Castle De'ath	n/k	30/10/65
7	The Cybernauts	n/k	16/10/65
8	The Gravediggers	n/k	9/10/65
9	Room Without a View	n/k	8/1/66
10	A Surfeit of H_2O	n/k	20/11/65
11	Two's a Crowd	n/k	18/12/65
12	The Maneater of Surrey Green	n/k	11/12/65
13	Silent Dust (aka Strictly for the Worms)	n/k	1/1/66
14	The Hour That Never Was (aka An Hour to Spare)	n/k	27/1/65
15	Too Many Christmas Trees	n/k	25/12/65
16	The 13th Hole	n/k	29/1/66
17	Small Game for Big Hunters	n/k	15/1/66
18	The Girl from Auntie	n/k	21/1/66
19	The Quick, Quick, Slow Death (aka The Light Fantastic)	n/k	5/2/66
20	The Danger Makers	n/k	12/2/66
21	A Touch of Brimstone (aka The Hellfire Club)	n/k	19/2/66

Steed and Emma Peel momentarily off duty.

22	What the Butler Saw	n/k.	26/2/66
23	The House That Jack Built	n/k	5/3/66
24	A Sense of History	n/k	12/3/66
25	How to Succeed at Murder Without Really Trying	n/k	19/3/66
26	Honey for the Prince	n/k	23/3/66

MACNEE/RIGG SEASON 5 (Colour)

	Title	Production completed	Transmission date
1	The Fear Merchants	Not known	21/1/67
2	Escape in Time	n/k	28/1/67
3	The Bird Who Knew Too Much	n/k	11/2/67
4	From Venus With Love	n/k	14/1/67
5	The See-Through Man	n/k	4/2/67
6	The Winged Avenger	n/k	18/2/67
7	The Living Dead	n/k	25/2/67
8	The Hidden Tiger	n/k	4/3/67
9	The Correct Way to Kill	n/k	11/3/67
10	Never, Never Say Die	14/2/67	18/3/67
11	Epic	27/2/67	1/4/67
12	The Superlative Seven	13/3/67	8/4/67
13	A Funny Thing Happened on the Way to the Station	22/3/67	15/4/67
14	Something Nasty in the Nursery	2/4/67	22/4/67
15	The Joker	11/4/67	29/4/67
16	Who's Who?	18/4/67	6/5/67
17	Death's Door	7/6/67	7/10/67
18	Return of the Cybernauts	15/6/67	30/9/67
19	Dead Man's Treasure	5/7/67	21/10/67
20	The £50,000 Breakfast	20/7/67	14/10/67
21	You Have Just Been Murdered	2/8/67	28/10/67
22	The Positive Negative Man	31/8/67	4/11/67
23	Murdersville	25/8/67	11/11/67
24	Mission Highly Improbable (aka The Disappearance of Admiral Nelson)	22/9/67	18/11/67
25	The Forget-Me-Knot [5]	19/1/68	12/1/69

[5] This episode is included in both lists for completeness and though it actually appears on the production company's records as the final Rigg story, it is, of course, widely considered to be the first Thorson story. In fact, the episode was filmed between December 1967 and January 1968, while the cross-over scene between Emma and Tara was actually filmed on 19 January 1968.

Tara King in a scene from Game.

MACNEE/THORSON SEASON 6

	Title	Production completed	Transmission date
1	Invasion of the Earthmen	21/11/67	27/4/69
2	The Curious Case of the Countless Clues (aka The Murderous Connection)	19/1/68	18/5/69
3	The Forget-Me-Knot	19/1/68	12/1/69
4	Split	1/2/68	9/2/69
5	Getaway	15/2/68	27/7/69
6	Have Guns Will Haggle	29/2/68	30/3/69
7	Look, Stop Me If You've Heard This One (But There Were These Two Fellers)	19/3/68	23/3/69
8	My Wildest Dream	1/4/68	7/9/69
9	Whoever Shot Poor George/Stroke XR40	17/4/68	16/2/69
10	You'll Catch Your Death (aka Atishoo, Atishoo, All Fall Down)	24/5/68	2/2/69
11	All Done With Mirrors	13/6/68	2/3/69
12	The Super Secret Cypher Snatch (aka Whatever Happened to Yesterday?)	14/6/68	26/1/69
13	Game	25/6/68	19/1/69
14	False Witness (aka Lies)	11/7/68	23/2/69
15	Noon Doomsday	30/7/68	16/3/69
16	Legacy of Death (aka Falcon)	9/8/68	9/3/69
17	They Keep Killing Steed	29/8/68	6/4/69
18	Wish You Were Here (aka The Prisoner)	12/9/68	25/5/69
19	Killer	27/9/68	4/5/69
20	The Rotters	8/10/68	20/4/69
21	The Interrogators	22/10/68	13/4/69
22	The Morning After	5/11/68	11/5/69
23	Love All	18/11/68	13/7/69
24	Take Me To Your Leader	29/11/68	15/6/69
25	Stay Tuned	13/12/68	8/6/69
26	Fog (aka The Gaslight Ghoul)	31/12/68	23/6/69
27	Who Was That Man I Saw You With?	10/1/69	31/8/69
28	Pandora	17/1/69	10/8/69
29	Thingumajig (aka It)	21/1/69	1/8/69
30	Homicide & Old Lace (aka Tall Story)	23/1/69	6/7/69
31	Requiem	13/2/69	17/8/69
32	Take Over	21/2/69	24/8/69
33	Bizarre	3/3/69	14/9/69

PRODUCTION CREDITS

Season One
Ian Hendry/Patrick Macnee
1961

Produced by:
Leonard White

The Avengers Theme composed & played by:
Johnny Dankworth

Story Editors:
Patrick Brawn & John Bryce

26 monochrome episodes

Season Two
Patrick Macnee/Honor Blackman
Julie Stevens/Jon Rollason
1962

Produced by:
Leonard White (Episodes 1 to 14)
John Brycc (Episodes 15 to 26)

Music by:
Johnny Dankworth

Story Editors:
John Bryce (Episodes 1 to 14)
Richard Bates (Episodes 15 to 26)

26 monochrome episodes

Season Three
Patrick Macnee/Honor Blackman
1963–64

Produced by:
John Bryce

Music by:
Johnny Dankworth

Story Editor:
Richard Bates

26 monochrome episodes

Season Four
Patrick Macnee/Diana Rigg
1965–66

Produced by:
Julian Wintle

In charge of production:
Albert Fennell

Associate Producer:
Brian Clemens

Music by:
Laurie Johnson

Story Editor:
Brian Clemens

Art Director:
Harry Pottle

26 monochrome episodes

Season Five
Patrick Macnee/Diana Rigg
1967–68

Produced by:
Albert Fennell & Brian Clemens

Executive Producer:
Julian Wintle

Music by:
Laurie Johnson

Production Controller:
Jack Greenwood

Music Editor:
Karen Heward

25 colour episodes

Season Six
Patrick Macnee/Linda Thorson
1969

Produced by:
Albert Fennell & Brian Clemens

Executive in charge of production:
Gordon L.T. Scott

Music by:
Laurie Johnson

Additional Music by:
Howard Blake

Production Controller:
Jack Greenwood

Consultant to series:
Julian Wintle

Story Consultant:
Philip Levene

Script Editor:
Terry Nation

Music Editors:
Karen Heward & Paul Clay

34 colour episodes

SEEING DOUBLE

Celluloid Mayhem to Order

EXCITING AND realistic action sequences punctuated every episode of *The Avengers* and, on countless occasions, the stars would be asked to perform a death-defying leap from a tall building; cling precariously by their fingertips to the bonnet of a fast-moving car; or leap from an out-of-control vehicle. Or did they? Of course not. The production company couldn't take the risk of having their most valuable assets – the stars themselves – injured by a mistimed stunt. Such an injury could have hospitalised the star for weeks or – in the case of a broken limb – months, and added thousands of pounds to the production costs in delayed shooting time, not to mention the extremely high insurance premiums. The really dangerous sequences were handled by 'doubles', those unsung heroes of celluloid mayhem who ensure that the impossible appears believable – the stunt artists.

Look again as Steed leaps to safety over the giant bulldozer blade in *The Fear Merchants*, or at Tara as she faces the motorcycle assailant before plunging from the clifftop in *All Done With Mirrors*. Perhaps the sight of Mrs Peel diving from the springboard in *The Bird Who Knew Too Much* quickened your pulse? If so, you're in for a surprise. 'Steed' was in fact Rocky Taylor, a professional stuntman who had handled all of Patrick Macnee's stuntwork throughout all the Rigg episodes – a role he continued in *Invasion of the Earthmen* until the role of Macnee's double was handed over for the entire Thorson series to Paul Weston.

Cyd Child, a stuntwoman who specialised in doing 30-foot leaps and falls from balconies, doubled Linda Thorson for the clifftop fighting scene. In fact, this stunt was as dangerous as it looks and the motorcycle passed close enough to tear a few threads from her costume! A regular with the series from 1965, Miss Child also handled all the 'rough stuff' for Diana Rigg. Close scrutiny will reveal that it is Cyd Child who manhandles the prison guard over her head before dumping him on the bed in the scene from *The Living Dead*. Miss Child also took up the reins as fight arranger for *The New Avengers* and did the occasional dangerous stunt for Joanna Lumley, although, as we shall learn, both Joanna Lumley and Gareth Hunt did about 90 per cent of their stuntwork themselves.

Steed versus 'Steed'. Having assumed Steed's identity, stunt double Rocky Taylor (right) tries to prevent the real Steed wrecking Arcos's plans in They Keep Killing Steed.

Doubling for Linda Thorson, stuntwoman Cyd Child does a graceful banister slide to join Steed at the foot of the stairs in Whoever Shot Poor George Oblique Stroke XR40.

These days, of course, stunt artists have gained some degree of recognition for their work and frequently receive on-screen credit for their input. However, this is quite a recent occurrence and, as most television programmes produced in the Sixties and early Seventies seldom acknowledged them, here are the names of some of the many stunt artists who made *The Avengers* one of the most exciting programmes of the last 25 years: Les Crawford, Eddie Powell, Cliff Diggins, Denny Powell, Bill Sawyer and Terry Richards.

Fight arrangers Joe Dunne and Cyd Child go through their paces prior to filming the finale of Stay Tuned.

As for the diving stunt, it was performed by stunt*man* Peter Elliot! Peter also doubled Diana Rigg in the riverside action sequence in *You Have Just Been Murdered* and, dressed as 'Tara King' and wearing make-up and a wig, it is him we see doing the trampoline jumps in the opening sequence of *Have Guns, Will Haggle* – a stunt that went wrong and left him with a dislocated shoulder blade. Oddly enough, two other stuntmen, Gerry Crampton and Frank Henson – both *Avengers* regulars – doubled Linda Thorson in two other scenes from this story.

Even those breathtaking fight sequences were never quite what they seemed. They were meticulously planned by fight arrangers Ray Austin (the Rigg stories) and Joe Dunne (the Thorson stories), who led both the stars and their doubles through endless rehearsals until a no-holds-barred on-screen punch-up could look convincing and a punch, supposedly 'connecting' with a villain's jaw, in reality stopped fractions of an inch from its target. Then, by clever camera angles and post-production editing, the blow would appear to land on the designated area of the actor's body. Once again the stunt doubles handled the really rough stuff, while close-ups of the stars were later edited into the finished scene, leaving the viewer with the impression that they had just witnessed a full-blown encounter between star and on-screen villain. This, of course, is hardly 'cheating', for it is what appears on screen that counts. If a little bit of camera trickery adds extra sophistication to the proceedings we should perhaps offer our thanks to those 'unseen' heroes who, by their expertise, add that touch of realism to the action.

FROM CELLULOID TO GREASEPAINT

IN APRIL 1971, almost two years after *The Avengers* faded from British television screens, the media began carrying reports of a new *Avengers* production – a stage show! John Mather, one-time head of the William Morris Agency in Europe, had negotiated with ABC/EMI to obtain the rights to transfer the popular television series to the British stage and, to quote Mather's words, 'Blast the British theatre into the Seventies.'

Mather acquired the services of one-time *Avengers* writer, Terence Feely, and producer/writer of the television series, Brian Clemens, to produce the script for the show.

'The script is ready,' said Mather. 'I now have the difficult task of finding the stage equivalents of the Patrick Macnees, the Honor Blackmans and the Diana Riggs of this world.'

Patrick Macnee *was* approached, but told me, 'I told them that I considered that *The Avengers* was a *television* product – not even a film product, and was essentially for the small screen which was, of course, one of its unique qualities. Slightly slapdash and casual, it wasn't crafted in the way that the Bond films are crafted. Bond films are really the ultimate in that form of mad, slightly callous, superficial, forceful, crazy, wild and fun-filled extravaganzas. But the stage is a place that should look dazzling and beautiful, but basically remain a place for the exchange of ideas, dialogue and characters – and not whiz, bang, wallop.'

By early May, Mather announced that Simon Oates (who had previously played a trendy, well-dressed scientist in BBC's *Doomwatch* production, and had appeared in several episodes of *The Avengers*) had been signed to play John Steed.

'I was very dubious about the bowler,' Simon Oates said at the time. 'I had the distinct feeling that if I wore the thing in public, a chap might rush up and kiss me.' (No one did – which isn't surprising when you consider that Mr Oates is 6 ft 4 in and a former Army heavyweight boxing champion.)

Kate O'Mara was chosen to play the evil Madame Gerda. She complained that the vinyl suit she had to wear for the role stopped her from sitting down, and creaked when she walked.

The part of Steed's new female partner in the show, Hannah Wild, took slightly longer to fill. It eventually went to blonde actress, Sue Lloyd.

When told that Hannah would have to fight ten girls while Simon Oates threw a villain into the orchestra pit,

Oates said to the producer, 'Tell you what, why don't I fight the girls and Hannah can have the bloke!'

The following is a slightly edited version of an article printed in the London *Evening News*, 2 July 1971, written by James Green.

NOW THE AVENGERS GO WEST

That sophisticated hokum series, *The Avengers*, which had the right chemistry of in-jokes and send-ups to become a TV cult, is all set to become a stage show. Directed by Leslie Phillips, using a helicopter, a Bentley, and back-projection on stage, it opens in Birmingham shortly and arrives in the West End on 2 August.

Not however, with Patrick Macnee as agent John Steed. When the TV series ended, unflappable Macnee took his bowler and carnation off to Los Angeles. In his place, Simon Oates, debonair and handsome, will bring his own brand of stiff upper lip to the role of Steed.

They have found him a new girl assistant, Sue Lloyd. Her job is to knock 'em out with looks or hooks. To date, four actresses have enrolled as Steed's Girl Friday. I have been interrogating them all. . . .

HONOR BLACKMAN, alias Mrs Cathy Gale, Avenger girl MK1. A 5 ft 6 in ash-blonde noted for kinky black leather gear, she says,

'I played Cathy for two years, and the kinky leather thing was an accident. At first I wore culottes but they looked awful. So I changed to tight pants. But when I threw a man over my shoulder they split up the middle, and there I was in front of the camera with my knickers hanging out. So we had another think. I already had leather trousers. Boots to match seemed a good idea, and it all happened from there. As it turned out we were way ahead of fashion. Cathy Gale was super for me and I enjoyed my time tremendously. She was an anthropologist originally, you know, and was brilliant at everything. Judo, guns, fencing . . . she could do the lot. We made her a widow because the producers didn't want a love interest with Steed, but as a widow she could flirt and there was always a feeling that someday romance might happen.

'I received some very strange fan mail as Cathy, some of it so weird they wouldn't let me see it. Some people seeing me thumping around in black boots, with no man

The Avengers logo as used in the theatre programme.

in my life, and practically carrying a whip, decided that I must be a lesbian, and I had some extraordinary offers.'

DIANA RIGG, alias Mrs Emma Peel, Avenger girl MK2. Chestnut-haired, single, 5 ft 9 in and statuesque, she specialised in sci-fi space clothes and sexy second-skin catsuits.

'I had two years as the widowed Emma and I've little idea how she differed from Cathy because I never saw Honor in the part and only saw a few of my own shows. My girl was a great character who used judo among other things to look after herself. She was also financially free.

'Escapist stuff, of course, but really pointing towards the future, because women today have become more realistic and self-sufficient. They are moving in the direction of Emma Peel.'

LINDA THORSON, alias Miss Tara King, Avenger girl MK3. Canadian, another five-feet-niner, unmarried, brown-haired, her trademark was fluffy, pink feminine dresses.

'I had 18 months as Tara and she was the only one of Steed's girls to be single. I used a lot of wigs and changed from blonde to brunette and redhead.

'I decided that she was in love with Steed. Any girl who would risk her life and spend that much time with a man must be in love. I think my interpretation influenced the producers and they let me play it that way.

'Viewers noticed that she was in love with him and, judging by the letters received, Steed's image changed as a result. He seemed to care, too.

'One problem was that fashions were changing and they didn't know whether to put me in minis or maxis. Usually they settled for midis.

'Another difference was that Tara didn't go in for karate but fought more like a girl – scratching, kicking and lashing out with her handbag.

'The part came early in my career, right after drama school. I'm glad I did it.'

SUE LLOYD, alias Hannah Wild, Avenger girl MK4. Unmarried, 5 ft 8 in, reddish-gold hair.

'When I walk out as Hannah Wild, it will be my first time on the London stage.

'I see Hannah as a highly intelligent girl with a certain hardness. Practical, yet with a lot of warmth. She's fond of Steed, but otherwise there's no man in her life. On the action front her accomplishments will include shootings, half-nelsons, and the occasional karate chop.

'Since Kate O'Mara as the villainess is in black shiny leather, they've given me a crimson leather fighting outfit. I also wear a golden leather suit and dusty pink costume.

'Obviously, having had so little stage experience, the first night will be doubly tense for me. What must help is that I did face a studio audience while making *His and Hers*.

'Some people think I'm a toughie . . . rather like Hannah Wild . . . but I don't agree. If I seem hard that's a cover. Because actually, I'm a big softie. What I've discovered is that the really dangerous girls who need watching are the wide-eyed innocents!'

THE AVENGERS ON STAGE

(Reprinted from the official theatre programme)
Is there anyone, watching television over the last ten years, who has not tuned in and listened to that familiar theme music without a thrill of anticipation? For John Steed is the modern Robin Hood, and we know in advance that he will not come to harm, even though he never made Marion.

Every week we have switched on to Steed and his faithful girl-friends – Cathy Gale, Emma Peel, Tara King – those cynical, leather-clad females who could kiss or chop you according to their moods.

Now Steed and his latest Avenger girl – Hannah Wild – are presented on stage in a fast-moving outrageous comedy, with all the panache and gloss of the imperturable Avengers, but with the sinister and exotic Madame Gerda, leader of the Forces of Evil, and her incredibly wicked gang of beautiful girls.

With the Avengers – anything can happen!

I count myself fortunate to have been present at the premiere at the Birmingham theatre, 20 July 1971. For those who missed seeing the show – or those who may have seen it, and would like a memory-jogger – here's a personal review of that first-night performance.

John Mather's promise that the production would have 'a very special look' was not just idle boasting. Nothing was overlooked in an effort to provide the audience with 'something different' in British theatre production and, as Mather had promised, to 'blast the theatre into the Seventies'.

The show had all the off-beat appeal of the successful television series: imaginative sets – 16 in all; colourful, trendy costumes; over 30 dolly-birds. It all helped to give the production an up-to-the-minute look.

The ambitious sets, designed by Michael Young, included a full-scale replica of Steed's vintage Bentley; Steed's luxury penthouse apartment; the top secret Operations Room of M15; the Brain Room of the Master Computer; Madame Gerda's Academy for Young Girls (complete with scantily-clad nymphets); even a helicopter landing!

Simon Oates, immaculate in his trendy suits, shooting jackets and Cuban heel shoes, made an excellent Steed.

Sue Lloyd, in her red, fawn and off-white trouser suits, made a luscious Hannah Wild, and Kate O'Mara, in her black shiny PVC suit and thigh-length boots, completed the trio as the evil (though rather too attractive) Madame Gerda.

The plot concerned the efforts of Madame Gerda, and her gang of young students, to overthrow the governments of the world and infiltrate their spy networks.

By using the Giant Computer Brain, Gerda has developed a method of making herself and her girls invisible. Only Steed is immune to her plot and is able to see the girls. This leads Mother to suspect that his prize agent has gone mad, and has Steed committed to hospital!

Needless to say, Steed escapes, only to find that Gerda and her gang have all the world's security ministers in their power.

After numerous battles with the enemy (the scenes in which Simon Oates ad-libbed his fights with his unseen assailants were hilarious), Steed finally convinces his chief that he is sane, and thwarts Gerda's evil plot. But not before he has been court-martialled (and we learn that his licence to kill has two endorsements on it!),

stripped of his rank of Major (and also stripped of his fountain-pen camera – for photographing fountain-pens!), and undergone various forms of torture (such as being whipped by a half-naked girl while tied to the Giant Computer Brain, which was a giant phallic symbol!).

Yes, the accent *was* on comedy, and Simon Oates and Sue Lloyd shared further funny moments. Steed and Hannah are set upon by three robot girls, and while Hannah tackles two of them, Steed and his assailant fall backwards over a sofa. A few moments pass, during which various articles of ladies' underclothing are thrown out, followed by a leg, an arm, etc. Finally, Steed emerges, saying 'That's the first time I've ever *un*screwed a girl. Still, she's (h)armless now!' Plus Simon Oates telling a dying robot to 'Get on with it, man, robots don't have death scenes', and then turning to Sue Lloyd to tell her that 'He died babbling of Green Shields!'

There were also many unscripted funny moments. In one, Miss Lloyd hit her opponent over the head with a plastic bottle, and had to stand and watch while it slipped from her hands and bounced across the stage. And Kate O'Mara fell flat on her bottom when the rope ladder she was climbing collapsed.

However, it was the first night (when things are expected to go wrong), and no one seemed to mind, least of all Simon Oates himself, who finished the show with the lines, 'Why not come back tomorrow night and see how the show really ends?'

The show ran its scheduled two-week trial run in Birmingham, then transferred to the stage of London's Prince of Wales Theatre, for a limited engagement. Very limited, unfortunately, since it only ran for a few weeks. As Sue Lloyd recalled recently, during *On Stage* (BBC2 TV, 15 August 1987), the 'prop' problems continued to plague the production. She told viewers of an amusing incident which happened during that run. 'It was a very ambitious show – perhaps too ambitious. Kate O'Mara was supposed to be invisible at certain times and special effects allowed her to vanish into special props which would part to allow her to step inside. There was this trick sofa, which had been designed to open and swallow her up. Unfortunately, what happened one night was that she pressed the button and nothing happened. After several uneasy moments she gave up trying and tiptoed off the stage. In the next scene Jeremy Lloyd came on and was supposed to be sitting down for a straightforward tea scene. He no sooner sat down when, wham, the sofa opened up like giant jaws and poor Jeremy disappeared into it. The problem was that he was too big to go all the way inside, and his head and shoulders were left sticking out at a ridiculous angle. Watching this, I couldn't keep my face straight any longer. Everyone was hysterical – none more than the audience.' (Perhaps the Prince of Wails would have been more appropriate?)

A couple of interesting 'facts' emerged from the show, though. Steed was the youngest of a family of eight – the other seven being girls. And he was christened John Wickham Gascoyne Berresford Steed!

Cast
(in order of appearance)

James (Steed's new butler) .... Julie Neubert
John Steed .... Simon Oates
Hannah Wild .... Sue Lloyd
Melanie .... Wendy Hall
Carruthers (an M15 agent) .... Jeremy Lloyd
Parsons (an M15 agent) .... Kenton Moore
Chummers (an M15 agent) .... Paul McDowell
Maitland (an M15 agent)................. John S. Landry
Walters (The Minister for Internal
  Security) .... Anthony Sharp
Madame Gerda .... Kate O'Mara
Victoria (one of Gerda's gang) .... Lisa Collings
Prunella (one of Gerda's gang)............. Gail Grainger
Wanda (one of Gerda's gang) .... Gypsie Kemp
Air Marshal Striker.......................... Derek Tansley
General Bull .... John S. Landry
Admiral Drake .... Tim Buckland
A Psychiatrist .... Derek Tansley
Military Police Sergeant .... Tim Buckland
Military Policeman........................ Paul McDowell
Mother, chief of M15....................... John S. Landry
Miss Lacey (his Secretary) .... Mary Llewellin
Nicola (one of Gerda's gang) .... Joanna Ross
Jasmine (one of Gerda's gang) .... Kubi Chaza
Emma (one of Gerda's gang) ....Helen Gill
Miranda (one of Gerda's gang) .... Heather Kydd
A Nurse .... Gail Grainger
Scarman (Gerda's bodyguard) ....Kenton Moore
A fantasy maid............................... Gail Grainger
A fantasy masochist .... Joanna Ross
A fantasy cricketer .... Kubi Chaza

**and various dignitaries and wives,
guards, secretaries, passers-by, etc.**

The Action of the Play
Act I
Scene I — John Steed's Penthouse Apartment – morning
Scene II — A helicopter – somewhere in Scotland – that night
Scene III — Steed's Bentley – that night
Scene IV — Top Secret Operations Room somewhere in Scotland – that night
Scene V — Whitehall Communication Centre – next day
Scene VI — Steed's apartment – later

INTERVAL

Act II
Scene I — An office at the Ministry of Internal Security – next day
Scene II — Steed's apartment – later that day
Scene III — Conversation à deux
Scene IV — Madame Gerda's Academy for Young Ladies – late afternoon
Scene V — Ministry of Internal Security – that evening
Scene VI — Steed's apartment – minutes later
Scene VII — Ministry of Internal Security – that night
Scene VIII — Brain Room of the Master Computer

PRODUCTION CREDITS
Director: Leslie Phillips
Producer: John Mather
Writers: Brian Clemens and Terence Feely
Designer: Michael Young
Fight Sequences: Tim Condron
Mr Oates' suits by: Bentley, Perry and Whitley
Miss Lloyd's costumes by: Berkely Sutcliffe
Publicity: Fred Hift Associates

STEED MK III

If the idea of *The Avengers* on stage strikes you as somewhat bizarre, what could be more strange than our bowler-hatted hero and his female aide appearing on radio?

Believe it or not, that is exactly what happened next in *The Avengers* saga.

A series of *Avengers* radio plays was produced for the South African Broadcasting Company by Sonovision Ltd. The first episode was broadcast in January 1972. Starring Donald Monat as John Steed, and Diane Appleby as Mrs Emma Peel, the stories were freely adapted from the original Patrick Macnee/Diana Rigg television scripts, plus one or two Macnee/Thorson stories (though the characters were always portrayed as Steed/Emma). Each episode was 15 minutes long and contained one complete story, or a serialised adventure lasting from five to eight episodes.

The tongue-in-cheek feel of the original television series was achieved by the use of a narrator (Hugh Rouse), whose interjections supplied most of the humorous aspects to each story.

The stories were adapted by Tony Jay and Dennis Folbigge, who also directed the series.

Episodes known to have been broadcast are: *From Venus With Love, The Joker, Dial a Deadly Number, The Quick, Quick Slow Death, A Sense of History, The Fantasy Game (Honey For the Prince), The Super Secret Cypher Snatch, The Morning After, Who's Who?* and *A Deadly Gift (The Cybernauts)*. Four other scripts were remitted to the company, but it is not known if these were ever used. These were: *The Correct Way to Kill, The £50,000 Breakfast, Wish You Were Here* and *Killer*.

THE AVENGERS RETURN

The New Avengers
Patrick Macnee/Gareth Hunt/Joanna Lumley 1976

A FTER THE failure of the stage production (it closed after only six weeks), *The Avengers* went into television limbo – at least as far as the British television channels were concerned, with only Channel 4 giving the filmed series an airing in 1983–84. It did, however, continue to appear on American television screens at regular intervals. Some stations even showed all the 83 filmed episodes on 83 consecutive nights, while others screened four episodes a day!

Six years passed, then, in 1975, Brian Clemens received a call from a French television and film executive, Rudolph Roffi, asking if Tara King was available to make a champagne commercial for French television. (Linda Thorson was still a big name in France at the time.)

Linda was contacted, as was Patrick Macnee, as a sort of tribute to *The Avengers*, and the commercial was made at Elstree Studios during the summer of 1975.

Six months after the commercial played on French television, Roffi, having discovered that *The Avengers* was no longer in production, rang Clemens to ask why. Explaining that although he and Albert Fennell had always believed that the show would one day reappear (hence the reason Clemens had kept their options open by having Steed and Tara shot into space: 'What goes up, must come down – eventually'), Clemens told the Frenchman that they had been unable to interest any British company in financing a new production, which would cost over £2,000,000 to produce. In the event, it was to cost at least double that sum.

A few weeks later, Clemens received a second call from France. It was Roffi, saying, 'I have the money. When can we start production?'

Within three hectic months, Clemens, Fennell and ex-*Avengers* music arranger, Laurie Johnson, had formed The Avengers (Film & TV) Enterprises Ltd., at the time the only truly independent TV company in the UK, in association with IDTV Paris. Plans were formulated to produce a new series of 26 films under the name of *The New Avengers*.

Aware that it would be difficult to mount any new *Avengers* series without the presence of stalwart Avenger, Patrick Macnee (as Clemens told the press at the time, 'Avenger girls can come and go, but if Patrick Macnee fell down a manhole tomorrow, it would be the end of *The Avengers* for good'), Clemens rang the ex-Avenger at his Hollywood home. At first, Macnee was hesitant to accept. He thought it was some gigantic joke and asked for more time to consider the offer.

However, he asked them to send a script. They never did. But, believing that he was still young enough and energetic enough to play a still-recognisable Steed, and convinced that he had something more to contribute to the role, within two weeks he had decided to face the challenge, come what might. (When he'd started out in the role back in 1960, he was a swashbuckling 38. Now he was 54.)

Finding a new *Avengers* girl to step into the shoes vacated by Honor Blackman, Diana Rigg and Linda Thorson was to prove as daunting as any of the cases investigated by Steed. Over 300 actresses were auditioned and Clemens eventually reduced the list of candidates to one dozen.

On 8 March 1976, Nigel Dempster's Diary page in the *Daily Mail* carried the following:

JOANNA SCOOPS THAT SUPER-ROLE AS STEED'S AVENGERS SUPER GIRL . . .

With aspiring hopefuls still clamouring for the female lead in the new Avengers series, which starts production next month, I can reveal that the role has now been filled. The debby-voiced Miss Joanna Lumley, 29, has been chosen to take over the part pioneered by Honor Blackman and subsequently inherited by Diana Rigg and Linda Thorson.

Joanna, who had previously been turned down as an *Avengers* girl – the role of Hannah Wild, in the stage production – was given three screen tests: one for reading, and two physical auditions, in which she played a scene with Gareth Hunt, who had already been chosen as Gambit, and a fight scene with a stunt man to see if she could handle the rough stuff. (Part of this audition appears in the title credits of the American transmission prints: Joanna, complete with brunette, shoulder-length hair, stands behind a door as a villain crashes into the room.) 'It was difficult getting to meet them,' she told me, 'because they apparently don't want me and it took forever getting into the audition. I tried very, very hard for it because I wanted to do it. I couldn't believe it when I heard I had landed the part.'

Originally, the new *Avengers* girl was to have been called Charly, but prior to filming, Clemens discovered that there was a perfume of that name on the market. Not wishing to spend lavish amounts of money endorsing another company's product, the name was changed.

Joanna herself is credited with suggesting the name Purdey – after the most revered and expensive shotgun in the world.

Prior to filming, Clemens told the media, 'Purdey will be a stockings and suspenders girl – giving lots of glimpses of thigh. She will be tough, yet vulnerable, with a huge sense of humour. The *Avengers* girls will have gone full circle with Joanna. So much so that she won't have to burn her bra – she can put it back on.'

It's not too surprising, then, that male viewers waited with baited breath (and eager anticipation) for their first glimpse of Steed's new Girl Friday.

Reality, however, isn't always that simple or – in the case of television hype – is seldom what we'd been led to believe. Although it soon became obvious to the more discerning viewer that Miss Lumley was indeed wearing 'single hose', regular views of stocking-tops and suspender tabs were all too conspicuous by their absence – with only the rooftop-climbing scenes in *Target* and the titillating close-up of Purdey's black stocking-tops in *To Catch a Rat* allowing the onlooker a clear (though all too brief) glimpse of thigh. Mind you, in fairness to Joanna Lumley, neither she nor her clothes designer Catherine Buckley were happy about this before filming started. As Joanna Lumley told me, 'They said she was going to be a stockings and suspenders girl. I said that if she was *the* most effective sleuth in the world, or part of some enormous Secret Service, then she would *have* to wear efficient and sportsman-like clothes. So it was filtered out, because when climbing over a barbed-wire fence or shimmying up a drainpipe and scaling a roof while wearing high heels and suspenders . . . well, *I* had to do it and it was lucky I didn't break my ankle.'

At the time, Joanna was sporting a mane of long blonde hair. Before filming began, however – and apparently against studio wishes – she had it cropped into the now familiar Purdey bob.

'It's fine,' said Joanna at the time, 'if you have long, healthy, shining hair like Diana Rigg, but look at mine – it's really quite tatty. As I'm going to be leaping about the place and working outside a lot, it's bound to go frizzy, so I thought I'd have it shortened.'

Purdey was a girl of the 1980s. Sexy – for a TV heroine, VERY sexy. Not promiscuous, but not a virgin either. An ex-ballerina, she made use of her high-kicking legs to dispatch her opponents in a series of athletic manoeuvres that relied as much on speed and surprise as on power and flexibility. She could use her hands, too, and shoot the pips out of an apple at twenty paces. And she could run like an Olympic athlete, drive anything from her orange drop-head sports car to a motorbike and acquit herself favourably on a paratrooper's assault course.

Purdey was tough. She dressed in frills and soft, flowing materials.

As you would expect from her unique personality, her permanent pad was different, too. She lived in the biggest, most sensuously decorated bed-sitter in the world. A gutted basement in London, refurbished in feminine art decor style and colours which accurately reflected its occupant. Right down to the fact that her bedroom door was little more than a hanging curtain of beads.

A third member of the team was added to the new format – Mike Gambit. After testing for the part, the role was given to 35-year-old Gareth Hunt, who told me that he played a scene written by Brian Clemens. 'It was really like an excerpt from one of the shows. I recall a funny moment when Joanna and I sat on one of the ornate tables they were using in the test, and broke it – but that wasn't in the script. Luckily we were both chosen for the series.'

Mike Gambit was different, too. A man of the next decade, there hadn't been a hero like Gambit before. He was hip, yet dressed quietly to merge easily with the high-power world of espionage and corruption in which he worked. He could be quiet and deceptively still – until he flared into action, when he could strike as fast as a cobra, using his lethally effective hands. He drove a fast car with consummate skill – experience of Formula One racing put to good use – and could turn his Jaguar XJS on a sixpence. He could move faster than the eye could follow and shoot any sidearm fast and straight.

Rumour had it that Gambit was once an Army man – a major in the Paras – and before that a mercenary, once wrestling crocodiles – until he decided to take up more exciting work!

Like Purdey, he lived in London – in a super modern

apartment, for which he'd chosen ultra-modern decor and every conceivable electronic device – right down to an automated bed!

Bowler hat, umbrella, buttonhole, immaculate dress, an appreciation of the better things of life – John Steed was still the suave, elegant man who *knew* that Britannia ruled and was still sworn to defend her from her enemies. But his circumstances had changed. He still had his mews flat in London but now preferred to spend most of his time in a big house in the country, 'Steed's Stud' as it was called, where, when not engaged in more dangerous tasks, like saving the world from destruction, he bred beautiful horses and entertained beautiful women.

He hadn't mellowed – just grown perkier.

He'd got a new car, too. The Bentley was still there, lovingly garaged for the occasional recreational spin (or so the publicity handout led us to believe – it wasn't seen!) but Steed had seen the light; villains had little respect for such splendid machinery and with each outing, the risk of a scratch – or worse, a bullet hole – increased. His current mode of transport blended the practical with the beautiful. The practical was a Range Rover, suitably converted for a man of Steed's impeccable style. The beautiful was the Big Cat, a wide-wheeled, highly polished road version of the Jaguar Racing Coupé; a docile monster capable of 200 mph, hand made and tailored, and a worthy stablemate for the Bentley.

The relationship between the new team was that of partners, equals, good friends, each as important as the other. Though they were poles apart – Steed locked in a cell would 'con' the jailer into opening the door, Gambit would kick it doown – one factor welded them together as a team, mutual respect. And a shared sense of humour.

The announcement that Steed was to have a new sidekick in the series left me with a feeling of unease. How, I wondered, would this association affect what had previously been seen as a winning format? I held reservations that the introduction of a third member to the team (particularly that of a male) would relegate Steed's character to that of a 'Mother' figure – a kind of 'Mr Waverley' to Gambit and Purdey's 'Solo and Kuryakin' - and leave Steed delegating the action to his younger protégés. Indeed, why change the format at all? Brian Clemens supplied the answer. Asked why he'd thought it necessary to introduce the character of Gambit, he told me: 'Because *The Avengers* has *always* changed – moved forward. Because also Patrick Macnee was that much older, we needed a younger man to handle at least some of the action. Don't forget, this was called *The NEW Avengers*, so we had to stay true to that, otherwise the critics would have hammered us for just serving up a new batch of the *OLD Avengers*.'

Certainly, considering that Patrick Macnee was 47 when the original *Avengers* series ceased production in 1969, and a seven-year gap separated the new series from its predecessor, it is hardly surprising that *Sunday Mirror* columnist Pat Boxhall posed the following question in the issue dated 11 January 1976: 'Can Steed make it

again?', then went on to say that as a one-time *Avengers* fan she was alarmed that Patrick Macnee (at 53, and having seen off three glamorous sidekicks) was still being asked to play the sophisticated Steed. She added that he was 'pushing his luck to put a fourth on his arm and did someone in those ivory television towers believe that time doesn't tick-tock for men?' Considering the facts, an understandable question.

Surprisingly, however, it appeared that time had indeed stood still for the ever ebullient Mr Macnee and although the media led us to believe that 'Steed has mellowed', in fact he'd hardly changed at all. True, he was slightly heavier – though only in the first few stories; by the time the second 13 episodes began production, Patrick had slimmed down and looked every bit as suave as the 'slimline' Thorson series model. True, the much loved four-and-a-half litre 1929 vintage Bentley – loaned to *The Avengers* production by a Huddersfield garage owner for the duration of the series – and Rolls-Royce trademarks were no longer in evidence, though a 'reference' to the former did appear in the episode *K Is For Kill* (the vehicle seen in the background as Steed telephones Mrs Peel was courtesy of some unused film footage, while the vehicle seen in the opening moments of that story was hired for one day's filming). But Steed's *character* had hardly changed at all. Still immaculate as ever, bowler-hatted, he continued to spread British good manners. In short, Patrick Macnee was back as Steed. Avenging, though it was certainly not better than before, was nevertheless well worth waiting for.

The New Avengers as a show differed little from the previous *Avengers* stories.

The bizarre qualities were still there to delight the viewer. These included a man whose mere touch could spell death; Nazis alive and well, and living as monks on a remote Scottish island; a sophisticated apparatus that transferred people's thoughts by scrambling their brain; a 'monster' rat; and even Steed's old enemy, the dreaded Cybernauts.

Brian Clemens explained: 'The situations are just as fantastic, but, this time, we carefully framed our stories so that, no matter how mind-blowing the plot, we make it believable. And that is the big change, if you want to point out the difference! The old series was a humorous spoof, with dramatic overtones. *The New Avengers* is dramatic, with humorous undertones. The previous series had a very loyal following, but we never got Middle America (or its equivalent across the world) – the sort of viewer who took a quick look then changed channels because they found the stories "silly". This time, I added more depth – annoyed the true *Avengers* fans – but picked up a few million others along the way.'

Clemens put the *Avengers*' amazing track record down to a 'happy knack right from the start'. He said, 'We were always at least two or three years in advance of our time. It was costume, without being period costume. We even upstaged James Bond, with karate, kung-fu, mini-skirts and women's lib, and we managed to stay ahead. This time we mean to top all that has gone before. Audiences have grown more sophisticated, and the successful show must get ahead of them. This is what we've tried to do –

to produce a show that is in the 1980s. A show that will seem as fresh as ever, but still stay ahead of its nearest emulators. The production values of the new series *are higher than any other television series in the world*. The use of location exteriors is a 100% improvement. You are going to be seeing a lot of Britain in the new series, but *Avengers-style*, weird, bizarre, unusual locations.'

Changes in fashion were not as predominant as in the earlier *Avengers* series. No black leather for Purdey. Instead she wore a wardrobe designed by London-born Catherine Buckley. These included silk dresses, gathered at the waist and tied at the shoulder, with skirts in pleated chiffon; a kimono in orange, black, green, red and yellow flower-print silk, with long sleeves and side slits; black cotton jump-suits, with an *Avengers* lion motif and the name Purdey trimmed in white and red (worn only once in the series); and a luxurious evening dress in red, green and blue lurex, with velvet top and lurex dangle pieces.

The original intention was to make Gambit a swinger – complete with jeans, bomber jackets, etc. (Gareth Hunt had expressed a preference for these). The end product, however, was a very up-to-the-minute man who wore expensive, well-cut, three-piece suits in a traditional business dark blue pin-stripe, and moth head checks and plain gaberdine, worn with smart ties.

Not even the producers dared to play around with Steed's attire. As ever, his wardrobe retained a wide selection of colourful bowler-hats, some of which were as useful as they were decorative. One, for instance, had a steel crown, which was ideal for protecting his head from attack and handy for knocking out the opposition. Another had a steel brim, which served as a deadly missile when thrown frisbee-style. A third bowler had a miniature receiver built into the crown. The tightly furled brolly was also still in evidence – a weapon in itself when used to hook an opponent's arm, or for fending off attacks. The umbrella also doubled as a swordstick, with a thin rapier blade hidden in its shaft. This, coupled with Steed's knowledge of fencing, was, like everything else about him, impeccable.

For the new series, Steed would be seen wearing – along with the familiar Edwardian suits – riding breeches, shooting jackets, blazers and sportswear.

Martial arts had long been the hallmark of *The Avengers* ethos, so Clemens and Fennell were determined to get the very best people to teach Joanna and Gareth how to create their own brand of havoc. Prior to filming, Cyd Child and Ray Austin (who had shared a long association with *The Avengers* series), were brought in as fight arrangers. They rigged up a gymnasium in the studio, and the two stars were subjected to a vigorous fitness training schedule.

Both had already been put through a commando training course to toughen them up but, because the producers wanted the gestures in the fight scenes to look completely authentic, Joanna was given an additional hour of ballet training each day, in which every movement of her fight sequence was carefully plotted, checked, worked out and rehearsed in slow motion as if for a ballet. For the scenes in which Purdey was seen in close-up kicking directly at the camera, Austin sometimes would have Joanna's leg held up by a tripod to achieve the correct height. Joanna Lumley recalled being given 'an *enormous* amount of training', while Gareth told me that he and Joanna were 'put through a six-week-long Olympic training crash course' to get them fit for the rigours that lay ahead. Brian Clemens reflected, 'If we had found Joanna when she was nine years old, by now she would have probably won a fistful of Olympic medals.'

Asked if they did their own stunts, Joanna replied, 'Yes. I steeled myself to do them because it is so much more interesting if you're getting involved with *all* the filming, rather than sitting back and watching someone else do all the juicy bits. The stunts I *didn't* do were those with motorbikes, because I can't ride a motorbike, and they couldn't cover me for insurance.' Gareth said, 'Joanna and I became very involved in it. One didn't feel that you were playing a character totally unless one *did* actually do a lot of the stunts yourself – and we were very fit. We were obviously not allowed to do the really dangerous stunts, like turning cars over. But we did do

certain things which we possibly *shouldn't* have done – like diving through windows. Even when one realises that "sugar glass" was used, it could still cut your head – as it did mine.'

One other major change was *The New Avengers* theme music. The opening few bars remained the same, a bouncy kettle-drum boom, followed by the familiar strains of the original *Avengers* theme, but this soon gave way to a faster, punchier, 1980s-style theme tune to signal that this was the *NEW Avengers*.

Before filming began, the producers issued the following production brief to writers and directors:

THE NEW AVENGERS
Some notes on style

Times have changed, and The Avengers must not only change with them but – hopefully – keep ahead of the game. PACE is the thing – exposition, in the main, will be kept down to a minimum and, although The Avengers, The NEW Avengers, will never be hidebound by the strict format of self-imposed restrictions, there ARE certain guidelines we want to abide by ... *unless a particular episode demands a different treatment.*

1) Wherever possible we will not see characters coming through doors – we will pick up the scene AFTER the normal how-do-you-do's are over. Cut – and we will be there ... unless of course the whole sequence is built around what actually lies behind the door, or in any other way makes a virtue of seeing someone come through a door.

2) Establishing shots per se – are OUT. For instance – an exterior shot of a house is not desirable if the only thing it is saying is ... 'Here is the house the next scene should take place in.' HOWEVER, if it says, 'Here is the house, and here is a villain creeping towards it ...' that's O.K. The shot MUST say something.

3) Inserts. Are not desirable. Not *isolated* inserts. If it is necessary to see the headline of the paper Steed holds, then see it with him – incorporate him with a pan or a tilt or even an over-the-shoulder with the insert. If we *have* to pick up an isolated insert later in the schedule, then the visual storytelling of the initial scene has gone awry.

4) The fights. Should be as indicated in the scripts – the new girl will be shot so as to capitalise on her grace and sexuality – coming in, of course, for close moments of impact.

The new man should be shot – from great stillness – into a blur of close shots – a blur of fast movement – and out again to the stillness we will come to associate with him before and after vigorous action.

Steed, of course, will continue as before – often resorting to sheer guile and the use of props to achieve his purpose.

5) STEED. Is the one, vital element from the old Avengers to be regarded as UNTOUCHABLE. He will remain much as before – save that there are now scenes in which to externalise a hitherto unexplored dimension to his character.

6) As before – and again, where possible – The Avengers will create its own world – so that the normal day-to-day traffic should be ignored. Shooting say, in London Airport, may give us problems – but in a case like that, then one should stay very firmly involved and shooting on OUR protagonists.

7) In conclusion; the NEW Avengers look will stem from a number of subtly different elements. One will certainly be the increased use of location exteriors. Two – MUST BE an increased pace in the narrative. PACE is paramount.

Given the choice between the fight that – no matter how much fun it provides – goes on too long – and the crisp action that leads to maximum IMPACT – we must lean towards the latter.

And one world of caution – we are aiming at a worldwide sale. This means walking a not too difficult tightrope of varying censorship restrictions. Generally speaking most of these problems have been ironed out at the script stage – but there must arise occasions when on the spot decisions have to be made ... and SHOT. When in doubt – the ultimate yardstick must be – is it in good taste? Never forgetting an equally important question ... is it ENTERTAINING?

Brian Clemens & Albert Fennell
January 1976

Another noteworthy entry in the same document details the draft scenario for what was intended to be the series' *original* title sequence. Far removed from the one we're accustomed to, this ran as follows ...

Through the middle of a frozen frame bursts the original title logo of *The Avengers*, coinciding with the familiar first few bars of Laurie Johnson's earlier *Avengers* theme. The logo grows larger until it fills the screen and an inverted 'V' and the word 'new' is inserted – both scrawled like graffiti – an afterthought. It now reads *THE new Avengers*. With the addendum 'new' comes the music, the NEW music, acknowledging the novelty.

The picture dissolves to a long shot of an empty horizon, where, striding briskly into shot, is the tall, immaculate, bowler-hatted figure of John Steed. Without slackening his pace, he adjusts his bowler to a jaunty angle and smiles:

STARRING PATRICK MACNEE AS JOHN STEED

As he exits past the camera, we return to the horizon where, hurrying into shot come Gambit and Charly; she, a step or two behind him, hurrying to close the gap between them:

Cut to a close-up of Gambit, striding purposefully along:

????? AS MIKE GAMBIT

Pausing, he looks back to where Charly has stopped to lift her skirt and adjust her stocking-top to its suspender belt – an intimate moment which ends as she glances up and catches Gambit's eye, at which point she drops her skirt back into place:

AND ????? AS CHARLY

Hurrying over to where Gambit waits, they both look ahead to Steed, still striding briskly along. Glancing knowingly at her companion, the new girl, unexpectedly, puts both fingers to her lips and whistles!

Steed stops in mid-step and turns to face them, then, casually placing the umbrella to his shoulder, he waits while his companions hurry to his side:

PRODUCED BY ALBERT FENNELL &˙ BRIAN CLEMENS

Together, they exchange smiles before – a team now, they turn in unison and stride away as one:

SUPERIMPOSE DIRECTOR & EPISODE TITLE

As we know, this sequence was abandoned in favour of the current 'silhouette' version. I asked Brian Clemens why. 'Because,' he replied, 'by that time the age of computer-graphics had arrived and we decided that as our product was a child of the Eighties, we would take advantage of the available technology.'

The production went before the cameras in April 1976, at Pinewood Studios.

Any initial success *The New Avengers* might have had was sabotaged before it ever reached the screen. The ITV network failed to reach agreement on when the programme should be shown.

Some channels opted for Sunday evenings, other for Tuesdays, and the remainder screened the show on Friday nights. (Quite a contrast to the prime-time Saturday evening spot which the original *Avengers* had always been allocated.)

Interviewed at the time, Clemens said, 'It is total madness. With a proper network showing we could have emptied the streets on our opening night. It is tragic because *The Avengers* was the best adventure series British television ever made. But isn't that just typical of Britain, to sabotage and to underrate that which we do best?'

The series did, however, receive worldwide orders and soon recovered its production costs.

It seems that the original plan was to film 26 episodes, with a short break following the completion of the 13th story, before continuing to film the final 13. This, however, was not to be. Largely because the series was being financed by French and Canadian money, both countries demanded that several of the second 13 episodes be made there. In the event three were filmed in France and four in Canada – although one of the Canadian syndicate of backers wanted twice as many. Then, during the recess, Clemens was contacted by Roffi, head of the French backers, who told him that the series would have to go back to the drawing board. It appeared that they felt that Purdey wasn't sexy enough. They wanted Joanna Lumley to put on a sexier act and dress in more sultry creations. 'Purdey is short of lip gloss, and her wardrobe is dull and drab,' said Roffi. Though they'd liked what they'd seen, the French had certain reservations and wished to see Purdey dressed in

A rare shot of Joanna Lumley for overseas promotion.

top French designs, like those of Yves St Laurent. 'In general terms,' Roffi told the British press, 'I think the stories could be sexier, more violent also, but still remain sophisticated.'

This inevitably led to problems. Parallels can be drawn between this situation and that of the earlier *Avengers* series, when the American buyers put money into making the Linda Thorson series, then promptly began to dictate the show's future format – until the consequences proved disastrous. Seemingly the French were bent on going the same route.

Joanna Lumley, angered by the criticism, blasted back, 'We don't want to see bottoms and breasts, do we? I think the public have had quite enough of that on TV and everywhere else. Aren't people bored with actresses who lick their lips trying to be sexy? It will be a pity if *The New Avengers* has to jump on the bandwagon because of the influences from other programmes. As an actress, I believe improvements can be made. But I've never thought I looked dowdy.

'My own dress designer is considered to be sexy and sophisticated by the French. But we did have some problems with the earlier shows because after the first three or four, it was a rush to get the right clothes. This time, more thought had gone into it. The French certainly have a way with women's fashions, so there will be a French selection when the series comes back.'

Patrick Macnee agreed that more sex and violence could signal the death of the show. 'Ours is a surrealistic Grimm's fairy tale sort of terror,' he said. 'If we start pumping bullets into people's stomachs, we're done for. And it's a joke that the French should ask for more violence when the Americans are so interested in buying the show. They've got the biggest no-no against violence – viewers are even striking against *Starsky and Hutch*.' (As things turned out, Macnee was proved correct. When the show eventually reached America – long after it had stopped production, CBS saw it as far too violent and screened it at 11.30 p.m.)

Changes were made, however, and as promised, about half of Joanna's new wardrobe for the 'second season' was of French origin. The rest, however, was chosen by Joanna herself. She visited the premises of Betty Jackson, at Quorum, and selected a string of beautiful dresses and skirts, including an assortment of mini-skirts, that she wore on and off the screen.

Purdey's hairstyle was changed, too. Gone was the smooth-as-glass mushroom bob. In its place was a shaggy but controlled hairstyle. John Frieda was the man responsible for both the original bob and the new cut.

Other changes were made, to give the second 13 stories their fair share of sexy moments. Purdey's role was made sexier. In one episode, *Obsession*, she met and fell in love with an old flame (who turned out to be a bad lot). We even got to see her in bed!

Purdey as she might have been, had the French backers got their way with her fashion designs.

Gambit's character was broadened and developed. He was given a succession of dolly-birds and other female admirers.

Even the formerly untouchable John Steed was revealed as a man with a past – and a romantic interest!

Clemens told me, 'It becomes clear that Purdey is carrying on with somebody. And Purdey's guardian angel – Mike Gambit – will receive more attention. We're strengthening his character, and giving him a collection of girls all to himself. He still fancies Purdey, of course. And she isn't exactly averse to him either! But as they work together – face death together – if they slipped beneath the sheets, might that not take the fine edge off their relationship? And as Purdey has pointed out, they just don't have the time. Mind you . . . one day! And Steed and Purdey are something again. After all, Steed is a handsome, virile, *experienced* man – and Purdey can't help but know that. Especially the "experience". That intrigues her. And Steed, undeniably, finds her very attractive. So give them the right set of circumstances and something *could* happen. Although those circumstances haven't arisen yet, it's always there.'

However, the modern-day knight in shining armour, who wore a bowler for a visor and carried an umbrella for a lance, Patrick Macnee, was unsure about Steed's new, romantic, role. 'When you're in your fifties, however good you look or feel, you've got to act your age,' he said. 'You're not really supposed to start leaping into bed with young ladies on the television screen. It would look ludicrous.' In fact, he wasn't too happy with Steed's new role at all. As he told me, 'I believed that I still had something more to contribute to the part. In fact, it wasn't until the second 13 stories that my voice was heard and I became more in keeping with the original Steed. I confess that I didn't like being "retired" to Steed's Stud – nice house and all that, but rather boring.' Clemens placated him and promised Steed's women would be of the more mature variety and Steed's character took on more of his old style.

THE EAGLE'S NEST

by Brian Clemens

John Steed	Patrick Macnee
Mike Gambit	Gareth Hunt
Purdey	Joanna Lumley
Von Claus	Peter Cushing
Father Trasker	Derek Farr
Karl	Frank Gatliff
Hara	Sydney Bromley
Brown-Fitch	Trevor Baxter
Lady with dog	Joyce Carey
Main	Neil Phillips
Stannard	Brian Anthony
Barker	Jerold Wells
Gerda	Trude van Dorne
Nazi Corporal	Peter Porteous
Ralph	Jerold Wells

Directed by Desmond Davis

PURSUED BY fishermen who use rod and line like whips – their hooks dipped in deadly poison – agent Stannard falls to his death, and when his body is later washed ashore, The New Avengers spring into action. Purdey and Steed follow Stannard's trail, while Gambit is delegated to stand in for the dead agent at a lecture being given by Von Claus, an eminent specialist in suspended animation. When Von Claus is abducted, Gambit is forced to fight and win against a young tough named Ralph. Before he can question his prisoner, the youth swallows a suicide capsule and Gambit is left holding one clue – a toupée that covered Ralph's tonsure. Claus meanwhile is taken to the lonely island of St Dorca, a retreat for monks (in reality Nazis intent on forming a new Third Reich). There, he is asked to attend one of the 'brothers' by Father Trasker, their benevolent leader. The treatment proves successful, and Von Claus retires for the evening. As he does so, Brother Karl enters the patient's room and switches off the man's life support system.

Gambit uncovers a link to the island – a plane that crashed there during its flight in 1945 carrying 'Germany's greatest treasure' onboard. Purdey discovers the wreckage, and she and Steed infiltrate the island. They are soon discovered and locked in cells below the monastery. Claus is now informed by Karl that his patient has suffered a relapse and they hurry to the man's side. However, becoming suspicious that the body isn't the same one he attended previously, Claus orders Karl to raise the sheet covering the patient's face. His suspicions are confirmed when the features of Adolf Hitler are revealed and Claus immediately protests his abhorrence at further treatment. However, when Karl informs him that his family are under arrest and will be killed unless he continues to attend the comatose figure, Claus sees no avenue of escape and prepares to administer the final life-giving injection into the Führer's body. Enter Purdey and Steed who, having engineered their escape, are in turn held at gunpoint by Father Trasker.

At that moment, Gambit breaks into the room and shoots Trasker. As he does so, the man's finger tightens on the machine-gun's trigger and the room is sprayed with stray bullets. Several enter the comatose body, effectively putting an end to Trasker's plans of a new Reich. Exit The New Avengers to the tune of 'The Colonel Bogey March'.

Gambit, Purdey and Steed exchange ideas and theories before following a trail that will lead them to the murderous Nazis who occupy The Eagle's Nest.

THE MIDAS TOUCH

by Brian Clemens

John Steed	Patrick Macnee
Mike Gambit	Gareth Hunt
Purdey	Joanna Lumley
Freddy	John Carson
Vann	Ed Devereaux
Hong Kong Harry	Ronald Lacey
Turner	David Swift
Lieutenant	Jeremy Child
Curator	Robert Mill
Garvin	Ray Edwards
Midas	Gilles Millinaire
Sing	Pik-Sen Lim
Doctor	Chris Tranchell
Tayman	Lionel Guyett
Simpson	Geoffrey Bateman

Directed by Robert Fuest

THE NEW AVENGERS are on hand to meet the arrival of 'The Fat Man's' plane. The man turns out to be 'Hong Kong' Harry, an old adversary of Steed's, but he is so fat that Steed fails to recognise him until Harry is downed by a sniper's bullet. Steed and his colleagues are astonished to see a flow of gold dust run from the wound in Harry's ample stomach. Harry's 'belly', they discover, contains over £750,000 worth of gold dust – all neatly packed in small sacks. This discovery leads the trio, together with Freddy, an ex-colleague of Steed's now down on his luck, to the deadly secret of Professor Turner, a man with a lust for gold. Turner, they later discover, has rendered Midas – an Adonis of a young man with a smooth and blandly youthful face – a carrier of every disease known to man. Although Midas himself remains immune, his merest touch on the naked skin spells death to any living thing. Harry's gold dust was meant as part-payment to be given to Turner at an auction of Midas' powers. The auction goes ahead as planned and, to demonstrate Midas' killing power, Turner orders the youth to wipe out the entire assemblage of guests. Vann, a foreign diplomat with demagogic ideas, is so impressed at the demonstration that he agrees to exchange a valuable collection of gold antiquities for Midas. The killer will then assassinate a visiting foreign princess, simply by being presented to her at the gold exhibition.

Steed gets a call from Freddy, but before they can meet, his colleague commits suicide after being touched by Midas during an escape attempt. Purdey, acting on her own, discovers a lead to the plot from a commando officer who used to work with Turner. She infiltrates Turner's office, but is overpowered by a guard and taken prisoner . . . and promised to Midas upon completion of his mission. Steed and Gambit find a lead to Purdey's abductors when Gambit breaks into a foreign embassy and proves his worth by beating the embassy guard in a karate match. They arrive at the gold exhibition at the very second that Midas is due to be presented to the princess and quickly proceed to mop up Vann and his cohorts while Purdey, heedful of her colleague's warning cry, 'Don't let him touch you', sets about Midas. A well-timed kick sends the death merchant reeling backwards into an empty mummy case and Gambit races over and slams the lid. The trio then turn their attention to Turner, who was accidentally touched by Midas during the fight and now writhes in plague-ridden agony.

HOUSE OF CARDS

by Brian Clemens

John Steed	**Patrick Macnee**
Mike Gambit	**Gareth Hunt**
Purdey	**Joanna Lumley**
Perov	**Peter Jeffrey**
Roland	**Frank Thornton**
Cartney	**Lyndon Brook**
The Bishop	**Derek Francis**
Spence	**Mark Burns**
Jo	**Geraldine Moffatt**
Suzy	**Annette Andre**
Olga	**Ina Skriver**
David	**Murray Brown**
Vasil	**Gordon Sterne**
Boris	**Dan Meaden**
Tulliver	**Jeremy Wilkin**
Frederick	**Anthony Bailey**

Directed by Ray Austin

A RUSSIAN DEFECTOR, Professor Vasil, is about to be returned to his homeland at gunpoint by fellow countryman and master-spy Perov. There is a sudden burst of confusion when a group of screaming pop fans, led by Purdey, stampede through the airport lounge in pursuit of their idol – Mike Gambit, masquerading as a pop star. During this confusion, Vasil is led to safety by John Steed. Because of this fiasco, Vasil is ordered home to face the Commissariat. Instead he feigns his death, and after his 'funeral' goes into hiding and sets operation House of Cards into action. The House of Cards is a code system designed by Perov in which Russian 'sleepers', infiltrated into the country during the last twenty years, are sent half-playing cards on receipt of which they become mindless killers, each with a designated target. The King of Hearts is the code to kill Steed; Gambit's name is on the Knave; and Purdey is in line to become the assassinated Queen.

Soon afterwards, close 'friends' of the trio begin to act strangely; Gambit is faced with a fight for his life during a 'friendly' karate session; Purdey saves Steed's life at the hands of his girlfriend; and further assassination attempts are thwarted. Their success, however, is not Perov's ultimate aim – this is to get Steed worried enough for Vasil's safety to race for his secret location and unwittingly lead Perov to the man responsible for his disgrace. Unaware that his car is being shadowed by Perov in a helicopter, Steed does just that and as he is preparing to move Vasil to a new safehouse the men find themselves under fire from Perov. Perov then threatens to kill both men by tossing a grenade into the cottage unless Steed sends out Vasil alone. Steed takes a desperate gamble and, wearing Vasil's clothes, steps through the doorway. He is immediately downed by a shot from Perov's pistol.

Enter Purdey by road and Gambit by air, piloting the Russian's vacated helicopter. Several low-flying swoops send Perov racing into Purdey's waiting arms but, anticipating an easy fight against a woman, the Russian viciously knocks Purdey to the ground. In total disbelief, she springs to her feet and sends Perov sprawling backwards with a right uppercut to the jaw, and as Gambit races to her side the girl exclaims indignantly: 'He *hit* me!'

Steed hears the last words of his friend David Miller, victim of Perov, foreign agent with a death list of names. A scene from House of Cards.

THE LAST OF THE CYBERNAUTS...?

by Brian Clemens

John Steed	**Patrick Macnee**
Mike Gambit	**Gareth Hunt**
Purdey	**Joanna Lumley**
Kane	**Robert Lang**
Malov	**Oscar Quitak**
Dr Marlow	**Gwen Taylor**
Professor Mason	**Basil Hopkins**
Goff	**Robert Gillespie**
Fitzroy	**David Horovitch**
Laura	**Sally Bazely**
Mrs Weir	**Pearl Hackney**
Second guard	**Martin Fisk**
Terry	**Eric Carte**
First guard	**Ray Armstrong**
Cybernaut	**Rocky Taylor**
Tricia	**Davina Taylor**

Directed by Sidney Hayers

JOHN STEED and Emma Peel had met them before – the Cybernauts. It was over ten years ago and they had nearly died. Steed had forgotten the incident, but when a man named Frank Goff – a man who helped Professor Armstrong construct the deadly robots many years ago – walks free from prison, Steed is once again embroiled in the unfinished business of The Cybernauts.

Months ago, The New Avengers were on the trail of double agent Felix Kane when, during a frantic car

Purdey has an unwelcome guest in the half-man cybernaut shape of Kane, in The Last of the Cybernauts?

chase, Kane's car had collided with a petrol tanker and burst into flames. Steed and his colleagues believed the man had died in the inferno, but Kane's will to survive was as massive and intense as the flames from which he was dragged. Now, confined to a wheelchair, with his horribly scarred face hidden behind masks, the evil, bland, smiling Kane is determined to accomplish his sole vendetta – the extinction of the New Avengers. Accompanied by Malov, his faithful retainer, Kane abducts Goff and he is forced at gunpoint to reactivate the Cybernauts that are found hidden in a cellar. One of the robots is then sent on a mission of death and destruction until it finally meets its own end at the hands of Gambit and Purdey.

Undaunted, Kane sends a second Cybernaut to abduct Professor Mason, a leading cybernetics expert. Mason is then forced to formulate a system of cybernetic limbs whereby Kane – his brain linked by electronic pulses to the Cybernaut's power – becomes half-man, half machine. Armed with his newly-found killing power and his burning hatred for the New Avengers, Kane then sets out to dispose of his immediate target – Purdey – his intention being to mutilate her body to such a degree that it will cause Steed mental anguish until he, too, meets death at Kane's powerful hands. Gambit, waiting for his colleague outside her flat, is unable to prevent Kane's advance and finds himself hurtled to the ground by a single blow from Kane's fist. Kane now turns his attention to Purdey's door and within seconds the door is smashed apart. Purdey is now faced with the fight of her life, and the two are soon embroiled in deadly combat. Enter Steed who, handing Gambit an aerosol spray, races to Purdey's defence. The can's contents are sprayed on to Kane's body and soon his flailing arms shudder to a halt until, finally, the monstrous figure becomes immobile. Kane's eyes burn with intense anger as he is shown the can's label, 'PLASTIC SKIN – good for 1,001 uses', and Steed utters the words: 'A thousand and *two*.'

TO CATCH A RAT

by Terence Feeley

John Steed	**Patrick Macnee**
Mike Gambit	**Gareth Hunt**
Purdey	**Joanna Lumley**
Gunner	**Ian Hendry**
Cromwell	**Edward Judd**
Quaintance	**Robert Fleming**
Cledge	**Barry Jackson**
Grant	**Anthony Sharp**
Finder	**Jeremy Hawk**
Operator	**Bernice Stegers**
Nurse	**Jo Kendall**
Farmer	**Dallas Cavell**
Mother	**Sally-Jane Spencer**

Directed by James Hill

SEVENTEEN YEARS ago, Irwin Gunner, an agent operating in the Eastern sector, came within an ace of exposing the identity of 'The White Rat' – a double agent who had betrayed his colleagues. But all Gunner had managed to do was to fire a bullet into his quarry's leg before the traitor got away, unidentified. Gunner's cover had been that of a trapeze artist. He was the 'flyer' and his partner Cledge, also an agent, the 'catcher'. Cledge, however, was in the White Rat's pay, and during a big top performance he had failed to catch his 'flyer' and Gunner fell to the sawdust below. For seventeen years he had lived with a loss of memory. Now, as the result of a knock on the head during a children's game, Gunner's memory is unfrozen and he immediately begins to transmit a message, 'The flyer has landed', to Steed's department – a message that, though transmitted in obsolete code, is urgent enough to have Steed send Gambit and Purdey racing across the countryside to locate its source. Unknown to Steed, the message had also been overheard by Cledge and the traitor who, reasoning that it can only be Gunner, decide he must die before exposing their secret. Cledge discovers their quarry, but Gunner kills him before transmitting a further message that he will 'cut off the Rat's tail'.

Later, when Purdey breaks into Cledge's flat, she discovers Cromwell, head of department DIC, rifling through Cledge's belongings. The man gets amorous, and Purdey is forced to cool his ardour by offering to repair his torn trouser leg. Meanwhile, Steed and Gambit decide to lay a trap for the traitor. They suspect Quaintance, a ministry official who walks with a pronounced limp, but when questioned, the man reveals that he received the injury while 'going over the wall'. Pressed further, he reveals that his replacement in the Eastern sector had been shot in the leg – by whom or why was never made clear. The replacement's name, they discover, is Cromwell. Purdey, meanwhile, is avoiding further advances from Cromwell who, having expressed interest in her colleague's plan to net the traitor, receives a phone call from Gunner and the couple race to his location. Fortunately, Gunner becomes impatient at their late arrival and rings a second time. The call is taken by Gambit and he and Steed race after their colleague. They arrive too late, and enter as Gunner, dying from Cromwell's gunshot wound, recovers consciousness long enough to complete his mission with a shot to Cromwell's heart – a shot that was fired seventeen years late.

CAT AMONGST THE PIGEONS

by Dennis Spooner

John Steed	**Patrick Macnee**
Mike Gambit	**Gareth Hunt**
Purdey	**Joanna Lumley**
Zarcardi	**Vladek Sheybal**
Turner	**Matthew Long**
Rydercroft	**Basil Dignam**
Waterlow	**Peter Copley**
Lewington	**Hugh Walters**
Bridlington	**Gordon Rollings**
Hudson	**Joe Black**
Foster	**Patrick Connor**
Tomkins	**Kevin Stoney**
Merton	**Andrew Bradford**
Controller	**Brian Jackson**

Directed by John Hough

AFTER TELLING Steed that Rydercroft, Controller of the Ministry of Ecology, is due to die at noon that day, Merton's body is found in coma and from the wreckage of his crashed car Purdey plucks a feather. Steed and his colleagues are in attendance as the plane due to take Rydercroft to Switzerland is about to depart. At 11.55 all is well . . . 11.56 and the plane is airborne . . . 11.58 . . . 11.59 . . . all is well aloft – visibility 100%, not another thing in the sky. But at noon the plane disappears off the radar screen. Among the fragmented pieces of the plane found scattered across the countryside is a small ring used for 'ringing' birds. On it are printed the words Sanctuary of Wings. Feathers by the hundred are also found, leading Gambit and Purdey to suspect that the plane was hit by a flock of wild birds. They discover that the bird sanctuary is run by a strange little man named Zarcardi, a man who, because of his unpopular ideas concerning bird conservation, has been ostracised by his fellow ecologists – the majority of whom now appear to be falling victim to bird attacks.

While Steed and Gambit visit Professor Waterlow, a man mentioned by the dying Merton, Purdey dons her motorcycle gear and speeds off to the bird sanctuary. Steed and the Professor are soon forced to seek refuge in a swimming pool when they are attacked by hundreds of screeching birds. Later, on leaving the Professor's home, Steed has to ward off a second attempt when a large bird, planted earlier by Zarcardi, tries to attack him during his drive home. The agent seeks refuge in the back of an open removal truck where, under cover of darkness, he traps the bird beneath his bowler. Purdey meanwhile enters a huge room filled with exotic plants and hundreds of species of birds. As she does so, a small bird alights on her hand and begins to chirp merrily away until Zarcardi, who has arrived back at the sanctuary and been 'informed' of Purdey's presence, proceeds to play a strange, flute-like instrument. The sound of it has an astonishing effect on the small bird, which immediately draws blood. Purdey now finds herself in a locked room, surrounded by hundreds of screeching feathered assassins.

Enter Steed and Gambit who, armed with baskets of the 'enemy' (cats), proceed to pluck the birds' feathers. During his attempted escape, Zarcardi falls to his death, for as the two agents exclaim: 'He could sing . . . but he couldn't fly!'

Steed retains his natural air of elegance even after playing Cat Amongst the Pigeons *with feathered assassins in a swimming pool.*

TARGET

by Dennis Spooner

John Steed	Patrick Macnee
Mike Gambit	Gareth Hunt
Purdey	Joanna Lumley
Draker	Keith Barron
Ilenko	Robert Beatty
Bradshaw	Roy Boyd
Jones	Frederick Jaeger
Myers	Malcolm Stoddard
Kloekoe	Deep Roy
Kendrick	John Paul
Lopez	Bruce Purchase
Talmadge	Dennis Blanch
Palmer	Robert Tayman

Directed by Ray Austin

WHEN FIVE top agents die of 'natural' causes, Steed, suspecting foul play, asks Dr Kendrick to investigate further. The doctor finds three tiny marks – barely pin-pricks – on the agents' bodies and confirms Steed's suspicions. Someone, it seems, is depleting Steed's department by curare poisoning. Meanwhile, Draker and his midget aide Kloekoe gloat in the shadows. Steed and Gambit recall that all the agents had recently applied for leave and all had taken their practical test – target practice on an intricate shooting range which is in fact a mock-up street, complete with shops and houses and cut-out characters of life-size figures. Each agent has to traverse the target range shooting down 'enemy' figures that suddenly spring up and avoid getting 'hit' himself, in which event a red spot appears on the 'hit' areas of the body. The test is further complicated by 'friendly' figures, and an agent shooting one of these has points deducted from his score. Only one man has ever achieved a 100% score – John Steed, and he did it three times in succession.

Determined to equal her colleague's record, Purdey sets off down the range shooting 'enemy' figures with ease until, on completing the course, she is informed by Bradshaw, the course controller, that she has in fact received one 'hit' and achieved only a 99% score. Disgusted by her performance, Purdey drives home – little knowing that the single 'hit' marks her for death. The course has been sabotaged by Draker and Kloekoe who, in cahoots with Bradshaw, are determined to prove to Ilenko, a compatriot, that they can decimate Steed's department personnel at will. Draker has loaded the 'enemy' figure's guns with tiny ampoules of glass dipped into a curare derivative, and once an agent is 'hit' the poison is released, bringing death within hours.

Draker's plans go awry, however, when Gambit plays a joke on Bradshaw – a joke that misfires and sends a spot-ridden Bradshaw reeling into Gambit's arms. Before dying, he whispers the words: 'Hat . . . Steed's hat . . . antidote', words that confirm Gambit's suspicions and send him and Steed racing to Purdey's side. Matters

worsen further when Steed himself falls victim to the drug – injected by Kloekoe during their visit to Purdey's flat – and it is left to Gambit to run the gauntlet of Draker's killing machine and Kloekoe's deadly blowpipe before recovering the antidote and saving his colleagues.

Agent Myers and remote controlled 'killer' Purdey in Target.

In Target, *Purdey takes to the rooftops to escape the deadly pistol fire of automated crackshots.*

FACES

by Brian Clemens and Dennis Spooner

John Steed	**Patrick Macnee**
Mike Gambit	**Gareth Hunt**
Purdey	**Joanna Lumley**
Prator	**David De Keyser**
Mullins	**Edward Petherbridge**
Clifford	**Neil Hallett**
Wendy	**Annabel Leventon**
Bilston	**David Webb**
Sheila	**Jill Melford**
Craig	**Richard Leech**
Torrance	**Donald Hewlett**
Attendant	**Robert Putt**
Tramp	**J G Devlin**
Peters	**Michael Sheard**

Directed by James Hill

It now becomes a case of who can Purdey trust? Is it *really* 'Purdey'. Is Steed really *Steed?* Which Gambit *is* Gambit? Matters are soon resolved when Steed exposes Craig, and Gambit, suspected by Purdey of being a double, saves face by throwing a well-timed punch to Craig's jaw as he holds Steed at gunpoint . . . proving beyond doubt that, though 'two-faced', there is only *one* Mike Gambit!

Opposite: *Purdy fights for her life at Base 47 – launching into a flurry of haymakers with pirouetting legs, flailing arms and fists to discover who is behind the Faces organisation. .*

Below: *The chase is on to find the man who has secrets which could shake the government to its foundations. Steed smashes a window to discover the mystery of* The Tale of the Big Y.

SPOTTING THE similarity between himself and Home Office official Craig, Terrison, a drifter, and his cohort Mullins kill the man and Terrison replaces him. They join forces with Dr Prator, a brilliant plastic surgeon, and begin to recruit down-and-outs from the Mission for the Distressed and Needy and use them to replace high-ranking government officials. The down-and-outs' faces must be similar to someone in the government and they are then brainwashed and sent to replace the victims. Craig's plans, however are soon threatened with exposure when their latest 'double' – a lookalike for Mark Clifford, a close friend of Steed's – dies within days of replacing the man, an event that brings Steed into the picture. Convinced that the Mission holds a clue, Steed delegates Mike Gambit to pose as an unkempt alcoholic and infiltrate the place. Gambit does so, and is soon spotted as an ideal replacement for 'Gambit'. Purdey, acting independently, visits the Mission disguised as a prim Salvation Army official and, finding a link with Craig, she returns masquerading as 'Lolita', a cheap and dowdy tart. Craig meanwhile orders Prator to find a 'double' for John Steed – an opportunity that swiftly arrives when a Steed 'lookalike' is found in a drunken stupor.

Informed by 'Lolita' that she is wanted by the police, Prator, aware that 'with some work' the girl could pass for Purdey, agrees to help her and she is taken to meet 'Mike Gambit'. Gambit, however, fails to recognise his colleague and, believing that Prator has discovered a replacement for Purdey, telephones Steed and tells him that Purdey's life may be in danger. Craig now orders Prator to advance the 'treatment' on their Steed 'lookalike', and later, satisfied that the 'double' is ready, he drives the man to Steed's country home, hands him a gun and orders him to dispose of Steed. A shot through an open window achieves that end, and the men drive away smiling.

TALE OF THE BIG Y

by Brian Clemens

John Steed	**Patrick Macnee**
Mike Gambit	**Gareth Hunt**
Purdey	**Joanna Lumley**
Harmer	**Derek Waring**
Irene	**Jenny Runacre**
Brandon	**George Cooper**
Turner	**Roy Marsden**
Roach	**Gary Waldhorn**
Poole	**Rowland Davis**
Minister	**Geoffrey Toone**
Mrs Turner	**Maeve Alexander**

Directed by Robert Fuest

BERT BRANDON had been trying to do a deal with the government for years. His information, he told them, would rock Whitehall to its foundations but they wouldn't bite and now, as Brandon leaves prison, he is determined to recover the document he had hidden and sell it to the highest bidder. The day he walks through the prison gates, four people are waiting: Poole and Roach – two foreign 'heavies' – Purdey and Gambit. Within hours, Brandon dies – hurled backwards into the rear seat of his car by the shots from Poole and Roach's automatics. The ensuing chase ends with Purdey being thrown headlong from her motorcycle into a rock a few feet away from the remains of Brandon's car – demolished by the two hoodlums during their unsuccessful search for Brandon's secret. Gambit races to Purdey's rescue and they remove Brandon's boots from the wreckage – boots that when X-rayed show traces of Diolyhyde, a chemical used in crop spraying. The clue leads them to Turner, a friend of Brandon's who supplements his earning by crop-dusting. Turner, however, soon finds himself on the run and chased by Poole and Roach, who are in turn pursued by Purdey and Gambit as they race to Turner's rescue. After the chase, Purdey is told by Turner's wife that Brandon visitced the farm and left a package to be posted to his daughter, Irene. Steed visits the girl and she willingly hands him the package, but to his surprise it contains only a western paperback called, *The Tale of the Big* Y. The book obviously holds a clue – but to what?

After much deliberation, the trio crack the code and realise that the 'tale' is in fact the 'tail' of the letter Y in Surrey, as denoted on an aviator's map of the county. However, their efforts to locate Brandon's secret are thwarted by Irene Brandon who, in cahoots with Turner, has reached the same conclusion. The trio stay one jump ahead, and are soon involved in a cross-country chase that eventually leads to Purdey being abducted by Poole and Roach who, having demanded the document in exchange for the girl, meet with a 'laughter-filled' end; Gambit playing a 'dangerous game' with Turner's plane; and Steed playing a deadly game of chess with Home Office official, Harmer, before exposing him as the traitor named in Brandon's document.

THE THREE-HANDED GAME

by Dennis Spooner and Brian Clemens

John Steed	**Patrick Macnee**
Mike Gambit	**Gareth Hunt**
Purdey	**Joanna Lumley**
Ranson	**David Wood**
Juventor	**David Greif**
Ivan	**Tony Vogel**
Larry	**Michael Petrovitch**
Professor Meroff	**Terry Wood**
Masgard	**Gary Raymond**
Tony Fields	**Noel Trevarthen**

Directed by Ray Austin

MASTER SPY Juventor and his aide Ivan have stolen a sophisticated apparatus that transfers the thoughts and physical skills from one person to another by 'scrambling' their brain – leaving the donors' bodies mindless vegetables. Their first victim is 'Taps' Ranson, a professional dancer, and Juventor then arranges a demonstration of the machine for Colonel Meroff, a foreign ambassador, in which Ranson's psyche is transferred into Meroff's body. Flushed with the machine's possibilities, Meroff offers Juventor ten million pounds to obtain details of 'The Three-Handed Game' – a top secret 4,000-word document which, designed by Steed, has been 'entrusted' to three agents, Masgard, McKay and Fields, each of whom has a photographic memory and, like a computer, can 'bank' endless information until called on to reveal it at a later date. Each agent has received one-third of the code – parts which, without the others, are useless.

Steed gets an idea of Juventor's plans from Larry, one of his field agents who, though succumbing to Juventor's machine, manages to reach Steed before being hospitalised. Juventor, however, is convinced that The New Avengers are on his trail, and permanently transfers his own psyche into Ranson's body before setting off to obtain the secrets from the agents. When 'Juventor's' body is found, Steed is suspicious of the ploy and delegates himself to guard Fields; Gambit is ordered to McKay; and Purdey is given the task of protecting Masgard. Masgard, a professional memory-man, is the first to receive the 'treatment' and his brain is scrambled after an evening performance, while Purdey 'clowns' about in the next room. Steed, too, is unable to prevent racing-driver Fields from imparting his third of the code, and Steed immediately doubles the guard on McKay, a young female artist. However, even the combined forces of Purdey and Gambit prove insufficient to halt Juventor's plans, and McKay's secret is soon added to Juventor's shopping list. In receipt of the complete code, the spy now rings Meroff and demands payment.

Juventor has, of course, reckoned without the combined forces of all three Avengers and, in a deserted theatre setting, he has to face a merry dance from Purdey's shapely legs and feet before she rings down the curtain on his plans.

Mike Gambit smashes renegade agent into submission whilst uncovering the secret of The Three-Handed Game.

SLEEPER

by Brian Clemens

John Steed	Patrick Macnee
Mike Gambit	Gareth Hunt
Purdey	Joanna Lumley
Brady	Keith Buckley
Tina	Sara Kestelman
Chuck	Mark Jones
Bart	Prentis Hancock
Bill	Leo Dolan
Ben	Dave Schofield
Fred	Gavin Campbell
Carter	Peter Godfrey
Hardy	Joe Dunne
Policemen {	Jason White
	Rony McHale
Dr Graham	Arthur Dignam

Directed by Graeme Clifford

THE NEW AVENGERS are told by Hardy, one of Steed's field agents, that something 'big' is about to happen connected with S.95, a new anti-terrorist weapon – a colourless, odourless gas which can put a man to sleep for a minimum of six hours unless he has been injected with the antidote – so they attend a demonstration of the gas. However, all seems to run smoothly and they leave. As they depart, Brady – previously disguised as Professor Marco, the inventor of S.95 – overpowers a guard and steals several canisters of the gas together with a supply of antidote capsules. Steed, spending the night at Gambit's apartment, is concerned when he unsuccessfully tries to renew contact with Hardy. His worries increase further when, during the early hours of the following morning, his colleague's 'pet' sparrow Charlie is found fast asleep on Gambit's window ledge. Suspecting a link with Hardy's message, Steed telephones Purdey and asks her to check the area outside her flat. Meanwhile, a helicopter flies low over the city releasing vast quantities of S.95 over a designated area and in the streets below, unhindered by the sleeping populace, Brady and his gang begin their joyride – looting major banking houses as they tour the deserted streets.

Purdey finds the neighbourhood full of sleeping figures and, returning to her flat, tries to relay her findings to her colleagues. Her attempt to do so is hampered by finding her flat door securely closed, and further contact is made impossible when Brady's men sever the telephone wires to the area. Now alone and dressed only in her slippers and pyjama suit, Purdey decides to drive to Gambit's apartment. Her colleagues reach a similar decision, and unwittingly pass her on her drive across town.

The scenario is now set for a cross-city chase between the trio and Brady's gang of cut-throats. A chase that is fraught with danger for the agents who, unarmed, are forced to ward off numerous attacks by Brady's armed cohorts. Dropping heavies as she goes, Purdey finally reaches the river. However, though the opposite side beckons safety, she is unable to find a crossing point and she continues her search. Meanwhile, her colleagues have reached 'high ground' (the Post Office Tower) and, spotting the gang's departure point, they soon overpower them. Then, dressed in their captives' clothing they make their way to a waiting helicopter – only to find Purdey asleep at the controls. Within minutes, they too fall fast asleep.

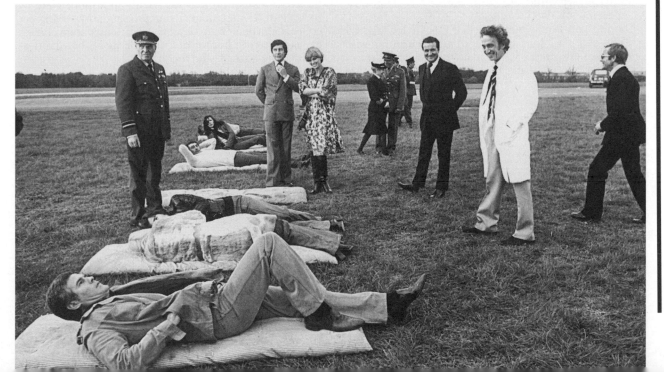

Gambit, Purdey and Steed watch volunteers for a demonstration of the deadly gas S.95 in Sleeper.

GNAWS

by Dennis Spooner

John Steed	**Patrick Macnee**
Mike Gambit	**Gareth Hunt**
Purdey	**Joanna Lumley**
Charles Thornton	**Julian Holloway**
Walters	**Morgan Shepherd**
Carter	**Peter Cellier**
Harlow	**John Watts**
Girl	**Anulka Dubinska**
Motor Mechanic	**Ronnie Laughlin**
Ivan Chislenko	**Jeremy Young**
George Ratcliffe	**Patrick Malahide**
Joe	**Keith Marsh**
Arthur	**Ken Wynne**
Malloy	**Keith Alexander**
Couple in car {	**Denise Reynolds** **Peter Richardson**

Directed by Ray Austin

TWELVE MONTHS earlier Steed and his colleagues had investigated the death of Marlow, an agent who had been on surveillance security duty at the Ministry of Agriculture. At the time there had been little evidence to link the agent's death to a clumsy robbery of secret papers connected with research into the growth of living things through radioactivity. Marlow's death, it appeared, had been coincidence. However, Thornton and his assistant Carter had been responsible for both crimes. Thornton had left six weeks later, but Carter stayed on and together they had entered into business alone. Unhampered by red tape, they had cut corners and taken risks to grow things to enormous proportions. Their experiments were meant to help mankind, but things started to go awry when Carter carelessly spilt some radioactive isotope and washed it down the sink. Since that day, reports of 'something nasty in the sewers' had started circulating, and when a gang of maintenance men disappear while checking the sewers The New Avengers are asked to investigate.

Gambit and Purdey discover that rats are few and far between in a place that would normally be teeming with them. They also meet Chislenko, their opposite number, and for once East and West unite against a common foe – whatever is down there, they decide, has grown ravenous and has started to hunt human prey. Meanwhile, alarmed that their mistake will lead to their exposure, Thornton and Carter arm themselves and enter the sewers to destroy their 'creation'. Carter soon falls victim to the unseen 'monster' and his colleague retreats to safety – only to find himself confronted by Chislenko who, believing the man to be responsible for the killings, tries to arrest him. The Russian is shot, and Thornton escapes.

Purdey searches the Ministry records and finds a connection with the previous break-in – a giant tomato! Her two colleagues meanwhile concoct a foul-smelling mixture that they hope will bring the 'monster' into the open, and enter the sewers. Hearing Thornton's shot, Purdey races to the scene and quickly finds herself held at gunpoint by the scientist and in danger of being used as 'live' bait. Racing to her rescue, Gambit puts paid to the beast – an enormous rat – with an armour-piercing rocket gun. Purdey shows her appreciation by serving her colleagues a giant tomato salad – a dish they soon confess is guaranteed to last for not just one meal, but the next . . . and the next . . . and the next . . .

DIRTIER BY THE DOZEN

by Brian Clemens

John Steed	**Patrick Macnee**
Mike Gambit	**Gareth Hunt**
Purdey	**Joanna Lumley**
Colonel Miller	**John Castle**
Sergeant Bowden	**Shaun Curry**
Travis	**Colin Skeaping**
General Stevens	**Michael Barrington**
Captain Tony Noble	**Michael Howarth**
Terry	**Brian Croucher**

Directed by Sidney Hayers

GENERAL STEVENS, arriving at Colonel 'Mad Jack' Miller's special 19th Commando Unit for a 'spot check', finds the place deserted but is later killed when Miller and his unit arrive back from a mysterious jungle campaign. The General's disappearance brings Steed, Gambit and Purdey into action. Gambit receives two reels of film in the post – films that contain scenes of jungle fighting in various parts of the world and, after several viewings, Purdey and Gambit find a common link between the newsreels. Colonel Miller had been filmed everywhere from the war-torn Middle East to the jungles of Latin America; the question is, how could Miller have been fighting in so many wars – especially when he is a serving British officer?

Miller's army record shows that his unit is made up from the dregs of army personnel – the rogues and malingerers – from which such unpromising material Miller has forged a formidable fighting unit. Steed suspects the unit is being hired out as mercenaries – Miller's own private army, in fact. Further investigations are called for, so Steed delegates Gambit to join the unit. Purdey visits Miller's base alone and, after questioning

his men, is arrested by Miller and accused of being a spy. Gambit, posing as a Major, arrives at the base and meets with more success when Miller tells him that his army record – allegations about missing army funds; appropriation of army property, etc – points to Gambit being either a fool or extremely cunning. His record is in fact despicable . . . and the best recommendation he could have to join the 19th Commando!

Steed, having checked on the equipment purchased by Miller for his next campaign, discovers that everything points to the Middle East – a place where banks are loaded with money and the mosques laden with gold. He is further concerned that Miller intends to leave the missing General's body on the spot, thus implicating the British Army and instigating the possibility of World War 3. The question now is, can Miller be stopped in time? Before that question can be answered, Gambit engineers Purdey's escape – only to find he has landed her into a minefield from which Steed is forced to extricate both his colleagues and the solution. Miller chooses a 'military' death, and Purdey is given an 'in flight' glass of champagne – courtesy of John Steed.

HOSTAGE

by Brian Clemens

John Steed	Patrick Macnee
Mike Gambit	Gareth Hunt
Purdey	Joanna Lumley
McKay	William Franklyn
Spelman	Simon Oates
Walters	Michael Culver
Suzy	Anna Palk
Packer	Barry Stanton
Vernon	Richard Ireson
Marvin	George Lane-Cooper

Directed by Sidney Hayers

STEED HAS planned an intimate dinner for two. His attractive guest arrives and he prepares the claret for the table. The telephone rings, and a voice informs him that Purdey is being held prisoner – to prove the point, her car is now parked in Steed's garage. He is told to play along or Purdey will die. Furthermore no one must know – least of all Mike Gambit. Racing to his colleague's flat, Steed finds the place deserted and is about to leave when a phone call orders him to take £5,000 to a specified rendezvous. He follows instructions and returns home to await further orders. A lock of Purdey's hair arrives in the morning post, and after several more calls and rendezvous he realises that they have all been 'dummy' runs. The gang wants something else – but what? The answer is quick to arrive and he is told that unless he steals the secret plans for The Full Allied Attack, Purdey will die. Later that evening, he enters the Ministry and photographs the plans held in McKay's safe.

McKay's interest is aroused when he is shown film of Steed making a money drop to the 'other side's' post office. Aware that his colleague often plays his own game, he lets the matter drop without further action. Later, however, when he finds an envelope containing £5,000 in Steed's mail he decides to have Steed followed. Steed gives his 'shadow' the slip and returns home to await the gang's next order. The gang send a man dressed as Steed to kill one of McKay's agents and when his body is discovered with Steed's gun by his side, McKay orders Gambit to bring Steed in for questioning.

Gambit's confrontation with his superior turns out to be a showdown between the 'Master' (Steed) and the 'Pupil' (Gambit), and the young agent is left gasping on the floor as Steed leaves to take the plans to the gang's location – a disused funfair that serves as home for Spelman, a Ministry official who is the mastermind behind the plot. Steed and Purdey soon find themselves under fire as they try to escape until Gambit, having located the gang's hideaway, arrives in style – racing to the rescue in an empty Ghost Train carriage. The trio soon mow down the opposition and, leaving Gambit to fight the gang's toughest thug, Steed allays Purdey's worries when he explains that 'Gambit is capable of beating *anyone*'. He does so – with style.

TRAP

by Brian Clemens

John Steed	**Patrick Macnee**
Mike Gambit	**Gareth Hunt**
Purdey	**Joanna Lumley**
Soo Choy	**Terry Wood**
Arcarty	**Ferdy Mayne**
Dom Carlos	**Robert Rietty**
Tansing	**Kristopher Kum**
Yasho	**Yasuko Naggazumi**
Marty Brine	**Stuart Damon**
Murford	**Barry Lowe**
Miranda	**Annegret Easterman**
Mahon	**Bruce Boa**
Williams	**Larry Lamb**
Girlfriend	**Maj Britt**

Directed by Ray Austin

ONE OF Steed's field agents, Willie, manages to switch on a tracking device when he is shot while on a mission, and when Purdey and Gambit find him his dying words are: 'Williams . . . drug drop . . . Wednesday . . . Windsor.' The New Avengers, together with Marty Brine, a CIA agent, are waiting when the drugs are delivered. During the resulting chase Brine is shot and the assassin falls to his death – the ten-million-pound packet of drugs lying at his feet. The delivery had been arranged by Soo Choy, a Chinese overlord, as part of his plan to impress the 'Syndicate' and enter the world of the highly profitable drugs trade. Now, however, Choy finds himself labelled 'dumbhead' by his intended partners and, desperate to regain his lost reputation, he plans to take revenge. Using Murford, a Ministry official, he transmits a special 'Red Alert' code to Steed's department – a code that sends Steed and his colleagues racing to a deserted airfield where they board a plane for 'Rendezvous' – a secret base to be used in a terrorist attack. The plane, however, is piloted by one of Choy's minions whom Gambit is forced to kill during the flight. The pilotless plane then crashlands in Choy's territory where, hearing news of the crash, Choy promises to give his syndicate friends the heads of his enemies.

Gambit is the first to recover consciousness and, finding that Steed's arm is broken, he improvises a sling. Then, armed with a home-made bow and arrows, the trio set out to play a deadly game of hide-and-seek with Choy's armed soldiers. After avoiding detection for some time and putting paid to a number of Choy's forces, Gambit is taken prisoner and brought before Choy who promises that his death will be a painful one.

The overlord has, however, reckoned without the resourcefulness of Purdey and Steed, who overpowers the leader of Choy's forces, dons the man's uniform and marches into Choy's headquarters with Purdey as his 'prisoner'. Choy's elation quickly turns to despair when Steed strips off his disguise and trains his rifle at the huge man's chest. Gambit seizes the opportunity to turn the tables on Choy, and as the trio depart with Choy in tow, a playful Purdey laughingly describes their catch as a 'real Chinese take-away'.

Having used his brolly like a spear, Steed rushes the killer while Gambit crouches to fire, in Trap.

DEAD MEN ARE DANGEROUS

by Brian Clemens

John Steed	**Patrick Macnee**
Mike Gambit	**Gareth Hunt**
Purdey	**Joanna Lumley**
Mark	**Clive Revill**
Perry	**Richard Murdoch**
Penny	**Gabrielle Drake**
Hara	**Terry Taplin**
Dr Culver	**Michael Turner**
Sandy	**Trevor Adams**
Headmaster	**Roger Avon**

Directed by Sidney Hayers

AFTER DECIDING to round off their evening with a nightcap Steed and Purdey enter Steed's home to find the place vandalised. The agent's valuable art and porcelain collection lies smashed in the fireplace and later a bomb explodes in Steed's garage – writing off his beloved Bentley. Further events happen in swift succession: a coffin bearing the inscription JOHN STEED – R.I.P. arrives at Steed's home; Gambit finds that Steed's school sporting mementoes have been destroyed; and Steed twice escapes death from a sniper's bullet – or were the shots meant as a warning? Someone, it seems, is intent on destroying all the things Steed cares for, trying to deny his very existence. Finally, Steed's mental anguish is stretched to the breaking point by a message that Purdey has been abducted and will die at 5 am that day.

Gambit discovers a clue to the abductor's identity –

Mark Crayford, an old school chum and ex-colleague of Steed's who, during an East-West border incident ten years previously, had 'crossed over' to the enemy. Steed had been forced to shoot him, and his bullet had lodged dangerously near to Crayford's heart. During the intervening years, the bullet had moved almost an inch, bringing the man close to death, and now Crayford has returned to wreak vengeance on his 'killer'. A clue to the man's whereabouts is also discovered on a tape-recording made during his Ministry medical. It contains references to 'The Victorian Folly' – a deserted bell tower in the country where, as children, Crayford had achieved his one and only victory over Steed. Purdey meanwhile finds herself chained to a wall of the tower and is forced to listen to Crayford's cravings as he rants on about his final victory over Steed, a victory that will be complete with Purdey's death. The hands on the clock read 4.48 and Purdey's fears increase.

Gambit informs Steed of his discovery and the two men race to the bell tower. As Steed enters, he uses his steel-lined bowler to deflect Crayford's shot. Undaunted, Crayford turns to face his nemesis and beams with delight at having his quarry in his gunsight. However, seconds later, when Gambit bursts into the room he is astonished to find his colleague safe, and confused to find Crayford lying dead on the floor. Purdey clears up the mystery when she tells him: 'Steed shot him . . . ten years ago.'

Gambit, assisted by Sandy, works overtime in the file room trying to find out where defector Mark Crayford is hiding, in **Dead Men Are Dangerous**.

MEDIUM RARE

by Dennis Spooner

John Steed	**Patrick Macnee**
Mike Gambit	**Gareth Hunt**
Purdey	**Joanna Lumley**
Wallace	**Jon Finch**
Elderly man	**Mervyn Johns**
Richards	**Jeremy Wilkin**
Victoria Stanton	**Sue Holderness**
Roberts	**Neil Hallett**
McBain	**Maurice O'Connell**
Dowager lady	**Diana Churchill**
Model girl	**Celia Foxe**
Man in seance	**Steve Ubels**
Mason	**Allen Weston**

Directed by Ray Austin

THE NEW AVENGERS are investigating the sudden death of Steed's friend and colleague, Freddy Mason – a man who had been acting as paymaster to a team of informers. Wallace, Mason's boss, had set up the informers' team and then, by a series of clever and elaborate disguises, had used the operation to line his own pockets. Now Wallace, knowing that Steed will dig and keep on digging until he has discovered his friend's killer, hires Richards, a professional killer, first to frame and then eliminate Steed.

Help comes from an unexpected source – Victoria Stanton, a 'fake' medium who suddenly realises her powers when she 'foresees' Steed's death. Gambit and Purdey refuse to take her warnings seriously, however, until she predicts that Steed will receive a communication from overseas; will unexpectedly have to walk to the rendezvous; and will attend a performance of the Royal Ballet – three events that uncannily happen later that day, and lead to Steed being suspected of having killed Cowley, a clerk in the accounts department. Stanton's next prediction warns Steed that he will kill Wigmore, an accountant brought in to investigate the department finances. Steed agrees to meet Wigmore but is clubbed down from behind and when Wigmore's dead body is discovered and the gun in Steed's hand proves to be the murder weapon, Steed is put under house arrest pending further investigation. Wallace and Richards continue to build up the evidence against Steed and arrange to have a large amount of cash deposited in the agent's night safe. Gambit, forewarned by Stanton of the event, is too late to stop the delivery being made and is forced to kill the man when he attempts to escape. Steed meanwhile convinces Purdey of his innocence, and promises that all will be made clear after he has broken into the paymaster's office that evening. He does so but, finding nothing, returns home.

Wallace and Richards decide that the time is ripe to play their trump card and have Steed's own gun left at the scene of Steed's death – his suicide will prove an admission of guilt. However, when Richards attempts to plant the weapon in Steed's home, the agent is waiting for him and places the man in custody. Purdey and Gambit arrest Wallace, who later confesses his guilt. When asked to 'forecast' the length of their prison sentence, Stanton falters before replying: 'How would I know?'

Purdey threatened by hired killer Richards in **Medium Rare.**

ANGELS OF DEATH

by Terence Feely and Brian Clemens

John Steed	Patrick Macnee
Mike Gambit	Gareth Hunt
Purdey	Joanna Lumley
Manderson	Terence Alexander
Tammy	Caroline Munro
Reresby	Michael Latimer
Pelbright	Richard Gale
Jane	Lindsay Duncan
Wendy	Pamela Stephenson
Coldstream	Dinsdale Landen
Sally Manderson	Melissa Stribling
Simon Carter	Anthony Bailey

Directed by Ernest Day

STEED AND PURDEY are on the scene when agent Martin returns to the West by crashing down a lonely border post – only to be gunned down moments later by a sniper's bullet. Before dying, Martin whispers: 'Angel of Death . . . the killer within'. Back home, The New Avengers attend a departmental meeting headed by Pelbright, a man who looks fit and well after a week on a health farm. However, immediately after opening a folder with a strange maze doodled upon it, Pelbright shows signs of stress and within minutes dies – from 'natural' causes. Further investigations reveal that forty-seven other agents had died in similar circumstances within the last two years. All had three things in common: each had held secret Ministry posts; all had died within days of each other; and all had died from 'natural' causes. Steed believes that there is a missing fourth factor – one that must be found soon.

Later that day, Steed and Head of Security, Colonel Tomson, are out clay pigeon shooting and the man tells Steed that he never felt better since returning from a week's course at a health farm. Suddenly, however, Thompson falls over dead. Later, when the post mortem points to death from 'natural' causes, Steed reasons that the missing fourth factor could be connected to the health farm and decides to book in for treatment. Purdey, reaching the same conclusion and acting independently, also pays the health clinic a visit. She is discovered while searching a room and soon finds herself strapped to a huge traction machine. Gambit meanwhile is reading the clinic's prospectus and decides that he, too, should investigate further.

Steed's arrival is greeted with elation by the clinic's staff and he soon finds himself the victim of 'the killer within'. The clinic is being used as a cover for a gigantic brainwashing complex, in which agents under stress are trapped in a maze and, like rats in a trap which smell food but can't get to it, they eventually go mad – or die – in their attempt. Steed is now trapped in the maze and being given the 'treatment'. Meanwhile Coldstream, a Ministry official responsible for the operation, orders his cohorts to interrogate Purdey. Purdey, however, has been rescued by Gambit and while her colleague mops up Coldstream's gang, she attempts to locate Steed. In the process she, too, finds herself trapped between the advancing maze walls and it is left to Gambit to become an 'Angel of Mercy' and rescue his colleagues in the nick of time.

OBSESSION

by Brian Clemens

John Steed	Patrick Macnee
Mike Gambit	Gareth Hunt
Purdey	Joanna Lumley
Larry	Martin Shaw
General Canvey	Mark Kingston
Commander East	Terence Longdon
Kilner	Lewis Collins
Morgan	Anthony Heaton
Wolach	Tommy Boyle
Controller	Roy Purcell

Directed by Ernest Day

WHEN PURDEY is asked to join Steed in a security team protecting an important delegation of visiting Arabs, to his astonishment she turns the assignment down flat. Unknown to her colleague, seven years earlier when Purdey had been a dancer with the Royal Ballet, she had met and fallen in love with Larry Doomer. They had planned to settle down and build a home, but that all changed when Larry's father, a troubleshooter with an oil company, had been killed by Arab soldiers. Larry had sworn revenge and, when his fiancée had been instrumental in preventing his assassination attempt, they had parted. Doomer had now become Squadron-Leader Doomer, the man in charge of the aerial demonstration for the benefit of the visiting delegation – the same crowd who murdered his father.

Steed insists that Purdey join him, and their arrival at the base is met with the news that the armoury store has been broken into. However, nothing appears to have been stolen – all the rockets are intact. As the agents cross to the display area, Purdey bumps into her old flame. The meeting is brief, and the girl gives Doomer the cold shoulder. The delegates watch as the planes swoop low over their targets and the rockets explode as planned – all save the rocket from Doomer's plane, which he later claims exploded in mid-air behind a thick cloud-bank. In fact the rocket now lies half-buried in a sand dune, from which it is hastily retrieved by Doomer's aides, Kilner and Morgan. Doomer, still obsessed with avenging his father's death, intends to fire the rocket at the Houses of Parliament during the Arab delegation's visit.

Doomer now goes missing and, believing that he is using the intended location of the home they planned together as a base, Purdey pleads with Steed to give her five minutes alone with Doomer before they close in. Her colleague refuses her request and Purdey speeds off alone on her motorcycle – having first shot out Steed's vehicle tyres. Doomer is about to launch the rocket from its site in a dug-out as she arrives. Purdey pleads with him to think again but Doomer, playing on their past relationship, defies her to stop him and raises his automatic. A shot from Gambit finally ends their affair, and Doomer falls dead at Purdey's feet. Enter Steed who, leaping to safety, drives his vehicle over the dug-out as the rocket begins its ascent. The resulting explosion showers the agents with debris as Purdey, her face stained with tears, leaves the scene alone.

Steed and Purdey support agent Martin, shot after blurting out information about the Angels of Death.

Purdey, Steed and the Controller in Obsession.

Gambit, temporarily discomfited, will eventually overcome the Unicorn, in The Lion and the Unicorn.

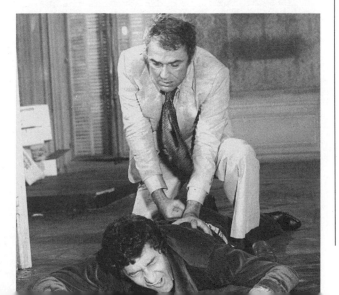

THE LION AND THE UNICORN

by John Goldsmith

John Steed	Patrick Macnee
Mike Gambit	Gareth Hunt
Purdey	Joanna Lumley
Unicorn	Jean Claudio
Leparge	Maurice Marsac
Henri	Raymond Bussieres

Directed by Ray Austin

STEED HAD insisted that the Minister wear a flak jacket. The expected attack takes place, but proves unsuccessful – the Unicorn's attempt on the Minister's life fails. Steed had come up before against the Unicorn – a ruthless, brilliant killer and one of the world's top five agents with a triple D rating – and he desperately wants to take him and his whole operation alive and undamaged. When Steed receives a tip-off that his quarry is heading for France, The New Avengers fly ahead and succeed in holding the man prisoner in his own penthouse apartment. However, suspecting that something is wrong when a prearranged signal fails to materialise, two members of his organisation stake out the building and, seeing Steed in the Unicorn's apartment, send a hail of bullets into the room. The bullets pass through a mirrored wall divider, shattering Steed's reflection and killing the Unicorn. To avoid open warfare, Steed decides to maintain the illusion that the Unicorn is still alive and throws a security ring around the building.

In return, the gang take a hostage of their own – a royal prince, abducted from a hijacked train. It looks like checkmate so Steed decides to play for time and asks the gang for twenty-four-hours in which to work out a swap-over agreement. Suspicious of the delaying tactics, one of the Unicorn's gang climbs down the building and, finding the Unicorn's dead body, races off to inform his colleagues. Gambit gives chase and waylays the man, but when he turns out to be both dumb and illiterate the Minister suggests that they should inform the gang of their leader's death and offer unlimited funds for the safe return of their hostage. Steed disagrees and says the exchange must go ahead as planned.

The gang are told to bring their hostage to the building and Steed informs them that the exchange will be made by having them place their hostage into an empty lift stationed on the ground floor, while he in turn will send down the Unicorn in a second lift. Matters become complicated, however, when Marco, the gang's spokesman, informs Steed that they have strapped an explosive device to the prince's body – a device that will be detonated at the first hint of a double-cross. Needless to say, Steed has 'rigged' the exchange and the prince is rescued unharmed, but not before Gambit and Purdey play a game of bluff and counter-bluff with the gang – a 'game' that ends explosively for the gang when Purdey displays her footballing talents and Steed inadvertently detonates the bomb.

K IS FOR KILL
PART 1: "THE TIGER AWAKES"

by Brian Clemens

John Steed	Patrick Macnee
Mike Gambit	Gareth Hunt
Purdey	Joanna Lumley
Colonel Martin	Pierre Vernier
General Gaspard	Maurice Marsac
Stanislav	Charles Millot
Toy	Paul Emile Deiber
Jeannine Leparge	Christine Delaroche
Kerov	Sacha Pitoeff
Turkov	Maxence Mailfort
Minister	Alberto Simeno
Waiter	Jacques Monnet
Minsky	Frank Oliver
Guard	Guy Mairesse
Secretary	Cyrille Besnard
Soldier	Krishna Clough
Salvation Army Major	Kenneth Watson
Monk	Tony Then
Penrose	Eric Allen

Directed by Yvon Marie Coulais

1965, AND a young Russian soldier bursts into an old Nissen hut, mows down a Salvation Army band and makes his getaway by leaping over a perimeter fence. In the process, he stumbles to the ground and dies – his face has changed to that of an old man! Steed rings Mrs Peel and tells her it is a mystery they may never solve until. . . .

1977 and three workmen drive into a garage workshop in France. Within minutes they have been gunned down by a young Russian officer and the garage destroyed by a grenade. Mrs Peel rings Steed who leaves for France with Purdey and Gambit. The garage owner tells them about the attack and Steed believes it is connected with the incident in 1965 – but how? Suddenly, they are disturbed by a series of distant explosions and together with Colonel Martin, a French policeman examining the incident, they race off to investigate. They arrive to find a château under attack from mortar fire directed by a young Russian officer. Gambit downs the man and when they examine the dead soldier's paybook, they discover that the man is fifty-two years old. Within seconds, the youthful face ages and the dead man's hair turns white.

A second château comes under attack and the events are repeated when a young Russian soldier, captured during the fighting, also ages within seconds of death. His paybook identifies him as being sixty-five years old. The autopsy reveals that each of the bodies had something buried in their brain – something that appears to be a small radio transmitter. Events are complicated further when General Gaspard, an elderly French officer, believes that he recognises one of the dead men as a man he served with before the war – an assumption that Steed disregards as nonsense until a scar on the man's cheek proves otherwise. The dead man received the scar from the Frenchman's sword thirty years earlier. As they prepare to depart, Steed receives a telephone call from Toy, the Russian Ambassador in Paris, and outside a new barrage of mortar fire rains down on the building.

K IS FOR KILL
PART 2: "TIGER BY THE TAIL"

by Brian Clemens

John Steed	Patrick Macnee
Mike Gambit	Gareth Hunt
Purdey	Joanna Lumley
Colonel Martin	Pierre Vernier
General Gaspard	Maurice Marsac
Stanislav	Charles Millot
Toy	Paul Emile Deiber
Jeannine Leparge	Christine Delaroche
Kerov	Sacha Pitoeff
Turkov	Maxence Mailfort
Minister	Alberto Simeno
Waiter	Jacques Monnet
Minsky	Frank Oliver
Guard	Guy Mairesse
Secretary	Cyrille Besnard
Soldier	Krishna Clough
Salvation Army Major	Kenneth Watson
Monk	Tony Then
Penrose	Eric Allen

Directed by Yvon Marie Coulais

STEED IS informed by Toy that a satellite has gone wrong and is transmitting a full-strength signal over France – a signal that is activating a secret unit of Russian commandos, codenamed 'K' agents, who were planted by the Russians years previously. He further believes that unless the men are stopped, it could result in the outbreak of World War 3. Sometime later, Colonel Stanislav, a Russian agent, visits the Russian Embassy and is informed by the Ambassador that the entire unit of 200 'K' agents have either been killed or taken prisoner. Unknown to the man, however, there were in fact 202 'K' agents – one of whom is Stanislav's

father – and the Russian leaves the room smiling. Later that day two agents, Turkov (Stanislav's father) and Minsky, emerge from their hiding place in a French distillery warehouse, seconds before Purdey and Gambit arrive on the scene. Stanislav, watching from the shadows, sees the two men make good their escape then returns to the Embassy. However, the Ambassador has received word that there are two further agents in the unit – agents that have been given a special mission. They must be stopped and Stanislav must be arrested on sight. Stanislav, however, orders the Embassy guards to arrest the Ambassador and the man barely escapes with his life. He races to inform Steed of his discovery and explains that the two remaining 'K' agents are to destroy two specific targets – men whose elimination would almost certainly plunge the world into war. Before he can give Steed the targets' names, the Ambassador is killed by a sniper's bullet. Steed, too, is hit, but the bullet is stopped by a cigarette case in his breast pocket.

Steed now calls a special meeting of all Government representatives, but fails to convince the men of the plot. He leaves, his only ally Colonel Martin. Gambit now visits the home of General Gaspard but is unable to stop Minsky from taking his life. Gambit kills Minsky and he too changes into an old man. Stanislav meanwhile meets his youthful-looking father and explains that now Minsky is dead his father must complete the mission alone. Steed and Gambit compare notes and arrive at the conclusion that Gaspard's death was a red-herring, intended to lead them away from the real target – the French President, who will be assassinated when he attends Gaspard's military funeral. However, the funeral has more than one dead body when Stanislav is killed by Gambit and Purdey, and Steed rings the death knell for Turkov.

Colonel Martin and The Avengers study a map to work out why a small army with outmoded equipment is attacking out-of-date military targets. A scene from K Is for Kill, Part 2: 'Tiger by the Tail'.

COMPLEX

by Dennis Spooner

John Steed	Patrick Macnee
Mike Gambit	Gareth Hunt
Purdey	Joanna Lumley
Baker	Cec Linder
Talbot	Harvey Atkin
Karavitch	Vlasta Vrana
Koschev	Rudy Lipp
Patlenko	Jan Rubes
Cope	Michael Ball
Greenwood	David Nichols
Miss Cummings	Suzette Couture
Berisford Holt	Gerald Crack

Directed by Richard Gilbert

STEED HAD a healthy respect for X41, the enemy agent codenamed Scapina, and at last it appears that he has made a mistake. The New Avengers are waiting as their Canadian contact parachutes in to reveal Scapina's identity. The man is gunned down, however, and all they find is a blurred photograph of a man leaving a large building – his face unrecognisable. Steed is contacted by Karavitch, a Russian agent, who informs him that he will hand over Scapina's identity for one million dollars. The rendezvous – Toronto, Canada. Arriving in Toronto, the trio check into an ultra-modern security building where Baker, the security chief, delegates two of his agents to accompany Steed when he meets Karavitch. But the meeting is blown and Karavitch is shot from a moving van, and when the marksman is taken to the security building he throws himself to his death from an office window. Purdey meanwhile is investigating the man's files in the building's basement control room – a fortress which can only be entered via a bullet-proof glass box in which identities are cross-checked automatically by the building's computer. Lost in her research, Purdey fails to notice when the doors of the room slide gently closed and the entire complex seals itself and starts to pump out the air.

It now becomes clear that the building itself – codenamed Special Computerised Automated Project Plan X41 – is Scapina; and Purdey is trapped in its innermost bowels as she runs from room to room desperately trying to find an avenue of escape. Locked outside and unable to break down the building's defence system, Steed recalls that though the building is locked tighter than a drum it must still accept mail to its basement control room. Armed with this knowledge, he begins to cram the post box with a lighter and dozens of boxes of matches. At first, Purdey is unable to grasp her colleague's motive, then realisation dawns and she gathers up dozens of envelopes and kindles a fire on the control room's conveyor belt. She soon finds herself showered with water as the room's sprinkler-system answers the fire alarm. The deluge overloads the computer's power circuit and the machine grinds to a halt as Steed and Gambit race to the girl's rescue under the cover of Steed's open umbrella, allowing Gambit to comment that he always knew that it would prove useful – one day.

Hot on the trail of the enemy agent codenamed Scapina, Gambit leapfrogs a perimeter fence in pursuit of a killer in Complex.

THE GLADIATORS

by Brian Clemens

John Steed	Patrick Macnee
Mike Gambit	Gareth Hunt
Purdey	Joanna Lumley
Karl	Louis Zorich
Peters	Neil Vipond
O'Hara	Bill Starr
Tarnokoff	Peter Boretski
Barnoff	Yanci Burkovek
Cresta	Jan Muzynski
Hartley	Michael Donaghue
Huge man	George Chuvalo
Rogers	Dwayne McLean
Ivan	Patrick Sinclair
Nada	Doug Lennox

Directed by George Fournier

THE NEW AVENGERS are in Toronto on a working holiday when they are asked to check up on Karl Sminsky, a Red Army Colonel and KGB agent who is rumoured to have spent two years in Siberia on a secret training mission and has now turned up in Canada again. Sminsky has arrived accompanied by two aides, but they seem to be behaving themselves. In reality, Sminsky has taken a training course with over one hundred and thirty men. That total had been reduced to two and, on their arrival, Sminsky and his aides had been followed by two security men, both of whom now lie dead.

Steed is informed of the security men's disappearance and sends Gambit and Purdey to check the countryside where their radios had suddenly gone dead. Meanwhile, Tarnokoff, a Russian diplomat, had made a formal protest about Sminsky's sudden disappearance, but Steed points out that as Sminsky is KGB he could be up to something Tarnokoff doesn't know about. Matters came

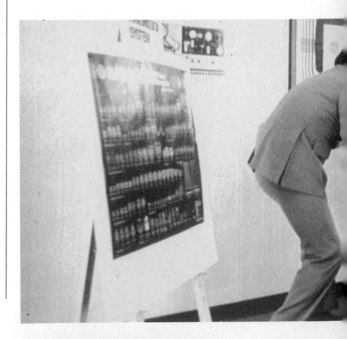

to a head when Sminsky's men attack two young Canadians in a small store. The two youths are killed barehanded by Sminsky's cohorts and Gambit remarks that they are up against some very special people. Gambit and Purdey find the dead security men and are joined by Steed. They are about to depart when Gambit recognises two faces in a saloon car as it drives by. Leaving Gambit to chase the saloon, Steed and Purdey head in the opposite direction and locate Sminsky's training headquarters. They are taken prisoner and told that they will be used as 'human targets', but Steed and Purdey quickly write off the enemy and find a tape-recording made by Sminsky which points to the Russian's mission – to break into the Canadian Security Building and smash the master computer files, effectively putting back the Canadian security system by twenty years. Gambit meanwhile loses his quarry and finds himself arrested for carrying an unlicensed gun.

Steed arranges his release, and the trio head for a showdown with Sminsky and his men – a battle that is hard fought until the highly trained agents eventually fade under the onslaught from Purdey and Gambit. Sminsky, however, concedes that his 'pupils' put up a good fight and tells Steed and his colleagues that they now face the 'Master'. Needless to say, when confronted with Gambit's fists and Steed's steel-lined bowler, even the 'Master' cannot overcome the inevitable, and Sminsky soon joins his colleagues.

In The Gladiators, *Steed and Purdey prove their worth against one of Sminsky's 'unbeatable' pupils.*

FORWARD BASE

By Dennis Spooner

John Steed	**Patrick Macnee**
Mike Gambit	**Gareth Hunt**
Purdey	**Joanna Lumley**
Hosking	**Jack Creley**
Bailey	**August Schellenberg**
Ranoff	**Marilyn Lightstone**
Malachev	**Nich Nichols**
Halfhide	**David Calderisi**
Milroy	**Maurice Good**
Doctor	**John Bethune**
Glover	**Anthony Parr**
Harper	**Les Rubie**
Clive	**Toivo Pyyko**
Czibor	**Richard Moffatt**

Directed by Don Thompson

THE NEW AVENGERS join forces with Canadian agent Bailey when he receives a tip-off that someone is being dropped at dawn. Czibor, a young Russian agent, parachutes in on schedule carrying a package which he manages to hide before dying of gunshot wounds. When the package is unearthed it is found to contain a Mark VI printed circuit control unit – proving that the Russians have moved ahead in missile guidance. Steed, however, is more concerned by the words 'Forward Base' spoken by Czibor before he died. His puzzlement increases further when Bailey's body is recovered from Lake Ontario.

Leaving Purdey and Gambit on stakeout to see who collects the package, Steed reburies the package and departs. Soon Halfhide, a known Russian agent, retrieves the package, makes his way to the water's edge, throws the package into the lake and leaves – followed by Gambit. Meanwhile, something odd happens on the edge of the lake and a local fisherman finds himself on dry land one moment and up to his neck in water the next. Purdey retrieves the package from the lake, but it appears to be a different model – a Mark V. Halfhide gives Gambit the slip and returns to the lake where Purdey is astonished to see the man jump in fully-clothed, only to reappear moments later wearing a dressing gown. Events become curiouser and curiouser: Purdey finds a bird's nest full of fish and, much to the amusement of the local populace, Steed goes fishing with a magnet. Something, it seems, is very odd about the place and Steed believes it is connected to Typhoon Agatha, which had hit the area in 1969.

While investigating the lake by dinghy, Purdey is abducted by a group of divers. She awakens in a strange underwater world – not a submarine but Forward Base, a place populated by Russian spies who, having built a small aquatic community disguised as a peninsula beneath the lake, are on constant alert for World War 3. Meanwhile, Steed's fishing expedition finally nets him a clue to the base and he informs the aquamen that unless they surface within minutes an anti-submarine flotilla will open fire on the base. Seconds later a surprised Steed watches as rows of enemy figures rise from the depths – closely followed by Purdey, automatic at the ready.

EMILY

by Dennis Spooner

John Steed	Patrick Macnee
Mike Gambit	Gareth Hunt
Purdey	Joanna Lumley
Collings	Les Carison
Phillips	Richard Davidson
Miss Daly	Jane Mallet
Kalenkov	Peter Torokvei
Mirschtia	Peter Arkroyd
Reddington	Brian Petchy
Arkoff	Don Corbett
First policeman	Sandy Crawley
Second policeman	John Kerr
Mechanic	Don Legros

Directed by Don Thompson

STEED IS determined to uncover the identity of the Fox so when Purdey discovers that the villain received regular funds from Arkoff, a courier, The New Avengers lie in wait at the next pick-up point – a deserted boat marina on Lake Ontario. After a short time a water-skier makes a fast and spectacular pick-up of the suitcase carrying the money. The skier is Gordon Collings, a liaison officer between the British and Canadian intelligence services – a man with enough 'inside' knowledge to keep himself one jump ahead of any pursuer. The man is eventually cornered in a filling station, but makes good his escape in a car that is later found abandoned. There are no fingerprints, but Steed recalls that the Fox had leapt over the car's roof during his escape and believes there is the possibility of a palm print. Collings hears about this and moves into action as Steed, Purdey and Gambit return to the garage workshop – but the car has gone. It belonged to a Miss Daly and is no ordinary car but a family heirloom nicknamed 'Emily' by its owner, and she has collected it and taken the car for a service. Fortunately, the agents arrive at the very second that 'Emily' enters the garage car-wash, and the valuable clue is saved from erasure when a quick-witted Purdey leaps on to its roof as the giant rollers edge the car into the bubbling foam. Reasoning that it would be safer to drive the car direct to Forensics, Steed tapes his bowler over the palm print and the agents set off for a jaunty cross-country trek, with the Fox's men hot on their heels and determined to use every means possible to stop them.

The incident-packed journey leads Purdey and Gambit into a 'moonshine' drinking session; the Canadian police on the trail of a car 'last seen wearing . . . a bowler?'; and to Emily herself guzzling gallons of home-made hooch until a barrage of mortar fire laid down by the Fox and his cohorts finally writes off Miss Daly's pride and joy. The valuable palm print is saved, however, and eventually leads the agents to their quarry.

The team repay their debt to Miss Daly by presenting her with a new vehicle, and the one remaining piece of 'Emily' as a memento. She in turn raises a few eyebrows when, correctly identifying the palm print on the memento as belonging to Collings, she informs them that she is quite proficient at reading palms, leaving the agents to consider whether their hazardous journey had really been necessary at all!

With Emily out of gas, Gambit and Purdey take off with their 'little brown jugs' of home brew.

PRODUCTION CREDITS

Series produced by
Albert Fennell & Brian Clemens

Music Composed by
Laurie Johnson

Production Supervisor
Ron Fry

Production Designer
Syd Cain

Story Editors
Bob Dearberg – Graeme Clifford
Eric Wraite – Alan Killick
Ralph Sheldon

Fight Arrangers
Ray Austin – Cyd Child
(Episodes 1 to 13)
Joe Dunne – Cyd Child
(Episodes 14 to 26)

Casting Director
Maggie Cartier

Fashion Co-ordinators
Catherine Buckley
(Episodes 1 to 13)
Jillie Murphy – Betty Jackson
Jennifer Hocking
(Episodes 14 to 26)

All 26 episodes produced by
Avengers (Film & TV) Enterprises Ltd
&
IDTV TV Productions
Paris

**The Four Canadian episodes carried
the following credits:**

(Opening Credits)
Albert Fennell & Brian Clemens
Present
The New Avengers
in Canada

Associate Producer
Ron Fry

Production Designers
Seamus Flannery – Daniel Budin

Stunt Co-ordinator
Val Musetti – Dwayne McLean

**Co-ordinating Producer
for Avengers (Film & TV) Enterprises**

Ray Austin

A Production of
The Avengers (Film & TV) Enterprises Ltd
&
IDTV TV Productions Paris
&
Neilsen-Ferns Toronto

Filmed on location in Canada

Emily carried an additional credit:
Produced in Canada by
Hugh Marlow & Jim Handley

Once again (possibly due to the programme being made by an independent company), Steed and his colleagues lost the battle of the ratings. The second 13 stories suffered the same fate as the first 13 – no network showing by the ITV network.

This time around *The New Avengers* did not even dent the viewing charts. But it did gain huge international sales and the producers immediately began negotiations to get financial backing for a further series.

Meantime, Brian Clemens handed two scripts he'd written to CBS television in America. The first of these, called *Escapade* (sub-titled *Avengers USA*), was the pilot story of an American version of *The New Avengers*. Only the pilot story was filmed. Starring Joanna Lumley lookalike Morgan Fairchild as Suzy, an American-based version of Purdey, and Granville Van Dusen as Joshua, a US Government equivalent of Steed, in between bouts of 'bed-hopping', the agents were selected by 'Oz', a computer, to undertake a case involving security secrets being sold to the highest bidder by a freelance agent. Produced by Quinn Martin/Woodruff Productions, and aired in America in 1978, a series failed to materialise.

One year later, on 2 September 1979, the *Sunday*

People carried the following (edited) article, by Tony Purnell.

STEED RIDES AGAIN – THANKS TO YANKS

John Steed, television's most successful secret agent, is all set to make a comeback.

Actor Patrick Macnee has his brolly, bowler and buttonhole booked to make another series of *The New Avengers* early in the New Year.

It looked like the end for the Old Etonian hero 18 months ago when no one would put up the cash to make more of the costly adventures.

But now the Americans have come to Steed's rescue.

Producer Brian Clemens explained: 'The show is a big hit in the States and the Americans have agreed to provide most of the finance for another 26 episodes. Other companies over here are also interested and it is now just a case of sorting out who puts in what.'

Patrick Macnee, 57, said, 'I have told Brian I will definitely be available. I have a great affection for *The Avengers*.'

In the last series, Patrick and Joanna Lumley were joined by dashing Gareth Hunt as Mike Gambit and it put Steed's nose out of joint. Patrick confessed, 'I was pushed rather into the background and complained. Gambit was taking over a lot of the stuff that Steed would have done. Changes were made and I was quite happy in the end. The three of us are great friends and there is a wonderful bond between us.'

Both Joanna and Gareth said they would be interested in making more *New Avengers*.

Brian Clemens said, 'It would be nice to have the three together again, but not essential. Avenger girls can come and go, but if Patrick Macnee decided to drop out of the picture, it would signal the end of *The Avengers* for good.'

CBS in America wanted to inject $140,000, and London Weekend TV (influenced no doubt, by the success of their joint venture with Fennell and Clemens' Avengers MK1 Productions – *The Professionals* series) agreed to put up the remaining cash, but that still left about £25,000 short for each episode.

Almost five months to the day of the announcement in the *Sunday People*, the following appeared in the *Daily Mail* of 9 February 1980, written by Paul Donovan.

STEED'S A WANTED MAN

The giant American network CBS, which is showing ITV's *The Avengers* coast-to-coast every Friday night, wants to turn the legendary series into a two-hour feature film.

And the bowler-hatted star Patrick Macnee – who made his first appearance as John Steed 20 years ago – said this week, 'I would be absolutely delighted to do it again.'

Mr Macnee, who spent his 58th birthday on Wednesday, flying home to Britain from Bombay after completing a movie, added that he was keeping himself free of commitments after mid-May.

As he spoke, Mr John Redway, the West End agent for both him and Brian Clemens – as well as ex-Avengers star Diana Rigg – was in New York discussing the project.

Said Mr Clemens, 'CBS are showing 13 episodes featuring Diana Rigg which were made around 15 years ago. It was way ahead of its time – and still stands up well today.'

Asked whom he would like as his leading lady in a possible film, Patrick Macnee replied, 'I love Diana Rigg, adore Honor Blackman and Linda Thorson and have the greatest admiration for Joanna Lumley. It's a profusion of riches, isn't it?

And that is where the story ended, until, on 15 March 1985, the *Broadcast* magazine, a weekly media journal, announced that Sarah Lawson, head of the newly formed Taft Entertainment Group, was considering the development of a pilot film for a new series of *The Avengers*, together with Brian Clemens, who would be writing the screenplay. Clemens confirmed that Patrick

Macnee would once again be heading the team as John Steed, but the new Mrs Peel was yet uncast. 'We are going back to grass roots, and it will be far more like the old *Avengers* rather than *The New Avengers*,' revealed Clemens. 'Patrick Macnee would like to re-create John Steed as a more avuncular figure,' said Sarah Lawson. 'He will have two younger operatives working for him, one English, one American, partly to provide a hook for viewers, partly to give it a more international flavour.'

As before, however, the project was dependent on a US network pick-up and though both Lawson and Clemens were optimistic of its chances, the project was given the cold shoulder once again.

This time, however, a script was written. Courtesy of Brian Clemens, the following extracts have been taken directly as they appear in his script for, as the series was to be known, *The Avengers – International*. The dialogue is reprinted exactly as it appears in Brian's script and has been selected to give the reader an introduction to the new characters. Shortage of space prohibits the reprinting of the entire script, but I have given a short story synopsis to familiarise you with the scenario.

REINCARNATION

Reports that someone is stalking John Steed – someone with murder on their mind, sends young undercover agent Samantha Peel on a merry cross-country chase that terminates aboard a fast-moving train somewhere in England.

Bobby Lomax, one of the most spectacular double-agents Steed ever encountered, a man who infiltrated M15 and rose to become its deputy controller – until Steed exposed him as a spy – is out to wreak revenge on our hero.

But how can this be? Isn't it fact that Steed shot and *killed* Lomax nine years earlier? Dead men don't return – do they? In this case it appears they do. Courtesy of a new brain transplant technique perfected by British scientist Professor Wyndham – now in the hands of Russian scientist Gross, a man with no love for Steed – those portions of the medically dead Lomax's brain which contain memory, personality and experience, have been transplanted into the body of a young man in his twenties, awakening the memory of the things denied to Lomax for so long; his black sobranie cigarettes, Scotch whisky, his incipient hay fever – and his intense hatred of John Steed, the man who ended his life almost a decade earlier.

But what happens when Lomax MK1 is killed a second time? Simple. You find a new recipient for the dead man's brain then, with surgery to change their physical features until Lomax Two bears no resemblance at all to Lomax MK1 (a shaved head, a *woman's* body), you unleash the new killer on its prey – if necessary, repeating the operation a third time.

And so Steed finds himself fighting for his life against THREE daunting enemies: each completely different, each as deadly as the other. His only clue to identification, his opponent's preference for black sobranie cigarettes – and, of course, his/her bouts of sneezing!

REINCARNATION

by Brian Clemens

ACT ONE

EXT. ROAD. DAY

As a Lotus Elan (same colour and model as that once driven by Emma Peel) comes screaming around a bend.

NOTE: At this stage we <u>do not</u> identify the driver – what we see is an exciting montage as:
Gloved hand shifts gears.
Feet hit brakes and throttle.
The car wheels bite the tarmac.
The car executes a perfectly controlled slide around a corner.

We NOW REVEAL that the Lotus is racing an express train – travelling a parallel road to the railway track.
We 'build' this visually exciting sequence – and then the parallel road turns away from the railroad track – enters a road running through a pine forest, so that the train is lost from sight.

EXT. FOREST. DAY
As the Lotus zooms right up at camera.

EXT. RAILROAD STATION. DAY
The train slows to a stop – PASSENGERS alight and embark.

EXT. ROAD. DAY
The Lotus swerves through several other cars as it speeds along.

EXT. RAILROAD STATION. DAY

CLOSE ON GUARD as he blows his whistle and:
The train starts to move away again.

EXT. OUTSIDE STATION. DAY
As the Lotus skids to a stop and:

ANOTHER, LOWER ANGLE as feet vault out of the car and run towards the station.

EXT. RAILROAD STATION. DAY
The train is really rolling now.

The GUARD turns and reacts as he sees the tall, slim figure of a WOMAN sprinting the length of the platform after the fast receding train. The WOMAN wears figure-hugging pants and top, and a close-fitting cap. The GUARD tries to intervene, but she evades him and JUST manages to grab at the last carriage of the train, JUST as it leaves the platform and, as she swings herself aboard, the GUARD stares after her.

INT. TRAIN. DAY

The WOMAN stands, her back to us, getting back her breath and then tugging off her cap and shaking loose a long mane of gorgeous hair. THEN she turns into the camera and, FOR THE FIRST TIME, we clearly see MRS PEEL.

SAMANTHA to her friends, 'SAM' to her intimates, she is young, beautiful and very sexy in a cool, 'Hitchcockian' mould. Her figure is superb, long and leggy – and her IQ matches up. One of the several daughters of an English Lord, she is titled in her own right, but prefers to be plain 'Mrs'. Her mode of dress can range from the kind of 'fighting/action' outfit she wears now – through the current mode of mannish suits, etc., – but when SHE wears them you would never, ever mistake her for a man! The other end of the scale are the wild, almost punkish clothes that the young covet, and can identify with. We will come to know that if she slipped into an old flour bag – on her it would look terrific. She is a natural 'clothes horse'.

Now, recovered from her drive and sprint, she sets off along the swaying corridor of the train.

CUT TO:

ELSEWHERE ON THE TRAIN. As MRS PEEL comes hurrying along – moving past the doors of several 'sleepers' now – reaching the right one – she opens the door and looks in at:

INT. SLEEPER. DAY

MRS PEEL'S RESTRICTED EYELINE IN TO WHERE:

STEED, wearing the kind of well-cut tweeds a gentleman takes to a country party, is sitting, looking at the barrels of a shotgun!

MRS PEEL reacts and instantly plunges into the small confines of the sleeper – she grabs the gun barrels – pushes them up – and at the same time slugs a terrific blow at the man holding them.

The man brilliantly fends off the blow – changes it into a handlock. Which MRS PEEL changes into her handlock – it is stalemate, and she finds herself looking into the face of CHRISTOPHER CAMBRIDGE.

> STEED
> That's it! That's enough!
> (he insinuates between them –
> pushing them apart about six inches)
> It's a draw.

He takes the shotgun from both their hands, and then introduces:

> STEED
> Mrs Peel – she's part of our mob.
> Christopher Cambridge – he's part of theirs.
> From across the Atlantic.

MRS PEEL & CHRIS regard each other appraisingly – she with some caution, he with a frankness we shall come to know well.

CHRISTOPHER CAMBRIDGE is a young, tall, handsome American. Edgar J. would have been proud of him, because everything about him is discreet – formal. With his height and physique he could hardly disappear in a crowd, but with his mode of dress, which is always a suit or jacket of expensive but discreet cut and colour, and almost always a collar and tie – and his deceptively quiet and self effacing manner – and most of all the eye glasses he wears from time to time – glasses, that, like Clark Kent, seem to heighten his attraction rather than conceal it – he does manage not to be a sore thumb. Which is a distinct advantage if you happen to be the ruthless, efficient, highly trained agent that Chris actually is. In a funny sort of way he is the American alter ego of the equally urbane and immaculate John Steed.

> MRS PEEL
> I'm sorry – when I saw the gun – I thought. . . .

> CHRIS (interjects)
> I thought the same – when you burst in here. . . .

> STEED
> I was merely showing him my Purdey.

MRS PEEL reacts to this name!

> STEED
> My shotgun. I'm going on a shoot – grouse,
> pheasant and, I'm assured, a Burgundy of
> unrivalled excellence.

> CHRIS
> But I've been telling you, Steed – we intercepted
> a message. . . .

MRS PEEL
So did we.

CHRIS & MRS PEEL
Someone is out to kill you!

INT. TRAIN. DAY

ANGLE ONTO A COMPARTMENT DOOR – we hear a loud sneeze, then the door opens and LOMAX ONE emerges into the corridor, wiping his nose on a tissue. He looks around warily – then sets off along the corridor. He looks very threatening indeed.

INT. SLEEPER. DAY
Like the Marx Brothers in Night At The Opera – STEED, CHRIS & MRS PEEL are still crammed into the tiny sleeper.

MRS PEEL
You must take this seriously, Steed.

CHRIS (simultaneously)
There's no doubt the message was genuine. . . .

STEED (simultaneously)
You're panicking unreasonably. . . .
(then:)
I mean, why would anyone want to kill me?

MRS PEEL
You're still on the active list. Very much so.

STEED
Yes, but I don't go scrambling over the Berlin Wall
anymore. Princes, Presidents and Prime Ministers,
they're my forte these days. Which is why I'm going on this
shoot – a personal invitation from the Prince of. . . .

CHRIS
Our intercept got a name.
(to MRS PEEL)
You didn't get a name?

MRS PEEL
If we did, I didn't stay around to hear it.

CHRIS
Bobby Lomax. He's the man coming to kill you.

STEED regards him – then laughs.

STEED

Now I know this is a storm in a teacup. Bobby Lomax!?
It would be a miracle!
He laughs again. MRS PEEL & CHRIS exchange a look.

STEED
I'm touched that you're both concerned, deeply touched –
but your trip was for nothing. Come on, at least I can buy you dinner.
He opens the door to the corridor, looks back at them and:

STEED (explains)
I killed Bobby Lomax five years ago!

MRS PEEL & CHRIS react – and now follow STEED out to:

INT. RESTAURANT CAR. NIGHT

CLOSE ON CHAMPAGNE as it pops – and we PULL OUT TO REVEAL STEED pouring wine for MRS PEEL & CHRIS who are both a bit watchful, both turning now as a YOUNG MAN enters the area.

STEED (notices – and smiles)
If Bobby Lomax were still alive, which he isn't –
he would be . . .oh . . .over sixty now. Grey and
stooped and sneezing.

(THEY react to this)

Suffered terribly with hay fever. Might have
been the death of him. If I hadn't. Cheers.
THEY drink, then CHRIS studies MRS PEEL
'Mrs Peel'? I seem to recall that name. . . .

MRS PEEL
The other Mrs Peel.

STEED
My partner – <u>Emma</u> Peel.

MRS PEEL
My mother in law.

CHRIS
Mother in law!?

STEED
Samantha – or 'Sam', as only I and three other people
are allowed to call her. . . .

MRS PEEL
Two.

Steed smiles at her and it is evident there is a special bond between them.

STEED
Two. Sam married Peter Peel – Emma's son – hence. . . .

MRS PEEL
I'm Mrs Peel, the second.

STEED
Not a blood relative – but in the same unique,
delightful mould.

CHRIS
I've never had the pleasure of meeting the
original – but I'll certainly drink to the second Mrs Peel.

They drink – then suddenly they react to a very loud sneeze nearby. THEY spin round, ready for trouble, and survey the rest of the car; a LARGE WOMAN is just dabbing her nose with a handkerchief – THEY regard her.

STEED
Two miracles.

(THEY look at him)

First you tell me Bobby Lomax is back from the dead –
and now apparently he has changed his sex as well!

It breaks the moment – THEY laugh along with Steed – and WE TAKE ANOTHER ANGLE – REVEALING – at the rear of the car LOMAX ONE, smoking a black sobranie.

EXT. HOTEL. NIGHT

A creaking sign announces "THE PRINCE OF WALES HOTEL"

PULL OUT TO REVEAL a typical 18th century hotel.

INT. HOTEL. NIGHT

STEED is up at the desk with MRS PEEL & CHRIS in attendance.

MRS PEEL
Steed. John. Please take this seriously.

STEED
No. You can if you wish, but I intend having a good night's
sleep – and being out on the moors early tomorrow.

CHRIS
At least let us check it out.

STEED
That's your prerogative.

DURING this the DESK CLERK has handed STEED a key, then banging the desk bell.

DESK CLERK
Where IS that porter!? Alfred!?

He hurries away to look for him.

MRS PEEL
You're a stubborn man.

STEED (Shakes head)
Wise. Long in the tooth. Experienced.

LOMAX ONE
Mr Steed?

STEED turns to look to where LOMAX ONE stands on the first of the stairs up, holding
Steed's suitcase and gun-case.

LOMAX ONE
This way, sir.

STEED flourishes his key – and sets off after LOMAX ONE, who starts to ascend the
stairs. MRS PEEL moves close to STEED.

MRS PEEL
What does it take to scare you!?

STEED
The Inland Revenue. Wine improperly decanted.
A surprise visit from my Aunt Agatha!

MRS PEEL
Stubborn. Pig headed. And carefree, courageous.
And not a bit long in the tooth!

She kisses him lightly on the cheek – STEED smiles, moves to ascend the stairs. MRS
PEEL remains, gazing after him – then CHRIS enters shot.

CHRIS
You like him a lot, eh?

(SHE nods)

Care about him?

(SHE nods)
What will you wear to his funeral?!
This brings her down to earth.

MRS PEEL
Check the place out?

CHRIS (Nods)
Check the place out.

MRS PEEL.
Someone grey, old and sneezing!

INT. HOTEL. NIGHT

MRS PEEL & CHRIS come back from separate ways and meet near the desk.

CHRIS
Anything?

MRS PEEL (Shakes head)
You?

CHRIS
No.

MRS PEEL
Better check the grounds.

CHRIS
Yes.

MRS PEEL
Don't pull your gun until we get outside.

CHRIS
I don't carry a gun.

MRS PEEL
You don't!?

CHRIS (Shakes head)
If I get into trouble, I fight with my feet.

MRS PEEL
Karate?

CHRIS
I run!

* * * * *

EXT. ROAD. NIGHT
As the Lotus comes speeding around a curve.

INT. LOTUS. NIGHT
MRS PEEL drives expertly and very fast. CHRIS alongside. He pats the car.

CHRIS
For an old one – she really moves.

MRS PEEL
It belonged to my mother in law.

CHRIS
Emma Peel? I hear she is really some lady.

MRS PEEL
Some dame.

(CHRIS reacts)
That's what she is now. 'Dame Emma Peel'
'For services rendered'. It's like a knighthood. . . .

CHRIS
We're not going to have that 'Tomato – tomato'
routine, are we? I know what a Dame of the British Empire is.
I went to Harvard, I am surprisingly well educated. For an American.

MRS PEEL
I'm sorry . . .

CHRIS
. . . I'm not asking for apologies – just the benefit
of the doubt.

Then suddenly he smiles his devastating smile and:

CHRIS
Truce?

MRS PEEL (Smiles)
Truce.
* * * * * * * *

EXT. STREET. DAY
The Lotus speeds along – with LOMAX TWO following in his car.

INT. LOTUS. DAY

MRS PEEL drives, CHRIS eyes her – hesitates, then:

CHRIS
How did you meet your husband – doing this
kind of work?

MRS PEEL
That came <u>after</u> I met him. I couldn't let my husband go
chasing after diabolical masterminds on his own, could I?
And leave me at home? So I tagged along. . . .

(she swirls the wheel hard)

I'm what you might call 'a talented amateur'.

CHRIS
<u>Very</u> talented.

She swings the wheel again, and:

EXT. STREET. DAY
The Lotus speeds around a corner – with LOMAX TWO still following.

INT. LOTUS. DAY

CHRIS
Where is he now? Your husband?

MRS PEEL
Peter? I wish I knew.

Her reply is sad, emotional – CHRIS regards her.

MRS PEEL
We went into Eastern Europe four years ago,
on an assignment. Since then – nothing.

CHRIS
That's too bad. So you don't know if. . . .?

MRS PEEL (Interjects)
. . . If he's alive or not.

CHRIS
Or if you're a widow or not?

She glances at him – and sees him regarding her very intently.

CHRIS
Or available or not.
* * * * * * *

MRS PEEL
Why do you wear those glasses? You don't seem to need them.

CHRIS reacts – picks up glasses from table – eyes them.

CHRIS
Do they bother you?

MRS PEEL
No, as a matter of fact they suit you – more than most anyway.
But – being American – I would have thought . . .contact lenses..?

CHRIS
Contacts don't show.

MRS PEEL (frowns)
That's the point, isn't it?

She moves back to him now, with a tray bearing shaker and glasses – she will pour two drinks as:

CHRIS
Funny thing about human nature. Nobody likes to hit
a guy wearing glasses – doesn't matter who it is, no
matter how ruthless, they always hesitate – maybe not for
more than one hundredth of a second, but they hesitate.
And that's all I need.

* * * * * * *

EXT. MOORS. DAY

CLOSE ON A SHOTGUN as it swings round to point at a tweed checked chest.

THEN WIDEN TO REVEAL a peppery DUKE pushing aside the gun held by THORNTON, an aged, dithery, myopic little man who wears thick pebble glasses.

DUKE
No, no, Thornton – not at me! The birds will show
over there – <u>over there</u> – driving 'em up from the north –
and <u>then</u> you'll see birds. Some of the biggest, plumpest. . . .
most delicious birds you've ever laid eyes on.

THORNTON
Ah!

He turns gun and gazes in that direction – a hillock close by.

DUKE
(moving away to take up his stand a way away:)
They'll be coming fast and AT you – and you'll see
them big as a house!

THORNTON
Ah!

He readjusts in anticipation – then hears an approaching sound – mounts his gun at the ready and then reacts as he sees:

Straight up from behind the hillock rises the huge bulk of a HELICOPTER – seemingly only a few yards away!

THORNTON, at the aim – blinks through his glasses at this huge 'bird' - and then he fires.

Even as he does so, the HELICOPTER passes right over head – with terrific noise and slipstream.

DUKE rushes into shot alongside a totally bemused THORNTON.

THORNTON
I missed. Biggest bird I've ever seen.
Gigantic! And I missed! It must be these glasses.

The DUKE strides angrily on.

CUT TO:

ELSEWHERE.

The HELICOPTER has landed – CHRIS & MRS PEEL alight. DUKE strides into shot.

DUKE
Disgusting behaviour – utterly reprehensible . . .
I really must protest . . .

CHRIS (Interjects)
I'm sorry.

DUKE
Ah – an AMERICAN – might have known..Do you
realise you have just ruined this shoot?
Man sets out for an afternoon's sport and. . . .

MRS PEEL (Over-rides)
We must find John Steed. He's in danger. . . .

DUKE
Steed?

LAURA (Off)
He went back to the house.

THEY turn to see LAURA standing there.

CHRIS
When?

LAURA
Oh, about ten minutes ago.

MRS PEEL
Alone?

LAURA
I don't think so. I saw John get into the Land-Rover –
but there was someone with him I'm sure – I
heard them sneeze.

CHRIS & MRS PEEL react to this, and, as they move:

INT. STATELY HOME/DRAWING ROOM. DAY

One of those large and gracious rooms one finds in such places – exquisitely furnished.

OPEN CLOSE ON A TABLE CIGARETTE LIGHTER – as it is snapped alight – and then presented to a black sobranie cigarette held between the delectable lips of LOMAX THREE! She is perhaps 35 or more, a typical British blonde beauty – cool and assured and sexily, yet unostentatiously flirtatious as the scene proceeds. WIDEN TO REVEAL STEED – very interested in her, lighting her cigarette.

STEED
You really shouldn't smoke you know.
It's a bad habit.

LOMAX THREE
(suggestively)
I keep promising myself I'll give them up – when
I find a more exciting substitute.

Her voice is a husky, sexy drawl.

STEED
I'm surprised I didn't meet you earlier.

LOMAX THREE (sneezes)
I didn't arrive here until this morning. 'Was in
Monte you know. And then they positioned me far over on the
West Tor . . .I thought it was going to be dreadfully dull.
Then I saw you.

                         STEED
          Will you be staying for the rest of the shoot?

                     LOMAX THREE
                      (regards him)
             I think perhaps yes. Now.

                         STEED
                     Catherine. . . .

                     LOMAX THREE
          Oh, please – call me 'Cathy'.

                         STEED
                       Cathy?

He picks up his drink and, introspective, he turns away.

                         STEED
          There was once another 'Cathy' in my life.

LOMAX THREE looks at his unprotected back and now pulls a tiny pistol from her purse
and an edge creeps into her voice as:

                     LOMAX THREE
                      I know.

                         STEED
                   I know you know.

Even as he speaks, he spins round and tosses his drink into LOMAX THREE'S face,
temporarily blinding her – he grabs for the gun.

                                                          CUT TO:

At this moment MRS PEEL & CHRIS enter – just in time to react to:

STEED pulls the gun from LOMAX THREE'S hand and delivers a terrific uppercut to
her jaw. A blow that sends her skidding along the floor to lie still.

STEED regards her.

                         STEED
          Hay fever AND black sobranie! That would have
                been too much of a coincidence.

Then he looks up as MRS PEEL & CHRIS move in towards him.

                         STEED
          You were right and I was wrong. TWO miracles.
               Bobby Lomax back from the dead. . . .

                       MRS PEEL
                . . . .And changed his sex.

                         STEED
          I never hit a woman before.

                        CHRIS
                  You still haven't.

THEY regard each other – start to smile and:

                                                    THROUGH TO:

EXT. STEED'S PLACE. DAY

As we shall see, one of his many homes – a country estate.

OPEN CLOSE ON STEED'S beloved 1927 green Bentley sports – PANNING OUT TO
FIND STEED, CHRIS & MRS PEEL coming riding across a field.

                                                          CUT TO:

THE AVENGERS RETURN 265

CLOSER SHOT
As all three reach a high hedge and jump it as one – clearly they are all experts on a horse.

CUT TO:

ANOTHER ANGLE.

As STEED reins in and CHRIS & MRS PEEL join him.

STEED
I forgot to tell you. . . .it's with the wish of someone
up there that you continue to work together. As a team
(THEY react – he addresses CHRIS)
It will mean working here and in Europe. . . .
(addresses MRS PEEL)
. . . .and even a few trips to the United States.
I think you'll make a very good team.

He rides away.

MRS PEEL & CHRIS regard each other. Then:

MRS PEEL
Mr Cambridge. . . .

CHRIS
(interjects)
Chris. You'd better start calling me Chris.
And I guess I'll call you Sam.

MRS PEEL
No! Not yet.

She turns and rides away. CHRIS blinks – then he too spurs his horse and rides after her.

CUT TO:

ANOTHER ANGLE.

STEED someway ahead – CHRIS & MRS PEEL riding almost together – as a team.

HOLD THIS IMAGE.

FINAL FADE OUT TO:

THE END

And that's where our story ends. Well, not quite. As recently as November 1988, reports were circulating that: Mel Gibson, of *Mad Max* and *Lethal Weapon* fame, has snapped up the film rights to the character and is very anxious to play the impeccable John Steed; and Universal Studios plan to reunite Patrick Macnee, Honor Blackman and Linda Thorson, in an Eighties TV version of the popular show, to be written by Michael Sloane, who calls it *The Avenging Angel*.

Of course we've heard it all before. This time, however, the odds are better than ever that at least one of the projects will progress beyond the storyboard stage.

During our conversation, Linda Thorson confirmed that she had been approached to star in the latter. She told me 'Michael Sloane wants to do an Avengers film, to be called *The Avenging Angel*. It's an episode where Linda Thorson and Honor Blackman meet at Steed's funeral. They've obviously never met before. They meet and they commiserate, and then go off to do something and then . . . well, I don't want to tell you the outcome. In fact Michael Sloane would love to do a brand new series of *The Avengers*. He's going to see the people who own the copyright and ask for the rights.'

And the Australian connection? I can confirm that Mel Gibson *has* acquired the film rights and production of the first ever *Avengers* movie is just around the corner – possibly immediately after the actor completes *Lethal Weapon II*.

Will *The Avengers* return? To reiterate Mother's last words from *Bizarre*, 'They'll be back. . . . You can depend on it.'

Personally, I can't wait.

DREAM MACHINES

CARS HAVE always played a major part in the *Avengers* stories, and it is difficult to conjure up a mental image of Steed and his colleagues without recalling their personal mode of transport. Emma's powder blue Lotus, the red and maroon speedsters of Tara and the gleaming Vanden Plas lines of Steed's vintage machines – all have now become a part of the *Avengers* folklore.

It was not always the case, however, and though Steed did drive a vintage vehicle in the latter part of the Blackman series, he was more likely to be found behind the wheel of a white Vauxhall saloon (registration number 7061 MK). His colleague, of course, professed a preference for two wheels – a powerful Triumph motorcycle (reg. 987 CAA) but she, too, could sometimes be viewed driving a sleek white MG sports. In each case, it is more likely that the cars had been 'driven' into camera range by the sweat and muscle of studio technicians. The series was, after all, taped live, and exterior inserts were kept to a minimum.

It is therefore fair to say that the cars really came into their own when, with the advent of the first filmed series in 1965, the creative brains behind the show decided to develop the idea of the stars driving a mode of transport that would, to some degree, reflect their own character traits. The ploy worked, and the cars quickly became a trademark of the series.

While everyone is probably conversant with the vehicles themselves, it appears that there is general confusion among the fans as to 'Who drove what – and where?' To that end, the following information should keep even the most avid and car-conscious fan satisfied.

Any attempt to list every vehicle used in the series would prove over-exhaustive, so I propose to limit my comments to the vehicles used by the stars themselves. As I do not profess to any expertise on the subject, I have resisted the urge to list every vehicle's technical data. Each vehicle's registration number is followed by a bracketed single number or group of numbers. These denote the episode in which that vehicle appeared, and should be used in conjunction with the corresponding episode numbers listed on pages 204-208.

THE AVENGERS

Model	Reg. No:	Comments
EMMA		
Powder blue Lotus Elan S2	HNK 999C	Throughout the b/w series
Powder blue Lotus Elan S2	SJH 4999D	Throughout entire colour series
STEED		
Bugatti	GK 3295	Two episodes Blackman Series Two
Vauxhall 30–98	XT 2273	Throughout the b/w Rigg episodes
Green 1926 4 ½ litre Bentley	UW 4887	Throughout the Rigg b/w series and episode (20) Rigg colour
Green 1928 Green Label Bentley	YK 6871	Rigg colour(1) [1]
Green 1926 Speed Six Bentley	RX 6180	(2–5–6–7–8–11–14–16–18–19–21) Rigg colour [2]
Green 1927 4½ litre Bentley	YT 3942	(22–24–25) Rigg colour and (3–4–6) Thorson [3]
Yellow 1927 Rolls Royce Silver Ghost	KK 4976	(5–7–8 to 14; 16 to 26) Thorson
Yellow 1923 Rolls Royce Phantom Tourer Mk1	UU 3864	(27–28–30–31–32) Thorson [4]
Olive-green Land Rover	WX 887	(8–10) Rigg colour
Trojan Bubble Car	CMU 574A	(24) Thorson
TARA		
Maroon AC Cobra 428	LPH 800D	(1 to 4; 7–8–9–12) Thorson [5]
Red Lotus Europa	PPW 999F	(6–11; 14 to 23) Thorson
Mini Moke	LYP 794D	(10) Thorson

Mrs Gale professed a preference for a powerful Triumph motorcycle . . .

MOTHER

Silver grey Rolls Royce	3 KHM	(30) Thorson
Brown Mini Moke	THX 77F	(26) Thorson

LADY DIANA

White MGB	BMW 300G	(19) Thorson

THE NEW AVENGERS

STEED

Olive green 5.3 litre Jaguar Coupé	NVK 60P	Throughout first season
Yellow Rover saloon	WOC 229P	Several episodes of the second season
Green Range Rover	TXC 922J	Several episodes of the series

GAMBIT

Red Jaguar XJS	MLR 875P	Throughout the series
White Range Rover	LOK 537P	Several episodes of the series

PURDEY

Yellow MGB Drophead Sports	MOC 232P	First season
Yellow Triumph TR7	OGW 562R	Several episodes of the second season
Yellow/Black Honda motorcycle	LLC 950P	Episode (5)
Red Honda motorcycle	OLR 471P	Episode (18)

The stars also drove various locally obtained vehicles in the episodes made on location in France and Canada.

[1] This model was featured regularly in the 1967 situation comedy series *George and the Dragon*, starring Sid James and Peggy Mount.

[2] In January 1984 this 1926 Speed Six changed hands for £49,500.

[3] Eight years later, this machine made a 'guest' appearance in the *New Avengers* story: *K Is for Kill*.

[4] Familiar? It should be. This model frequently turned up in both *The Benny Hill Show* and *The Morecambe and Wise* programmes.

[5] Steed in a low-slung sports car? That might have been the case. The AC Cobra 428 was, in fact, pencilled in to be the agent's regular transport throughout the entire Thorson series. Thankfully, the producers decided to retain his vintage image. (What's more, on 12 January 1965, the producers of the original *Avengers* series were offered the loan of a new TVR sports car. After considering using this as Steed's regular mode of transport, a decision was taken in favour of staying with the vintage models.)

. . . although on occasion she joined Steed for a sortie in a vintage Bugatti.

Patrick Macnee in 1927 Rolls Royce Silver Ghost.

What's this? Steed on a bicycle? The elegant hero of ABC's popular thriller series The Avengers *takes a cycle ride by the river in* Brief For Murder.

MERCHANDISE – A LICENCE TO SELL

A full guide to Avengers/New Avengers spin-offs

ONE ASPECT of promoting *The Avengers/The New Avengers* both here and abroad was merchandise. The production companies earned royalties from the sales of *Avengers* 'tie-ins', and during the Sixties/Seventies numerous items of related merchandise were licensed. The market was soon saturated with merchandise issued by the biggest and most popular names in the trade. Books, annuals, comic strips, toys, dolls, miniatures of Steed's Bentley and Emma's Lotus, records – aficionados of the series had a field day and quickly found they needed bottomless pockets to keep in step with the amount of merchandise the shows had spawned.

The following list includes items of merchandise known to have been issued, and other items that, though licensed, never appeared on the retailers' shelves. The most comprehensive guide ever published, it will prove invaluable to the serious collector.

Obviously, with the passage of time, many of the items listed have disappeared or lie 'lost' and forgotten in someone's attic. However, many items do still exist, and a morning spent searching the shelves of your local junk shop or a visit to a nearby jumble sale can unearth many a priceless item.

THE AVENGERS

Toys and Related Items

The Corgi Gift Set No 40 is perhaps the best known – and certainly the most collectable – of these. Issued in 1966 at a list price of 16/9d (86p), this contained replicas of Steed's 1929 Bentley and Emma's Lotus Elan.

The Corgi catalogue (complete with reproductions of the two cars plus two miniature photographs of Steed and Emma) described the package in this way: 'Steed's Bentley has been impeccably reproduced right down to the bonnet strap, spiked wheels and detailed interior, with a figure of John Steed at the wheel. Emma's Lotus Elan, complete with standing figure of Emma, is fitted with opening bonnet, plated engine and detailed interior with tip-up seat and suspension.' The company actually went so far as to include three moulded plastic umbrellas. The complete set was offered in an attractive presentation box which had artwork of Steed and Emma on both top and sides, and when opened it revealed a display unit with further artwork.

For some inexplicable reason, Corgi insisted on issuing the set with a red (not racing green) Bentley and a white (not powder blue) Lotus, so a word of caution to anyone being offered a set containing a *green* Bentley: Corgi issued a further Bentley model in 1967, and though this contained a bowler-hatted figure behind the wheel it is in fact based on another television series, *The World of Wooster*, and has no connection with *The Avengers*.

Incidentally, though Corgi relicensed the *Avengers* set in 1969 and planned to issue a further model, no further set was issued owing to the model's dyes being destroyed in a fire at the factory.

The Avengers Jigsaw Puzzles, a set of four, was manufactured by Thomas, Hope & Sankey exclusively for Woolworth's in 1966. Each puzzle consisted of 340 pieces and was 11 x 17 inches in size.

This highly prized and much sought after set was based on episodes from the first (Rigg b/w) filmed series. Each contained an artist-depicted scene on both puzzle and box.

The first in the series, *No Escape*, shows Steed and a rather obese gentleman fighting as they hang precariously out of an open railway carriage door. Mrs Peel, viewed in the next compartment, holds her opponent in an armlock. Although we're given to believe that this is based on *The Gravediggers*, Mrs Peel's attire (a white beret, complete with 'target' motif) points to it being based on *The Town of No Return* – though no such scene appeared in either story!

The second puzzle, *Castle De'ath*, features a scene from that episode, and depicts Steed, complete with kilt and sword, warding off an attack by a fearsome-looking bearded opponent as he descends a stone staircase. Emma is featured in the background pinning a second thug to the floor with her foot while holding him at gunpoint.

Puzzle number three, *In The Basement*, contains a scene based on *Death at Bargain Prices*, and shows a leather-clad Mrs Peel throwing a villain down a flight of

stairs in the basement sports department of a large store. Her colleague stands over a second prostrate figure, brolly at the ready.

The final puzzle, *Archery Practice*, depicts Steed pinned to a large outdoor archery target by an arrow, while a leather-clad Emma holds the archer at gunpoint. The scene is based on *The Master Minds*.

The John Steed Swordstick was also issued in 1966. Described in the manufacturer's catalogue as 'a plastic toy sword stick, for use also as a water pistol', this is extremely rare. (The same company also issued a miniature Steed bowler hat to complement the above.)

The Emma Peel Doll, which was manufactured in Hong Kong, was a 10-inch-high plastic doll, dressed in black leather trousers, a short black woollen coat, white roll-neck sweater and black leather boots. The suit was based on the plastic airman's outfit worn by Diana Rigg in *A Surfeit of H$_2$O*, and came complete with a white plastic base and metal strut to support the doll when standing. The figure is shown holding a gun in her right hand.

Other outfits are contained in the package. These range from two further pairs of trousers – one of brown leather, the second in dark grey wool; a white plastic tunic; a black plastic coat; a white plastic rainer (trimmed in black); and a pair of black mittens. The box has a clear plastic front and is yellow with the words THE AVENGERS in large print. When the doll is removed from the box, a black silhouette of Steed is depicted on the rear of the packaging.

Other items licensed, but never issued, were: **A Shooting Round Corners Gun** (Chad Valley 1965); **The Avengers Stationery Pad**; A set of **View Them Yourself** film strips; An **Avengers Bagatelle**; and an **Emma Peel Dress Cut-Out Book.**

Books

Between the years 1963 and 1969, twelve paperback books were issued to tie in with the television transmissions. Each of these contained an original story based on the characters from the series, and are highly sought after by collectors. The twelve titles are listed in chronological order.

The Avengers by Douglas Enefer (Consul Books, 1963). This features the only story to star Steed and Cathy Gale.

Deadline by Patrick Macnee & Peter Leslie (Hodder & Stoughton, 1965).

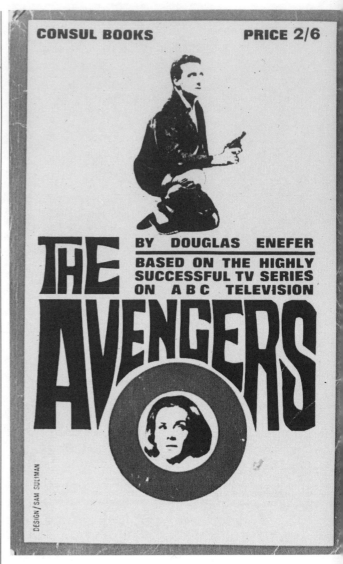

Patrick Macnee and Peter Leslie.

Dead Duck by Patrick Macnee & Peter Leslie (Hodder & Stoughton, 1965). Both these titles, starring Steed and Mrs Peel, are regarded as the best in the series, and are extremely rare.

Nine other paperbacks, officially listed as *The Avengers* series, were issued between 1967 and 1969. The first four titles were published jointly in both the UK and USA, while the remaining five titles were distributed in the American market only.

\#1 **The Floating Game**
\#2 **The Laugh Was On Lazarus**
\#3 **The Passing of Gloria Munday**
\#4 **Heil Harris**

All four titles by John Garforth (UK: Panther Books and USA: Berkley Medallion Books, 1967).

\#5 **The Afrit Affair**
\#6 **The Drowned Queen**
\#7 **The Gold Bomb**

All three titles by Keith Laumer (Berkley Medallion Books, 1968).

\#8 **The Magnetic Man**
\#9 **Moon Express**

Both by Norman Daniels (Berkley Medallion Books, 1968 and 1969).

An interesting point is that although Berkley Medallion issued only nine titles, they did in fact license twelve.

Four titles were also issued in France, and four in Germany (**Der Wreckers**), and these are the same as the UK Panther Book titles.

An oddity in the book line was a short (112-page) novel that appeared in Australia in 1980. Written and published privately by down under *Avengers* buff, Geoff Barlow, this contained a brand new adventure in the lives of Steed and Mrs Peel – or, *Steade* and *Peale*, as the author called them – and was a cracking read and infinitely better than most of the previous titles. (Incidentally, EMI, then *The Avengers* copyright holder, graciously allowed this book to remain on the market – provided no further copies were published after the initial print run. Anyone thinking of publishing, or

using *in any way* the characters or situations from the series is well advised to *think again*!)
The Saga of Happy Valley by Geoff Barlow (1980).

Annuals

The first comic annual to feature *The Avengers* was published in 1962. Entitled **TV Crimebusters** (TV Productions), this is of particular interest to aficionados of the series as it is the only publication to feature a story starring the original team of John Steed and Dr David Keel. *The Avengers* story, a seven-page story called *The Drug Pedlar*, is of added interest as the strip includes eight stills from the 1961 series and the strip depicts Steed's style of dress during that period.

1967 saw the publication of the first 'official' *Avengers* annuals. Titled, naturally enough, **The Avengers**

(Souvenir Press/Atlas Publications), this contains 92 pages of picture strips and text stories plus various features on the series with Steed and Mrs Peel. The cover depicts Steed and Emma battling it out with two uniformed (Russian?) soldiers on a castle staircase. Also included are 40 b/w and colour photographs. Incidentally, I've come across references to a second Steed and Emma Peel annual. However, this was not an official publication and was 'bootlegged' by a group of American fans and circulated from their home base in 1966.

The second annual, and the first to feature Tara King, was published in 1968. This contains 80 pages and the cover features a head-and-shoulders shot of Steed wearing a dark suit while sporting the proverbial bowler, brolly and red carnation, plus two smaller drawings of Tara. The annual includes 25 b/w and colour photographs.

A third annual was issued in 1969, again featuring Steed and Tara, and contains the same number of pages as the previous year's annual. The cover depicts a full-face shot of Steed while Tara, gun at the ready, peers over his left shoulder. This contains 25 b/w and colour photographs.

Other notable publications include: **Meet The Avengers** Star Special 15 (World Distributors 1963). Advertised as 'an exciting behind-the-scenes visit with the stars

of ABC's Top TV Show', this contains 44 pages of text features on the Patrick Macnee/Honor Blackman series. Also included are interviews with both the stars and production staff, and the publication is rounded off with over 30 b/w photographs. This is probably the rarest of all the publications and has appeared on dealers' lists at an incredible £12!

Various TV-related annuals carried features on the series. The best of these are: **Television Show Book** (Purnell, 1965) with a four-page feature on the Macnee/Blackman series; **Television Stars** (Purnell, 1965) containing four pages of text and pictures from the Macnee/Rigg series; **Girl Television & Film Annual** (Odhams Press, 1964) with features on Patrick Macnee and Honor Blackman; **Star TV & Film Annual** (Odhams, 1966) with two features on Honor Blackman, and the following year's annual which contained a feature on Diana Rigg.

Comics

The Avengers also featured in numerous comic strip publications. The most notable of these were the stories printed in full colour in **Diana** (1967). Lasting for a period of 26 weeks, this two-page strip pitted Steed and Mrs Peel against such adversaries as: Madame Zingara, a woman who had discovered a method of weaving trance-inducing material which, when woven into a dress for Mrs Peel, turns Steed's colleague into a mindless Zombie; modern-day Vikings loose on the streets of London; Black Heart and her deadly band of midgets; a power-crazed scientist bent on destroying England by the use of 'brainwashed' pet animals; The Mad Hatter, where Steed's bowler becomes a deadly weapon; and the Sinister Six, a group of six notorious criminals who are bent on destroying The Avengers.

The artwork on this strip was of the highest quality throughout and is a pure delight, making this set a highly prized and eagerly sought after item.

Other comic strip titles include **The Avengers No 1** (Thorpe & Porter, 1966). Published in the UK market, this 68-page, all b/w comic contained four picture strips: *The Mohocks*, *The K Stands for Killers*, *No Jury – No Justice* and *Deadly Efficient*. All four stories featured Steed and Mrs Peel.

John Steed – Emma Peel (Gold Key, 1968). This one-shot, 32-page, all-colour comic was published in the USA and contained two picture stories, *The Roman Invasion* and *The Mirage Maker*. Although the cover title is as above, the comic was actually registered as **The Avengers No 1**, but this was changed to avoid conflict with the Marvel Comics Group title of that name.

TV Comic (Polystyle) regularly used an *Avengers* comic strip between 1965 and 1971. The first *Avengers* story appeared in issue no 720 (2 October 1965) and strips featuring Steed and Mrs Peel (and later Tara King) continued to appear on a semi-regular basis until the early Seventies. *Avengers* strips and text stories also appeared in the company's TV Comic annuals.

Further adventures of Steed, Mrs Peel and Tara King could also be found in the London Express Features syndicated comic strip and as *Der Wreckers* in Germany. (Strangely, a 34-page b/w comic of this name, containing the last two stories from the Thorpe & Porter, *The Avengers No 1* title, turned up as issue no 2106 of the Scandinavian *TV Classics* title!)

Magazines

The TV Times Diana Rigg Spectacular – an 8-page all-colour magazine supplement, was published by the popular UK television journal *TV Times* in 1969. The magazine, devoted entirely to the *Avengers* star, contained features including 'Diana Rigg On Stage', and the centre-page spread pulled out into a giant size 'bioscope' of Diana's career. 18 b/w and colour photographs.

Seven years later, the same company produced a **TV Times Souvenir Extra – The New Avengers** (1976). Published to coincide with the arrival of *The New Avengers* on our screens, this contained hundreds of photographs and 'Patrick Macnee's Life Story.'

Possibly the rarest (and certainly the oddest) magazine was the 12-page **Man's Journal** dossier, which told the story of Steed's search for Miss Chlorophyll Jade! Presented free with the April 1966 edition of *Woman's Journal*, and issued to promote the new Terylene gentleman's fashion line being sold by the Austin Reed high street chain, this b/w and colour rarity gave us *The Strange Case of the Green Girl*, an opus from the pen of Brian Clemens, in which Steed, played in pictures throughout by Patrick Macnee, found himself hot on the trail of Mr X – an Arch-Fiend (and Diabolical Master Mind, to boot), who had captured the delectable Miss Jade (played by actress Jane Birkin).

Well worth looking for is **Tele Series**. Published in France, this 80-page full colour magazine, devoted entirely to coverage of popular television, is the best of its kind around. Issues 11 & 12 (January & February 1988) carried 14 pages on *Chapeau Melon et Bottes de Cuir*.

Finally, though not really an *Avengers* item, worthy of note is **Honor Blackman's Book of Self Defence** (Andre Deutsch, 1965). The introduction is written by Honor herself and contains references to *The Avengers* and the 'Cathy Gale' connection. The book contains over 130 b/w photographs of Honor Blackman being put through a catalogue of judo routines by Black Belt judo expert Joe Robinson, and is well worth keeping an eye open for.

Records

High on the aficionados 'most wanted' memorabilia list are records containing the original (or cover) versions of 'The Avengers Theme' or incidental music pertaining to the programme. However, the majority of these have long since been deleted. Nevertheless, I have catalogued the records in their chronological order of release.

Singles

The Avengers Theme by Johnny Dankworth & His Orch. Columbia DB4695, 1961.
The original theme from the Hendry/Macnee series.
The Avengers by Johnny Dankworth & His Orch. Fontana Tf442, 1963.
A revised edition of the above; used for the Macnee/Blackman series.
The Avengers by The Laurie Johnson Orch. Pye7N 17015, 1965. *
TV Themes (featuring the Johnson original theme). Pye NEP24244 (extended play), 1966.
The Avengers by The Joe Loss Orch. HMV/POP1500, 1966.
TV Themes – A Gift From Pascall Murray (A special 'give-away' containing the original Johnson theme). MCPS ATV1(B) (Extended Play) 1969.
Kinky Boots by Patrick Macnee/Honor Blackman. Decca F11843, 1964.
Kinky Boots by Patrick Macnee/Honor Blackman. Cherry 62, 1983. A reissue of the above, in picture sleeve.
Kinky Boots by Patrick Macnee/Honor Blackman. A 'Maxi-Single' reissue of the above, in picture sleeve.

(This also contains a cover version of 'The Avengers Theme' by the Roland Shaw Orch. 12 Cherry 62, 1983.)

Albums

The Avengers and Other TV Themes by The Johnny Gregory Orch. (Contains a cover version of the Dankworth 'Avengers Theme'). Wing WL1087, 1961.

The Big New Sound Strikes Back Again by The Laurie Johnson Orchestra. Pye 7N 17015. Contains 'The Shake'.*

Themes For Secret Agents by The Roland Shaw Orch. (Contains a cover version of the Johnson 'Avengers Theme'). Decca PFS 4094, 1966.

The Avengers Theme & Other TV Music (Contains the original Johnson theme). Hanna Barbara. 1966.

The Avengers & Other Favourites by The Laurie Johnson Orch. (Contains the original Johnson theme.) Marble Arch MAL695, 1967.

Time For TV by The Brian Fahey Orch. (Contains a cover version of the Johnson theme.) Studio Two/EMI Two175, 1969.

Theme From The Avengers by Jerry Monats Harmonicats (Contains a cover version of the Johnson theme). Hallmark CHM629, 1969.

Themes And .... by The Laurie Johnson Orch. (Contains the original Johnson 'Tara King' Theme, plus the 'Tag Theme' music). MGM/CS 8104, 1969.

The Phase 4 World of Thrillers (A compilation album containing the Roland Shaw version). Decca SPA 160, 1971.

50 Popular TV Themes by The Bruce Baxter Orch. (A double album, containing a cover version of the Johnson theme). Pickwick 50/DA315, 1977.

Music From The Avengers/The New Avengers & The Professionals by The Laurie Johnson Orch. (Contains selected incidental music from all three series, plus the title theme music. These are not the original dubs, but newly recorded.) UK: Unicorn-Kanchana PRM7009. USA: Starlog/Varese Sarabande ASV/95003, 1980.

Although the contents were the same in both the UK and USA, the cover wasn't. The UK sleeve opened into a double sleeve and contained numerous photographs from the series. The US version was issued in a single sleeve which portrayed Steed and Emma framed by a pair of scales.

Original TV Hits of the Sixties Advertised as a 'Collectors Edition', this contained the Brian Fahey Orchestra cover version from 'Time For TV'. Filmtrax/Moment 105, 1986.

* 'The Shake' track from this album is in fact a more primitive form of Laurie Johnson's *Avengers* theme. First recorded in 1965, to cash in on 'The Shake' dance craze, it was re-recorded in its now world famous form as 'Theme from The Avengers'.

Miscellaneous

During the mid Seventies, Derann Film Services, a midland-based home movie supplier, issued four *Avengers* titles for the home movie market. The episodes were supplied on Super 8mm film and were: *From Venus With Love, The Living Dead, The Positive-Negative Man* and *Return of the Cybernauts*. Each was issued in two formats: a full version on 3 x 400 ft reels, and a 15-minute 'condensed' version on 1 x 400 ft reel. Sadly, these prints have now been discontinued, prior to which they were offered at a 'bargain' price of £54.95 per

A shop window display for the Jean Varon Avengers pack.

45-minute episode. To achieve the 45-minute length, Derann edited out the opening and closing 'teaser' scenes. The result was most acceptable, and copies of these prints are now being offered at collector's marts for upwards of £60.

A company called Centaur Films also produced a full-length print of *The £50,000 Breakfast* for the home movie market. The six-reel colour print also had optical sound.

Perhaps not so widely known is that the production company (EMI) licensed six Super-8mm titles to an American company, Sundstand, which supplied many of the world's airlines with in-flight movies. The titles, issued between 1975 and 1978, were: *From Venus With Love*, *Escape in Time*, *The Bird Who Knew Too Much*, *Something Nasty in the Nursery*, *The £50,000 Breakfast* and *The Positive-Negative Man*. They were then supplied to the French airlines UTA and Air Afrique and were issued in dual language prints so that passengers could listen to the original soundtrack of a French over-dub. This contract expired in 1980, and all six prints were destroyed.

Special merchandising rights were also given to various other outlets. In 1969, *Spillers*, the producers of a world-famous brand of pet food, ran a consumer-orientated promotion campaign using *The Avengers* to promote their product. The campaign took the form of a detective/spy story of approximately 1,000 words, and entrants were invited to select certain salient points in the story that related to the questions asked on the entry form. Over 6½ million packs were distributed to major stores throughout the UK.

In Germany, two major fashion houses joined forces to promote a man-made fashion tie-up. The companies, ICI and Povel, went on to issue both men's and women's wear in the 'new' material. Also in Germany, an enterprising West German umbrella manufacturer, Knirps, used Patrick Macnee's Steed character to promote his new line. He made two commercials, and specially selected *Avengers* film clips were used.

Never slow to realise that related merchandise was a money-earner (the production company earned royalties on all items sold), the copyright owners held their own fashion display at a well-known London hotel in 1967. The event, devised and coordinated by Edser Southey Design Associates and produced by Michael Edser, promoted over 54 'Avenger-wear 67' items. Among these were the entire range of 'Emmapeelers' (the catsuits worn by Diana Rigg in the series), and a range of Pierre Cardin 'Steed' attire, plus shoes, hats, gloves, scarves and bags, etc. Of particular interest to *Avengers* buffs was the special entrance 'ticket' supplied for the occasion.

The entrance 'ticket' for the 1967 London fashion show.

Set of Avengers wrist watches, as issued.

This took the form of a standard-size playing card and featured a joint image of Mrs Peel and Steed as the Queen and Knave of Hearts. 'Steed' shirts in Bri-Nylon, styled in Savile Row and complete with bowler and brolly motif; a cheque-book-shaped catalogue from John Temple Tailoring, including Patrick Macnee complete with dolly bird (and gun?); Avengers wrist watches – two models, The Avenger at £4.19s.6d and The Great Avenger at £5.10s – the list is endless. Sadly, most of these items are now lost or destroyed, or in the case of dresswear, worn out and discarded.

And it continues: Patrick Macnee and Linda Thorsen appeared in two separate 20-second television commercials for Amplex Roll-on Deodorant and Fresh Breath Capsules (courtesy of film clips from the series), which ended in November 1988.

One of the items licensed though never issued would have been high on the list of collectables by aficionados. This was a set of two separate bubble-gum cards, containing over 144 colour photographs (one set each for Patrick/Diana, Patrick/Linda). These were licensed by a West German sweets and confectionery company in 1970 to tie-in with the German television screenings.

Other merchandise licenses considered in 1966 were: a daily strip feature in the *Daily Mirror* or *The Sun* – and the subsequent publication of same in paperback form; Avengers Painting Books; 'Emma Peel' shoes; Avengers wallets, badges, etc; a fob-watch; Avengers men's toiletries; a cosmetic gun with lipstick in barrel and compact in butt; and a mascot for Emma Peel.

THE NEW AVENGERS

Toys and related items

Like its predecessor, *The New Avengers* production company cast its eyes towards the merchandise market and numerous items of interest were issued.

Dinky Toys issued two die-cast model cars in 1977. The first of these, Model No 112 **Purdey's TR7**, was, according to *The Dinky Toy Price Guide* (Ernest Benn, 1982), issued in two different formats. One has silver flashes on its doors and sides, with black and silver trim and white interior. A black letter 'P' is on the bonnet and the model was designed with a double 'V' in silver in front of it. The second version is green, and has the word Purdey on the bonnet.

The second model, No 113 **Steed's Special Leyland Jaguar**, was advertised in the Dinky catalogue, but was never officially issued – although several prototype models were illegally 'spirited-out' of the factory and are therefore very rare and worth a great deal of money. In medium green, greenish blue or medium blue with gold stripes along each side, the model is also known to exist with a long orange flash, silver wheels and bumpers. With white or fawn interior and a figure of 'Steed' at the wheel.

THE NEW AVENGERS

750 Pieces

- No. 5592
- Four designs
- Puzzle Size 24" x 18¼" 61 x 46.3cm
- Box Size 12¼" x 8¾" x 1½" 31.1 x 22.3 x 4.1cm
- Outer Pack 4 dozen Cube .156 cu m
- Gross weight 21.3 kilos

A similar fate – that of being stolen from the factory – befell Model No 307 **The New Avengers Gift Set**. Never officially released, this contained Purdey's TR7 and Steed's Special Leyland Jaguar, plus a novel fly-off assailant.

Also highly collectable are two **Revell Plastic Assembly Kits: Purdey's TR7** and **Gambit's XJS** (1979). The first, issued in yellow and black plastic, and the second, in red and black, were both 1.25 scale models and came in easy-to-assemble kit form and nicely produced boxes with photos of Purdey and Gambit on each.

The New Avengers also spawned some children's games. Of these, **The New Avengers Mission Kit** (Thomas Salter, 1976) is the most collectable. This was issued with a photograph of the trio on the lid and contains a plastic gun and silencer, plastic holster, hand-grenade, magnifying glass and an assortment of cardboard cut-outs that in turn make up a 'code-breaker'. Also included are a paper passport and, or so the manufacturer would have us believe, a plastic camera that actually works.

'An exciting game for 2–4 players' is the way **The New Avengers Board Game** Denys Fisher, 1977) was described. The game comes complete with a nicely designed board, a bowler hat and umbrella spinner, plus playing models. In fact the game is as 'exciting' as Ludo!

There is also **The New Avengers Shooting Game** (Denys Fisher, 1976). Intended for 2–4 players, this comes in an attractive presentation box and contains cardboard cut-out figures, a clockwork-operated window set in a cardboard cut-out house and the object of the game (based no doubt on the story *Target*) is to shoot cardboard silhouettes out of the windows, provided the enclosed guns and pellets work!

Arrow games issued a set of four **New Avengers Jigsaw Puzzles** in 1976. Each measures 24 by 18½ inches and comes complete with artist-depicted designs. The first of these has Steed, Purdey and Gambit in the foreground against an action backcloth of a car, helicopter and burning buildings. The second puzzle portrays Purdey giving an action-packed kick to Kane's Cybernaut, while Steed and Gambit race to her rescue. Puzzle three displays a montage of the New Avengers and a Cybernaut, and the final puzzle depicts Steed leaving Number 10 Downing Street.

Female fans of the series could also buy the official **Purdey Doll**, though I suspect that many males were also tempted to do so. Manufactured by Denys Fisher, the figure was dressed in the purple leotard worn by Joanna Lumley in *The Eagle's Nest*, complete with tights, shoes and a patterned skirt. Further outfits were advertised on the back of the package. In the words of the manufacturer, 'Purdey leads such an exciting life, she needs an outfit for every occasion'. For special dates, there was a cream trouser suit with chiffon trimmings; for glamorous occasions, an elegant black dress with fur stole or a green halter-neck dress with long flowing scarf; for relaxing, a rust-coloured jump-suit or a red catsuit; and for practical wear, a suede trouser suit with matching hat and scarf. The 10-inch doll was sealed in a plastic bubble on a cardboard display board, which had an artist-depicted drawing of Joanna Lumley on the cover.

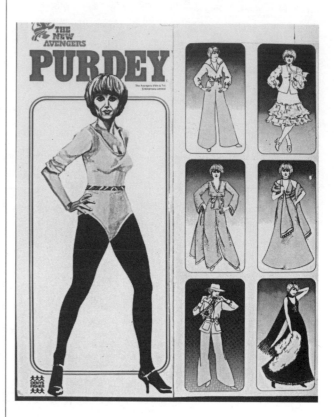

Books

Only six *New Avengers* paperbacks were issued during the course of the series and, unlike the *Avengers* books which contained original stories based on the characters, the *New Avengers* books were novelisations based on selected episodes from the series. All six titles were published by Futura Books and, in chronological order, were:

House of Cards by Peter Cave. 1976.
The Eagle's Nest by John Carter. 1976.
To Catch a Rat by Walter Harris. 1976.
Fighting Men by Justin Cartwright. 1977.
The Cybernauts by Peter Cave. 1977.
Hostage by Peter Cave. 1977.

The last three titles were not published in the USA, so these are marginally more valuable for collectors.

Another notable publication is **John Steed – An Authorised Biography**, Vol. 1, 'Jealous in Honour' by Tim Heald (Weidenfeld & Nicolson, 1977). This contained a fictionalised account of Steed's childhood and early career, and though well-written and interesting – particularly a chapter in which Steed dumps the college bully (a certain James Bond) on his backside – the book fails to give any account of Steed's earlier

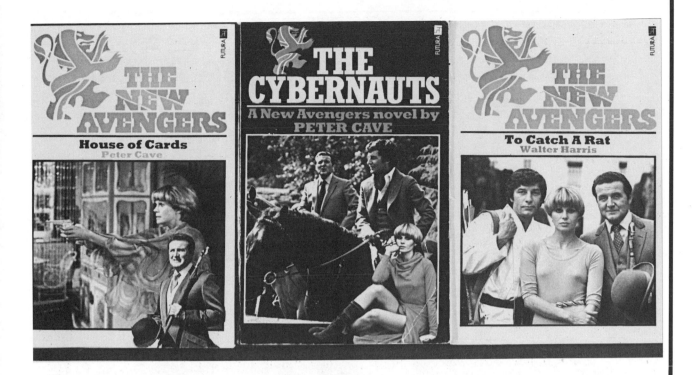

undercover activities and *ends* with his first meeting with Cathy Gale. Though the book was meant to be the first in a series, disappointing sales stopped further editions being issued.

No list would be complete without mention of Patrick Macnee's delightful and hilarious autobiography, **Blind in One Ear** (Harrap 1988). Written by Patrick himself, the Avengers star talks intimately about a life that has been every bit as extraordinary – if not more so – than any of his roles in the theatre, film or television. *The Avengers* is, of course, well-documented. A delight!

Annuals

In 1977, Brown and Watson published the first of two *New Avengers* annuals. This contained 64 pages of text and picture stories, and was complemented by over 40 b/w and colour photographs. The second annual was issued a year later, and followed the same format, but this time contained over 50 photographs.

For the *Avengers* completist, the same company produced a 1979 annual called **TV Detectives**, which contained two pages on Gambit and Purdey.

Comics

Only one *New Avengers* comic album was issued. Printed in France under the title **Chapeau Melon et Bottes de Cuir** (Collection TeleJunior No 1, 1977) this contained six full colour stories. The art was second to

none, although, oddly, Steed was shown throughout driving his Bentley! (The 'Le Repaire de l'Aigle' – *The Eagle's Nest* strip – was issued as giveaway in the April (No 14) edition of the French magazine 'Tele-Series' mentioned earlier.)

Records

Only two singles were released between 1976 and 1980. The first of these, The New Avengers Theme by The Laurie Johnson Orchestra, EMI 2562, was a faithful version of *The New Avengers* theme, and carried an extra bonus in the form of A *Flavour of The New Avengers* on side two. This gave extracts from a couple of the episodes, complete with a car-chase in stereo. Another plus factor was that the single was issued in a full-colour picture sleeve.

It was 1980 before a second 'official' version of the *New Avengers* theme was issued. Once again in picture sleeve, this contained **The New Avengers Main Title Theme**, played by the London Studio Orchestra, conducted by Laurie Johnson, and is a single version of the same track from *The Avengers/The New Avengers/The Professionals* album mentioned earlier. (Unicorn-Kanchana C15.)

To my knowledge, only one album was released during this period. This was issued by *Reader's Digest* and contained a new recording of the *New Avengers* theme, played by The London Festival Orchestra, conducted by Burt Rhodes.

Miscellaneous

Other notable *New Avengers* items include a rub-down set of transfers from *Letraset* (1977). This contains a scene from the episode *Last of the Cybernauts ..?* and depicts Kane and his metal-headed sidekicks in pursuit of Steed, Purdey and Gambit.

Scandecor Posters issued a giant-size poster of the trio in 1976, but this was quickly sold out. No replacement poster was ever issued. Fashionwise, very little (if anything?) was offered during the series' lifespan, though Joanna Lumley did model for a window-display manne-quin and her face could be seen in dozens of women's fashion-house windows. Then, of course, Patrick Mac-nee endorsed 'Right Guard' body deodorant and Colibri lighter products, and made · two television ads for Vauxhall motors, in which he was seen pushing two Vauxhall models into a garage forecourt!

Fan Magazines

Although I have already covered the professional maga-zines available, one aspect of published merchandise that certainly warrants a mention here is *Fanzines* – which perhaps I should define. As the name implies, the word was coined by collectors to describe a fan magazine – a publication produced by fans for fans. These can range from the simple quality of the 'homegrown' product (usually produced on a duplicating machine) to the more professional (and expensive) typeset product. In some cases, magazines are produced by over-zealous fans who, though their intentions are sincere, often cannot afford to maintain the finance needed and these magazines seldom survive two or three issues.

Strange though it may appear, despite its enormous popularity, *The Avengers* never received as much fanzine coverage as other popular shows of the period. However, one or two magazines were issued during (and after) its lifespan, and of these a few are worthy of mention. Probably the best of those issued during the Sixties was one produced in the USA called **En Garde**. It was produced quarterly and ran to eight issues, with numbers 1 to 4, 5 and 6 being of particular interest to fans of the show. A second well-produced American magazine was

The Avengers/Patrick Macnee Fan Newsletter. Produced between 1978 and 1980 by young *Avengers* enthusiast Heather Firth, each issue came complete with rare photographs, beautiful artwork, interviews and interesting text features on the stars.

A second 'fan-sheet' appeared during that period, **Gareth Hunt/Joanna Lumley 'Avengers' Fan Club**. Published by USA enthusiast Cindy Phares, this ran to over 14 editions and contained lots of interesting *Avengers* material, again with well-produced photos of the stars and first-class artwork.

One year later, a UK fan club, **The Avengers Appreciation Society**, produced two fanzines based on the show (June/Autumn, 1981). The first was an 8-page introductory issue, while the second contained 20 pages of features and photographs.

In April 1982, David Caruba, hooked on the series when it first began syndication in the USA during the early Seventies, issued the first photocopied edition of **With Umbrella, Charm and Bowler** (being the American translation of the German name for *The Avengers* – 'Mit Schirm, Charme and Melone') and this was followed four months later by issue 2. By January 1983 the magazine had proved so popular that the publication was continued in a professionally printed newspaper format, and the fanzine increased in both circulation and page count. However, even *quality* fanzines reach a crisis point, and W.U.C.B. was soon to fold – to be replaced by David Caruba's commercially produced magazine for secret agent connoisseurs, **Top Secret**. Though not strictly an *Avengers* magazine, this nevertheless contained some of the best *Avengers* features ever printed – with issue 1 carrying a stunning full-cover picture of Steed and Mrs Peel. Sadly both magazines are no longer in print.

Last but not least (in my opinion!) of the current *Avengers* magazines is **On Target – The Avengers**, on which I served as editor. Making its debut in 1983, this rapidly progressed from an A5 duplicated fanzine, into a slicker, 28-page A4 format which ran to 10 issues, plus a 56-page 'All Interview Special', until, in 1987 the title was changed to **Stay Tuned**. Three issues later, this, too, ran into financial difficulties, and the final edition was published in December of that year.

There is every possibility that **Stay Tuned** will re-appear during this year. In the meantime, Geoff Barlow (author of *The Saga of Happy Valley*, see p.273) is currently writing, and proposes to issue, further books of this nature shortly. For further details write to him direct at: 64 Southampton Road, Carole Park, Queensland 4300, Australia.